The Rural West Since World War II

The Rural West Since World War II

R. Douglas Hurt
Editor

University Press of Kansas

1998 by the University Press of Kansas
All rights reserved

Published by the University Press of Kansas (Lawrence, Kansas 66049), which was organized by the Kansas Board of Regents and is operated and funded by Emporia State University, Fort Hays State University, Kansas State University, Pittsburg State University, the University of Kansas, and Wichita State University

Library of Congress Cataloging-in-Publication Data

The rural West since World War II / R. Douglas Hurt, editor.
     p. cm.
   Includes bibliographical references and index.
   ISBN 0-7006-0877-X (cloth : alk. paper). — ISBN 0-7006-0878-8
(pbk. : alk. paper)
   1. West (U.S.)—History—1945– 2. West (U.S.)—Rural conditions.
978'.033—dc21   97-39054

British Library Cataloguing in Publication Data is available.

Printed in the United States of America

10 9 8 7 6 5 4 3 2 1

The paper used in this publication meets the minimum requirements of the American National Standard for Permanence of Paper for Printed Library Materials Z39.48-1984.

For
Mary Ellen, Adlai, and Austin

Contents

Acknowledgments

This study has been aided by the efforts of Anne Effland, who searched the photo files of the U.S. Department of Agriculture for images that would help tell the history of the rural West in the twentieth century. Sandra Schackel provided photographs from her own collection. Kim Allen Scott, Debbie Nash, and Jodee Kawasaki at the Montana State University Archives and Special Collections aided the photograph research. Shirley Kahn at Sunkist Growers, Inc., and Karolyn Wayman and Barbara Van Cleve in Santa Fe also generously provided essential photographs. David B. Danbom and an anonymous reader gave the manuscript a careful reading and made incisive comments that led to the improvement of this study. I am grateful for the support of everyone who contributed to this book.

Introduction

The American West has fascinated scholars, students, and the public for a long time. During the late nineteenth century, historians became increasingly interested in this vast region, and they primarily interpreted the history of the West in the context of Frederick Jackson Turner's frontier thesis, largely viewing it as an area where American social, political, and economic institutions were reborn and perpetuated in a frontier environment. As a result, many historians considered the West only as a frontier. By the early twentieth century, however, the frontier lay in the distant past. Although cattle and cowboys still roamed the range and growers still sought cheap, temporary agricultural labor, and while landowners and state governments struggled over water law, the economic and social structure of the West had begun to change dramatically. The population of the West increased as migrants from all parts of the nation sought economic opportunity and a new life. Quickly they transformed towns into cities and changed the face of the countryside. The private and institutional control of water became not only an economic problem but also an urban, political issue. Corporate expansion and consolidation helped coin the term "agribusiness." Lumber and mining companies greedily and rapaciously cut and gnawed away at the region's rich natural resources. With the onset of the Great Depression, the federal government initiated a multiplicity of programs that not only provided employment but also left its own indelible institutional mark on the region.

Although the federal government owns nearly 54 percent of the land in the Far West, ranging from a high of 80 percent in Nevada to a low of 33 percent in Montana, and while many Americans associate this region with urban sprawl, retirement communities, and beaches as well as the forestry, fishing, and mining industries, the West remains a rural and agricultural region unsurpassed for its sweeping vistas, isolated towns, and bountiful fields. It is a region of vast rangelands in the Rocky Mountains and on the Intermontaine Plateau, sprawl-ing wheat lands in eastern Washington and Oregon, and sun-drenched cotton and vegetable fields and vineyards in California.[1]

Without question the Far West is an important agricultural region. By 1995, California ranked second only to Texas in the growing of cotton, and it led the nation in the production of tomatoes used for processing, such as ketchup and sauce. Similarly, farmers in Washington raised more apples and, with Oregon, sweet cherries than horticulturists in any other state. Only Florida outranked California for the production of oranges and grapefruit, although California and Arizona raised the entire lemon crop. In addition, California, which often epit-omizes western agriculture, led all states in the production of table, wine, and raisin grapes, as well as the raising of freestone and cling peaches. Washington, California, and Oregon, respectively, produced more Bartlett pears than any other states.[2]

The western states also ranked among the leaders in the number of cattle and calves raised, with most cattlemen grazing or feeding fewer than 500 head. Montana and California led the nation in cattle operations averaging more than 500 head. Wyoming trailed only Texas in sheep and lamb production for both meat and wool. Moreover, only farmers in Wisconsin milked more cows and produced more fluid milk and milkfat than dairymen in California. Dairy-related agribusinesses in the West were also leaders in food production. Once again, California led the nation in the production of ice cream, and it ranked second to Wisconsin in the making of butter and cheese.[3]

In 1995, based on the U.S. Department of Agriculture's definition of a farm, that is, an operation that sold $1,000 or more of agricultural products during a year, California led the West in the number of farms, with 80,000 covering 30 million acres, mostly in cropland, and California's farmers irrigated more acreage than anywhere in the United States. California also led the West in farm real estate value, averaging $2,215 per acre, because of population pressures for urban expansion. In July 1995, the West also led the other regions of the nation in the employment of agricultural labor, but even here California far surpassed any other state with the employment of 225,000 farmworkers.[4]

Western agriculturists have also relied heavily on the federal government for a host of price support and income supplement programs that date from the New Deal, especially the Agricultural Act of 1938, which remained the founda-tion for federal agricultural programs. Western farmers avidly sought price-supporting loans from the Commodity Credit Corporation, which, since its inception in 1933, had become the chief price-supporting agency of the United States Department of Agriculture. In this regard, California farmers led the nation with the receipt of $666.6 million in Commodity Credit Corporation loans for 1993. Despite such government price support programs and high levels of agricultural production for both crops and livestock, western farmers bore considerable indebtedness from the purchase of land and machinery, as well as annual operating expenses. In 1995, California ranked third behind only Iowa and Illinois in the number of farm real estate loans from banks, with a total of $1.4 million, and it led the nation in non–real estate farm loans, with $3.4 million. Like farmers in other regions, westerners have turned to cooperative marketing and purchasing organizations to increase prices, reduce costs, and improve their managerial and business abilities. Cooperative organizations are particularly strong in California, Washington, and Oregon.[5]

In addition to the organization of farmers and growers in cooperative associations, large-scale agricultural production, processing, and marketing became known as "agribusiness" during the postwar years. Insurance and oil companies also invested in land to reap capital gains. Corporation-owned farms commanded more capital and better access to credit than individual farmers and weathered economic hard times with less financial difficulty than small-scale agriculturists, although weekend farmers remained largely invulnerable to national commodity price indexes, interest rates, and fluctuations in foreign market demands.

Large-scale and corporate farms often hired migrant labor to harvest truck and orchard crops and work in the vineyards along the West Coast. Since World War II, most migrant agricultural workers have been Mexicans or Mexican Americans. Low wages, long hours, and poor living conditions encouraged migrant workers to organize and bargain collectively, especially in California. In February 1972, after several attempts of the migrants to organize in groups such as the National Farm and Labor Union, Agricultural Workers Organizing Committee, and Farm Workers Association, Cesar Chevez established the United Farm Workers of America (UFW), which became the most successful association for agricultural laborers. Although the organizational activities of the UFW were fraught with violence, the union improved wages and working conditions. Even so, by the late twentieth century most migrant or seasonal agricultural workers did not belong to the UFW because they did not believe the union met their needs.[6]

While great changes have occurred in western agriculture since World War II, the small towns and settlements in the rural West that are inextricably tied or closely linked to agriculture also changed significantly. The Rural Electrification Administration enabled farmers and rural residents to organize cooperatives for the purpose of bringing electric power to the countryside. Electricity meant that farm and rural homes could have lights, hot water heaters, and electric stoves, all of which improved the standard of living. Expanded telephone service, along with new technological developments such as television and computers, helped link the rural West with urban America. Still, many young people left the towns and countryside for the cities, and businesses failed, leaving empty stores and darkened main streets. Often the county seats remained the only viable commercial and service centers for farmers, livestock raisers, or small-town residents. Out-migration also decreased the tax base in many areas and created difficulties for the maintenance of schools, roads, bridges, and other public services in the countryside. Even so, many people chose to remain on the land or to live in small towns because they preferred rural living.[7]

Employment in the rural West often involves the production of goods rather than services, such as "value-added" meat packing and food processing. These jobs, however, are dead-end, minimum wage, nonunion positions in branch plants that do not return the profits to the local community. As a result, many agriculturists and town residents now talk about the "sustainability" of agriculture and town life. Environmental concerns also influence the many decisions that agriculturists make regarding plowing, harvesting, and livestock raising, as well as the use of herbicides, pesticides, and fertilizers, which, in turn, link sustainability to biology and ecology. In contrast, the sustainability of rural towns depends on the "intentions," that is, the conscious decisions that people make to determine social and economic structures and the quality of life in their communities. Certainly, rural life in the West has become more diverse since World War II. In some areas, such as Arizona and southern California, rural life is no longer primarily identified with farming. Rather, it is defined by tourism, recreation, and retirement communities, all of which bring more income into rural areas than agriculture.[8]

While historians and other scholars have documented many of these developments with careful detail for the years prior to World War II, they have given little attention to the American West, particularly the rural West, since the war. Studies of the post-1930s West primarily have emphasized the war years, urban growth, mining, lumbering, and the contributions of ethnic groups to the region's history. In many respects this lack of scholarly attention to the rural West should not be surprising because most historians have been raised and trained in urban environments. Consequently, their focus often has been on city-related affairs, and they have not been particularly interested in the agricultural or rural history of the Far West. Yet the history of the rural West since World War II is important because many of the political, economic, and social issues that have concerned the region since that time also have influenced the national debate on a host of matters from the civil rights movement to environmental controls and from welfare programs to the regulation of corporations, all of which affect the making of public policy. Simply put, the rural West remains a vital part of this increasingly urban region and nation. Anyone who neglects the history of the rural West, especially since World War II, cannot adequately understand the social, cultural, economic, and political mosaic, that is, the history, of the United States.[9]

This collection of essays is designed to provide an overview of the rural West since World War II in order to show that agriculture, rural life, and agrarian politics have been inextricably linked to the economy and culture of the region even though the modern West has been disproportionately urban in population and city-driven in relation to economic, social, and political developments since 1945. The task of the ten scholars who have contributed to this book has been to discuss the most important historical developments relating to their area of expertise for the rural West. For the purposes of this study, the rural West is defined as the agricultural, small-town, and reservation West. Moreover, the West or Far West is defined as the Rocky Mountain and Pacific Coast West, which includes portions of eleven continental states—Arizona, California, Colorado, Idaho, Montana, New Mexico, Nevada, Oregon, Utah, Washington, and Wyoming. In cases where the Great Plains also compose a portion of these states, the authors were asked to analyze only those areas that fall within this geographic definition of the Far West in order to give greater focus to their subject.[10]

Some of the topics found in this collection will be familiar to students of American history in general and the Far West in particular—the cattle industry, agriculture, migrant labor, water policy, and environmentalism. Other subjects— small towns, social change, women ranchers, reservation life, and agribusiness—may offer new areas for reflection. In each case the authors provide a fresh look at major aspects of the rural West's history since World War II. Most important, this collection of essays is intended to provide a road map for scholars, students, and general readers of western history to indicate what has been done and to suggest other avenues for research.

To begin, David Rich Lewis traces the social and economic changes that have affected the Indian reservations since World War II. During the late twentieth century, Native American cultural groups or, more colloquially, tribes, remained an important cultural part of the rural West. Lewis notes that whereas few Indians practice farming or livestock raising, most maintain a rural identity. He argues that the tribes have confronted a formidable bureaucracy in the Bureau of Indian Affairs (BIA) that often has sought to scale back its services to the reservations. Lewis has found that tribal governments have increasingly bypassed the BIA to improve education, housing, health, and economic development programs on the reservations and, by so doing, protect Indian rights and tribal autonomy. Many tribes also have attempted to bring economic improvements to their reservations by developing tourism, casino gambling, and extractive industries, such as lumbering, coal and uranium mining, and the drilling for oil and natural gas, as well as seeking greater unity of purpose through pan-Indian organizations. Still, the Indians in the American West rely on the federal government for considerable economic support, which often denies them complete self-determination on the reservations. Moreover, while many Indians have migrated to urban areas in search of jobs and a higher standard of living, they often maintain a sense of cultural and community attachment to the reservations and the rural West.

Next, Paula M. Nelson traces social changes in communities via the adoption of new technology, such as electricity, telephones, and sewer systems, that made the lives of rural westerners little different from those of urbanites. She finds that the corresponding centralization of economic life in the large towns left many small communities on the verge of collapse. Nelson cogently notes that although volunteerism rather than professionalism remains strong in rural communities, urbanites who move to rural areas in the West do not have a tradition of community interaction and support that helps maintain the social fabric of the small towns. Moreover, while the automobile made communication easier, it also encouraged school and church consolidations and the loss of community spirit and identification. Rural westerners were caught in a dilemma. They wanted improved education for their children, but they did not want to lose their sense of place and cultural identity. Westerners have confronted social and economic change by organizing groups and associations that promote community interaction. Despite the efforts of westerners to maintain the economic and social viability of small towns, Nelson contends that modernization and urbanization have drawn away leaders, children, and others who sought better opportunities in urban areas, while city residents have found a refuge in the countryside. These movements have significantly changed the nature of small towns despite the attempts of longtime residents to maintain an unhurried lifestyle, rural social values, and a sense of place in the western landscape.

While white and Indian residents of the rural West sought both economic security and a sense of place, environmental concerns became increasingly important to both groups after World War II, but especially since the 1970s, when a new group called "environmentalists" began to shape the public debate over matters of conservation and ecology. Here James E. Sherow skillfully traces the development of the environmental movement in the West. He notes that environmentalists see the natural world as holistic, that is, inextricably interconnected. They have attacked the use of petrochemicals for pesticides, herbicides, and fertilizers because they upset the ecological balance and damage water supplies. Environmentalists have also challenged the social benefits of dam construction that destroyed wildlife habitat and ruined local agricultural practices. Moreover, they have also consistently argued that more science and technology does not mean better living but instead environmental ruin. Sherow contends that while environmentalists and farmers often have been at odds in the West, agricultural policy has begun to reflect the concerns of environmentalists, and many agriculturists have begun to give attention to ecology in their practices, especially regarding the use of petrochemicals. Sherow finds sufficient reason to remain hopeful that western farmers and environmentalists will achieve greater success in reaching common ground in the twenty-first century.

Thomas R. Wessel provides an overview of agricultural policy since the Agricultural Adjustment Act of 1938, which established the foundation for American farm policy. Since that time, agricultural policy has influenced the lives of farmers, urbanites, and town dwellers, particularly in relation to income for farmers and food prices for others. Wessel notes that while westerners have been underrepresented in the House and Senate agricultural committees, they have wielded considerable power. They also have dominated the House Interior and Insular Affairs Committee, which had oversight jurisdiction for the public lands administered by the department of the Interior. Both the Department of the Interior and the Department of Agriculture administer grazing permits for western livestock owners through the Bureau of Land Management and the Forest Service, and cattle raisers have clashed with these agencies over grazing fees, access to the range, and water use since the New Deal. But agricultural policy primarily attempted to deal with surplus production and low prices through acreage controls, government purchases, and price supports. These efforts proved costly and ineffective, and in 1996 Congress provided for an end to government price support and acreage-reduction payments to farmers over a seven-year period. Whether this attempt to reduce the cost of agricultural policy and encourage farmers to diversify will be effective remains unknown, but Wessel provides an unsurpassed assessment of the long and difficult process of agricultural policy development and its effect on farmers and cattle raisers in the West.

Although historians have given increasing attention to the role of women in the West, their studies focus primarily on the nineteenth century. Indeed, few historians have studied women in the twentieth-century West, and until now no one has analyzed the role of women in the rural West since World War II. Here Sandra Schackel argues that women have always been important to the success of western farms and ranches, but after World War II technological change altered their lives, particularly with the adoption of electrical appliances that made their days easier. At the same time, hardware technology in the form of tractors, combines, and hay balers helped decrease the need for women to labor in the fields or to feed as many hungry workers at harvesttime. As a result, many women found themselves relegated to the roles of full-time homemakers, although they continued to think of themselves as partners in the farm or ranch operation, and they maintained a strong attachment to the land and rural life. Western women also sought employment in nearby towns, often out of economic necessity, using their income to help support the farm or ranch operation. By basing her research on oral interviews, Schackel has given her analysis of women's roles in the rural West an immediacy not found in other studies.

The human condition in the late twentieth-century rural West also involves water and the right to use it. Indeed, water has been the lifeblood of the American West during the twentieth century, and water policy has shaped the political debate throughout much of the region, especially in California. There, state and federal governments and private interests clashed as growers competed with urbanites for the use of water and the control of rivers and reservoirs. Here, Donald J. Pisani, the foremost historian of water policy in the West, analyzes the efforts of the federal government to provide large- and small-scale farmers with sources for irrigation by damming the major rivers. Irrigation, however, increased the price of land, making it attractive to investors and real estate developers, and plentiful water supplies encouraged industrialization and urbanization, all of which threatened the economic viability of the family farm. Pisani carefully analyzes the successes and failures of the Bureau of Reclamation, the Columbia Basin Project, and the U.S. Army Corps of Engineers in providing irrigation and flood control throughout the West. Usually the large-scale farmers benefited from these efforts to the detriment of the family farm. Pisani argues, however, that technological change and dramatic increases in the amount of capital necessary for farmers to earn a living, as well as irrigation and federal water policy, also played major roles in the demise of the family farm throughout the West.

If one does not immediately associate acrimonious debates over water with the late twentieth-century rural West, the mental images of migrant and seasonal farm-workers have become stereotypes for many Americans. Although migrant workers and the growers have experienced considerable confrontation since World War II concerning wages, hours, and working conditions, as well as the unionization of migrant and seasonal workers, the history of migrant labor is more complex than the study of bread-and-butter issues for both workers and growers. Here Anne B. W. Effland traces changes over time in the ethnic composition of the migrant labor force in the Far West. Effland discusses the purpose and problems of the bracero program and the growing preference of the growers for Hispanic farmworkers rather than Asian, African American, or Anglo-American workers. She also traces the development of educational and health care opportunities for the migrants, analyzes the legislation designed to improve agricultural labor relations in California and other western states, and discusses the effects of technological change on those agricultural workers. She concludes by addressing the significance of contemporary immigration reform.

Rapid changes in agricultural science and technology have also affected western agriculture since World War II. New forms of science and technology have helped farmers increase productivity, efficiency, and income, while forcing many, including agricultural workers, from the land and making farming too costly for small-scale operators. In her essay, Judith Fabry traces the major technological and scientific changes in western agriculture by focusing on both hardware and biotechnology from tractors, which became important during the 1940s, to the use of hybrid seeds, growth hormones, chemical fertilizers, herbicides, and pesticides, which farmers commonly used by the 1990s. Fabry discusses the systems approach to western agriculture, emphasizing the adoption of feedlots, artificial insemination, and embryo transplants. She also traces the introduction of biotechnology, that is, the development of genetically altered plants and animals. Fabry clearly notes the importance of these changes in western agriculture, but she cautions that unknown consequences from biotechnology may harm western farming in the absence of the wise use of all new forms of agricultural science and technology.

Next Mark Friedberger discusses the major components of the western livestock industry, analyzing the feedlot system for producing "tailored beef," the development of "drylot" dairies, and the production of grass-fattened cattle.

Friedberger contends that competition became the driving force for technological and managerial innovation in the beef cattle and dairy industries following World War II. He also compares the methods used by ranchers in the southwestern desert with those in the mountainous north, as well as the intrusion of outsiders who desire to become ranchers for a hobby and the influence of the federal government, particularly in relation to grazing fees. Friedberger leaves no doubt that livestock raising in the twentieth-century West has become more complex and precarious than ever before.

Harry C. McDean concludes this collection of essays by tracing the development of agribusiness in the West. McDean notes that after World War II agribusiness became more than the businesses that financed, marketed, transported, distributed, and sold agricultural products and farm machinery, seeds, feed, and fertilizer. Rather, agribusinesses developed into large multinational, capital-intensive corporations that avidly sought diversification and expansion within and beyond the agricultural marketplace. Indeed, most agribusinesses had few close links to farming and often no regional, that is, specific, connection with the West. Most agribusinesses played the gamesmanship of diversification followed by divestiture, similar to corporate practices across the nation. Although the world of agribusiness is complex, McDean skillfully traces the emergence of the Bank of America as the largest agricultural lender in the West and the entry of Tennaco as a major competitor for the purchase of western lands for the production of gas and oil, as well as grapes and almonds. Biotechnology firms also have become an important part of western agribusinesses, joining the more traditional technological companies such as John Deere, Caterpillar, and J. I. Case. McDean discusses these operations, as well as the major changes in the most successful agricultural cooperative—Sunkist—in addition to Gallo Wineries, Ocean Spray Cranberries, Inc., and American Crystal Sugar Cooperative. Overall, McDean concludes that the history of agribusiness in the late twentieth century is more the story of high finance, management ethics, and business gamesmanship, all on a national and international scale, rather than the story of regional food production and marketing.

These essays, then, will give the student and scholar of the twentieth-century American West a place to begin. Anyone pursuing the history of the rural West since World War II should find them to be not only a useful reference but also a point of embarkation for further research. Indeed, the rural West remains large and wide-open both in terms of space and as a field for historical inquiry.

NOTES

1. Richard H. Jackson, "Federal Lands in the Mountainous West," in *The Mountainous West: Explorations in Historical Geography,* ed. William Wyckoff and Lary M. Dilsaver (Lincoln: University of Nebraska Press, 1995), 253–55.

2. *Agricultural Statistics, 1995–96* (Washington, D.C.: Government Printing Office, 1995–96), II-2, IV-23, V-3, 9, 12, 18, 24. For an excellent survey of the twentieth-century West, see Michael Malone and Richard W. Etulain, *The American West: A Twentieth-Century History* (Lincoln: University of Nebraska Press, 1989).

3. *Agricultural Statistics, 1995–96,* VII-2, 13–14, 36, 44; VII-7, 16–17; VIII-7, 16–17.

4. Ibid., IX-4, 6, 8, 14.

5. Ibid., X-10, 18; XI-12.

6. Dick Meister and Anne Loftis, *Long Time Coming: The Struggle to Unionize America's Farm Workers* (New York: Macmillan, 1977); J. Craig Jenkins, *The Politics of Insurgency: The Farm Workers Movement in the 1960s* (New York: Columbia University Press, 1985); Patrick H. Mooney and Theo J. Majka, *Farmers' and Farm Workers' Movements: Social Protest in American Agriculture* (New York: Twayne, 1995), 150–214; R. Douglas Hurt, *American Agriculture: A Brief History* (Ames: Iowa State University Press, 1994), 365–69.

7. D. Clayton Brown, *Electricity for Rural America: Fight for the REA* (Westport, Conn.: Greenwood Press, 1980); Hurt, *American Agriculture,* 325–26; David B. Danbom, *Born in the Country: A History of Rural America* (Baltimore: Johns Hopkins University Press, 1995), 221–23; Don F. Hadwiger and Clay Cochran, "Rural Telephones in the United States," *Agricultural History* 58 (July 1984): 221–38.

8. Malone and Etulain, *The American West,* 236–38; Earl Pomeroy, *In Search of the Golden West: The Tourist in Western America* (New York: Knopf, 1957); John A. Jakle, *The Tourist: Travel in Twentieth-Century North America* (Lincoln: University of Nebraska Press, 1985).

9. Gerald D. Nash, *The American West in the Twentieth Century: A Short History* (Englewood Cliffs, N.J.: Prentice-Hall, 1973); Gerald D. Nash, *World War II: Reshaping the Economy* (Lincoln: University of Nebraska Press, 1990); Gerald D. Nash, *The American West Transformed: The Impact of the Second World War* (Bloomington: Indiana University Press, 1985); John M. Findlay, *Magic Lands: The Western Cityscapes and American Culture* (Berkeley: University of California Press, 1992); Carl Abbott, "The Metropolitan Region: Western Cities in the New Urban Era," in *The Twentieth-Century West,* ed. Gerald D. Nash and Richard W. Etulain (Albuquerque: University of New Mexico Press, 1985), 71–98; Thomas R. Cox et al., *This Well-Wooded Land: Americans and Their Forests from Colonial Times to the Present* (Lincoln: University of Nebraska Press, 1985); William G. Robbins, *American Forestry: A History of National, State, and Private Cooperation* (Lincoln: University of Nebraska Press, 1985); William G. Robbins, "The Western Lumber Industry: A Twentieth-Century Perspective," in *The Twentieth-Century West,* ed. Gerald D. Nash and Richard W. Etulain (Albuquerque: University of New Mexico Press, 1989), 233–56; Harold K. Steen, *The U.S. Forest Service: A History* (Seattle: University of Washington Press, 1976); Leonard J. Arrington and Gary B. Hansen, *"The Richest Hole on Earth": A History of the Bingham Copper Mine* (Logan: Utah State University Press, 1963); Russell R. Elliott, *Nevada's Twentieth-Century Mining Boom: Tonopah, Goldfield, Ely* (Reno: University of Nevada Press, 1966); Harry H. L. Kitano, *Japanese Americans: The Evolution of a Subculture,* 2d ed. (Englewood Cliffs, N.J.: Prentice-Hall, 1976);

Rodalfo Acuna, *Occupied America: A History of Chicanos,* 3d ed. (New York: Harper and Row, 1988).

10. Danbom, *Born in the Country,* xi; Richard White, *"It's Your Misfortune and None of My Own": A History of the American West* (Norman: University of Oklahoma Press, 1991), 574.

1

Native Americans: The Original Rural Westerners

David Rich Lewis

American Indians were rural long before rural was socially or academically fashionable. At the time of European contact, the vast majority lived in dispersed bands and extended family congregations. With a few notable exceptions, even village dwellers across the country maintained density levels within what would be considered rural limits. They lived close to the earth in both the physical and metaphysical sense. They shaped and in turn were shaped by their natural environments. They cultivated the land. Nearly half of all native groups participated in some form of agriculture, producing between 25 and 75 percent of their total subsistence needs. After contact, Indian policies such as removal, reservation, and allotment emphasized agrarianism, intensifying Indian rural isolation in an industrial age.[1]

Given the agrarian bent of Indian policy, it is not surprising that American Indians remained rural decades after the majority of United States citizens gave up rurality and moved to the city. "Do you realize," Clyde Warrior is reputed to have told a group of people skeptical about the idea of rebuilding traditional Indian communities in the 1960s, "that when the United States was founded, it was only 5 percent urban and 95 percent rural and now it is 70 percent urban and 30 percent rural?" His listeners nodded, missing his point. "Don't you realize what this means? It means we are pushing them into the cities. Soon we will have the country back again."[2]

"Country," in Warrior's biting militant humor, is both nationalist and the antithesis of urban. It is the rural homeland of American Indian experiences past and present. In 1930, only 10 percent of the native population lived in cities. A decade of depression and New Dealing later, only 5 percent did—many having returned to their reservation communities, where poverty was more familiar and survivable, where government work programs actually improved predepression economic levels. During the 1940s, American Indians began to leave their rural homelands, pushed by growing reservation populations and the lack of opportunities, pulled by the promise of defense and industrial jobs. But this urbanizing process has been slower than many imagined. In 1950, 80 percent of Indians still resided in rural communities, as did 70 percent a decade later and 55.4 percent in 1970. As late as 1980, 51 percent of American Indians still lived outside standard metropolitan areas, far exceeding whites (26.7 percent), African Americans (19.9 percent), Hispanics (12.4 percent), and the national average (25.2 percent), making them the most rural of all major American ethnic groups. Not until 1990, seventy years after the rest of the nation recognized its urbanity, did a majority (51 percent) of the 1,959,234 American Indians and native Alaskans finally reside in urban settings.[3]

At the same time, Indians were western, primarily the result of five centuries of contact, conquest, and consolidation onto the least wanted lands of the arid American West. In 1910, 95 percent of the 291,014 Indians and Alaskan natives lived west of the Mississippi River, 55 percent in the western census region. In 1950, 57 percent of the 377,273 natives lived in the West. Today, four decades later, 75 percent of all Native Americans still live west of the Mississippi, 47 percent in the West.[4]

Just as citizens of the American West have tended to think of themselves as rural, so too have Native Americans, even as the entire West has entered a more urban, more cosmopolitan age. Today, only 437,358 Indians and Alaskan natives (22 percent) reside on the 314 reservations and trust lands. Nearly as many live in nearby border towns. Few practice extensive farming, livestock raising, or other agricultural pursuits, yet most maintain a rural identity and other shared rural characteristics: geographic isolation, seasonal and handwork labor, limited access to goods and resources, strong family, community, and land values, and a certain acceptance of the natural forces they face.[5]

Yet for all their rural westernness—or perhaps because of it—contemporary Indians have received relatively little attention from social scientists. Russell Thornton and Mary Grasmick pointed out this imbalance in the sociological literature in 1980, noting that Indians had been left to anthropological and historical study, relegating them to a traditional past rather than a usable present. Rural sociologists in particular seem more interested in the experience of rural blacks or women than in Indians. When they focused on Indians, it was generally as a comparison for rural poverty levels. Only recently have more complete studies of reservation economies and development options emerged. Likewise, rural historians have left the study of Indians to western or Native American scholars rather than incorporating them into their own growing field. Given this situation, room exists for interdisciplinary dialogue, contemporary analysis, and comparative synthesis. Moreover, it is clear that Indians have been and continue to be rural peoples even while becoming more urban, and that their contemporary experiences deserve attention in that context.[6]

"Indian Affairs is comparable to a Grade B movie," wrote Vine Deloria, Jr.

"You can go to sleep and miss a long sequence of the action, but every time you look at the screen it's the same group of guys chasing the other guys around the same rock." It seems that policy makers have always been chasing what they perceived as an "Indian problem" around and around. The contemporary situation of rural Indians can only be understood in this policy context.[7]

From the beginning, the pendulum of American Indian policy has swung back and forth between different philosophies and methods—warfare and treaty, assimilation and exclusion, collectivism and individualism. Sovereign and autonomous at the time of contact, American Indians were reduced by disease and warfare, trade, treaties, and legal rulings to "domestic dependent" nations. Removal, reservation, and allotment followed, resulting in the alienation of most of their lands. Indians' inherent rights to self-determination and natural resources devolved to "reserved rights" based on treaties subject to the plenary power of an increasingly capricious Congress. As their political and subsistence alternatives narrowed and populations dwindled, Indians found themselves abandoned on the periphery of American society. While Congress granted them citizenship in 1924, seven states still refused to let Indians vote fourteen years later; Arizona and New Mexico held out yet another decade before the Supreme Court overturned disenfranchisement clauses in their state constitutions.[8]

Between 1933 and 1945, Commissioner of Indian Affairs John Collier turned Indian policy on end, suspending the individualization of land that stripped Indians of over 80 percent of their reservation holdings between 1887 and 1928. His vehicle, the Wheeler-Howard Act, or Indian Reorganization Act (IRA) of 1934, held out the promise of self-determination for Indian peoples: the creation of their own tribal governments, the consolidation and reacquisition of Indian lands, the restoration of cultural freedoms. In reality, the results were as mixed as tribal responses to the IRA. The IRA's $4.2 million revolving land acquisition fund helped but fell woefully short of restoring the preallotment Indian estate. Furthermore, the imposition of alien governmental forms and laws frustrated tribes. Supervision of tribal council decisions by the secretary of the interior allowed only limited sovereignty, not true self-determination.[9]

After World War II, the policy pendulum swung hard to the right as budget-conscious Republicans, anti–New Dealers, assimilationists, and western congressmen joined forces to rid the nation of its legal trust responsibility toward Indians. In 1946, Congress created the Indian Claims Commission to clear federal liability for past treaty violations and land claims through dollar settlements. But the act had the unintended side affect of reaffirming tribal identities, even pan-Indian identities, showing tribes the persistent power of their nineteenth-century treaties. Tribal successes in court (about $800 million awarded in 370 claims between 1951 and 1978) gave many a voice and a new monetary base from which to operate, resist termination, and pursue genuine self-rule.[10]

Termination as policy became reality in 1953 with House Concurrent Resolution 108. Congress and the Bureau of Indian Affairs (BIA) identified a number of tribes to be "freed from Federal supervision and control," and ultimately withdrew recognition from 114 groups, including the Klamath and the 61 bands and tribes of western Oregon, the Mixed-Blood Ute and Southern Paiutes of Utah, and the California Rancherias. Nationally, termination involved 13,263 Indians and 1,365,801 acres of trust land. Congress also passed Public Law 280 (1953), which transferred criminal and civil jurisdiction on certain reservations to state governments, and then shifted responsibility for education and health from the BIA to private schools and the U.S. Public Health Service.

Relocation, the second half of this termination policy, was intended to move Indians into cities as a means of ending Indian rural poverty and tribal identity. The Navajo, San Carlos Apache, and other tribes with growing populations, insufficient arable land, and severe poverty conditions readily participated. However, the program was underfunded and struggled to situate relocatees with adequate jobs, housing, and support. It became, in the words of Philleo Nash, commissioner of Indian affairs from 1961 to 1966, "essentially a one-way bus ticket from rural to urban poverty." By 1960, 33,466 Indians had been relocated under the program. Another 100,000 Indians moved to cities on their own after World War II, pushed by the lack of rural reservation opportunities, pulled by the promise of jobs. Western cities like Los Angles, San Francisco, Phoenix, Seattle, Denver, and Salt Lake City attracted large numbers of Indians who formed the basis for an activist generation to come. Many, however, continued to move between reservation and city and back again, trying to make a living and a life. Of the 3,273 Navajo who relocated under the program between 1952 and 1961, 37 percent returned to the reservation because of problems with jobs, language, and alcohol. Nationally the figure was closer to 60 percent.[11]

By the early 1960s, the failures of termination were painfully visible, especially in the negative experiences of groups like the Klamath. Factionalism, liquidation of Klamath timber resources, and ill-advised per capita distributions left them more dependent than before. Likewise, termination had not rid them of the BIA, a bureaucracy that refused to die or even decline. At this juncture the rhetoric, if not the reality, of self-determination reemerged as Indian policy was swept up in the liberal reform atmosphere of President Lyndon B. Johnson's Great Society programs. Controversial sections of the 1968 Civil Rights Act protected individual Indian rights but also were interpreted by the courts (*Santa Clara Pueblo v. Martinez,* 1978) to protect tribal autonomy. Tribal councils began to bypass the BIA altogether, tapping into federal grants for redeveloping poor rural communities through job training, education, housing, health, and infrastructure development. In the process, increasingly sophisticated tribal leaders emerged to capture funds and direct these programs. So did tribal bureaucracies, a growing source of employment for reservation peoples.[12]

As liberal funding began to dry up in the late 1960s, Indian activism increased. Pan-Indian organizations like the National Congress of American Indians, the National Tribal Chairmen's Association, the Native American Rights Fund, and the Council of Energy Resource Tribes stepped up their calls for greater Indian autonomy. The National Indian Youth Council and the American Indian Movement—composed of a growing contingent of young urban Indians incited by the histories and rural reservation conditions their families fled— took their demands to the streets. Western state governments responded with their own agencies to address internal Indian matters, but the real issues were national in scope.[13]

In 1975, Congress passed the Indian Self-Determination and Educational Assistance Act, President Richard M. Nixon's formal call for "an orderly transition from federal domination of programs for and services to effective and meaningful participation by the Indian people," without the threat of termination of the government's trust responsibility. The act promised to strengthen tribal governments by ensuring their access to federal grants and their rights to contract for and redesign federal reservation programs involving education, housing, welfare, natural resource administration, and infrastructure improvements. By 1980, 370 tribes contracted for the operation of $200 million worth of reservation programs, receiving an additional $22.3 million to cover overhead expenses. Over half of all rural reservation jobs were tied to these program funds. While the act increased Indian control within their own communities, the BIA and state governments remained unwilling to relinquish institutional authority or jurisdiction, thereby limiting genuine tribal self-rule.[14]

Likewise, the courts have contributed to the ambiguous nature of tribal sovereignty in practice. *McClanahan v. Arizona State Tax Commission* (1973) confirmed that "the trend has been away from the idea of inherent Indian sovereignty as a bar to state jurisdiction and toward reliance on federal preemption" as established by treaty. In other decisions such as *Oliphant v. Suquamish Tribe* (1978), *Montana v. U.S.* (1981), *Brendale v. Confederated Tribes and Bands of the Yakima Nation* (1989), and *Duro v. Reina* (1990)—all cases involving western Indians—the Supreme Court has held that tribes lack the "territorial sovereignty" to regulate nontribal members or nonmember lands within their own reservations. These decisions reflect the confusion emanating from inconsistent congressional policies and the growing influence of conservative states' rights sentiments. The intrusion of states into jurisdictional questions on rural reservations has and will continue to muddy the already murky waters of Indian sovereignty and law, something Chief Justice John Marshall recognized and tried to thwart 160 years ago.[15]

What has emerged in the last thirty years is a singular paradox in Indian sovereignty: a new level in the reality and rhetoric of tribal autonomy, yet a simultaneous expansion of the federal trust responsibility to supervise Indian actions and resources. These mutually exclusive positions have been accepted, even demanded, by tribal peoples, in part as a hedge against the risks of self-rule and the threat of state jurisdiction. A noted native scholar is said to have described the situation like this: if the government decided to load all non-natives on ships and leave the United States in accordance with Indian wishes, Indians would be crowding the shore waving their fists at the departing ships crying, "Come back here! You're running out on your trust responsibility!" Apocryphal or not, the story captures the Catch-22 situation many tribes face as they attempt to assert real self-rule.[16]

Indians have had good reason to worry about the risks of self-rule—it was called the "Reagan eighties," a hard period for rural Americans in general. Despite his "government-to-government" rhetoric and the promise to "pursue the policy of self-government for Indian tribes without threatening termination," Ronald Reagan and his secretary of the interior, James Watt, castigated rural reservation Indians as symbols of the "failure of socialism." Having contracted for many of the services and duties of local self-government, tribes found their operating grants slashed. Total funding (only 0.04 percent of the federal budget in 1980) fell from $3.5 billion to $2 billion between 1982 and 1983. On rural western reservations, tribes were left to deal with reductions in, or inconsistent funding for, previously contracted services. Education and human service budgets were hard hit. The BIA venture capital grants fell from $11 million in 1975 to just over $3 million in 1982, while BIA administrative costs rose from $57 million to $75 million. Under Reagan the BIA budget for 1986 was $62 million less than that for 1985, and another $68 million less in 1987. Reagan's promise of private-sector help never materialized or came in the form of inequitable leases and extreme natural resource mining. Tribes, along with other state and rural governments, discovered that Reagan's "New Federalism" amounted to termination by accountants. As one tribal planner put it, "Trickle-down economics feels a lot like being pissed on."[17]

Nothing much has changed during the last two embattled presidential administrations. Assurances of a "government-to-government" relationship go hand in glove with the revelation of BIA mismanagement of trust funds and state attempts to extend their jurisdiction but not their responsibility. Conservative balanced budget rhetoric promises further budget cuts for Indian programs. We still seem to be circling that same old rock. The rhetoric, if not the reality, of sovereignty has come at a high price and may climb even higher as we enter this brave new world of conservative Republican legislative control.[18]

While self-determination remains the basic policy and has enhanced the role of tribal governments, its tragic flaw, as W. Roger Buffalohead pointed out, "is that there is so little actual Indian self-determination in Indian country because the consensus rides on the destiny of national political and economic trends rather than on the will or needs of Indian people." "We are the poorest of the poor, living in the richest country on the planet," laments Walter Echo Hawk. "We are strangers to economic development." In the last fifty years, rural reservation Indians have grown tired of being the poorest and most dependent group in the United States. Over the years, they have pursued a range of development strategies, but few have been sufficiently successful to erase the deficit imposed by nineteenth-century policies designed to turn Indians into idealized yeoman farmers and farm families.[19]

Indian reservation agriculture was never a very successful proposition in the arid West. The lack of assistance, water, and markets, along with Indian resistance and the alienation of reservation lands, had stifled farm efforts by the late 1920s. Hope returned during the New Deal and World War II as federal dollars and projects chipped away at the isolation of reservations and the insularity of the entire rural West. Reservations drew special attention during World War II for their underdeveloped natural and human resources. While 25,000 Indian men and women served in the military, another 46,000 worked in war support industries, 22,000 of them operating their own farms or wage laboring for regional agribusinesses. Twenty percent of all Navajo participated in defense industries, while 900 of 5,095 Pimas and two-thirds of the 6,200 Tohono O'odhams relocated off reservation for agricultural labor, military service, or related war industries.[20]

Agricultural production on reservations more than doubled between 1940 and 1945, in part due to increased leasing as well as improved market prices. Gross Indian farm income and home consumption reached $49 million in 1947, up from $1.8 million in 1932. Despite livestock reduction programs, drought, and diseases that decimated herds throughout the West in the 1930s—particularly on the Tohono O'odham and Navajo reservations—Indian ranching expanded during the 1940s. Taking advantage of revolving funds for livestock and land consolidation, tribes including the Northern Cheyenne, Arapaho, Gros Ventre, Yakima, Uintah-Ouray Ute, Tohono O'odham, Navajo, Mescalero, Jicarilla, and San Carlos Apache formed livestock associations to promote ranching and coordinate land use and stock sales. In 1945, Indian ranchers grossed more than $16.3 million (up from $1.3 million in 1932) and consumed another $9.2 million worth of beef at home. At war's end, two-thirds of reservation families relied on agriculture for more than half of their income. Even then, average income was only $918 in 1947, dropping to $500 in 1949, compared with the $2,500 averaged by white farmers.[21]

Declining postwar prices and markets hurt Indian agriculture and leasing, but so did Congress's terminationist policies. In the 1950s, it cut revolving credit funds for Indian farmers and ranchers, stepped up loan repayment schedules, expedited the alienation of individual trust lands, encouraged leasing, and scrapped reservation extension programs. "I think," recalled Conner Chapoose, a Northern Ute extension aide, "that's just about the time we needed the supervision." Small tribal herds such as those controlled by the Gros Ventre and Assiniboin at Fort Belknap, the Northern Cheyenne, and Isleta Pueblo were particularly vulnerable to termination. Government officials argued that they were inefficient, mismanaged, and promoted communalism instead of individual ownership and free enterprise. The BIA hindered tribal efforts to repurchase alienated and heirship lands and build viable communal herds or farms.[22]

Across the rural West, Indian farmers and ranchers struggled to make a living in marginal environments. Aridity, seasonal extremes in climate, over-grazing, erosion, and isolation from markets were hallmarks of most reservations. Small allotted field size, checkerboard inholdings by non-Indians, and complicated heirship cases, that is, disputes over inherited lands, made efficient use of the land difficult at best. At Wind River Reservation, one heirship case involved 104 descendants, while at Hoopa Valley in California more than 64 claimants shared rights to one four-acre allotment, making any use of the land—individually or by the tribe—impossible. Necessary water rights and irrigation projects passed into non-Indian control, fell into disrepair, or were beyond tribes' means to construct and maintain. Indian access to outside capital and technical training was limited, and white operators consistently outproduced Indians on the same land. On the Blackfeet Irrigation Project in 1954, Indians produced 56 percent less wheat, 25 percent less barley, and 61 percent less alfalfa than white farmers. Between 1948 and 1956, Indian crop production on the Yakima Reservation averaged $89 per acre, compared with $126 by non-Indians on leased land and $222 by non-Indians on alienated reservation lands.[23]

By the 1960s, the lure of leasing and wage work, combined with the disincentives of rural farm lifestyles, costs, lack of water, and competition from white operators and corporate agribusinesses, pushed Indians away from agriculture. Congress liberalized lease terms on trust lands, approving leases of up to ninety-nine years that brought Indian landowners only a fraction of their true value. In 1968, Indians used less than 30 percent of their irrigated fields, 25 percent of their dry lands, and 80 percent of their range. Gross production on Indian lands was about $300 million, only $114 million (38 percent) accounted for by Indians. Heirship status complicated use of over 6 million acres (11 percent) of Indian lands. Some tribes maintained cooperative livestock or farming enterprises (San Carlos, Isleta, Northern Ute, and Tohono O'odham, among others), but even the most successful ones involved fewer and fewer people. Individuals pursued subsistence operations with techniques, crops, and animals that mirrored cultural rather than market-oriented choices. Whereas 50 percent of Indians maintained full-time agricultural operations in 1940, only 10 percent did so by 1960. By 1970, only 6.2 percent of Indians lived on farms, roughly the same proportion as whites, yet higher than that for Mexican Americans (1.6 percent) or African Americans (3 percent).[24]

In 1980, Indians controlled 52 million acres, 42 million in tribal ownership. Only 7,211 full- or part-time Indian farmers remained in 1982. Their average age was 50.4 years; only 946 were younger than 35 years, and only 775 were women. Indian farmers sold $98.4 million in crops from 705,378 acres of cropland, as well as $138.5 million in livestock. The majority were small subsistence operators: 4,252 had fewer than 140 acres, and only 1,270 controlled more than 500 acres; 4,750 sold less than $10,000 annually, while 1,476 sold more than $20,000. Besides the lack of capital and access to technology, water limited most operations in the West. In 1983, litigation over non-Indian appropriation of groundwater and surface water involved 100 Indian communities in more than sixty water basins. Despite several federal aid programs available to Indian farmers, farming decreased and leasing increased under the Reagan administration. Between 1983 and 1985, Indian farm land use dropped from 38 to 35 percent and grazing land use dropped from 92 to 83 percent.[25]

Recently, some groups have tried to reinvigorate reservation agricultural economies. In 1987, the Intertribal Agriculture Council formed to promote agricultural land use, but its proposals to consolidate arable land and facilitate tribal operations have been blocked by the BIA's concern for individual over tribal land rights. Other organizations like the Southwest Indian Agriculture Association have pursued funding for irrigation projects, while the InterTribal Bison Cooperative is touting the commercial and cultural value of raising buffalo. Beyond a handful of successful tribal farms and ranches, hopes for widespread Indian agriculture are dim.[26]

While many Indian families continue to live in rural areas and spend part of their time working land or livestock, most earn a living in other ways—a familiar pattern for rural westerners in general. In the 1940s, many Indians entered the military or worked in the defense industries. In the 1940s and 1950s, a few worked as extras in the Hollywood Westerns filmed in the Southwest. Most simply existed on the per capita distributions of tribal claim case moneys or resource and lease revenues. Recognizing the limits of agricultural economies in the arid West, the BIA and tribal governments encouraged tribal members to relocate to cities in the 1950s and 1960s to make a living. Others found jobs in local border towns, precipitating a pattern of commuting from rural reservation home to urban center for work and the disjuncture of daily life in two worlds. This has become particularly evident among Indians in the Rio Grande valley who reside in their own pueblos and commute daily to Los Alamos, Santa Fe, or Albuquerque for work.[27]

In an effort to provide jobs at home and halt what was perceived to be a "brain drain" of educated Indians from reservation to city, western tribes with little to offer besides open land and an ample supply of low-wage, nonunion labor attempted to attract outside corporations or to set up their own manufacturing enterprises. They received some help from the Indian Vocational Training Act of 1956, that allowed the secretary of the interior to create vocational training programs or to subsidize private industries that provided on-the-job training for rural reservation Indians. Despite limited funding, the program proved more cost-efficient than similar ones designed for non-Indians (like the Job Corps).[28]

The pace of reservation industrialization increased in the 1960s. Prior to 1960, only 4 industrial plants were located on Indian lands. That number rose to 137 in 1968 and to 225 by 1972, employing between 391 and 6,239 Indian workers. Favorable lease deals arranged between businesses and tribal councils as well as government programs like the Area Redevelopment Administration (ARA, 1961) and the Economic Development Administration (EDA, 1965) which focused on job creation through grants for infrastructure improvements—roads, utilities, industrial parks, shopping centers, and other services—made reservations more attractive to industry and tourism. Between 1965 and 1970, the EDA spent $78 million on 107 reservations. Likewise, the Office of Economic Opportunity (OEO) extended antipoverty programs and training grants to reservations, spending $22 million on Indian community action programs in 1968 alone.

Most of the industrial employers attracted to reservations were military contractors, relying on heavy defense spending during the Vietnam era. Laguna Pueblo made electronic components for Burnell and Company of New York; Navajo made semiconductors for Fairchild Camera and Instrument Company; Zuni made computer parts for the AIRCO Corporation; and Fort Peck Assiniboin and Sioux reconditioned small arms for the U.S. Air Force through Dynalecton Corporation. In the early 1970s, as recession and military cutbacks slowed the economy and closed plants, tribes took them over and tried to operate their own tribal enterprises, joint-venture partnerships, and small businesses ranging from arts and crafts, to wood products and metal fabrication, to pharmaceuticals and textiles, to fireworks and native foods. Federal assistance became even more important for these nascent businesses, which relied on grants and preference contracts as spelled out by Nixon's Self-Determination Act and the Comprehensive Employment and Training Act (CETA).

Not all industrial operations on rural reservations were as successful as hoped. Isolation from markets, limited rural infrastructures, and lack of training continued to be a problem. Many firms employed Indian workers but non-Indian managers, and when cultural patterns of work, absenteeism, and low education levels interfered with productivity, white bosses hired more non-Indians. Tribal operations themselves were a mixed success in producing lasting jobs and income for rural reservation peoples. Bureaucratic mismanagement (both tribal and federal) plagued many of these operations, while inconsistent federal assistance made long-term planning difficult. The Reagan administration's cutbacks in funding and its vastly scaled-down Job Partnership Training Act of 1981 hurt tribal and individual Indian-owned operations dependent on federal assistance. Today, rural tribes are still eligible for a number of development grants from agencies such as the U.S. Department of Agriculture's Rural Development Administration, but the number and dollar amount continue to decline.[29]

Reservation development in the rural West has taken other paths as well. Tourism and recreational sports such as hunting, fishing, and skiing are becoming important sources of income for groups like the Jicarilla, Mescalero, and

White Mountain Apache. Navajo and Havasupais are cashing in on tourists visiting the Grand Canyon and Four Corners region. Near Glacier National Park and Little Bighorn Battlefield National Monument, Blackfeet and Crow are pursuing the benefits of seasonal tourism. But bigger still has been the impact of high-stakes bingo and casino gaming on reservation communities. Florida Seminoles got the bingo-ball rolling in 1979, and others followed suit, pushing the limits of tribal sovereignty and federal law. Concerned about the "moral" impacts of gaming and the threat of organized crime (but more worried about the competition Indian operations posed to existing state lotteries), Congress clamped down on tribal operations in 1988. The Indian Gaming Regulatory Act established three classes of operations, forcing tribes to negotiate restrictive compacts with state governments.[30]

Despite regulations that many claim abridge tribal sovereignty, tribes have embraced gaming as economic development. Hotel-casino complexes are popping up on reservations across the country. As of June 1993, tribes operated 209 legal gaming establishments, an estimated $6 billion annual industry creating needed jobs and cash flow for both Indian and non-Indian communities. In the rural West the Ak-Chin of Arizona, the Mi-wuk and various Rancheria and Mission bands in California, the Shoshone-Bannock in Idaho, the Southern Ute in Colorado, the Gros Ventre, Assiniboin, and Crow in Montana, Tesuque and Isleta pueblos and the Jicarilla Apache in New Mexico, Western Shoshones and Paiutes in Nevada, the Siletz in Oregon, and the S'Klallam, Nooksack, Colville, and Spokane in Washington all run gaming operations of varying sizes. Given their rural locations, few are as successful as Indian casinos in and around Seattle, Albuquerque, and Phoenix, or as the Pequot's Foxwood Casino in Connecticut, which draws from the New York metropolitan area, but they do provide some employment and income for the tribes—income used for a variety of development projects from housing to land acquisition to tribal aid programs. While not without its critics and inherent weaknesses, gaming offers rural tribes some hope for the economic self-sufficiency necessary to assure native self-determination.[31]

Unfortunately, gaming has not and will not magically solve reservation underdevelopment. While things have improved, rural Indian poverty and its manifestations are long-term problems. In 1945, one-third of rural reservation families had annual incomes under $500, and nearly all earned less than $1,000. In 1959, 60 percent of rural Indian families (compared with 30 percent of all rural families) earned less than $3,000. In 1968, 20 percent of reservation Indians received welfare payments, four times the rate of non-Indians. On the sixteen largest reservations in 1969, poverty rates ranged from 42 percent at Wind River to 78 percent at Papago. Median income for rural reservation Indians in 1970 was about $4,500, 62 percent of what urban Indians made and less than 41 percent of non-Indian income. One-third of Indian families lived below the poverty line, compared with 11 percent of families nationally. In

1980, rural Indian family median income was $13,055—still 78 percent of urban Indian and 63 percent of white family income. Rural poverty rates were 29 percent, compared with 20 percent for urban Indians and only 7 percent for whites. By 1990, median Indian family income was $21,750, 62 percent of the national median; 31 percent of rural Indians lived in poverty, compared with 16 percent of all rural dwellers, 15 percent of urban Indians, and 13 percent of all Americans.

Reservation unemployment has hovered between 30 and 50 percent from 1940 to the present. At Tongue River and the Rocky Boy reservations, unemployment in 1958 reached 81.5 and 90 percent, respectively. In 1972, reservation unemployment exceeded 40 percent, eight times the national average. While nationally Indian unemployment was 13.2 percent in 1980, reservation unemployment was 31.4 percent. That figure climbed as high as 38 percent by 1990, yet another 46.3 percent of rural Indians were underemployed and 26.2 percent with full-time jobs were living near the poverty level. As of 1988, Indian peoples had a shorter life expectancy than the national average, were 2.3 times more likely to die in automobile accidents, had 3.4 times the rate of chronic liver disease and cirrhosis, 2.6 times the rate of diabetes mellitus, 5 times the rate of tuberculosis, and were 1.3 and 1.6 times more likely to die from suicide or homicide. Between 1969 and 1988, Indian alcoholism mortality rates were from 3.8 to 7.7 times the national average. Poor nutrition and health care along with inadequate housing, utilities, and water systems, plague rural reservation dwellers. While educational levels have improved dramatically, only 65.5 percent of Indians aged twenty-five and over had high school diplomas in 1990, 10 percent below the national average. The cycle of rural poverty has become a way of life for many who find few viable alternatives close to home.[32]

"It is clear that Indians do not want to be poor any more," Philip S. Deloria told listeners in 1983. "The real issue in this country has been over the control of land and natural resources and the relationship of Indians to the economy." Removed to unwanted and apparently worthless reservations in the nineteenth century, Indians and their neighbors later discovered that many of these lands were rich in resources. Today, Indians control 30 percent of the coal west of the Mississippi River, 50 to 60 percent of uranium resources, 4 to 6 percent of proven oil and gas reserves, 15 million acres of timber, extensive fish and wildlife resources, and an unquantified amount of water, which is as precious as life itself in the arid West. Yet ownership has not ensured absolute control. Their retreat from small-scale agriculture and growing dependence on leasing and the global boom-and-bust economy of extractive resource industries has involved tribes in long legal battles. It has also forced tribes to reconsider a balance between development that generates income rather than jobs, and the benefits of their rural environment. In many ways their situation parallels that of the larger rural West, which both desires and fears development, values yet despoils their own environment.[33]

In the last fifty years, and at times in the face of tremendous social and political pressures, tribes recaptured many of their hunting and fishing treaty rights. Particularly in the Pacific Northwest, Indians have reclaimed access to rivers and beaches where they once carried on subsistence activities. In Washington and Oregon, several tribes have developed sophisticated fishery management systems, which include commercial outlets for native fishermen. Others like the Mescalero Apache, Pyramid Lake Paiutes, and Wind River Shoshones and Arapaho have developed scientific and culturally sensitive programs for managing their own faunal resources. The Jicarilla Apache boast a wildlife management program that has become a model for the state of New Mexico, using aerial surveys and radio telemetry to keep track of big game. Through management they hope to blend traditional subsistence resources with modern commercial use.[34]

Timber has been an important resource for a handful of western tribes. In the 1930s, surveys estimated that 90 percent of all merchantable Indian-owned timber was in four western states—Washington, Oregon, Arizona, and Montana—with lesser amounts in California and New Mexico. In the post–World War II boom, Indian timber found ready markets, creating jobs for thousands of rural reservation dwellers in the woods and processing plants. The Navajo, Fort Apache, Hoopa Valley, Colville, and Warm Springs Indians all developed successful forest products industries between 1950 and 1990. But as has occurred in other rural western communities, overcutting, market declines, and mismanagement, along with mandates for watershed and endangered species habitat preservation and the desire to balance forest use for economic need with preservation for cultural need have derailed some tribal operations.[35]

Of all resources, water is fast becoming the most important Indian asset in the arid West, but only after years of having little control over it. Twentieth-century reclamation, irrigation, and big dam projects have both flooded reservations and left them high and dry, affecting Indian farms, fisheries, and sacred sites. Over the years Indian water has been siphoned off for urban growth, agribusinesses, and power generation—for the transformation of the rural West. While the *Winters v. U.S.* (1908) decision assured Indians primary water rights, it never quantified those rights, and the issue of how much water tribes have legitimate rights to use or possibly sell has become crucial in the arid West. Indian claims may exceed 45 million acre-feet of water annually, with a market value of $20 to $50 billion. Future development, control, and water marketing by Shoshones, Ute, Paiutes, Navajo, Pimas, Tohono O'odhams, Ak-Chins, and others promise a massive redistribution of water (and money in lieu of water), raising critical economic and environmental issues for the entire western region.[36]

In the late twentieth century, coal, oil and gas, uranium, and a host of other minerals made a handful of tribes very wealthy. In 1955, six western tribes— Navajo, Jicarilla, Blackfeet, Wind River, Fort Peck, and Fort Berthold—received 45 percent of the $29.9 million generated by reservation mineral development. In 1958, the Jackpile uranium mine paid $1.75 million in royalties to Laguna Pueblo and wages to 400 Laguna and Acoma employees. Oil and gas income exceeded $66 million on all Indian reservations in 1964. Coal leasing took off on the Navajo, Hopi, Crow, and Northern Cheyenne reservations in the late 1960s. By 1975, disputes over inequities in long-term lease rates, the limited number and duration of jobs held by Indians, and the desire to control mineral development led to the formation of the Council of Energy Resource Tribes (CERT), representing twenty-five reservations (today, forty-nine groups and four Canadian affiliates). Renegotiated leases and the ability to levy severance taxes on resources have generated more income, if not jobs, for these tribes. While oil and gas income has declined from over $140 million in 1983 to $81.96 million in 1990, coal income has increased 160 percent since 1985, totaling $60.79 million in 1990—largely the result of renegotiated leases.[37]

These forms of natural resource exploitation and processing have generated some jobs for rural reservation dwellers and billions in revenues for tribes, but they have also divided tribes and unleashed some of the most environmentally destructive forces on fragile arid ecosystems, threatening native health and sacred places. Coal strip mining is only one of the more visible threats. At sacred Black Mesa, the Peabody Coal Company leases 64,858 acres from the Navajo and Hopi tribes. Each year it ships 7 million tons of coal seventy-eight miles by electric railroad to the Navajo Generating Station near Page, Arizona. It pumps another 5 million tons through an eighteen-inch-diameter, 273-mile-long coal slurry pipeline to the Mohave Generating Station near Laughlin, Nevada. Each year the pipeline consumes over 1.4 billion gallons of water, pumped from an aquifer 3,000 feet beneath the arid Hopi reservation. The power stations sell most of the electricity to Las Vegas and southern California customers, while casting a visible haze over the Grand Canyon and Four Corners region. Despite the employment and $9 million in royalties they receive each year (70 percent of their tribal budget), Hopi are still critical of this use of water, especially as it lowers their water table and hurts traditional farming. "We're not against southern California getting electricity," Hopi chairman Vernon Masayesva said in 1990. "It just seems foolish to be using water as a transportation method from a desert climate where you have an average rainfall of six to seven inches."[38]

Other types of resource mining can be equally destructive. Since the end of World War II, uranium mining and processing on the Navajo, Laguna, and Spokane reservations have contaminated soil and water and poisoned the health of rural Indian families who worked in or lived near those facilities. Oil and gas exploration across the Mountain West and in Alaska scars thousands of acres of land with service roads, drill sites, and pipelines, not to mention oil and drill-waste spills. Pollution from off-site resource exploitation is another threat to reservation Indians—the impact that the Exxon *Valdez* spill, the Alaska pipeline, or drilling on the North Slope and Arctic National Wildlife Refuge has on native subsistence resources; the impact of cyanide heap-leach gold mining on the neighboring Fort Belknap Reservation; the impact of radioactive contamination from atomic weapon production, testing, and storage across the West.[39]

What worries some observers is that in order to generate needed income, tribes without abundant natural resources have explored or agreed to become national dumping grounds. There are already an estimated 1,200 hazardous waste sites located on or adjacent to reservations, and that number is growing. The California Campo are proceeding with a 600-acre solid waste recycling center and landfill to handle 3,000 tons of nontoxic waste per day from San Diego County. Navajo and Kaibab-Paiutes in Arizona accepted, then backed out of, deals with Waste-Tech Services, a subsidiary of Amoco Oil, to host hazardous waste incinerators. Using $100,000 study grants, the U.S. Department of Energy (DOE) has enticed tribes and rural communities in the West to explore storing high-level nuclear waste in monitored retrievable storage (MRS) facilities until a permanent national DOE site at Yucca Mountain, Nevada, can be licensed. The Skull Valley Goshute, Mescalero Apache, Northern Arapaho, Fort McDermitt Paiute-Shoshones, Yakima, and other native groups applied for or received grants before Congress halted the process in 1993. Since then, the Mescalero have signed an agreement with Minnesota's Northern States Power Company representing thirty-three nuclear energy companies to establish a private MRS for 40,000 metric tons of spent fuel. The deal promises an estimated tribal profit of $250 million, with total revenues exceeding $2 billion over the forty-year life of the project. Several disputed referenda later, the tribe is still bitterly divided on how to proceed.[40]

The atmosphere has become so charged that even the decision to explore this MRS siting raises a howl of protest. "It's genocide aimed at Indian people who will suffer the consequences of poisoning our rivers and our land with nuclear waste," Klickitat chief Johnny Jackson of the confederated Yakima Nation told a 1992 gathering of tribal leaders. "Even if tribes say they just want to study it, the government intends to hook tribal governments with the money. I know from experience that the government never gives you money for nothing." Russell Jim (Yakima) agrees that when need dictates immediate resource exploitation rather than carefully planned development, tribes threaten themselves with "self-cannibalism." The concern that such development strategies might destroy reservation environments is genuine, tempered by the knowledge that rural Indians desperately need some alternative to poverty and unemployment. This conundrum faces rural communities throughout the West, but such decisions are particularly difficult for rural peoples with few alternatives, people whose cosmologies and identities are so tied to the land.[41]

In addition to these concerns, place is an important element in American Indian identity. Native creation stories often describe human emergence into this world at a specific location, or they underscore the importance of certain geographic features that bound and give meaning to a native world. Tribal control of land holds Indians together physically and culturally as identifiable groups, safe from the cultural submersion that has stalked other ethnic Americans. Reservations provide a way and a place for Indians and Indianness to continue. "Everything is tied to our homeland," said D'Arcy McNickle. "Our language, religion, songs, beliefs—everything. Without our homeland we are nothing."[42]

Yet Indian place and identity have never been static. In order to survive the descendants of Columbus, Indians have demonstrated enormous cultural flexibility and resilience in the face of changing location, land use, and lifestyles. From the nineteenth-century plethora of tribal identities, a truly pan-Indian identity has begun to emerge—one that actually gives meaning to the collective misnomer imposed by that lost Italian. Across the country, Indians have transcended tribal lines through pan-Indian organizations, political activism, urban community centers, national cultural events like the powwow, and a burgeoning body of Indian literature and art to realize a commonality of experience and purpose. There is a renewed pride in Indianness once hidden to escape ridicule or suppression. One might argue over how deep and clear this pan-Indian identity runs because, on the other hand, the West has seen a conservative retribalization—the revitalization of specific tribal identity, of language and ceremonies, of the meaning of homeland and a lifestyle that was overwhelmingly western and rural, on the periphery of urban pan-Indian/non-Indian society.

What has emerged recently is a painful struggle over Indian identity: Who, what, and where is "Indian," and who decides? At issue is the right to self-identification versus the sovereignty of tribes to recognize their own. Part of the problem is expressed in the competition between rural and urban, resident and nonresident tribal members for control of customs, tribal assets, and leadership. Larger forces fuel this process. Rapid population growth (a quintupling since 1940), mobility, intermarriage and multiple tribal affiliation by blood, tribal blood quantum games, and the emergence of separated mixed-blood groups have and will continue to generate factionalism within tribes, necessitating the periodic and painful redefinition of tribal identity and Indianness. The identity purges presently going on within the American Indian Movement (AIM), the contention between Northern Ute and their mixed-blood affiliates, and the long road to federal recognition by Southern Paiute bands are only a sample of the contemporary identity debates in the West.[43]

Underlying Indian identity problems are the persistent symbols and stereotypes perpetuated in both Indian and non-Indian cultures. Indians have always been used as symbols in opposition to Euro-American culture. On the one hand they were savage, deficient, and disappearing; on the other they were noble, environmental, and stoic. Twentieth-century movies and literature reinforced stereotypes of both Indians and the West—mounted

Plains warriors in a Monument Valley setting. Meanwhile, the pan-Indian powwow culture that has emerged is likewise heavily Plains-oriented in symbol and practice, more urban in focus than the rural powwow-rodeo culture that emerged on western reservations. Corporate America has used Indian images (again, largely Plains) to market products from tobacco to cooking oil to firearms to malt liquor. Schools and professional sports teams have adopted Indian mascots as symbols of their fierceness, pride, and authenticity. Today, natives themselves are moving to copyright and protect those symbols from exploitation and for their own use.

The counterculture of the 1960s, modern environmentalism, and the New Age revolution all created an explosion of interest in Indian philosophy and identity. They have also introduced new forms of commercialism and racism as a growing number of "wannabes" commandeer native arts, rituals, and places. In some cases they are led by Indians offering for-profit spiritual leadership outside the cultural context or sanction of their group. In the process these cultural "wannabes" appropriate the Indian public voice and message, emphasizing the mythic and relegating Indians to an idealized past, refusing to allow them to be or become modern. In the end, such stereotypes and misrepresentations mask the modern Indian reality and misdirect non-Indian society's relationships with and responses to Native Americans as modern peoples, as rural peoples living in the American West.[44]

One reality that has emerged in recent years as the differences between urban and rural America accelerate is the commonality among rural westerners—the emergence of a rural identity that may at times bridge race. Peter Iverson points out how increasingly Indian and non-Indian ranchers in the West have more in common with each other than with their urban counterparts. Their rural solidarity transcends cowboy clothing and music. They face the same problems of isolation, environment, and market forces beyond their control. They share a sense of place and an oral history of the land, of cultural as well as physical stewardship and ownership through generations. They both rely on and distrust government. They work the land and then work other jobs in order to keep working the land. They share a pride in their choice of livelihood and a hope for improvement even as they watch kin move to the cities. As Iverson sees it, they respectively have become "native to their lands" as they have become marginalized by urban society.[45]

Rural settlement and land-use patterns, then, continue to be the hallmark of western reservations even as the number of rural reservation dwellers dwindles. This divergence contributes to the difficulty that Indians as individuals and tribes have in defining themselves and their future. Will rural traits, identities, and values give way to more urban ones? Is the change approaching like a truck pulling uphill, or has it already passed, trailing in Doppler the sound of ruralness? Is there even an option, let alone a clear distinction, anymore in a world reduced in time and space by technology?

"I'm not sure what the Indian story is anymore," admits Jicarilla Apache Richard TeCube. "We're not feathers and buckskin. People live in houses with running water, pitched roofs. It's done, you can't take it back now. How does the influence countrywide filter down to an isolated reservation community? TV, books, movies. We have powwows and ceremonies all across New Mexico—packed with people from all over. That mobility is a profound influence." Mobility, the lure of jobs, and the possibilities of urban life have all chipped away at Indian ruralness but have not destroyed it. Gail Russell, Chemehuevi/Apache director of the Indian Walk-in Center in Salt Lake City, points out, "By living in urban areas, Indian people have seen that what they have is meaningful and precious. If there was an economy on the reservation, they would choose to live there. They would not *choose* to live in the cities." Culture and community rooted in place still hold sway.[46]

Most agree that a native future depends on living life simultaneously in two worlds, rural and urban, Indian and non-Indian. "If Apaches are going to be here in two hundred years—and be Apache—they're going to need to maintain both worlds, cross the bridge by day and come back safe at night," says Wesley Bonito. "If they don't, the world will just absorb us." Tribal educational programs are one way to bridge that gulf. Wilma Mankiller (Cherokee) counts on "a cadre of well-trained young people to help us enter the twenty-first century on our own terms." For others the ultimate rural future remains the continuity of earth and place in memory—the stories of elders who lived on and worked native land in a rural West. "This has always been our land," insist elders from Zia, Jemez, and Santa Ana pueblos. "We know these matters not merely because our grandparents told us vague stories when we were children, but because our parents and grandparents, and their parents and grandparents before them, made sure to tell us so exactly and so often that we could not forget."[47]

In the beginning and the end this connection with the land, with a rural landscape, defines the experience of western Indians. It is the basis for Indian identity and any aspiration for a tribal future. Its importance includes yet transcends simple economic worth as a place to be and become Indian. "Once in his life, a man ought to concentrate his mind upon the remembered earth," writes Kiowa novelist N. Scott Momaday. "He ought to give himself up to a particular landscape in his experiences, to look at it from as many angles as he can, to wonder about it, to dwell upon it. He ought to imagine that he touches it with his hands at every season and listens to the sounds that are made upon it. He ought to imagine the creatures that are there and all the faintest motions of the wind. He ought to recollect the glare of noon and all the colors of the dawn and dusk." This intimate experience with the land is what separates urban and rural America, just as it binds rural westerners together on land that was the Native West long before it was the rural West.[48]

NOTES

1. R. Douglas Hurt, *Indian Agriculture in America: Prehistory to the Present* (Lawrence: University Press of Kansas, 1987). While "Native American" has become a favored academic term, most native peoples refer to themselves as Indians.

2. As quoted by Vine Deloria, Jr., *Custer Died for Your Sins: An Indian Manifesto* (New York: Avon Books, 1969), 167–68.

3. Arlene Hirschfelder and Martha Kreipe de Montaño, *The Native American Almanac: A Portrait of Native America Today* (New York: Prentice Hall, 1993), 28; C. Matthew Snipp, *American Indians: The First of This Land* (New York: Russell Sage Foundation, 1989), 83; C. Matthew Snipp and Gary D. Sandefur, "Small Gains for Rural Indians Who Move to Cities," *Rural Development Perspectives* 5 (October 1988): 22; Joane Nagel, Carol Ward, and Timothy Knapp, "The Politics of American Indian Economic Development: The Reservation/Urban Nexus," in *Public Policy Impacts on American Indian Economic Development,* ed. C. Matthew Snipp (Albuquerque: University of New Mexico, Institute for Native American Development, 1988), 61.

4. The western census region includes Arizona, California, Colorado, Idaho, Montana, Nevada, New Mexico, Oregon, Utah, Washington, Wyoming, Alaska, and Hawaii, the parameters of "West" in this study. See Paul Stuart, *Nations Within a Nation: Historical Statistics of American Indians* (New York: Greenwood Press, 1987), 57; Edna L. Pasano, *We the . . . First Americans* (Washington, D.C.: U.S. Department of Commerce, Economics and Statistics Administration, Bureau of the Census, 1993), 3; David Harris, "The 1990 Census Count of American Indians: What Do the Numbers Really Mean?" *Social Science Quarterly* 75 (September 1994): 584.

5. Pasano, *We the . . . First Americans,* 1; C. Matthew Snipp and Gene F. Summers, "American Indians and Economic Poverty," in *Rural Poverty in America,* ed. Cynthia M. Duncan (New York: Auburn House, 1992), 155–56; Peter Iverson, "Cowboys and Indians, Stockmen and Aborigines: The Rural American West and the Northern Territory of Australia Since 1945," *Social Science Journal* 26 (January 1989): 8; Peter Iverson, *When Indians Became Cowboys: Native Peoples and Cattle Ranching in the American West* (Norman: University of Oklahoma Press, 1994), 182–224; Michael P. Nofz, "Rural Community Development: The Case of Indian Reservations," *Rural Sociologist* 6 (March 1986): 69; Robert P. Swierenga, "Theoretical Perspectives on the New Rural History: From Environmentalism to Modernization," *Agricultural History* 56 (July 1982): 495–96.

6. Russell Thornton and Mary K. Grasmick, *Sociology of American Indians: A Critical Bibliography* (Bloomington: Indiana University Press, 1980), 1–7; Melissa L. Meyer and Russell Thornton, "Indians and the Numbers Game: Quantitative Methods in Native American History," in *New Directions in Native American History,* ed. Colin G. Calloway (Norman: University of Oklahoma Press, 1988), 19; Robert P. Swierenga, "The New Rural History: Defining the Parameters," *Great Plains Quarterly* 1 (Fall 1981): 211–23. This observation is borne out in my own literature searches and in an e-mail conversation with Matt Snipp of the University of Wisconsin–Madison, one of the few (and best) rural sociologists actively involved in such research and writing. With the exception of Doug Hurt's superb overview in *Indian Agriculture in America,* rural/agricultural historians have done no better. I would argue that most contemporary

issues facing tribal groups transcend the West—a disputed term itself—and are more universal than regional, more temporal than spatial. For the purposes of this essay, however, I will confine my examples to this "West."

7. Vine Deloria, Jr., as quoted by Peter Nabakov, ed., *Native American Testimony: A Chronicle of Indian-White Relations from Prophecy to the Present* (New York: Penguin, 1991), 408.

8. Alan L. Sorkin, *American Indians and Federal Aid* (Washington D.C.: Brookings Institute, 1971), 7; Howard M. Bahr, Bruce A. Chadwick, and Joseph H. Stauss, *American Ethnicity* (Lexington, Mass.: D. C. Heath, 1979), 375. For the general outlines of Indian policy, see Francis Paul Prucha, *The Great Father: The United States Government and the American Indians,* 2 vols. (Lincoln: University of Nebraska Press, 1984); Frederick E. Hoxie, *A Final Promise: The Campaign to Assimilate the Indians, 1880–1920* (Lincoln: University of Nebraska Press, 1984); Donald L. Parman, *Indians and the American West in the Twentieth Century* (Bloomington: Indiana University Press, 1994).

9. Kenneth R. Philp, ed., *Indian Self-Rule: First-Hand Accounts of Indian-White Relations from Roosevelt to Reagan* (Salt Lake City, Utah: Howe Brothers, 1986), 15–109.

10. Imre Sutton, ed., *Irredeemable America: The Indians' Estate and Land Claims* (Albuquerque: University of New Mexico Press, 1985); Philp, *Indian Self-Rule,* 114–28, 150–60.

11. Philleo Nash, "Relocation," in *Indian Self-Rule: First-Hand Accounts of Indian-White Relations from Roosevelt to Reagan,* ed. Kenneth R. Philp (Salt Lake City, Utah: Howe Brothers, 1986), 166. See also Snipp and Sandefur, "Small Gains for Rural Indians," 22–25. On termination and relocation see Donald L. Fixico, *Termination and Relocation: Federal Indian Policy, 1945–1960* (Albuquerque: University of New Mexico Press, 1986); Parman, *Indians,* 123–47; Kenneth R. Philp, "Stride Toward Freedom: The Relocation of Indians to Cities, 1952–1960," *Western Historical Quarterly* 16 (April 1985): 175–90; Joseph Jorgensen, "Federal Policies, American Indian Polities, and the 'New Federalism,' " *American Indian Culture and Research Journal* 10 (Spring 1986): 1–13; Prucha, *Great Father,* 2:1013–84.

12. Parman, *Indians,* 139–41; Susan Hood, "Termination of the Klamath Indian Tribe of Oregon," *Ethnohistory* 19 (Fall 1972): 379–92; Public Law 90-284 (1968), 82 *U.S. Statutes* 73–92; *Santa Clara Pueblo v. Martinez* (1978), 436 *U.S. Reports* 49–83; Conference of Western Attorneys General, *American Indian Law Deskbook* (Niwot: University Press of Colorado, 1993), 151–66; William A. Brophy and Sophie D. Aberle, comps., *The Indian, America's Unfinished Business* (Norman: University of Oklahoma Press, 1966); Sorkin, *American Indians;* Parman, *Indians,* 150–51; Philp, *Indian Self-Rule,* 191–250; Prucha, *Great Father,* 2: 1087–1110.

13. Donald L. Parman, "Indians of the Modern West," in *The Twentieth-Century West: Historical Interpretations,* ed. Gerald D. Nash and Richard W. Etulain (Albuquerque: University of New Mexico Press, 1989), 164–65; Parman, *Indians,* 148–74; Philp, *Indian Self-Rule,* 228–50; Alvin M. Josephy, Jr., *Now That the Buffalo's Gone: A Study of Today's American Indians* (1982; reprint, Norman: University of Oklahoma Press, 1984), 215–63; Francis P. Prucha, "American Indian Policy in the Twentieth Century," *Western Historical Quarterly* 15 (January 1984): 13.

14. Public Law 93-638, 88 *U.S. Statutes* 2203–17 (1975); George S. Esbner, Jr., "Shortcomings of the Indian Self-Determination Policy," in *State and Reservation: New Perspectives on Federal Indian Policy,* ed. George Pierre Castile and Robert L. Bee (Tucson: University of Arizona Press, 1992), 212–23; Nofz, "Rural Community Development," 73–75; Prucha, *Great Father,* 2: 1139–62; Philp, *Indian Self-Rule,* 251–59.

15. Conference of Western Attorneys General, *American Indian Law Deskbook,* 98–150; Ward Churchill and Glenn T. Morris, "Key Indian Laws and Cases," in *The State of Native America: Genocide, Colonization, and Resistance,* ed. M. Annette Jaimes (Boston: South End Press, 1992), 13–21. Charles F. Wilkinson, *American Indians, Time, and the Law* (New Haven, Conn.: Yale University Press, 1987), 29, 61–63, notes that, despite apparently contradictory opinions, Indian sovereignty has done well in the courts.

16. Prucha, "American Indian Policy," 16–18; Parman, "Indians of the Modern West," 165; Robert L. Bee, "Riding the Paper Tiger," in *State and Reservation: New Perspectives on Federal Indian Policy,* ed. George Pierre Castile and Robert L. Bee (Tucson: University of Arizona Press, 1992), 144.

17. "Indians Rap Watt's Socialism Remark," *Wisconsin State Journal* (Madison, Wisc.) 20 January 1983, A1; Nabakov, *Native American Testimony,* 405; Marjane Ambler, *Breaking the Iron Bonds: Indian Control of Energy Development* (Lawrence: University Press of Kansas, 1990), 3–5, 8; quote in Nabakov, *Native American Testimony,* 406; Nofz, "Rural Community Development," 72–75; Jorgensen, "Federal Policies," 10–13; C. Patrick Morris, "Termination by Accountants: The Reagan Indian Policy," in *Native Americans and Public Policy,* ed. Fremont J. Lyden and Lyman H. Legters (Pittsburgh: University of Pittsburgh Press, 1992), 63–84.

18. "President Bush Issues Indian Policy Statement," *Indian News, Week-in-Review* 15 (17 June 1991): 1; "President Bill Clinton's Address to Native American Leaders," *Native Peoples* 7 (Summer 1994): 5–6; "Mismanagement Uncovered in Audit of Indian Trust Fund," *Deseret News* (Salt Lake City, Utah), 8 October 1989, A21; Bunty Anquoe, "BIA Mismanagement Blasted," *Indian Country Today* (Rapid City, S.Dak.), 8 April 1992, A1. For an example of the wholesale attack on the BIA and Indian funding by the new Republican-controlled Congress led by House Speaker Newt Gingrich, see Bunty Anquoe, "BIA Funding Axed by House GOP Lawmakers," *Indian Country Today,* 2 March 1995, A1; Bunty Anquoe, "Congress Hams It Up While Slashing Tribal Programs," *Indian Country Today,* 20 April 1995, A1.

19. W. Roger Buffalohead, "Self-Rule in the Past and the Future: An Overview," in *Indian Self-Rule: First-Hand Accounts of Indian-White Relations from Roosevelt to Reagan,* ed. Kenneth R. Philp (Salt Lake City, Utah: Howe Brothers, 1986), 271; Walter Echo Hawk, "Healthy Environment, Healthy Environment: American Indian Lessons," in *A Society to Match the Scenery: Personal Visions of the Future of the American West,* ed. Gary Holthaus et al. (Niwot: University Press of Colorado, 1991), 63.

20. Iverson, "Cowboys and Indians," 2–3; Alison R. Bernstein, *American Indians and World War II: Toward a New Era in Indian Affairs* (Norman: University of Oklahoma Press, 1991); Parman, *Indians,* 107–17; Sorkin, *American Indians,* 104–5; Jeré Franco, "Beyond Reservation Boundaries: Native American Laborers in World War II," *Journal of the Southwest* 36 (Autumn 1994): 241–54.

21. Hurt, *Indian Agriculture*, 195–98; Parman, *Indians*, 116–17; Iverson, *When Indians Became Cowboys*, 116–81.

22. Conner Chapoose, Interview, September 1960, no. 10:17, Dorris Duke American Indian Oral History Project, Marriott Library Manuscripts Collection, University of Utah, Salt Lake City; Iverson, *When Indians Became Cowboys*, 155–61; Brophy and Aberle, *The Indian*, 80–81, 92–95.

23. Brophy and Aberle, *The Indian*, 73–80; David Rich Lewis, *Neither Wolf Nor Dog: American Indians, Environment, and Agrarian Change* (New York: Oxford University Press, 1994), 115; Hurt, *Indian Agriculture*, 211.

24. C. Matthew Snipp, "Public Policy Impacts and American Indian Economic Development," in *Public Policy Impacts on American Indian Development*, ed. C. Matthew Snipp (Albuquerque: University of New Mexico Press, 1988), 5; Nagel, Ward, and Knapp, "Politics of American Indian Economic Development," 42–44; Hurt, *Indian Agriculture*, 195–208; Iverson, *When Indians Became Cowboys*, 155–81; Sorkin, *American Indians*, 18, 66–78; Brophy and Aberle, *The Indian*, 63, 80–81; Lewis, *Neither Wolf Nor Dog*, 19–20, 168–76; William P. Kuvlesky, Clark S. Knowlton, Thomas J. Durant, Jr., and William C. Payne, Jr., "Minorities," in *Rural Society in the U.S.: Issues for the 1980s*, ed. Don A. Dillman and Daryl J. Hobbs (Boulder, Colo.: Westview Press, 1982), 105–6.

25. Hurt, *Indian Agriculture*, 226–27; C. Matthew Snipp, "American Indians and Natural Resource Development: Indigenous Peoples' Land, Now Sought After, Has Produced New Indian-White Problems," *American Journal of Economics and Sociology* 45 (October 1986): 466–67; Morris, "Termination by Accountants," 71; Hirschfelder and Montaño, *Native American Almanac*, 216–17.

26. Henry W. Kipp, *Indians in Agriculture: A Historical Sketch*, prepared for the Task Force of the American Indian Agricultural Council, 7 August 1987; National Indian Agricultural Working Group, *Final Findings and Recommendations*, prepared for the Assistant Secretary of Indian Affairs and the Intertribal Agricultural Council, December 1987; Bunty Anquoe, "BIA Opposes Agriculture Bill," *Lakota Times* (Rapid City, S.Dak.), 30 September 1992, A3; "SWIAA Addresses Indian Agriculture Problem," *Indian Country Today* (Southwest edition, hereafter SW), 23 February 1995, B4; Amy Onderdonk, "Indians Hope Buffalo Can Revive Tribes' Fortunes," *High Country News* (Paonia, Colo.), 24 (4 May 1992): 6.

27. Parman, *Indians*, 107–15, 142–43; Brophy and Aberle, *The Indian*, 70; Snipp and Summers, "American Indians and Economic Poverty," 163–65; Nagel, Ward, and Knapp, "Politics of American Indian Economic Development," 53–54; Stephen Trimble, *The People: Indians of the American Southwest* (Santa Fe, N.Mex.: School of American Research Press, 1993), 116–17, 436–39.

28. Sorkin, *American Indians*, 107–19.

29. Larry Burt, "Western Tribes and Balance Sheets: Business Development Programs in the 1960s and 1970s," *Western Historical Quarterly* 23 (November 1992): 475–95; Snipp and Summers, "American Indians and Economic Poverty," 165–74; Alan L. Sorkin, "Business and Industrial Development on American Indian Reservations," *Annals of Regional Science* 7 (December 1973): 115–29; Sorkin, *American Indians*, 80–96; Brophy and Aberle, *The Indian*, 96–102; Trimble, *The People*, 338–39; David Rich Lewis, "Still Native: The Significance of Native Americans in the History of the

Twentieth-Century American West," *Western Historical Quarterly* 24 (May 1993): 211–17; Marjorie P. Snodgrass, *Economic Development of American Indians and Eskimos, 1930 Through 1967: A Bibliography* (Washington, D.C.: U.S. Department of the Interior, Bureau of Indian Affairs, 1968).

30. Les Daly, "Beyond Santa Fe," *Atlantic Monthly* 272 (December 1993): 54–58; Cheryl Atwell, "Sunrise: An Environmentally Sound Apache Enterprise," *Native Peoples* 7 (Winter 1994): 70–76; Art Latham, "Jicarilla Apache Sets Their Sights on Big-Game Resort," *Indian Country Today,* 16 March 1995, B3; Trimble, *The People,* 189–90, 218–23, 245–96; John Young, "Crow Pursue Little Bighorn Tourist Attraction," *Indian Country Today,* 2 February 1995, A1; Burt, "Western Tribes," 483–84.

31. "Indian Gaming: Law and Legislation," *NARF Legal Review* 10 (Fall 1985): 1–5; Pauline Yoshihashi, "Indian Tribes Put Their Bets on Casinos," *The Wall Street Journal,* 5 August 1991, B1; "IG Says 209 Gaming Halls—106 Are Casinos," *Indian News, Week-in-Review* 18 (7 January 1994): 4–5; Bunty Anquoe, "New Casino Regulations Backed by Washington, Tribes," *Indian Country Today,* 6 July 1995, A1. See also "Winner's Circle," special supplement, *Indian Country Today,* 10 November 1993; Henry Tatum, "With Casinos, Native Americans Get Revenge," *Salt Lake Tribune,* 30 October 1994, D1; Gary Sokolow, "The Future of Gambling in Indian Country," *American Indian Law Review* 15 (Spring 1990): 151–83; Eduardo E. Cordiero, "The Economics of Bingo: Factors Influencing the Success of Bingo Operations on American Indian Reservations," in *What Can Tribes Do? Strategies and Institutions in American Indian Economic Development,* ed. Stephen Cornell and Joseph P. Kalt (Los Angeles: American Indian Studies Center, 1992), 206–38; National Indian Policy Center, *Reservation-Based Gaming* (Washington, D.C.: National Indian Policy Center, 1993).

32. Parman, *Indians,* 117; Brophy and Aberle, *The Indian,* 68, 141, 160–70; Helen W. Johnson, "Rural Indian Americans in Poverty," in *Native Americans Today: Sociological Perspectives,* ed. Howard M. Bahr, Bruce A. Chadwick, and Robert C. Day (New York: Harper and Row, 1972), 25–27; Bahr, Chadwick, and Stauss, *American Ethnicity,* 151, 156, 159–60, 165, 170–71, 198–204, 362; Sorkin, *American Indians,* 7–8, 162–65; Stuart, *Nations Within a Nation,* 95–120, 145–202; Snipp, *American Indians,* 206–65; Snipp and Summers, "American Indians and Economic Poverty," 155, 169–71, 174; Marlita A. Reddy, ed., *Statistical Record of Native North Americans* (Detroit: Gale Research, 1993), 485, 663, 685–91, 723, 771, 812–15; Nagel, Ward, and Knapp, "Politics of American Indian Economic Development," 53; Paul A. Kettl, "Suicide and Homicide: The Other Costs of Development," *Northeast Indian Quarterly* 8 (Winter 1991): 58–61; Rural Sociological Society Task Force on Persistent Rural Poverty, *Persistent Poverty in Rural America* (Boulder, Colo.: Westview Press, 1993), 175–78.

33. Philip S. Deloria, "What Indians Should Want: Advice to the President," in *Indian Self-Rule: First-Hand Accounts of Indian-White Relations from Roosevelt to Reagan,* ed. Kenneth R. Philp (Salt Lake City, Utah: Howe Brothers, 1986), 319, 321; Ambler, *Breaking the Iron Bonds,* 4–6, 29; Joseph G. Jorgensen, ed., *Native Americans and Energy Development II* (Cambridge, Mass.: Anthropology Resource Center, 1984); Hirschfelder and Montaño, *Native American Almanac,* 214–18.

34. Donald Parman, "Inconsistent Advocacy: The Erosion of Indian Fishing Rights in the Pacific Northwest, 1933–1956," in *The American Indian Past and Present,* 4th ed., ed. Roger L. Nichols (New York: McGraw-Hill, 1992), 235–50; Josephy, *Now That*

the Buffalo's Gone, 177–211; Fay Cohen, *Treaties on Trial: The Continuing Contro-versy over Northwest Indian Fishing Rights* (Seattle: University of Washington Press, 1986); Mary B. Olson, "The Legal Road to Economic Development: Fishing Rights in Western Washington," in *Public Policy Impacts on American Economic Development,* ed. C. Matthew Snipp (Albuquerque: University of New Mexico Press, 1988), 77–112; Trimble, *The People*, 292; David H. Getches, "A Philosophy of Permanence: The Indi-ans' Legacy for the West," *Journal of the West* 29 (July 1990): 56–61.

35. Alan S. Newell, Richmond L. Clow, and Richard N. Ellis, *A Forest in Trust: Three-Quarters of a Century of Indian Forestry, 1910–1986* (Washington, D.C.: U.S. Department of the Interior, Bureau of Indian Affairs, Division of Forestry, 1986); Rich Nafziger, "A Violation of Trust?: Federal Management of Indian Timber Lands," *Indian Historian* 9 (Fall 1976): 15–23; Joe D. Dillsaver, "Natural Resources: Federal Control over Indian Timber," *American Indian Law Review* 5 (Summer 1977): 415–22; Hirsch-felder and Montaño, *Native American Almanac,* 217–18; Trimble, *The People,* 285; Ruth Rudner, "Sacred Geographies," *Wilderness* 58 (Fall 1994): 12–20; Brenda Norrell, "Navajo Want Better Protection Laws for Trees, Endangered Species," *Indian Country Today,* 18 August 1993, A3.

36. Richard Lowitt, *The New Deal and the West* (Bloomington: Indiana Univer-sity Press, 1984), 81–99, 122–37, 157–71; Norris R. Hundley, "The *Winters* Decision and Indian Water Rights: A Mystery Reexamined," *Western Historical Quarterly* 13 (January 1982): 17–42; Parman, *Indians,* 172–74; Brian Collins, "The Public Gets a Chance to Revamp Dams Built 50 Years Ago: Native Americans Are in the Best Posi-tion to Alter the Way Dams Are Operated," *High Country News* 23 (2 December 1991): 1; Steven J. Shupe, "Indian Tribes in the Water Marketing Arena," *American Indian Law Review* 15 (Spring 1990): 185–205; Daniel McCool, "The Northern Utes' Long Water Ordeal," *High Country News* 23 (15 July 1991): 8; James Bishop, Jr., "Tribe Wins Back Stolen Water," *High Country News* 24 (15 June 1992): 1. See also F. Lee Brown and Helen M. Ingram, *Water and Poverty in the Southwest* (Tucson: University of Arizona Press, 1987); Daniel McCool, *Command of the Waters: Iron Triangles, Federal Water Development, and Indian Water* (Berkeley: University of California Press, 1987); Thomas R. McGuire, William B. Lord, and Mary G. Wallace, eds., *Indian Water in the New West* (Tucson: University of Arizona Press, 1993); Richard White, *The Organic Machine: The Changing World of Indians and Whites, Salmon, and Energy on the Columbia River* (New York: Hill and Wang, 1995).

37. Ambler, *Breaking the Iron Bonds;* Brophy and Aberle, *The Indian,* 85–86; Snipp, "American Indians and Natural Resource Development," 467–70; Snipp, "Public Policy Impacts," 11–18; Hirschfelder and Montaño, *Native American Almanac,* 214–15; Iverson, "Cowboys and Indians," 6–7.

38. Masnyesva as quoted in George Hardeen, "Is Peabody Coal's Slurry Sucking the Hopis Dry?" *High Country News* 22 (5 November 1990): 6; Karin Schill, "Coal Firm May Pull Its Straw Out of Aquifer," *High Country News* 26 (18 April 1994): 4; Keith Schneider, "Grand Canyon Air Plan Is Challenged by Utility," *New York Times,* 2 February 1991. See also Trimble, *The People,* 94–97, 165–67, 170–75; Philip Reno, *Mother Earth, Father Sky, and Economic Development: Navajo Resources and Their Uses* (Albuquerque: University of New Mexico Press, 1981).

39. Winona LaDuke, "Indigenous Environmental Perspectives: A North Ameri-

can Primer," *Akwe:kon Journal* 9 (Summer 1992): 52–71; Barbara R. Johnston and Susan Dawson, "Resource Use and Abuse on Native American Land: Uranium Mining in the American Southwest," in *Who Pays the Price? The Sociocultural Context of Environmental Crisis,* ed. Barbara Rose Johnston (Washington, D.C.: Island Press, 1994), 142–53; Norman A. Chance, "Contested Terrain: A Social History of Human Environmental Relations in Arctic Alaska," in *Who Pays the Price? The Sociocultural Context of Environmental Crisis,* ed. Barbara Rose Johnston (Washington D.C.: Island Press, 1994), 170–86; Peter H. Eichstaedt, *If You Poison Us: Uranium and Native Americans* (Santa Fe, N.Mex.: Red Crane Books, 1994); Keith Schneider, "A Valley of Death for the Navajo Uranium Miners," *New York Times,* 3 May 1993, A1; Rudner, "Sacred Geographies," 21–22; Greg Bechle, "Mountains of Cyanide," *The Progressive* 54 (September 1990): 14; Robert Tomsho, "Dumping Grounds: Indian Tribes Contend with Some of Worst of America's Pollution," *Wall Street Journal,* reprinted in *Ute Bulletin* (Ft. Duschesne, Utah), 11 December 1990, 5; Keith Schneider, "Nuclear Complex Threatens Indians," *New York Times,* 3 September 1990; Richard W. Stoffle and Michael J. Evans, "American Indians and Nuclear Waste Storage: The Debate at Yucca Mountain, Nevada," in *Native Americans and Public Policy,* ed. Fremont J. Lyden and Lyman H. Legters (Pittsburgh: University of Pittsburgh Press, 1992), 243–62.

40. Parman, *Indians,* 173; Tomsho, "Dumping Grounds," 5; "EIS Favors Recycling Center/Landfill," *Indian News, Week-in-Review* 16 (18 December 1992): 4; Valerie Tailman Chavez, "Native Americans Battle with Toxic Waste," *Indigenous Woman* 1 (Summer 1991): 15–16; Paul Schneider and Dan Lamont, "Other People's Trash: A Last Ditch Effort to Keep Corporate Garbage Off the Reservation," in *Native American Resurgence and Renewal: A Reader and Bibliography,* ed. Robert N. Wells, Jr. (Metuchen, N.J.: The Scarecrow Press, 1994), 232–45; Caroline Byrd, "Radioactive Dollars Draw Tribes," *High Country News* 24 (21 September 1992): 6; Avis Little Eagle, "Tribes Meet to Discuss Role of Nuclear Waste," *Lakota Times,* 8 April 1992, A1; Tony Davis, "Apaches Split over Nuclear Waste," *High Country News* 24 (27 January 1992): 12–15; Bunty Anquoe, "Mescalero Apache Sign Agreement to Establish Facility for Nuclear Waste," *Indian Country Today,* 10 February 1994, A1; George Johnson, "Apaches Reject Plan to Store Nuclear Waste," *New York Times,* 2 February 1995, A12; Tony Davis, "Flip-Flop on Storing Nuclear Waste Shakes Up Tribe," *High Country News* 27 (29 May 1995): 6. See also Jon D. Erickson, Duane Chapman, and Ronald E. Johnny, "Monitored Retrievable Storage of Spent Nuclear Fuel in Indian Country: Liability, Sovereignty, and Socioeconomics," *American Indian Law Review* 19 (Spring 1994): 73–103.

41. Jackson as quoted in Valerie Taliman, "Tribes Denounce Interest in Nuclear Wastes," *Lakota Times,* 22 April 1992, A6; Russell Jim, "The Legacy of the Termination Era," in *Indian Self-Rule: First-Hand Accounts of Indian-White Relations from Roosevelt to Reagan,* ed. Kenneth R. Philp (Salt Lake City, Utah: Howe Brothers, 1986), 180. See also Ward Churchill and Winona LaDuke, "Native North America: The Political Economy of Radioactive Colonialism," in *The State of Native America: Genocide, Colonization, and Resistance,* ed. M. Annette Jaimes (Boston: South End Press, 1992), 255, who use the terms "self-liquidation" and "auto-genocide"; Marjane Ambler, "Opponents of Nuclear Waste Share Strategies: Indian Reservations Not Targets," *Lakota Times,* 20 May 1992.

42. Quoted in Josephy, *Now That the Buffalo's Gone,* 132.

43. Jerry Reynolds, "Indian Writers: Real or Imagined," 3 parts, *Indian Country Today,* 8 September, 15 September, 6 October 1993; Carole J. Standing Elk, "Center for the Spirit: On Wannabes, Bogus AIM Leaders," *Indian Country Today,* 5 January 1994, A5; Avis Little Eagle, "Bellecourts Targeted by New AIM Dissidents," *Indian Country Today,* 13 April 1994, A1; Nancy Hobbs, "Mixed-Blood Indians Seek Reinstatement in Ute Tribe," *Salt Lake Tribune,* 1 August 1993, B1; Ronald L. Holt, *Beneath These Red Cliffs: An Ethnohistory of the Utah Paiutes* (Albuquerque: University of New Mexico Press, 1992).

44. Lewis, "Still Native," 220–24.

45. Iverson, *When Indians Became Cowboys,* xii–xv, 182–224; Peter Iverson, "Cowboys, Indians, and the Modern West," *Arizona and the West* 28 (Summer 1986): 107–24.

46. TeCube and Russell as quoted in Trimble, *The People,* 453, 437.

47. Bonito and Pueblo elders as quoted in Trimble, *The People,* 286, 38; Wilma Mankiller, "Education and Native Americans: Entering the Twenty-First Century on Our Own Terms," *National Forum* 71 (Spring 1991): 6.

48. N. Scott Momaday, "The Man Made of Words," in *The Remembered Earth,* ed. Geary Hobson (Albuquerque: University of New Mexico Press, 1981), 164–65.

2

Rural Life and Social Change in the Modern West

Paula M. Nelson

In *The American West Transformed,* Gerald Nash explains the impact of World War II on the West and celebrates the population explosion and the dynamic urban society that resulted from the conflict. No longer an underdeveloped colonial region with little recognizable culture, the West in 1945 was "the pace-setting region of the nation." In the years since, the West has continued its growth as an urban oasis society. The old rural economy and way of life has declined precipitously. A survey of 218 western counties in 1940 indicated a farm or ranch population of 785,002; in 1990 only 172,243 still lived on farms and ranches.[1]

What have these changes meant for those who lived on farms, on ranches, and in small towns? Hard at work in occupations that produced goods at the most basic level or, in the towns, in occupations serving the economic needs of producers, rural westerners have found their economic and cultural world under attack by forces they could not identify or control. World War II only acceler-ated the inexorable course of urbanization, centralization, and specialization that has been remaking rural society everywhere in the United States since the 1880s. A tremendous irony lies in the fact that rural westerners embraced the modernization and urbanization of their world wholeheartedly, not recognizing that it brought with it the seeds of their own economic and social destruction. Who could have known that there were so many long-term implications in the simple purchase of an automobile?

The rural West today is engaged in a battle over its future. The old-style community, which stemmed from nineteenth-century values and structures, and which was centered around a culture of work and the use of natural resources, is losing ground to a new vision of the West based on urban values and a leisure-time culture that sees preservation and restoration of the scenery as a primary goal. In the best case, newly arrived urbanites tend to view the old rural community as a quaint anachronism. In the worst case, urbanites perceive it as parochial, exploitative, and ludicrous. As T. J. Gilles, agriculture editor of the Great Falls *Tribune* put it in 1992, "Those of us who grew up here need to realize that we are now in the place of the Indians and the Eskimos. . . . Some new people have come to take the land from us. They [have] a higher and better use for it."[2]

What does it mean to say that the rural West has become modernized and urbanized? At the most basic level these terms refer to the new technologies that have eased workloads, lessened geographic and cultural isolation, and provided material comforts similar to those in urban areas. This process did not occur for everyone at the same pace nor to the same degree, but the trend has been clear and the impact profound.

Prior to World War II, most rural westerners lived far more physically demanding lives than their urban neighbors and enjoyed far fewer amenities. Distance and isolation shaped the lives of many farm and ranch residents. The gulf between rural and urban lives was well understood. In 1940, Lucille Anderson, who grew up in a small Arizona mining town, married a cattleman whose ranch was "only eight dirt road miles" from her home. "The distance," according to Anderson, "could have been eight thousand miles." The stark contrast between urban life and the rugged West had a great appeal to some urbanites. Dude ranches, where city folks could "rough it," had been popular vacation destinations since the turn of the century. Eulalia Bourne, who ranched in Arizona with the help of friends and family, reported the occasional visits of city people whom she did not know; they motored up her rough dirt road in search of western "atmosphere."[3]

For those whose livelihood depended on crops or cattle, the scenery, the "quaint" dependence on nineteenth-century technologies, and the facts of distance and the struggles with nature were not "atmosphere" but life. Most enthusiastically embraced technological change and rejoiced over the growing ease of daily existence. Such changes came late by standards of most areas in the East and Midwest. Oscar and Emma Swett, for example, had no road to their ranch in northeastern Utah until 1926. Prior to that time, neighbors rode horseback to Linwood to get the mail and supplies for everyone in the ranch community. The ride took four hours each way. Even with the road, the Swett family did not purchase a motorized vehicle until 1942, when the high cattle prices of the war years made them more prosperous. Their Dodge truck could take them all the way to Vernal and back, thirty miles each way, in one day.[4]

The family adopted other technologies as they became available and affordable. In the 1930s, they purchased a battery-powered radio but ran it sparingly. In the early 1950s, the Swetts installed a gasoline-powered Delco electric generator plant and used it to run electric lights for reading at night. In the mid-1950s, they piped running water into the house and became the first in their community to build an indoor bathroom. Because their water source, a spring, was up the hill from their home, they could use the force of gravity to aid the system. After highline electricity reached them in 1960, the Swetts purchased a refrigerator, a television, and other appliances. Oscar continued to use horses rather than mechanized equipment to work the ranch, however. The Swett place had always been a subsistence operation. Expensive machinery would have put them out of business.[5]

The pace of modernization depended on location and density of population. In the Blue River community outside Blue, Arizona, modernization arrived late. Highline electricity reached the scattered ranches in 1957. Prior to that time, local families relied on kerosene lamps and woodstoves, although some bought kerosene refrigerators and Delco battery light plants to provide power as early as the 1940s. In the more densely settled, irrigated farm regions of southern Idaho, electricity came in the late 1930s, when farm families organized under the Rural Electrification Administration policies of the New Deal. In the more established farming areas, roads tended to be improved; families purchased cars and trucks more quickly and in general could take advantage of new technologies more easily.[6]

Today, distance continues to shape life for many rural westerners and inhibits the modernization process. An Oregon ranch woman, writing in 1978, reported that her family had been wired for electricity for less than ten years but still had no phone service. Some ranch families did not have highline electricity in the late 1970s and instead relied on home generators. There were ranch women who lived as far as thirty-two miles from a paved road and seventy miles from a town. Nevada ranch women surveyed in the late 1980s had undependable phone service with multiple party lines. Some phone lines were "strung just on large sticks." Others included ranches eighty miles apart on the same party line. By the late 1980s, there were still a quarter-million rural westerners without access to phone service. High costs and confusing regulations deter phone company expansions. In the mid-1980s, a Colorado rancher who agreed to pay the full costs of phone service to his home received a bill for $47,597.[7]

For people in the small towns of the West, modernization and urbanization have been a mixed blessing. Since a concentrated population allowed economies of scale, larger, well-located towns had electricity, water, and sewer systems. The larger the town, the more quickly these comforts were achieved. The smallest towns sometimes never got beyond the private well and outhouse stage. Improvements came late in many places. In 1938–39, the Works Progress Administration (WPA) built an underground water pipeline for the town of Antimony, Utah. Prior to this, residents there had "had to carry their water from ditches for all their household needs." Antimony received highline electricity in 1946 to replace the gas and coal oil lamps and occasional Delco plants. Also in 1946, the county paved the twenty-mile-long "narrow, twisting dirt road" that led to the town.[8]

Electricity arrived in Pingree, Idaho, in 1935, "improving the standard of living." Water quality generally remained poor. The children at the school once "burped gasoline" after taking drinks at the fountain. From then on, each child brought a quart of water from home. An open sewer "blew a terrible stench" into the school when the weather was windy.[9]

Fredonia, Arizona, experimented with a privately owned electric company beginning in 1932. Each family wanting electricity purchased a pole and a cedar post to hold it in place. Because participants believed wrongly that the pole gave them stockholders' rights in the company, the advent of electricity led to twenty years of serious internal wrangling in the town. The frazzled owners finally sold out to California-Pacific Utilities in 1952. The utility installed true streetlights in Fredonia in 1954 to replace the 100-watt bulbs that had marked only the corners of the streets.[10]

For towns, however, the issue was not so much modernization of the immediate environment, although that was important, as the impact of larger economic and social forces on their very viability. By 1950, it was clear that there had been winners and losers in the competitive economic struggles of modern life. The centralization of economic functions into larger towns left smaller communities struggling for survival. The modernization of farm and ranch life allowed rural residents to travel greater distances at a faster pace. Small trade centers could not compete with the selection, prices, and sheer entertainment value of larger towns. Most small towns came up losers.

When did this happen? Elvin Hatch suggests that World War II accelerated the structural changes already occurring in small-town life. In his study of the small central California town of "Starkey" (a pseudonym), he notes that the village of "fewer than 200 households" had "enjoyed a sense of confidence in itself and its virtues and goals" prior to World War II, in spite of the rise in urbanization and its accompanying cultural change. The war created an economic and social boom; the town was alive with activity. Once the war ended, however, the "normal" patterns that returned finally made clear to Starkey residents the changing status of rural people in the overall scheme of things, and reflected the technological gains and higher expectations of society as a whole. Almost everyone had a car, for example, and the prosperity of the postwar era allowed states to build better roads. As the recognition of imminent economic failure dawned, Starkey residents lost faith in the goodness of their town and their way of life. They internalized the negative views of themselves that urban people held. Anyone who was truly someone, they began to believe, would not be caught dead in Starkey. Buildings began to decline; there was little incentive to patch and repair. Starkey began to live up to its low expectations of itself.[11]

Starkey was not alone. When Ivan Doig moved to Ringling, Montana, with his grandmother in 1949, he found "the scant bones of a town." The town was founded in high hopes at the turn of the century, but two destructive fires in the

1920s and 1930s burned most of the business district to the ground. What remained was a few houses with about fifty residents, "a saloon, a gas station, a post office, Mike Ryan's store [and] the depot." Except for the fall livestock shipping season, "the handful of people who lived there out of habit" and the needs of "the few ranchers who used it as their gas and mail point," there was no need for Ringling at all.[12]

Twenty miles up the road, White Sulphur Springs was doing better but still faced an uncertain future. In the late 1940s, "the town didn't look too perky." Here the impact of the Great Depression and World War II had been largely negative: "Obviously nobody had built anything or painted anything or cleaned anything for twenty years." Grand edifices, built in the nineteenth century when the future looked bright, now stood derelict and dangerous, "the relic faces of White Sulfur, the fading profiles of what the town had set out to be." When Doig lived there it was a livestock town with a stable population of about 1,000 and no real hopes for better. It served the needs of another 1,000 people scattered on (the appropriately named) Meagher County ranches. By the 1990 census, only 190 people remained on those ranches. White Sulphur Springs has survived this massive loss of population; it had a population of 1,300 people in 1990. Its location on a federal highway near several recreation areas has helped it to survive, if not flourish.[13]

A study of ranch women in Nevada done in the late 1970s tried to assess the services offered to ranch families by communities of various sizes, as well as the choices these women made when they sought out services such as shopping and medical care. The investigator discovered that ranch families used nearby towns for "convenience centers for their unexpected, small purchases." They went to the cities for all major purchases. One subject, when asked about the closest small town, Austin, remarked, "Austin isn't a town. When I go to town I mean Reno." Her family willingly traveled sixty-five extra miles to get the selection and prices they wanted. With almost everyone abandoning local loyalties for the variety, lower costs, and multitude of choices larger towns and cities provide, small towns struggle and decline or die. Modernization and urbanization, while providing comforts and contacts with the broader world that all town dwellers enjoy, have profoundly challenged the small town's primary reason for existence.[14]

To some degree, modernization and urbanization have also shaped the social patterns of the rural West. Both critics and admirers of the rural westerners' way of life agree that their social world is built on nineteenth-century principles and systems. The family remains strong, local people and issues matter, and residents strive to be good neighbors and serve the community. Voluntarism, rather than professionalization, still dominates social organization. Yet there have been changes. As people have left the farms and ranches in larger numbers, country people have looked to the towns to be their social centers. As towns lost their economic functions, the school and its activities have become the vital center of local identity. Television and other modern pastimes have also altered social patterns. As one Idaho woman noted, "The neighbors are no longer dependent upon the Busy Bee [Club] for social activities." A Utah woman explained that "television is one distraction" that reduced attendance at Daughters of the Utah Pioneers meetings.[15]

As more and more urbanites move into the rural West to escape the trials of city life and enjoy the West's beauty, they bring along different values and goals. Urbanites often do not try to fit in to the existing social fabric. Longtime residents feel threatened by the changes that make their own communities unfamiliar places. Farmers, ranchers, and townspeople alike worry that their way of life will disappear; they suspect that many urbanites hope it will. Factionalism and discord, always present to a degree in rural life, continue as rural residents fight for a piece of the limited pie. Some are too worn out to participate. Cynicism, fatalism, and inertia are now common to rural culture. Other rural westerners are deeply angry about their declining status.

In the days before automobiles and radio, the rural social world was highly localized because it had to be. Without the assistance of labor-saving technology on the farm or ranch, days were spent in hard work. Chores had to be done. Every day and every season had their rhythms and patterns. Families worked together for the good of all. Neighbors helped each other with larger tasks. There was little time for leisure. Without good roads to ease the hazards of travel, what little free time there was tended to be spent in the immediate neighborhood or in the closest towns. Because of their isolated locale, the Swett family, for example, lived as people had a generation before. When the Swett children were growing up in the Greendale community of northeastern Utah, they enjoyed the visits of neighbors who stopped by their ranch in the evenings, when chores were done. Occasionally the neighborhood held dances in the schoolhouse, "accompanied by the music from Sanford Green's hand-cranked phonograph machine." Thanksgiving and Christmas were important holidays; the neighbors all contributed food and gathered at one home or another for dinner. The neighborhood also enjoyed birthday parties and surprise parties. The Greendale community socialized most frequently in the winter; in the summer they were too busy and too tired.[16]

By World War II, modernization and its accompanying centralization and consolidation reached even to Daggett County, Utah. After the family bought their truck in 1942, trips to town became important occasions. Both Oscar and Emma usually went, and the children still living at home were glad to go along. The truck enabled them to go to the July 24th rodeo in Manila as well, where "everybody gathered around, a lot of old friends came, people to see!" The ability to travel was becoming increasingly important for sociability. The Greendale school, the former community center, closed in 1942, and over the next decade the original homesteaders moved away until only the Swetts remained.[17]

The closing of the Greendale school typified developments across the rural

West, as one-room schools run by small local districts began to disappear. The one-room school was an artifact of nineteenth-century American life that had served its purpose well. Flexible and relatively inexpensive, it represented an education system concerned with basic knowledge and local control. Patron-run school districts sprang up wherever the density of settlement required. When people moved in or out of a community, the building could be moved to accommodate the new center of population. Neighbors sometimes wrangled over school location, costs, or the quality of a particular teacher's methods, but schools and their teachers more often provided the social glue that kept communities together. By World War II, however, the problems became far greater than school location or teacher hiring. There was a sense that the small rural districts and the neighborhoods that supported them were backward and unable to give students a proper education for modern times. In the late 1950s, the Salt Lake City *Tribune* brought the entire fifty-one-member student body of the Antimony, Utah, school to Salt Lake City for a tour of city delights. The published photographs of the students included such captions as "Never ate in a cafe," "Hasn't seen elephant," "Never eaten ice cream soda," or "Wants to talk on telephone." The author of the memoir worried that the newspaper had made him and his classmates seem "culturally deprived." He did not believe they were.[18]

With the large-scale population migrations of the 1930s and 1940s, massive school consolidations occurred across the rural West. The New Deal rural resettlement programs removed thousands of people in some areas; the attractions of high-paying defense jobs lured other thousands away. State governments, in some cases, stepped in and mandated new standards for student numbers, physical plant, and curriculum for grades one through eight that forced the closure of some schools. Residents left without schools nearby had to scramble to make other arrangements for the education of their children. The increasing emphasis after World War II on education beyond grade eight created further burdens for western families.[19]

The initial response was separation of older children. The system of boarding out youngsters in towns to enable them to attend high school became increasingly common from 1910 through the 1920s. That process accelerated as more teens aspired to high school education, and it began to include younger children when local grade schools closed. The Swett children had always boarded with relatives or friends in Manila or Vernal in order to attend high school. When the Greendale school closed, the youngest Swett child, Wilda, was still a small girl. She spent eleven winters in town under the care of her adult sisters in order to attend grade school as well as high school. Her father always made it down the mountain to retrieve her on the last day of school, no matter what the condition of the road. Ivan Doig lived with friends of the family at times, when his father and grandmother worked on Montana ranches at long distances from school. At age nine he began what he recalled as "a theme of my life, staying in town in the living arrangement we called boarding out." His father paid someone, "friend or relative or simply whoever looked reliable," to care for him during the school week. On weekends when the weather was good, his father drove the rugged miles into town to take him to the ranch. In the mid-1950s, Doig attended high school in the farming town of Valier but boarded in the smaller, nearer town of Dupuyer, "nine dirt road miles" from the current ranch home. His grandmother, recognizing the impossibility of winter travel to their rented foothills ranch, asked the first person she saw in Dupuyer to board him. Fortunately, she chose well, and the arrangement was of great benefit to the teenager.[20]

The problem of distances between students and schools became so vexing that the state of Oregon built a boarding high school that received national publicity in 1950. The Crane School served the 6,600-square-mile Harney County School District in southeastern Oregon. A note that accompanied a photo of the students dancing in the recreation room commented: "To freshmen such social evenings are unfamiliarly wonderful."[21]

The advent of school buses helped with the transportation problems of the rural West but exchanged them for the problem of boredom, since the commutes often required as much as two hours each way to school. In 1982, twenty-two local children attended grades one thorugh six in Arbon, Idaho (there used to be "several schools" in the Bannock Valley). To get there one bus driver traveled sixty-six miles a day on the southern route; the other driver traveled eighty-four miles a day north of town. After sixth grade, students took the bus to American Falls or Malad, each approximately forty miles from Arbon.[22]

The Arbon experience is typical of many ranching areas in the West. Blue, Arizona, continued to operate a one-room school in 1987. When the children reached high school age, they rode the bus to Round Valley High School. The local chronicler believed this to be progress comparable to the old system of boarding out but noted that busing did "take a good chunk of time out of a day for travel." In the 1970s, dryland farmers on the Uncompahgre Plateau in western Colorado ran a one-room school for the four school-age children in their midst. Their school held "summer vacation" from January through March because of the fierce winter weather conditions in the region. During the same period in northwestern Colorado, parents from three states, (Colorado, Utah, and Wyoming) sent their children to a one-room school out in the open country forty miles by dirt road from the nearest town. They had no buses, and parents had to drive "as much as twenty-five miles one way, four times a day, or about five hundred miles a week." The nearest high school was in Craig, Colorado, eighty miles away. In this neighborhood, families split up during the school year, with high school–aged children moving to Craig.[23]

In the ranch country of Nevada there are school buses, but they travel only the main roads. Ranches can be scattered miles up dirt lanes well away from the route. Nevada families sometimes teach their youngsters to drive by the age of twelve in order to spare their parents the daily trips to meet the bus. When the children are old enough to drive legally, some families allow their children to drive themselves to school. The two McGilvray teenagers, who lived on the family ranch in southern Oregon in the mid-1970s, drove thirty-eight miles each way every day to school, although bad roads in winter sometimes prevented their attendance. As a one-room school teacher from Colorado put it, "Education is a hard-earned thing out here."[24]

Town schools provided many more opportunities for learning and recreation, although programs varied by the size and wealth of the district. By the 1940s, even profoundly rural districts tried to adopt the systems and structures progressive reformers had been advocating since the turn of the twentieth century. Athletics and other student performance activities such as music, drama, debate, and speech found favor with locals for their sheer entertainment value, and they also built community loyalty and pride. The development of high schools and their activities shifted community commitment away from the building of a strong economic function—an effort that appeared more and more fruitless in the changing national order—to successful representation by student athletes, first and foremost, and then by student musicians, actors, and scholars.[25]

In the rural West, high school athletics caught on big in the 1940s and 1950s. In Monticello, New Mexico, for example, basketball games were popular, although the school did not have an indoor basketball court. All games had to be played away at high schools that could afford gyms. Because the athletic districts were arranged geographically rather than by school size, Monticello's seven players had to face Las Cruces, a much larger town, in the tournaments. "As you can imagine," the Monticello principal remembered, "Monticello didn't go far in the tournament." The growth of high school sports in Monticello helped spur athletic interest in the elementary county schools in rural Sierra County. Every Friday brought a competition in one of three sports—volleyball, softball, or basketball. "Since no money was available for such activities, the teachers took the children to other schools in their own cars at their own expense," noted a longtime Sierra County teacher. In 1955, the county schools and Monticello High School closed; the newly consolidated district centered at Truth or Consequences, the only school with adequate facilities.[26]

Bob Pace of Bonners Ferry, Idaho, remembered the competitive atmosphere of his high school years. The football and basketball teams played to a large following. Local businesses, "including the bank," closed for football games, which were held on Friday afternoons in the era before lighted fields. When the basketball team won third place in the state tourney, the "band, school, and it seemed, the entire town, was out to meet the train." In Jerome, Idaho, in 1947, the manager of the movie theater interrupted the show to announce the local high school's basketball game win. "There followed much yelling and back whacking."[27]

In a world centered on school activities, families at a distance from the consolidated school had to make great sacrifices to allow their children to participate, or else their children sacrificed the opportunity to play or perform. The ranching McGilvray family in southern Oregon made sure their daughter, Annie, participated in track, although she was needed to work at home. "Living so far out and having so many things to do this time of year, it's hard to let her go," Shirley McGilvray wrote, "[but] girls and boys alike that don't have outside activities are missing the best years of their lives." Annie McGilvray also participated in Junior Rodeo and was the 1974 Junior Rodeo Queen. The Van Slyke family near Glide, Oregon, enjoyed daughter Lindsey's cross-country activities and arranged their schedule to help her compete. On one occasion Mrs. Van Slyke fed the cattle earlier than usual to allow her to drive to Eugene for the district track meet. The Van Slyke's daughter and son also belonged to the Future Farmers of America (FFA) and were active in 4-H activities. In Nevada, isolated rural families still use the boarding-out system for children who wish to participate in activities. Long distance and two-hour bus rides made living at home impossible.[28]

Besides their value as a medium for entertainment and community identity, schools also provided an opportunity for adult participation, commitment, and uplift. With the growth of school programs and the increasing emphasis on the significance of a well-rounded education, parent-teacher organizations became important. The Parent-Teacher Association (PTA) is the best known such organization, but it was not necessary for local people to join the national group and pay its dues to serve the needs of the schools. By altering the name a bit (Parent-Teacher Organization, or PTO, was popular), local concerned citizens could gather regularly to support the school and their children without the cumbersome regional and national organization. In Fredonia, Arizona, for example, parents and teachers established a PTA (later called PTO) to oversee development of the school and its offerings. The group met over potluck suppers to discuss ways to raise money and expand opportunities for the students. The PTA imported speakers for uplift, held carnivals and book fairs to raise money, and in 1976, brought a college theater troupe to town to perform *1776*. They "lost money on the project [but] considered it worthwhile." As college attendance became common, the Fredonia PTO awarded scholarships to any Fredonia graduate enrolled in college. In Holbrook, Idaho, in the 1950s, the PTA sponsored a trip for schoolchildren to the Bear River Migratory Bird Refuge (Utah), with lunch at the Brigham City Park and a visit to the Intermountain Telephone Office. "Ice cream cones and a safe journey home completed a happy day," the rural correspondent to the *Idaho Enterprise* concluded. (The Holbrook school closed in 1971; "it was no longer economical to keep the school open.")[29]

State laws mandate school attendance. Parents and neighbors must do whatever is necessary to provide for education for their children, no matter what problems must be overcome. In contrast, church membership is voluntary, yet many rural westerners exert tremendous effort to attend services and participate in the active life of their churches. Although the twentieth century has witnessed growing secularization in American culture, churches in the rural West fill the hunger for a spiritual life, as well as the hunger for community. What has changed, however, is the status that membership in a particular church once conveyed. The secularization of society has greatly reduced the influence of churches and their teachings. Before World War II, the "better" people, the leaders, of Starkey, California, had been Methodists, and it was generally accepted that the church and religion in general "ought to play a major role in small town life." But after World War II in Starkey, "it was being said that the [Methodist] Church was no longer the center of the community . . . [and] that it no longer enjoyed a sort of hegemony over local affairs that were wholesome and family oriented." By the mid-1960s, "the Church did little more than serve the emotional and social interests of its members."[30]

In the 1950s, experts in the sociology of churches believed that it took a base population of at least 1,000 per congregation to carry on effective church work. By this standard, much of the rural West had too many churches and too few people to support them. Yet many congregations persevered, unwilling for doctrinal reasons or from considerations of distance and neighborhood loyalty to give up their churches. The trend since World War II, however, has been toward smaller memberships in open-country churches; small towns, larger towns, and cities have enjoyed membership growth. The same forces that led to economic consolidation into larger towns and cities, and the consolidation of small schools into larger regional ones, have shaped church life as well. Even the Church of Jesus Christ of Latter-day Saints (LDS), the most organized and all-encompassing of the West's many denominations, has suffered from the steep declines in the agricultural population since World War II. The Bannock Valley, for example, "at one time had 5 L.D.S. Churches, one in each area. Now [1982] there is one, which is the Arbon Branch." Some members had to travel "over 22 miles for their meetings." In Hanna, Utah, "the last meeting to be held in our little Ward was held November 5, 1963 with many tears shed by all. . . . It was a sad time but we know it was the will of the Lord." The Church merged the Hanna Ward with the larger Tabiona Ward.[31]

What do rural churches do? A study of rural churches in Montana completed in 1956 explained that churches, besides their religious function, were also important for "recreation, education and charity. . . . Often in the more rural settings churches offered about the only reason and means for the social gathering of large numbers of far-flung neighbors." In Montana during this period, churches were "Montana's most numerous rural organizations." The most successful churches offered the most services per week and had the largest number of organizations. Churches sponsored such groups as the Ladies Aids, youth groups, missionary societies, boys' and girls' scouting programs, choirs, Sunday schools, and Bible studies. The most successful churches also had installed running water, central heat, and kitchens. Montana churches without these facilities lost 31 percent of their membership between 1945 and 1955. Large churches in towns were much more likely to provide the facilities, services, and social opportunities that modern worshipers had begun to demand.[32]

The LDS Church provided the most comprehensive religious and social structure in the modernizing West. Organized into wards at the local level, with regional "stakes" linking these wards, Mormon families had a hierarchy of leadership that helped them focus on the group and recognize the need for community in their lives. Church activities provided an abundant social life. The Relief Society for Women, the Young Men's and Young Women's Mutual Improvement societies, the Singing Mothers, the Daughters of the Utah Pioneers, and other church organizations filled the schedules of the faithful. The Mormons' love of music and dancing also helped them break down the monotony of farm life. In the Holbrook Valley in southern Idaho, there were church-sponsored dances nearly every week. The three wards in the valley alternated sponsorship of the entertainment. The wards of the Curlew Stake in that same region held weekly softball games as well.[33]

Mormon communities celebrated the Fourth of July with picnics, parades, and patriotic programs (as did the Gentile communities). The Twenty-fourth of July, however, the holiday that commemorates the arrival of Brigham Young and the Saints to the Salt Lake Valley, was even bigger, with rodeos, parades, and celebrations of pioneer life and achievement. The Mormons in Hagerman Valley, Idaho, for example, put on a grand celebration in 1947. The parade, as Inez McEwen recounted it, consisted of several "sagebrush bands loudly tooting, . . . leathery cowboys riding, a float or two," and some flag-bearing veterans of World War I marching in time. The Mormon women served a lunch of ham, mashed potatoes and gravy, cabbage salad, and lemonade at the church, although many farm families brought their own picnic lunches and ate at the park. For entertainment there were foot races "for boys and girls, for old men and fat women" and a rodeo that brought everyone to their feet again and again. To conclude that gala day, the organizers put on a fireworks show and a dance. Before they could attend, however, farm families had to go home to do the chores: "come death, birth or Pioneer Day, the cows had to be milked and the pigs fed."[34]

That commitment to the church continues. In Buckeye, Arizona, the LDS Church created a ward in 1954, when there were 150 members. By 1982, "the membership had outgrown the facilities"; the congregation was divided into two geographical wards and the building enlarged. In Central Arizona, the congregation planned July 24th rodeos and "eat yourself into a new church" banquets to raise money for a church building. They reached their goal and dedicated the building in 1950; the ward remodeled it in 1980. The Central Ward entertained other wards with their original "road shows" throughout the

1950s, 1960s, and 1970s. The road shows included "singing, dancing and speaking" with home-designed costumes and scenery. Dozens of people took part. Since the 1950s, the Central Ward members have marked the Twenty-fourth of July with a children's "Around the Block Parade" in which the young ones costumed as pioneers, or sometimes as Indians, parade. It is part of a larger Gila Valley celebration of the occasion. The Mormons in Tabiona, Utah, continue to maintain a relief society, a Young Men's and a Young Women's Mutual Improvement Society, a Sunday school, and a Daughters of the Utah Pioneers chapter, as well as their regular church meetings. Their calendar of events for late winter, 1972, included a ward Valentine party, the Mormon men's basketball team sportsmanship award, a party for the young women and their mothers, a regional parent and youth night, and a ward speech festival featuring a history sketch of each member family. The link between religious faith, shared history, and community commitment makes membership in the LDS Church a central factor in each member's life.[35]

Religion was also the vital center of a distinctive Mexican American culture in the rural West. Except for the original Native American peoples, the Spanish-speaking peoples who moved north from Mexico are the oldest settlers in the region. Their rural villages have dotted the southwestern landscape for as long as 400 years. In the twentieth century, some villagers, as well as new immigrants from Mexico, have joined a caravan of migrant workers following the harvests across the West. Sometimes migrants have dropped out of the caravan to find permanent homes in new locations, bringing their distinctive culture with them.[36]

Mexican Americans are largely Roman Catholic, although in recent years the Pentecostals and other evangelical Protestant sects have made inroads. Roman Catholicism provided an integral part of the Mexican American worldview, although many lived in isolated rural villages that saw a priest only once or twice a month when he came in to say Mass. Mexican Americans observed the church holidays and in some regions developed distinctive religious groups, such as the male Penitentes, whose purpose was the performance of penance rituals to mark Holy Week. Special feast days, especially the Feast of Our Lady of Guadalupe, provided opportunities for worship and community celebration. Hispanic religious observances included not only a mass, but also singing, dancing, drinking, games of chance, and other festivities. Church weddings also linked the individual, the family, the church, and the community.[37]

In the Monticello area of New Mexico, Saint Ignacio Day (5 February) brought special celebrations. Residents attended mass and walked in procession around the town square. Later in the day the community held a rodeo, a barbecue, and a dance, "with everyone from miles around in attendance." In the late 1970s, six local ranch families organized the festivities. The Las Placites community, also in Sierra County, New Mexico, celebrate Saint Lorenzo Day on 10 August. The owners of the Sedillo ranch provide the fiesta for their neighbors, complete with rodeo, dances, and "the special barbecue that is Charlie Sedillo's secret." Hundreds attend.[38]

Modernization and urbanization have reshaped Mexican American life as much as Anglo life. In the 1970s, Amadeo Martinez, clerk of Costilla County, Colorado, complained of "the heritage that is going. . . . [The children] don't even speak Spanish anymore . . . and we don't tell stories about the old days either. The kids would rather watch television." Since the mid-1960s, "nearly one fourth of the population have left the valley in search of city jobs." Pagosa Junction, which in its heyday had 100 people and regular train service, was down to 3 in the late 1970s; the last train came in 1968. The church, however, still had occasional masses; the same priest had attended to the spiritual needs of the region since 1932. As of 1979, a bar with a gas pump outside were all that remained of the once-busy business section of Monticello, New Mexico.[39]

As Hispanic people relocated to cities, migrant camps, or towns, the Catholic Church and the extended family remained central to their lives. The Spanish language, in spite of Amadeo Martinez's complaints, continues to be widely spoken. Urban Anglo cultural pressures, however, have made inroads. Mexican American young people sometimes resist family norms and desire the clothing, money, and freedom that they observe Anglo teenagers enjoying. Peer values become a stronger force in their lives, and loyalty to family values breaks down. Assimilated Hispanic leaders are sometimes resented "for rejecting their ethnic roots. . . . Sadly, the poverty-stricken Mexican Americans misdirect their hostility toward Mexican Americans who have become successful."[40]

Rural westerners have created many organizations beyond the school and the church to uplift, entertain, and provide services and amenities. In this they have built upon the noble American tradition of voluntary association. Nineteenth-century Americans tended to be a mobile lot; the creation of lodges and other such groups provided a reference point for newcomers to a community. A Mason from New York could join the lodge in his new home in Ohio. He immediately held something in common with his new neighbors, and such commonalities helped maintain order and stability in an otherwise tumultuous society. During the Progressive Era associationalism ran rampant. People of like interests joined together to promote the common welfare. Voluntarism, the idea that private individuals can work together to effect social change, built upon the old-fashioned idea of neighborhood cooperation to solve problems. This history of cooperation for individual and social betterment combined with the rural penchant for keeping busy led to a proliferation of groups for people of all ages and interests. Although interest in a particular organization might wane over time, other organizations would spring into place to fill the void.[41]

Active, committed individuals were vital to this process. Time and again the county histories detail the influence of one or two individuals in an organization or community. In Antimony, Utah, for example, "between 1947 and 1953 Antimony had a very active and interesting scouting program. Phil Albin was the scout master." Once his tenure ended, the scouts lagged. From the same memoir: "In the fall of 1948 two new teachers came to Antimony. . . . They brought a few innovations into the school, mainly dancing." The children learned and their parents caught on, and "it was not long before Antimony had a square dance team." The dancers traveled to other towns to spread the square dance gospel, and the whole valley danced "until after [the teachers] left in the mid-1950s." One Antimony man, Archie Gleave, recorded his own voluntary contributions to this region. He had been "mayor for eight years, . . . on the welfare board for five years," served on three other boards for several years, and had been a town councilman for fourteen years. He had also "worked and got the TV started, got the cemetery mapped out and the water at the cemetery; also got crosses for the graves and cleaned it up; helped get the road oiled, . . . helped with the playground, . . . the tennis court [and] put up the Christmas lights for the town." The smaller the town, the fewer people there were to carry the load. Mr. Gleave had done his share.[42]

The Cowbelles of Blue, Arizona, did their share as well. Organized in 1954 by the wives of area cattle ranchers, this women's group planned to promote beef. They did so with such programs as the delivery of beef roasts to nursing homes, to the mail carrier, and to all new fathers, and with skits and filmstrips in the schools, floats in parades, and booths at the fair. They quickly found other community service projects as well. The Cowbelles brought phone service to Blue in the 1960s, made "large donations" to the hospital, maintained the cemetery, sponsored a lending library, and made vests lettered with BARB WIRE BOYS for the local dance band. The Cowbelles' husbands seemed to become a sort of auxiliary organization. In the 1970s, the husbands dug a grave and provided a headstone for a local man who otherwise would have ended up in a pauper's grave in a distant town. The husbands also dug a "new landfill dump," fenced it, and built the access to it. The women assisted "by serving them food and cold drinks." The twenty or so Cowbelles were still around in 1986 doing good works and urging people to eat beef.[43]

Across the rural West, it is still important for residents to contribute to the community. In Starkey, California, in the 1960s, Elvin Hatch estimated that 54 percent of the population were aware of and involved in community affairs. Another 28 percent were partially engaged in the life of the town; only 19 percent lived on the social periphery. When the town held its annual barbecue to raise funds for local projects and build community solidarity, 100 adults, out of a population of "fewer than 200 households," contributed time and labor. Community commitment can take a variety of forms. In the Bitter Valley community near Starkey, residents included a bachelor farmer in their list of community members. He rarely attended social events but always "donated money, materials, tools, equipment—even the labor of his hired men."[44]

Service to the community, of course, can attract criticism. Rural communities are known for their infighting and factionalism as locals argue over schools, churches, town budgets, or other community issues. Individuals or groups that take the lead sometimes find themselves targets of faultfinders who wanted things done differently. In extreme cases, disagreements can poison the community atmosphere to the point that nothing gets done and potential leaders withdraw or even move away. In most circumstances, however, parties disagree about the means to reach the same goals—the creation of the best community possible for all. It takes a certain kind of person to thrive in a rural community, one who recognizes the value of its intensely personal relations and is not troubled by the negatives these relations sometimes bring.[45]

Urbanites sometimes fail to understand the organizational and associational impulses of rural communities. A study of "Middlewest," Idaho, published in 1995, states that "a good case for provincialism could be built" based on the "quaint aspects of life in Middlewest." The author cites two examples—the chamber of commerce holiday turkey raffle and the library ice-cream social held to raise money for that institution—as proof of quaint or parochial life. "The local dairy donated the ice cream. The women's auxiliary of the library baked cakes. The head librarian declared the event a success, though it raised less than $300." To longtime residents or to rural people anywhere, these activities would be neither parochial nor quaint.[46]

Recent arrivals in the town compared it unfavorably in many ways with their previous urban California homes. "Sally could only laugh at the Christmas parade, because it lacked class," the investigator reported. (The same woman lambasted local fashion as well. "I thought all the polyester had been used up years ago, but now I know they shipped it all to Middlewest.") Neither Sally nor the investigator seemed to recognize the meaning behind the parade, instead basing their evaluation on parade images taken from television, movies, or perhaps the professionally managed, multimillion-dollar Rose Bowl Parade. Home talent can never measure up to that ideal.[47]

Ed Marston, editor of the environmental newspaper *High Country News* and resident of the rural West for several years, says that it "presents few handholds" for urbanites who wish to live there. "If Rotary, Kiwanis or the Elks is not your cup of tea, . . . or if you are a woman with an independent streak, you will find yourself short of groups to join." Marston concludes that the rural West "has been on a separate track for decades, and may be fundamentally different from America," an artifact of nineteenth-century life. Its ability to sustain itself as such, however, is coming to an end, he believes. The question, as he sees it, is whether "the economic demands of the twenty-first century require such large changes that the underlying social base will be altered beyond recognition."[48]

The painful results of modernization and urbanization in the rural West have been the removal of many leaders, or their children, to greener pastures, the tremendous reduction in the number of followers needed to get things done, and the growing suspicion among rural people that their efforts do not matter and will come to naught anyway. Those feelings manifest themselves, to greater or lesser degrees, in feelings of isolation, resentment, and stoicism; the feelings are frequently exacerbated when new population growth occurs in the form of fleeing urbanites, who mix an airy condescension with an odd attachment to the supposed values of the urban areas they have so recently fled. Islands of successful rural life continue to exist, but they are vulnerable to small changes that can effectively spell their doom. The rural West continues its tradition of precarious defiance of the odds.

NOTES

1. Gerald D. Nash, *The American West Transformed: The Impact of the Second World War* (Bloomington: Indiana University Press, 1985), 14. U.S. Bureau of the Census, *Sixteenth Census of the United States: 1940 Population and Housing* (Washington, D.C.: Government Printing Office, 1942–43), vol. 2, parts 1, 2, 4, 5, and 7; 1990 data come from U.S. Department of Commerce, Bureau of the Census, Data User Services Division, *1990 U.S. Census CD-ROM Summary,* CD 90-3, A03; CD90-3A 09; CD 90-3A58.

2. Daniel N. Vichorek, *Montana Farm and Ranch Life,* Montana Geographic Series, no. 18 (Helena, Mont.: American and World Geographic Publishing, 1992), 103. Other sources that address this theme include Ed Marston, ed., *Reopening the Western Frontier* (Covelo, Calif.: Island Press, 1989), a book made up of essays that originally appeared in *High Country News,* an environmental newspaper; Richard Baker, *Los Dos Mundos: Rural Mexican Americans, Another America* (Logan: Utah State University Press, 1995); Jim Carrier, *West of the Divide: Voices from a Ranch and a Reservation* (Golden, Colo.: Fulcrum, 1992), a reprint of a series of articles written for the *Denver Post;* and Ruth Rudner, *Greetings from Wisdom, Montana* (Golden, Colo.: Fulcrum, 1989).

3. Lucille S. Anderson, *The Life and Times of a 1940 Cattle Rancher's Bride Who Learns to Be Bridle-Wise* (Phoenix, Ariz.: Lucille Anderson, n.d.), 1; Eulalia Bourne, *Women in Levi's* (Tucson: University of Arizona Press, 1967), 118; Nathaniel Burt's parents ran a Wyoming dude ranch for several years. He tells about growing up there in *Jackson Hole Journal* (Norman: University of Oklahoma Press, 1983).

4. Eric G. Swedin, "The Swett Homestead: An Oral History, 1909–1970" (M.A. thesis, Utah State University, 1991), 63, 81, 101.

5. Ibid., 99, 108, 117, 118, 102. Rural people sometimes used the term "highline" electricity to distinguish that coming by wire from distant generators from electricity generated at home or in small towns with Delco plants.

6. Cleo Cosper Coor, comp. and ed., *Down on the Blue: Blue River, Arizona, 1878–1986* (Goodyear, Ariz.: Valley West Printing for the Blue River Cowbelles, 1987), 234; Louis J. Clements, *Centennial Farm Families,* vol. 1 (Rexburg, Idaho: Upper Snake River Valley Historical Society, 1991), 10–14, 35–36, 51, 97, 113–18.

7. Shirley A. McGilvray, *Crazy Ranching* (n.p.: Shirley A. McGilvray, 1978), 2; Carolyn Anne Sprague, "Nevada Ranch Women: A Study in the Management of Isola-

tion" (Ph.D. diss., University of Illinois–Urbana-Champaign, 1984), 144, 174; the telephone pole quote comes from Evelyn L. Pickett, "Women in the Empty Quarter: A Study of Changes and Challenges as Related to Women's Experiences in the Nevada Ranching Industry from the Mid–Nineteenth Century to the Late Twentieth" (M.A. thesis, University of Nevada–Reno, 1988), 74; Ed Quillen, "For Whom the Bell Tolls," in *Reopening the Western Frontier,* ed. Ed Marston (Covelo, Calif.: Island Press, 1989), 267.

8. M. Lane Warner, *Grass Valley, 1873–1976: A History of Antimony and Her People* (Salt Lake City, Utah: American Press, 1976), 54, 59.

9. The People of Bingham County, *Bingham County History* (Blackfoot, Idaho: Bingham County Historical Society Book Committee, 1990), 257–58.

10. Gracia N. Jones and Janice F. DeMille, *History of Fredonia, Arizona, 1885–1985* (Hurricane, Utah: Homestead Publishers, 1986), 113–15.

11. Elvin Hatch, *Biography of a Small Town* (New York: Columbia University Press, 1979), 4, 113–17.

12. Ivan Doig, *This House of Sky: Landscapes of a Western Mind* (New York: Harcourt Brace Jovanovich, 1978), 127.

13. Ibid., 81, 87; *1990 U.S. Census CD-ROM Summary.*

14. Sprague, "Nevada Ranch Women," 183.

15. Boundary County Historical Society, *History of Boundary County, Idaho* (Bonners Ferry, Idaho: Boundary County Historical Society, 1987), 151; Tabiona and Hanna [Utah] Communities, *Footprints in a Beautiful Valley: A History of Tabiona-Hanna* (Springville, Utah: Art City Publishing, n.d.), 58.

16. Swedin, "The Swett Homestead," 66, 94.

17. Ibid., 103.

18. Andrew Gulliford, *America's Country Schools* (Washington, D.C.: Preservation Press, 1991). Gulliford provides a beautifully illustrated history of the institution; Warner, *Grass Valley,* 60.

19. U.S. Bureau of the Census, *Fifteenth Census of the United States: 1930. Population* (Washington, D.C.: U.S. Government Printing Office, 1931–32), vol. 2, parts 1 and 2; *Sixteenth Census of the United States: 1940 Population and Housing;* U.S. Bureau of the Census, *Census of Population: 1950. A Report of the Seventeenth Decennial Census of the United States* (Washington, D.C.: Government Printing Office, 1952), vol. 2, parts 3, 6, 12, 26, 28, 31, 37, 44, 47, 50; Nash, *American West Transformed,* 17–74. One example is the Oneida County area of Idaho; see Carol Eliason, comp., *Holbrook and Surrounding Areas History Book, 1878–1987* (Blackfoot, Idaho: Neves Printing, 1987), 33. Oneida County lost 22 percent of its population between 1930 and 1940 and another 38 percent between 1940 and 1950.

20. Swedin, "The Swett Homestead," 104, 112; Doig, *This House of Sky,* 94, 182.

21. *Life* 29 (16 October 1950): 117–18, 120. The only other dormitory high school in the lower forty-eight states is on the Great Plains in Jordan, Montana. Dayton Duncan, *Miles from Nowhere: Tales from America's Contemporary Frontier* (New York: Viking Penguin, 1993), 38. Parents have tried other solutions. In Nevada, one family enrolled their son in an accredited home correspondence course. Sprague, "Nevada Ranch Women," 76.

22. Laurie Jean Ward, *Bannock Valley* (Providence, Utah: Keith W. Watkins and Sons, 1982), 13.

23. Coor, *Down on the Blue,* 236; National Geographic Society, *American Mountain People* (Washington, D.C.: National Geographic Society, Special Publications Division, 1973), 144; Nancy Wood, *The Grass Roots People* (New York: Harper and Row, 1978), 156.

24. Sprague, "Nevada Ranch Women," 86; McGilvray, *Crazy Ranching,* 18; Wood, *Grass Roots People,* 156.

25. Hatch, *Biography of a Small Town,* 265.

26. Sierra County Historical Society, *History of Sierra County New Mexico* (Truth or Consequences, N.Mex.: Sierra County Historical Society, 1979), 27–28.

27. Boundary County Historical Society, *History of Boundary County Idaho,* 156; Inez Puckett McEwen, *So This Is Ranching* (Caldwell, Idaho: Caxton Printers, 1948), 213.

28. McGilvray, *Crazy Ranching,* 51; Tracee Van Slyke, "Ranching, Logging, Grocery Keep Oregonians on the Go: The Way We Live," *Farm and Ranch Living* 17 (December/January 1995): 26; Sprague, "Nevada Ranch Women," 76; Pickett, "Women in the Empty Quarter," 78–79.

29. National Congress of Parents and Teachers, *The Parent-Teacher Organization: Its Origins and Development* (Chicago: National Congress of Parents and Teachers, 1944), is an early overview of PTA history; Jones and DeMille, *History of Fredonia, Arizona,* 77; Eliason, *Holbrook and Surrounding Areas History Book,* 35–36, 33.

30. Hatch, *Biography of a Small Town,* 264, 174.

31. A'Delbert Samson, "Church Groups in Four Agricultural Settings in Montana," Montana Agricultural Experiment Station, *Bulletin 538,* March 1958, 14, 38, 17; Ward, *Bannock Valley,* 15; Tabiona and Hanna, *Footprints in a Beautiful Valley,* 129. A good general introduction to Mormonism can be found in Leonard J. Arrington and Davis Bilton, *The Mormon Experience: A History of the Latter-Day Saints* (New York: Knopf, 1979).

32. Samson, "Church Groups," 3, 15–25.

33. Tabiona and Hanna, *Footprints in a Beautiful Valley,* 56, 93–129; People of Bingham County, *Bingham County History,* 125–37; Central Centennial Book Committee, *A Century in Central* (Central, Ariz.: Central Centennial Book Committee, 1983), 16–21; Eliason, *Holbrook and Surrounding Areas,* 68.

34. McEwen, *So This Is Ranching,* 154–57.

35. Edith Mae Sandell Christian, *Buckeye: The First 100 Years, 1888–1988* (Visalia, Calif.: Jostens Printing and Publishing Division, 1988), 42; Central Centennial Book Committee, *A Century in Central,* 18, 37, 59; Tabiona and Hanna, *Footprints in a Beautiful Valley,* 97.

36. A classic account of Mexican American migration and society is Carey McWilliam, *North from Mexico: The Spanish-Speaking People of the United States* (Philadelphia: Lipincott, 1949). An updated version is available from Praeger Press (New York, 1990). In the 1940s, Mexican Americans were a popular subject of study among sociologists, who worried about their cultural differences. See Quincy Guy Burris, "Juan, a Rural Portrait: Unassimilated Spanish-Americans of the Southwest," *Survey Graphic* 33 (December 1941): 499–503, as an example.

37. Sarah Deutsch, *No Separate Refuge: Culture, Class, and Gender on an Anglo-Hispanic Frontier in the American Southwest, 1880–1940* (New York: Oxford University Press, 1987), 50–51; Baker, *Los Dos Mundos*, 77.

38. Sierra County Historical Society, *History of Sierra County, New Mexico*, 20.

39. Wood, *Grass Roots People*, 83–84, 92; Sierra County Historical Society, *History of Sierra County, New Mexico*, 18.

40. Baker, *Los Dos Mundos*, 57–82, 83–84.

41. Don Harrison Doyle, *The Social Order of a Frontier Community: Jacksonville, Illinois, 1825–70* (Urbana: University of Illinois Press, 1978), 156–93; John Whiteclay Chambers III, *The Tyranny of Change: American in the Progressive Era, 1900–1917* (New York: St. Martin's Press, 1980), 119–25.

42. Warner, *Grass Valley*, 61, 73.

43. Coor, *Down on the Blue*, 2–3.

44. Hatch, *Biography of a Small Town*, 124, 184, 4, 151.

45. Jones and DeMille, *History of Fredonia, Arizona*, 113–15, tells one such story with the battle over electric power. Hatch, *Biography of a Small Town*, discusses this theme throughout.

46. Baker, *Los Dos Mundos*, 37–39. The tone of Baker's book is highly disrespectful of the people of "Middlewest"; he creates a caricature, not a true portrait. Even the condescending "Sally" had to acknowledge that the community was neighborly and helpful. Her husband's fellow workers visited him in the hospital, which surprised them, and she admitted that their neighbors offered them all sorts of assistance without being asked; see pages 39–40. The couple admitted that they had no intention of returning to California.

47. Ibid., 37–39.

48. Ed Marston, "The Rural West: An Artifact of the Nineteenth Century," in *Reopening the Western Frontier*, ed. Ed Marston (Covelo, Calif.: Island Press, 1989), 31, 29, 32; Thomas E. Sheridan, *Arizona: A History* (Tucson: University of Arizona Press, 1995), describes the shift of "the state's political, economic, and ideological center of gravity from the countryside to the city." Rural Arizona and its citizens became "the Other Arizona. . . . The Other Arizona was by turns recreational, utilitarian and aesthetic. But it was almost always subordinate to Urban Arizona" (pp. 303–6, 316). Ted K. Bradshaw provides the technical details of the urban-rural split in "In the Shadow of Urban Growth: Bifurcation in Rural California Communities," in *Forgotten Places: Uneven Development in Rural America*, ed. Thomas A. Lyson and William W. Falk (Lawrence: University Press of Kansas, 1993), 218–56.

3

Environmentalism and Agriculture in the American West

James E. Sherow

Following World War II, Aldo Leopold reflected on the conservation practices initiated during the New Deal and found them lacking in an important respect. Farmers, he believed, had to redefine their relationship to land in order to realize true conservation. An older set of values, Leopold feared, governed farmers' views of their landscapes. He criticized an ethic based solely on "economic self-interest." Farmers, he pointed out, recognized their social obligations in funding roads, public schools, churches, and local sports programs but failed to see their responsibility to the land itself. Even when farmers employed conservation methods, they "continued only those practices that yielded an immediate and visible economic gain for themselves." Leopold charged farmers with disregarding practices unprofitable to themselves, even when they were beneficial to the community.[1]

Leopold included forests, wetlands, streams, and their biosystems in his notion of community. A "land-use ethic based wholly on economic self-interest," he warned, endangered this greater community of which farmers were an integral part. "A thing is right only when it tends to preserve the integrity, stability, and beauty of the community, and the community includes the soil, waters, fauna, and flora, as well as people." He charged adherents to "cease being intimidated by the argument that a right action is impossible because it does not yield maximum profits, or that a wrong action is to be condoned because it pays." According to Leopold, farmers lacked *an ecological conscience.*[2]

Leopold articulated the stand environmentalists would take against farm operations in the Rocky Mountain West after World War II. Eco-activists saw themselves confronting a vast opposition of government agencies, farm organizations, land-grant universities, and farmers and ranchers, all attempting to master the land through market-culture values, reductionist science, and technological manipulation.[3]

Environmentalists presented an alternative view, one that many academics, government bureaucrats, and farmers eventually began to embrace. "Greens" saw the world in a holistic light: everything is connected in some manner to everything else, and the whole is greater than the sum of its parts. Fields, livestock, wild animals and plants, and the workings of society all lived intertwined within a biosystem. Change one, and all the other parts of the life system changed. This community of life thrived when people considered what was best for all of the parts.

This line of reasoning directly challenged the prevailing view, one that saw the world largely as a machine. Through the scientific method and applied technology, people could reduce the world to its basic components, and they could control and manipulate these in keeping with their social goals and aspirations. For farmers this usually meant reducing the biology of crops to their basic component parts and manipulating these for greater efficiency and larger yields. Many farmers and agricultural economists sought efficiency in three basic ways. First, they reduced labor costs through greater uses of machinery; next they applied petrochemicals to control insects and encourage plant growth; and finally they increased landholdings to maximize economies of scale. Farming became an industrial enterprise to be managed in the same manner as a factory. In essence, environmentalists' holistic worldview came to loggerheads with many farmers' reductionistic one.

This contest is easily illustrated in the post–World War II West. For example, conservationists and farmers shared similar concerns over mounting soil erosion in dryland farming, but they dealt with the problem in different ways. Many farmers and agricultural scientists have long disagreed with environmentalists over the uses of petrochemicals for insect control and the proper scale of farm machinery. Responding to these environmental concerns, some farmers have blended organic techniques with small-scale uses of farm machinery and have retained profitable operations.

The quarrelsome nature of western water development has highlighted the differences between a mechanistic and holistic approach to farming more than any other issue. Environmentalists long questioned the ecological and social effects of big dams and railed about the depletion of groundwater and surface flows in streams. Moreover, these critics questioned whether western law is appropriate to the health of ecosystems in the region.

In the postwar period, the struggle between these worldviews seldom strictly divided environmentalists and farmers into two contending camps. In the last decade or so, institutions in western states and federal agricultural policies, with the support of organic farmers and environmentalists, showed a trend toward "sustainable agriculture" and ecosystem protection. Nonetheless, others within the Sagebrush Rebellion and Wise Use Movement bemoaned these trends. Often drowned in the shrill rhetoric of this noisy opposition are those people working at the grassroots level to reconcile the economic realities of farming with maintaining rural communities and their ecosystems.

In 1945, this farmer near Ashton, Idaho, worked to keep the ditches in his irrigated potato field running free. Contour-plowed and -planted fields such as this help prevent wind and water erosion. These conservation techniques are common throughout the West. *Courtesy, United States Department of Agriculture.*

Environmentalists in the West have been quick to point out the harsh consequences of mechanistic farming practices. Consider soil erosion in the Palouse, a productive wheat region on the western fringe of the Rocky Mountains. Dryland farmers in this eastern portion of Washington have grown and harvested some of the highest wheat yields in the nation. Recently, researchers such as R. I. Papendick, D. L. Young, D. K. McCool, and H. A. Krauss have documented farmers' inclinations to maximize profits by increasing crop yields. Through the extension service at Washington State University, agricultural economists and scientists provided the technical knowledge and suggestions for creating farms with large investments in machinery and chemicals in the chase for efficiency and profits.[4]

Wheat farming in the Palouse reflected a widespread belief in reductionistic science and an unfettered faith in mass production. Many farmers presumed their market was a mass-consuming society more worried about grocery prices than about quality or how their purchases affected the land and people where the crops were grown. In 1994, some farmers, such as Darrell O. Turner, the president of the Washington State Farm Bureau, continued to see agriculture in terms of economically competitive food production. The 1940s through the 1960s, Turner claimed, were golden years when extension agents and researchers from agricultural universities provided farmers with the technical knowledge and means to raise bumper crop yields.[5]

Recently, however, changes to the land have called into serious question the ability of farmers in the Palouse, and throughout the Rocky Mountain West, to sustain the farming practices of the last fifty years. An inch of topsoil normally takes 500 years to accumulate, yet in the Palouse some farmers' fields have lost an inch of topsoil every eighteen months. In three years' time, on an acre where such erosion occurred, the accumulation of 1,500 years of soil building, some 300 tons worth, flew with the winds and flowed in the streams. On some slopes as much as 90 to 200 tons disappeared in a single winter.[6]

Scholars such as Sara Ebenreck have claimed these farming practices were shortsighted and ultimately unproductive and nonsustainable. Only recently have farmers and scientists in the agronomy departments such as those at Washington State University listened to Ebenreck and others. In 1994, Karl Stauber of the U.S. Department of Agriculture (USDA) noted this attitudinal shift toward farming. Land-grant universities, Stauber noted, "have faculty members that are very much interested in [an] integrative approach." This newer breed of researchers have read, and taken to heart, the writings of Aldo Leopold, Rachel Carson, and Jim Hightower, who responded to prevailing assumptions about the uses of chemicals and farm machinery.[7]

By the end of World War II, many farm researchers believed the use of chemicals would solve most farm production problems, particularly crop losses to insects. F. C. Bishopp, who grew up on a ranch in Colorado and later served as the assistant chief in charge of research in the Bureau of Entomology and Plant Quarantine in the Department of Agriculture, believed people were in a "constant battle against insects." The challenge was nothing less than human survival itself. He championed the "spectacular" results of agents like DDT, while at the same time recognizing their potential ill effect on "beneficial forms of life." Yet Bishopp would use this weapon, along with others, in "carefully planned" strategies to combat insects. He was waging a war, and reductionistic science was his arsenal.[8]

Besides the domination of nature, post–World War II researchers stressed the economics of technological efficiency in crop production and harvests. Advanced designs in tractors, combines, hay balers, and sugar beet and corn harvesters promised reductions in labor costs and higher returns. As the noted soil scientist Charles E. Kellogg optimistically prophesied, "Science can make abundance physically possible." Technological and industrial change grow out of science, Kellogg claimed, and result in efficient farming.[9]

Drawbacks, Kellogg recognized, also existed within the promise of scientific agriculture. He fretted over farmers' finding their old ways obsolete and themselves unable to render a livelihood in an increasingly complicated market system. He called attention to how efficient farming might result in "disparities of opportunity." Some farmers would profit at others' expense in the pursuit of

Tractors have been the most important hardware technology to influence western agriculture. Since 1940, however, technological change has created considerable division between environmentalists and farmers. In 1971, this farmer in the Hamblin Valley near the Hart Mountains in Utah plowed sagebrush. By the late twentieth century, environmentalists often demanded that farmers plow less to help conserve the soil. *Courtesy, United States Department of Agriculture.*

"immediately practical objectives." Perhaps the drive toward lower labor costs, increased applications of chemicals, and greater use of technology had some unintended social and environmental consequences.[10]

The bountiful predictions of Kellogg and Bishopp came to fruition, but their harsh projections also bore fruit. By the 1960s and 1970s, environmentalists rallied around two clarion calls to reform, one from Rachel Carson's *Silent Spring* and the other from Jim Hightower's *Hard Tomatoes, Hard Times.* Carson warned about the harsh environmental effects of DDT. Hightower roundly criticized economists and scientists in agricultural colleges who promoted mechanized agriculture. He said the emphasis on machines destroyed small farmers and their land.

Dependence on chemicals, so environmentalists argued, bore out many of Rachel Carson's predictions. Dale McDonald related how the use of petrochemicals significantly increased farmers' risk of developing cancer and other serious illnesses compared with nonfarmers. Anthony Brown noted the harsh effects of pesticides on arthropods, including beneficial species such as honeybees. His point illustrated both the unintended ill effects of petrochemical use on the ecosystem of which the crops were a part, as well as the economic loss resulting from declining honey production in association with alfalfa. Moreover, researchers with the National Research Council pointed to over 440 insect and mite species, like the Colorado potato beetle, that became resistant to pesticides after 1945.[11]

R. Neil Sampson's warnings about the use of the mechanical potato harvester echoed what Hightower and Leopold feared about the greater use of technology. Sampson noted how Idaho farmers once planted in contoured fields. But the newly invented potato harvester, which cut labor costs, worked poorly on hillsides. Consequently, farmers took out their contours and planted rows up and down the hills rather than across. This planting technique increased soil erosion from an average of less than 10 tons to nearly 100 tons per acre. Sampson feared such methods would simply kill the soils and ruin agriculture in the region.[12]

With more unwise topsoil and petrochemical practices, greens, that is, environmentalists, questioned the development of water in the West. In 1954, the well-known Texas historian Walter Prescott Webb chastised westerners for their wasteful water practices. Webb angered westerners by elegantly refuting the remaking of the West in the image of the Midwest corn belt through federally subsidized irrigation. His insight led to one inescapable conclusion: western agricultural production was limited and constrained by scarce supplies of water. Irrigated agriculture, as practiced and envisioned, rested on wobbly legs at best, and its vigor, much less its growth, was unhealthy and unwise at best and destined for ruin at worst. Webb implored westerners to put on the brakes— to slow down their pell-mell rush toward consuming more water than the environment could supply.[13]

Webb's critique of progress in the West perturbed many people. They rejected out of hand any calling into question the domination of nature in the pursuit of growth. Westerners based their assumptions on faith in reductionistic science overcoming any, and all, ecological and social impediments to growth in an arid land. Representing this mind-set, Michael Creed Hinderlider, who had just retired from thirty years as the state engineer of Colorado, had always believed technology and science could make water an "untiring slave" on behalf of agriculture. Growth, in crop production, profits, and population, prefigured power and opportunity. Nonetheless, as in dryland farming and ranching, new approaches in science and social thought would call into question the assumptions undergirding water development.[14]

Irrigation promoters and advocates often advanced their cause using the rhetoric of Jeffersonian republicanism even if farmers seldom practiced their ideals. Those people who practiced smaller, community-oriented irrigation found themselves more hard-pressed to maintain their way of life each year after 1945, and environmentalists soon linked the destruction of riparian ecosystems to the decline of irrigated agriculture and small farming communities throughout the Rocky Mountain West. At the same time, the influence of large-scale agribusiness began to be felt at the state and national levels of economics and government. Even the people managing this form of irrigation had to face the effects of altered ecosystems on their farming practices and the growing criticisms of environmentalists who called into question the social and ecological affects of mainstream irrigation in the Rocky Mountain West.

Consider the plight of Hispanic Americans in northern New Mexico and southern Colorado. For nearly four centuries, many of these people who resided in the villages along the western slope of the Sangre De Cristo Mountains and in the Rio Grande valley above Albuquerque, New Mexico, combined elements of Pueblo Indian culture with Spanish traditions to form a tight community-based society. In general, their small irrigated farms fit nicely into the region's ecosystems. As U.S. District Judge Encinias noted in 1990, "The people [Hispanics], the land and the water are inextricably bound together and will be until Santa Fe is entirely paved over. It is this culture which is our greatest pride and not without considerable value, though not measurable directly in dollars." Encinias saw land and water as the basis for community and family rather than as a commodity with a market value.[15]

Environmentalists, novelists, and scholars have quickly pointed to how changes in the landscape can bring about social and ecological problems in Hispanic American agricultural practice. Anglo-American policy has generally treated land as a commodity, suitable for market transactions. Even the conservation policies of the federal government have treated land and water in this manner. Forest Service policies regarded trees, grass, and minerals in terms of economic production, and reclamation certainly treated water as a commodity subject to agricultural and urban markets.

Environmentalists and Hispanic Americans often joined forces to preserve a community-based agriculture centered around the *acequia madre* (mother ditch). Beginning in 1971, at the Rio Grande del Rancho project just south of Taos, New Mexico, Hispanic Americans and environmentalists formed the Tres Rios Association and successfully staved off the formation of the Indian Camp Dam irrigation district. Membership in the conservancy district would have ruined small-scale Hispanic American farmers, and their water rights would have been used for other purposes. More recently, the Citizens for San Luis Valley Water in Colorado foiled American Water Development's plan to transport groundwater to Denver and Colorado Springs. American Water Development, with powerful investors Maurice Strong, a Canadian businessman, Richard Lamb, former governor of Colorado, and William Ruckelhaus, former director of the Environmental Protection Agency, failed to convince the Colorado Supreme Court that tapping deep groundwater would leave waterfowl habitat, the Great Sand Dunes National Monument, and the Hispanic Americans' community irrigation practices unaffected. By the mid-1990s, even some state judges had begun to consider the interconnections within, or holism, of an ecosystem.[16]

In the immediate aftermath of World War II, however, environmentalists could claim few victories, especially in halting the mechanistic march toward dam building in the West. Concrete plugs seem to grow out of every river bottom, backing flows and creating artificial lakes in the middle of deserts. Between the early 1930s and the early 1970s, the Bureau of Reclamation alone constructed over 200 projects. Critics certainly called into question the need for these monoliths, but most westerners believed the intertwined ideals of social and economic progress through dam building overrode the need to consider alternatives.[17]

Environmentalists mounted only two real victories over dam building prior to the 1980s. The Bureau of Reclamation's plans for a dam at Echo Park and its threat to Dinosaur National Monument prompted a storm of protest from David Brower and Sierra Club members, in coalition with a score of other dam opponents in other conservation groups, and even within the Army Corps of Engineers. The other victory came in defeating the construction of Bridge and Marble Gorge Dams in the mid-1960s. These structures would have affected the Colorado River in Grand Canyon National Park. In this fight against "big dam foolishness," the Sierra Club lost its tax-exempt status but won enough public support to force the bureau to retreat. Nevertheless, bureau engineers and hydrologists planned and built scores of other large dams and irrigation projects throughout the Rocky Mountain West.[18]

Not until the passage of the Endangered Species Act and the National Environmental Policy Act of 1969, which require impact statements detailing the probable effects of a governmental project on the surrounding ecosystems, did environmentalists have an effective tool for confronting dam building. Since then, the bureau has been stopped from building several dams—for example, Two Forks, which was intended primarily to supply Denver's growing water needs and also to supplement irrigation supplies in the Platte River Basin.[19]

Moreover, environmentalists argued that a physical limitation to dam building existed in the American West. As Marc Reisner pointed out, "Glen Canyon [Dam site] was inferior to Hoover, as Auburn was vastly inferior to Shasta (but four times as expensive, even allowing for inflation), the Bureau was now being forced to build on sites it had rejected forty, fifty, or sixty years earlier." As Pat Dugan, a bureau engineer, reflected in the 1980s, "Every site we've built on since [1940] would probably have scared hell out of nineteenth-century engineers." But the dam-building technology used in the 1960s and 1970s, so he insisted, made these structures safe. However, he erred in judgment.[20]

One failure in Idaho bore environmentalists' concerns on a deadly crest of floodwaters on 5 June 1976. The Teton Dam collapse wreaked havoc all along the Snake River valley. The bureau built this dam on a questionable geologic site, and the contractors ignored warning signs about weak dam links into the canyon sidewalls. Supporters of the dam, most of them agriculturists from the valley, hailed the completion of Teton as a savior from irrigation water shortages. When the dam collapsed, these same people had far more water than they could handle in one setting. A twenty-foot-high wall of water moving over fifteen miles per hour smashed through the town of Wilford, leaving only one hollowed-out shell of a building behind in its wake. Residents in three other cities felt the brunt of the flood; eleven people died, while survivors endured over $2 billion in estimated damages to their homes, businesses, and fields.[21]

Incredibly, few people were swept away when the Teton Dam broke, and those who remained later endorsed rebuilding it. Even in the late 1980s, John Keys, the regional bureau director, advocated rebuilding Teton Dam, this time in concrete. In spite of the disaster, farmers continued to have unquestioned faith in the ability of technocrats to harness even the most dangerous sites. The bureau, so members of the Fremont-Madison Irrigation District clamored, had a "moral" responsibility to rebuild the dam. Environmentalists such as Tim Palmer, however, labeled such plans "a cement-mixer's fantasy," one that ignored threats of seismic tremors and the potential destruction of the Snake River. For dam promoters, technology can overcome all limitations, whereas for environmentalists, technology faces severe and ever-mounting limitations.[22]

The Big Lost River, a tributary of the Snake River in Idaho, may be in danger of being truly lost forever. Over the years, thirteen dams altered the flow of the Snake River to the point of rendering it absolutely dry in stretches. Irrigation laid the base for lucrative markets in potatoes, sugar beets, barley, wheat, mint, and hops. In 1955, Governor Robert Smylie put it bluntly: "We are seeking—we always have been and we always will—the ways and means of developing every drop of water that tumbles from the snow packs of the Snake River watershed." Flood irrigation was not enough, and farmers began an unrestrained pumping of groundwater in the late 1960s.[23]

Groundwater pumping clearly illustrates the differences between environmentalists and irrigators over water use. Frank Zyback's center-pivot irrigation system and improved pump technology made groundwater easily accessible, making agriculture possible in many arid lands. Irrigators eagerly sought inexpensive parcels in valleys formerly only grazed or untended. They drilled wells and pumped what they termed an "inexhaustible" supply of water. They gave little, if any, thought to ecological consequences, which brought them into conflict with environmentalists concerned with changes to springs and riparian ecosystems.[24]

In the halcyon days after World War II, water law in the American West served only one unquestioned principle: the application of water for economic gains. Generally, western water law recognized three forms of use: domestic, agricultural, and industrial. In fact, most state water codes made it impossible for anyone to use water for other purposes. Environmentalists lacked the legal means to protect streamflows, riparian ecosystems, wetlands, or endangered species.[25]

Environmentalists took note of these institutional limitations and, in the

1960s, advocated wide changes to state and national laws. Reformers targeted groundwater law, nonsource pollution control, and instream flow protection. Farmers, however, have oscillated in their support of environmentally inspired water law changes. They have found themselves between two realms: one in which the technological control of nature and agribusiness prevails, and the other in which a holistic and sustainable ethic holds sway. Farmers persuaded by the latter view worked most effectively with environmentalists, whereas those taken by the former often stand in opposition.

Only the people of one state have seen fit to define a holistic connection between groundwater and surface flows. New Mexicans made this part of their state water law in a supreme court decision in 1958. The "Templeton doctrine recognized that all the waters of a basin, whether above or below the ground, deriving from a common source, were one and the same and should be treated as such." This seems a commonsensical approach, but few Rocky Mountain states have effective regulation of groundwater, much less a recognition of its connection to surface flows.[26]

Growing problems over the connections between groundwater pumping and surface flows in the Snake River Basin underscore environmentalists' concerns with what makes for an ecologically sound administration of water use. Even though state law forbade pumping beyond the recharge rate of an aquifer, the disappearance of flows in Big Lost River showed the ineffectiveness of state regulation on this score. As late as 1995, the Idaho legislature thought it unnecessary to link groundwater and surface flows for administrative purposes. But in the last decade, Lew Rothwell, a thirty-five-year irrigator on Big Lost, and Charlie Traughber, a fly fisherman for twenty years, bitterly criticized state officials' administration of water uses affecting Big Lost. As conditions along the Big Lost deteriorated, environmentalists feared legal disputes would mount, endangered species such as salmon would perish, and riparian ecosystems would become dry as a bone.[27]

The plight of Milt Thompson in Diamond Valley, Nevada, serves well as another example. In 1993, Thompson owned a 2,700-acre ranch, where Diamond Springs had once flowed. Ranchers had used this water source since 1859, and Thompson continued its use until the 1980s when the springs began to dry up. Thompson could identify the source of his problem, but he could not find a remedy.[28]

Beginning in the late 1950s, irrigators began buying sagebrush lands under the provisos of the Desert Land Act of 1877 and putting these lands into the production of alfalfa. Promoters, including the state engineer's office and real estate speculators, ignored the limitations to groundwater recharge rates; by 1962, irrigators had acquired permits to 87,000 acre-feet of water to an aquifer with a recharge rate of no more than 30,000 acre-feet a year. In the early 1990s, 90 farms operated around 170 wells that pumped nearly 66,000 acre-feet of water onto 22,000 acres annually. Predictably, Diamond Springs began to falter, and Thompson began to wage a lonely battle against the state engineer's office for allowing water rights beyond the "safe yield" of the aquifer. More recently, Thompson has linked his crusade with environmentalists like Sierra Club members and Citizen Alert, and Indian peoples; together they have challenged the extensive pumping of water in Diamond Valley. Now, city planners from Reno and Las Vegas have plans to mine these same aquifers for urban uses. Thompson has a bleak vision of the future for himself and for Diamond Springs.[29]

More often than not, action to stop or slow water development has ruined political careers. Jimmy Carter's administration, supported by environmental activists, worked to halt what he considered wasteful, unneeded water projects throughout the West. His actions angered western irrigators and their politicians. Many, if not all, of the projects had questionable cost-benefit ratios and posed severe threats to existing ecosystems. Carter lacked organized public and political support to accomplish his ends, and his attack, even with the spectacle of Teton Dam fresh in people's memories, fell victim to frenzied pork-barrel politics. Carter did prevent some federal money from flowing into the construction of new reservoirs, but his efforts were not enough to end the building, and they initiated the erosion of his political power and popularity.[30]

Only recently have the leadership and the goals within the Bureau of Reclamation received support from environmentalists. Nothing illustrates this trend better than President Clinton's appointment of Dan Beard as the commissioner of the Bureau of Reclamation. Unlike Floyd Dominy, who in the 1960s led the bureau in a dam-building frenzy, Beard hoped never to build a big dam and would not mind removing dams, especially ones "that have ruined salmon habitat." He hoped to transform the bureau, "to make us more environmentally sensitive and responsive to the needs of the contemporary West." He proclaimed the end of big dam building. Still, Beard survived only two years as commissioner, resigning his office in September 1995. Now the question lingers in the minds of many environmentalists: Has the bureau really changed direction?[31]

Environmentalists have had more success in shaping policy in the USDA than they have with the Bureau of Reclamation. Beginning with the Carter administration, agricultural economists such as Garth Youngberg and Charles Benbrook advocated an organic approach toward farming. In 1979, Benbrook published an article in the *Journal of Soil and Water Conservation* that advanced new approaches for soil and water conservation; Youngberg, while working for the USDA, wrote "Report and Recommendations on Organic Farming" in 1980. At the time, these men's ideas were poorly received, and Youngberg quit the department as a result.[32]

By the mid-1980s, however, environmentalists had enough support in Congress to have several of their planks included in the 1985 farm bill. This legislation implemented the conservation reserve program, sodbuster and conservation compliance, and wetland protection. By the end of the decade, ideas from greens such as William Lockeretz, who championed a holistic, organic approach to agriculture, helped to shape the regulations designed for greater wetland protection and water quality enhancement in the farm bill of 1990.[33]

The inclusion of environmentalists' aims in the 1985 farm bill failed to win the wholehearted acceptance of farmers. Many agriculturists drew strength from a general, growing hostility toward greens in the West. In 1979, the state legislators of Nevada, capitalizing on growing anger with greens, passed a measure designed to gain state control over federal Bureau of Land Management (BLM) lands in the state, thereby launching the Sagebrush Rebellion. At heart these disgruntled westerners may have simply wanted to halt, or even turn back, environmental regulations shaping their use of the public domain. In many respects, conservatives such as James Watt, President Reagan's first secretary of the interior, desired a federal policy premised on the more mechanistic approach of Gifford Pinchot's conservation, an approach centered on the use and economic development of natural resources. The Sagebrush rebels resented the ecosystem preservation and maintenance approach to the environmental legislation of the 1970s. They saw in such laws impediments to economic growth in the West.[34]

The Sagebrush Rebellion spilled over into a debate over agricultural policy, too. Read Smith, a farmer from St. John, Washington, recalled how he and others resisted efforts by agents of the Soil Conservation Service (SCS) to force compliance to the farm bills. As Smith recalled, "The SCS field staff took some real heat." By the early 1990s, most farmers, Smith observed, had accepted conservation compliance, even if they did not like it. Chuck Merja, a farmer from Sun River, Montana, echoed Smith's fears about growing environmental regulation interfering with their liberties and called the SCS the "conservation cop." He believed the farm bill of 1985 would fundamentally change the role of the SCS from farm advising to "top cop," looking for farmers in noncompliance with soil, wetland, and petrochemical regulations.[35]

More recently, especially with the rise of the Wise Use Movement spearheaded by Ron Arnold, some antienvironmentalists have resorted to violence against greens. Fred Walking Badger had protested the use of pesticides and other petrochemicals on the Gila River Reservation. Walking Badger's position had gained considerable support among those Pimas who feared petrochemicals harmful effects on wildlife, their gardens, and their health. He sought to force nontribal cotton growers and the tribal council to quit using pesticides. In May 1994, just before public hearings on this issue, he disappeared. In June, law enforcement agents found the burned-out hulk of Walking Badger's car, and federal authorities began a murder investigation but had precious few leads.[36]

All these examples serve to illustrate how mechanism has vied with holism, and what some of the consequences have been for agriculture in the West. During the post–World War II period, holism exercised little influence as a guiding light until the last ten or so years. Despite some vocal opposition, a growing number of farmers found holistic farming practicable, profitable, and worthy of support in the political arena. They began finding themselves in a rapprochement with environmentalists.

In the years after 1970, the grape-growing business owned by Steven Pavich and his sons' families demonstrated how organic farming, favored by environmentalists, worked within a market economy. In 1986, Pavich's family alone grew 1 percent of the grapes harvested in the United States. They achieved this feat in central Arizona, one of the driest and hottest regions in the American West.[37]

The Paviches considered their grape growing an exercise in enhancing community life. They developed a holistic approach after becoming thoroughly frustrated by the poor returns from their petrochemical-based farming in the early 1970s. Their organic practices included summer cover, which increased organic matter in the soil and decreased the effects of solar radiation on the soil. Their no-till farming encourages the population of "beneficial insects" such as assassin bugs, which prey on vine-destructive insects like heliothus.

The Paviches' grapes cost more to grow, resulting in higher prices for consumers. At times the Paviches faced problems with wholesalers who simply purchased produce according to price. But "give the consumer the option of having something that is better," Steven Pavich retorted, "and they don't mind paying a few cents more a pound for it." The growing sales of Paviches' grapes attested to Steven Pavich's faith in growing organic grapes.

Pavich's farms reflected not only the possibilities of organic farming but also a greater concern with the use of water, the most valuable resource for agriculture in the arid West. They used irrigation wells and flood irrigation, but also experimented with a fan-jet system, which created less water use, little soil compaction, lower incidence of root rot, and a uniform distribution of water throughout an entire field. As capital permitted, Pavich intended to extend fan-jets to his other fields.

More recently Ed Marston, an environmental advocate and the editor of the *High Country News,* spearheaded a rapprochement with conservative farmers in Colorado. He visited monthly a group of "Wise Use" people from the area of Delta and Montrose, Colorado. Among seemingly implacable foes such as these, Marston had constructive discussions about how to live together. Environmentalists and wise-users have, he believed, "complementary blind spots." Wise-users refused to see how badly past land-use practices damaged western lands, while environmentalists too often saw wrecked ecosystems but not the people and communities tied to these lands. Marston advocated "internal" reform for the West—reform touching all institutions, including "schools and universities, its media, its local government, its corporations, and its citizen groups." In some of these settings this reform impulse had already taken root.[38]

In the late 1980s and early 1990s, land-grant universities, often accused by environmentalists of purveying land-destroying mechanistic farming, started taking a more holistic view of agriculture. This trend, while not the major

concern of most schools, made its weight felt within the ivory tower and beyond to the farmers served through the Extension Service. This movement, as
the plight of the holistic advocates at Washington State University illustrated,
faced many difficult obstacles, but undaunted reformers worked to reshape the
premises of agricultural research.[39]

In 1989, the school of agriculture at Washington State University asked the
legislature for $6.6 million to fund a Center for Sustaining Agriculture and
Natural Resources. The school failed to win wholehearted support from environmentalists and agriculturists, and the proposal flopped in the urban-domi-
nated legislature. Karl Stauber, a deputy undersecretary in the Department of
Agriculture, saw Washington State University caught in a difficult position.
Land-grant schools "have faculty members that are very much interested in
[holistic agriculture]. But they have a constituency calling on them for the same
reductionist approach . . . yet the societal pressures are calling for [agricultural
schools] to behave in a different way." Stauber's interpretation explains the
situation in Washington. "There's a lot of resentment," said Darrell O. Turner,
president of the Farm Bureau. "We don't rely on the university." On the other
hand, Cha Smith, of the Washington Toxics Coalition, believed extension agents
were "little more than conduits of the chemical industry." Caught in the middle,
David Granatstien, the director of the center, continued to push for "economically viable, environmentally sound and socially acceptable agriculture." With
some funding from the university, he and his small staff pursued "applied"
research and the cultivation of ties to agriculturists and environmentalists.[40]

In the post–World War II period, Aldo Leopold's summons to think more
holistically about agriculture has met with mixed success in the American West.
Some farmers, fearful of either change or economic loss, hold dearly to a
mechanistic and commodity approach to farming. Others followed Leopold's
advice and implemented practices based on principals wider than "economic
self-interest." Moreover, farm policy and practices began to reflect environmentalists' concerns with petrochemicals, soil erosion, farm technology, and water
development. In some instances, greens and farmers met and worked together
on common ground. Perhaps emerging from this movement will be a new
western regionalism, one reflecting Leopold's notion of a greater community,
including soil, water, plants, and wildlife as well as people.

NOTES

1. I want to express my deep appreciation to Bonnie Hamer, who helped me
think through this topic and write about it more clearly than otherwise would have been
the case. Aldo Leopold, "The Ecological Conscience," *Journal of Soil and Water Conservation* 5 (January 1950): 110. Other writers had echoed Leopold's theme. Bernard
DeVoto, in his classic piece, "The West Against Itself," *Harper's Magazine* 194 (Janu-

ary 1947): 1–13, wrote: "While [westerners] move to build [an economy on the natural resources of the West, developed and integrated to produce a steady, sustained, permanent yield], a part of the West is simultaneously moving to destroy the natural resources forever."

2. Leopold, "The Ecological Conscience," 112.

3. In the last twenty-five to thirty years, a growing number of authors have advocated some form of organic, alternative, or sustainable agriculture. They are quite explicit in their stance. For example, Michael Allaby and Floyd Allen, in *Robots Behind the Plow: Modern Farming and the Need for an Organic Alternative* (Emmaus, Pa.: Rodale Press, 1974), 8, state: "Much of the organic movement and much of this book exists as a challenge to, and an indictment of, reductionism." Sir Albert Howard, as quoted in *Robots Behind the Plow,* pleaded for a holistic approach toward agriculture: "Instead of breaking up the subject into fragments and studying agriculture in piecemeal fashion by analytical methods of science [reductionism], . . . we must adopt a synthetic approach and look at the wheel of life as one great subject [holism] and not as if it were a patchwork of unrelated things" (p. 60).

Probably the two leading advocates of alternative agriculture are Wendell Berry and Wes Jackson. Even though they are not in the West, their thinking has greatly influenced the debate over how to farm. The leading publisher of books on organic farming is the Rodale Press, which also publishes the journal *Organic Farming and Gardening* (1953–present). Other useful journals include *American Journal of Alternative Agriculture* (1986–present); *Agriculture, Ecosystems and Environment* (1978–present); and *Agriculture and Human Values* (1984–present). A few of the books on the subject that also contain useful bibliographies are Judith D. Soule and Jon K. Piper, *Farming in Nature's Image: An Ecological Approach to Agriculture* (Washington, D.C.: Island Press, 1992); National Research Council, *Alternative Agriculture* (Washington, D.C.: National Academy Press, 1989); Jay Staten, *The Embattled Farmer* (Golden, Colo.: Fulcrum, 1987); and R. Neil Sampson, *Farmland or Wasteland: A Time to Choose* (Emmaus, Penn.: Rodale Press, 1981).

Two Department of Agriculture yearbooks, *Using Our Natural Resources: 1983 Yearbook of Agriculture* (Washington, D.C.: Government Printing Office, 1983); and *Agriculture and the Environment: The 1991 Yearbook of Agriculture* (Washington, D.C.: Government Printing Office, 1991), contain a wealth of information on agriculture and the environment.

Television producers also have found the debate over agricultural production a compelling topic. Two productions illustrate the point: "Down on the Farm," produced and directed by Noel Buckner, Janet Mendelsohn, and Rob Whittlesey, NOVA, 1984; and "Common Ground: A Documentary Report on How Alternative Agricultural Practices Are Improving the Economics and the Ecology of American Farms," produced by Leslie Reinherz, Graham Chedd, and the Chedd-Angier Production Company and directed by Leslie Reinherz, A National Audubon Society Special, 1987.

4. Robert I. Papendick et al., "Regional Effects of Soil Erosion on Crop Productivity: The Palouse Areas of the Pacific Northwest," in *Soil Erosion and Crop Productivity,* ed. R. F. Follett and B. A. Stewart (Madison, Wisc.: American Society of Agronomy, Crop Science Society of America, and Soil Science Society of America, 1985), 318–19.

5. Lisa Jones, "Between Past and Future: Washington State University Tries to Get There from Here," *High Country News* 26 (14 November 1994): 9.

6. "Down on the Farm," transcript, 4; and Papendick et al., "Regional Effects of Soil Erosion on Crop Productivity," 305.

7. Sara Ebenreck, "Stopping the Raid on Soil: Ethical Reflections on 'Sodbusting' Legislation," *Agriculture and Human Values* 1 (Summer 1984): 7–8; Jones, "Between Past and Future," 9; Aldo Leopold, *A Sand County Almanac: And Sketches Here and There,* with an introduction by Robert Finch (New York: Oxford University Press, 1989); Rachel Carson, *Silent Spring* (Boston: Houghton Mifflin, 1962); and Jim Hightower, *Hard Tomatoes, Hard Times: A Report of the Agribusiness Accountability Project on the Failure of America's Land Grant College Complex,* with a foreword by Senator James Abourezk (Rochester, Vt.: Schenkman Books, 1978).

8. F. C. Bishopp, "The Tax We Pay to Insects," in *Science in Farming: Yearbook of Agriculture, 1943–1947* (Washington, D.C.: Government Printing Office, 1947), 613–15.

9. R. B. Gray, "Some New Farm Machines," in *Science in Farming: Yearbook of Agriculture, 1943–1947* (Washington, D.C.: Government Printing Office, 1947), 815–16; Charles E. Kellogg, "What Is Farm Research?" in *Science in Farming: Yearbook of Agriculture, 1943–1947* (Washington, D.C.: Government Printing Office, 1947), 17.

10. Kellogg, "What Is Farm Research?" 18.

11. Dale McDonald, "Chemicals and Your Health: What's the Risk?" *Farm Journal* 111 (Mid-January 1987): 8–11; Anthony Brown, *Ecology of Pesticides* (New York: Wiley, 1978), 55–57; National Research Council, *Alternative Agriculture,* 124.

12. Sampson, *Farmland or Wasteland,* 59.

13. Walter Prescott Webb, "The American West, Perpetual Mirage," *Harper's Magazine* 214 (May 1957): 24–31.

14. James E. Sherow, "The Chimerical Vision: Michael Creed Hinderlider and Progressive Engineering in Colorado," *Essays and Monographs in Colorado History* (Essays no. 9), 1989, 45.

15. Helen Ingram and Cy R. Oggins, "Water, the Community, and Markets in the West," Western Water Policy Project, Discussion Series Paper, no. 6 (Boulder, Colo.: School of Law, University of Colorado, 1990), 5–6. Also see Clark S. Knowlton, "Land Loss as a Cause of Unrest Among the Rural Spanish-American Village Population of Northern New Mexico," *Agriculture and Human Values* 2 (Summer 1985): 25–39; F. Lee Brown and Helen Ingram, *Water and Poverty in the Southwest* (Tucson: University of Arizona Press, 1987); and Stanley Crawford, *Mayordomo: Chronicle of an Acequia in Northern New Mexico* (Albuquerque: University of New Mexico Press, 1988).

16. Brown and Ingram, *Water and Poverty,* 61–62; Barry Noreen, "Rural Area Beats Back Water Diversion Plan," *High Country News* 26 (30 May 1994): 5.

17. Marc Reisner, *Cadillac Desert: The American West and Its Disappearing Water* (New York: Viking, 1986), 172. Many other works exist on water in the West. The following is only a small sampler from a large and growing bibliography: Ira G. Clark, *Water in New Mexico: A History of Its Management and Use* (Albuquerque: University of New Mexico Press, 1987); Robert G. Dunbar, *Forging New Rights in Western Water* (Lincoln: University of Ne-

braska Press, 1983); Philip L. Fradkin, *A River No More: The Colorado River and the West* (Tucson: University of Arizona Press, 1968); Robert Gottlieb and Margaret FitzSimmons, *Thirst for Growth: Water Agencies as Hidden Government in California* (Tucson: University of Arizona Press, 1991); Stanley Howard, *Green Fields of Montana: A Brief History of Irrigation* (Manhattan, Kans.: Sunflower University Press, 1992); Norris Hundley, Jr., *The Great Thirst: Californians and Water, 1770s–1990s* (Berkeley: University of California Press, 1992); Russell Martin, *A Story That Stands Like a Dam: Glen Canyon and the Struggle for the Soul of the West* (New York: Henry Holt, 1989); Wallace Stegner, *The American West as Living Space* (Ann Arbor: University of Michigan Press, 1987); and Donald Worster, *Rivers of Empire: Water, Aridity and the Growth of the American West* (New York: Pantheon, 1985).

18. Reisner, *Cadillac Desert,* 293–300. Also see Mark Harvey, *A Symbol of Wilderness: Echo Park and the American Conservation Movement* (Albuquerque: University of New Mexico Press, 1994); Elmo Richardson, *Dams, Parks and Politics: Resource Development and Preservation in the Truman-Eisenhower Era* (Lexington: University Press of Kentucky, 1973); and Martin, *A Story That Stands Like a Dam.*

19. Ed Marston, "Ripples Grow When a Dam Dies," *High Country News* 26 (31 October 1994): 14–15.

20. Reisner, *Cadillac Desert,* 397.

21. Ibid., 403–25.

22. Tim Palmer, *The Snake River: Window to the West* (Washington, D.C.: Island Press, 1991), 78–81.

23. Steve Stuebner, "No More Ignoring the Obvious: Idaho Sucks Itself Dry," *High Country News* 27 (20 February 1995): 8–11.

24. Donald E. Green, "A History of Irrigation Technology Used to Exploit the Ogallala Aquifer," in *Groundwater Exploitation in the High Plains,* ed. David E. Kromm and Stephen E. White (Lawrence: University Press of Kansas, 1992), 41–42.

25. In the last two decades, some state legislatures have expanded beneficial use to include recreational and/or instream flow rights. These rights, however, always take lesser priority than domestic, agricultural, and industrial uses because of their more recent enactment.

26. Clark, *Water in New Mexico,* 309–12.

27. Stuebner, "No More Ignoring the Obvious," 8–11.

28. Jon Christensen, "Now Dust Is His Crop, Says Nevada Rancher," *High Country News* 25 (9 August 1993): 1, 10–12.

29. Ibid.

30. Reisner, *Cadillac Desert,* 317–43.

31. For background on Floyd Dominy see Reisner, *Cadillac Desert,* 222–63. On Daniel Beard see Marc Reisner, "The Fight for Reclamation," *High Country News* 27 (20 March 1995): 1, 8–10, and "A Progressive Bureaucrat Signs Off," *High Country News* 27 (24 July 1995): 19.

32. U.S. Department of Agriculture, *Report and Recommendations on Organic Farming (July 1980),* prepared by USDA Study Team on Organic Farming; Charles Benbrook, "Integrating Soil Conservation and Commodity Programs: A Policy Proposal," *Journal of Soil and Water Conservation* 34 (July–August 1979): 160–67; and

Kenneth A. Cook, "The Environmental Era of U.S. Agricultural Policy," *Journal of Soil and Water Conservation* 44 (September–October 1989): 362–66.

33. William Lockeretz, *Issues in Sustainable Agriculture* (Washington, D.C.: Rural Economy Policy Program, The Aspen Institute, 1988).

34. The Sagebrush Rebellion resembles protests in the West over federal land policy during the late 1940s and early 1950s, and Bernard DeVoto's reaction presaged environmentalists' arguments in the 1990s. See Bernard DeVoto, "The Easy Chair," *Harper's Magazine* 194 (June 1947): 543–46; and R. McGreggor Cawley, *Federal Land, Western Anger: The Sagebrush Rebellion and Environmental Politics* (Lawrence: University Press of Kansas, 1993).

35. Jeffrey Zinn, "How Are Soil Erosion Control Programs Working?" *Journal of Soil and Water Conservation* 48 (July–August 1993): 257; "Other Comments . . . on Agricultural Sustainability," *Journal of Soil and Water Conservation* 48 (July–August, 1993): 306–7.

36. David Helvarg, *The War Against the Greens: The "Wise-Use" Movement, the New Right, and Anti-Environmental Violence* (San Francisco: Sierra Club Books, 1994); Karin Schill, "Missing: Another Tribal Environmentalist," *High Country News* 26 (17 October 1994): 3.

37. "Fresh Grapes in California and Arizona: Stephen Pavich and Sons," in *Alternative Agriculture* (Washington, D.C.: National Academy Press, 1989), 350–73; and "Common Ground," transcript, 10–11.

38. Ed Marston, "We Can't Save the Land Without First Saving the West," *High Country News* 26 (26 December 1994): 15.

39. Jones, "Between Past and Future," 8–9.

40. Ibid., 8–9.

4

Agricultural Policy Since 1945

Thomas R. Wessel

Agricultural policy in the post–World War II years has consisted of variations on a single theme, with three dominant notes and several minor chords. Since 1933, the federal government has set the tone for agricultural production in the United States through programs to maintain farm income, control production, and provide relatively cheap food for consumers. The basic governmental approach to agricultural policy was established during the 1930s depression by imbedding commodity price supports, acreage manipulation, and income maintenance in permanent legislation. The Agricultural Marketing Agreement Act of 1937 established a working relationship between the U.S. Department of Agriculture (USDA) and producers of perishable crops. Basically, import controls and marketing quotas summarized the program's approach and have remained largely unchanged since its enactment. The Agricultural Adjustment Act of 1938 defined government agricultural policy and, along with some sections of the Agricultural Act of 1949, has remained the permanent congressional authorization for agricultural programs. Virtually all legislation since 1938 has been through amendment to the original 1938 and 1949 acts.

The vast soil and climatic variations that characterize the Mountain and Pacific States provide the basis for extraordinarily diverse agricultural enterprises, from citrus fruits in Arizona to hard winter wheat in Montana. Somewhere within the region, farmers produce nearly every product that enters the United States domestic market. The region contains both Nevada, which contributes only marginally to the nation's agricultural output, and California, the single most productive agricultural state in the Union. Consequently, every aspect of general agricultural policy influences the economic well-being of farmers in the Mountain and Pacific States.

Although highly diverse, Mountain and Pacific State farmers and ranchers share a common interest regarding two policy areas: government policies concerning water development and use of public grasslands. All of these states rely heavily on irrigation water or access to public lands administered by the USDA or the Department of the Interior. Indeed, farming interests in the far western states often exert considerably more energy to influence water and grazing policies than they expend on general agricultural policy.

In the post–World War II years, Mountain and Pacific State agriculture reflected a general restructuring that characterized all of United States agriculture. The total number of farms declined dramatically from nearly 500,000 in 1945 to just over 250,000 in 1992. While the number of farms declined, the average size increased along with rapid specialization and increased investment in technologies designed to replace hand labor. The decline in farm labor, although significant everywhere, was greatest in California, where farmers employed sophisticated machine technology to harvest crops once harvested entirely by hand. The decline in farm labor is reflected in the increased value of farm equipment. In California, for example, the largest user of farm labor, the value of farm equipment rose from $928 million to more than $4 billion in the period between 1964 and 1992.[1]

Nonagricultural interests involved in agricultural policy determination are also resident in the western states. Environmental groups, concerned with the loss of wild and scenic lands through water development and the erosion of grasslands, competed with agricultural interests in devising policy in the postwar years. Although environmentalism eventually captured the attention of Americans throughout the country, environmentalists were already major players in the West by 1945.

Surprisingly few political leaders from the Mountain and Pacific States chose to focus their attention on agricultural policy matters in Congress. Only one western congressman, Thomas Foley of Washington (1975–81), chaired the House Committee on Agriculture, while as late as 1965 only one western senator, Joseph Montoya of New Mexico, sat on the Senate Committee on Agriculture and Forestry. Indeed, given the importance of agriculture to the region, the western states were generally underrepresented on the House and Senate agricultural committees. Nevertheless, the congressmen who sat on the House Agricultural Committee exercised a degree of influence that belied their numbers. Along with Foley, Congressmen Leon Panetta and Tony Coelho of California occupied important leadership positions within the House as well as their positions on the Agricultural Committee. Southern and midwestern politicians, however, dominated agricultural policy after the war.[2]

While underrepresented on the House and Senate Agricultural Committees, Mountain and Pacific State congressmen dominated the House Interior and Insular Affairs Committee. For most of the postwar period, a western congressman chaired the committee. In 1965, for example, when Morris Udall of Arizona chaired the House committee, eleven of sixteen members representing the Democratic majority and ten of thirteen members of the Republican minority were from the Far West. The House Interior and Insular Affairs Committee had principal oversight jurisdiction for the Department of the Interior, which, along with the USDA, administered grazing permits on public lands. By 1992, the Forest Service of the Department of Agriculture administered more than 6,700 grazing permits in the Mountain and Pacific States, while the Bureau of Land Management in the Department of the Interior administered more than 11,000 grazing permits in these states. Western livestock raisers never reconciled themselves to public landownership, particularly those lands susceptible to grazing. The relationship between western livestock organizations and the federal government remained tense throughout the postwar period and occasionally resembled open warfare.[3]

Western livestock interests began an effort to gain control of grazing lands well before the end of World War II. Senator Patrick McCarran of Nevada conducted a series of hearings throughout the West during the war years that generally were calculated to attack the Grazing Service and the General Land Office of the Department of the Interior. By 1946, McCarran and livestock interests had persuaded President Harry S. Truman to reorganize the two Interior Department agencies into a single Bureau of Land Management with considerably less authority than had existed in the parent organizations. The creation of a more sympathetic Bureau of Land Management, however, was simply the opening skirmish in an effort to transfer the western public grazing ranges to state or private ownership.[4]

Stockmen and the federal government agencies responsible for grazing ranges clashed on nearly every subject regarding the range. Cattlemen conceded no need for federal regulation of predator control, length of grazing on the range, the numbers of cattle permitted, the fees paid for the privilege, requirements for range restoration, or even who owned the land. As early as 1943, stockmen and western public officials demanded that the federal government "return public lands to the states." The notion that all federal land became state property when a territory entered the Union echoed through western land controversies during the next fifty years.[5]

Western livestock interests failed to gain complete control of the public grazing areas but were able to moderate significantly the Bureau of Land Management and Forest Service efforts to decrease livestock on the public range and increase grazing fees. Generally, livestock groups argued that grazing fees should be no more than necessary to create sufficient funds to pay the cost of administering grazing permits. If the agencies wanted additional funds for range improvements, they should seek funding from general tax revenues. In 1949, Congress passed the Anderson-Mansfield bill for just that purpose.[6]

While western stockmen and their congressional allies worked to gain more control over the grazing ranges, other western farmers urged the federal government to impound more water in western rivers for diversion to agricultural uses. Their efforts were largely successful. Between 1944 and 1992, the three Pacific States brought an additional 4 million acres under irrigation. The Mountain States added 2.5 million acres.[7]

The efforts of western farmers to obtain more water, with maximum local control at public expense, mirrored the efforts of stockmen to control the public grazing ranges. Two fundamental questions underlay the development of western water for irrigation. Who should pay for the development, and what limits should exist for an individual user? Western growers, particularly those from California, answered the first by looking to the federal government for finance, and the second by insisting that water be supplied to whatever amount of land they owned.

The federal government had been in the business of developing water projects in the West for most of the twentieth century. After World War II, the process accelerated. After 1946, Congress appropriated more than $250 million a year for western water projects, nearly nine times the amount expended in the last year before World War II.[8]

Much like the debate concerning grazing fees, water users insisted, generally successfully, in keeping the cost of water to themselves at low levels. Usually they paid the cost of annual distribution and maintenance, while the federal government paid the cost of construction for dams and distribution networks. The fees for water were often less than 10 percent of actual costs.[9]

Agricultural water users circumvented acreage limitations as well. The Reclamation Act of 1902 set a residency requirement and a limit of 160 acres for individual users. The sponsors of the act envisioned a West filled with numerous relatively small, irrigated farms in the Jeffersonian tradition. By 1946, few held any illusions about Jeffersonian yeomanry in the West, but the limitation remained the law. Pressure from western water users and their congressional allies forced the Reclamation Service to adjust administrative rules to allow both husband and wife to qualify as individual users and later extended the ruling to include all family members. California farmers, often large oil and insurance companies, sold land, then leased the land back as one way of circumventing the limitation. In many areas, particularly California's Imperial Valley, large farming interests obtained an administrative exemption from the acreage limit. For all practical purposes, water users obtained federally subsidized water for virtually any amount of land they could acquire.[10]

In the meantime, the end of wartime legislation compelled Congress to address questions of general agricultural policy. The Agricultural Adjustment Act of 1938 incorporated much of the general structure of the original Agricultural Adjustment Act of 1933 and features of the Soil Conservation and Domestic Allotment Act of 1936. Although comprehensive and complex in detail, the Agricultural Adjustment Act of 1938 essentially relied on acreage quotas, marketing agreements, and nonrecourse loans to support prices. Although the concept of parity as a measure of appropriate agricultural prices had been used in all of the New Deal programs, the Agricultural Adjustment Act of 1938 was the first legislation to embed the idea in statute. Under the nonrecourse loan provision, the Commodity Credit Corporation (CCC) took possession of crops when the market price failed to exceed the loan rate. By 1940, the CCC was choking on stored commodities.[11]

The advent of World War II made the question of how long farmers would tolerate such severe control programs moot. By early 1940, the government relaxed production controls, and in 1941 it enacted "lend-lease" legislation that drew down agricultural reserves. That same year, Congressman Henry B. Steagall of Alabama successfully authored an amendment that mandated 90 percent parity support for those crops which the government had requested farmers to increase production. The Steagall amendment required such support for two years following the end of hostilities. President Truman declared the war officially ended on 31 December 1946. Consequently, 90 percent parity support extended to the end of 1948.[12]

Renewed debate on agricultural policy began in earnest as wartime price supports neared an end. Domestic demand for food and fiber, in part a reaction to the end of wartime rationing, and foreign assistance programs such as the Marshall Plan kept agricultural prices relatively high during the immediate postwar years. The government resorted to price supports and acreage restrictions sparingly from 1946 to 1948. For some that policy confirmed their belief that market forces alone would provide both ample supplies of agricultural goods and a price level that ensured farmers a reasonable profit. Others, however, compelled by memories of the swift fall in prices that accompanied the end of World War I and the phenomena of low prices and surplus production that characterized the 1930s, were skeptical. Both ideology and experience drove the initial postwar agricultural policy debate. After 1945 the West also witnessed the beginning of an erosion in the coalition of farm organizations and congressional supporters that had fashioned New Deal agricultural legislation.

Agricultural policy until 1948 generally reflected a strong coalition between southern cotton interests and midwestern and western grain farmers. In the 1930s, the coalition came together under the leadership of Edward O'Neal, an Alabama cotton planter and president of the American Farm Bureau Federation. The Farm Bureau benefited substantially through its close connection with the USDA's Extension Service and support of southern and western congressmen. Cracks in the coalition were evident by the end of the war, but they widened considerably when O'Neal retired in 1947. O'Neal championed high price supports and strict adherence to acreage allotments as a means of controlling production. His experience with depression-level prices for cotton beginning in the 1920s undoubtedly colored his persistent support of agricultural policies based on the Agricultural Adjustment Act of 1938.[13]

In 1947, Allan B. Klein, an Iowa feed grain producer and cattle feeder, succeeded O'Neal as president of the Farm Bureau. Klein represented more closely the interests of western livestock raisers and midwestern livestock feeders, who were not interested in seeing feed grains maintained at high levels. Klein moved the Farm Bureau toward support of lower, flexible price supports and limited acreage controls only when surpluses became excessive. Allied with the new Farm Bureau position were a growing number of urban congressmen who reacted to the sharp increase in consumer prices in the postwar years and saw no value in high price supports for their city-bound constituents. Others argued for an immediate return to price and supply decisions set by market forces.[14]

Congressional debate in 1948 centered on high fixed support for agricultural prices and the institution of a lower, flexible support system. Few in Congress gave serious thought to totally abandoning government price supports quickly. Nevertheless, the three views on the future of government programs sufficiently fragmented farm state representatives so that none of the three alternatives could muster a majority. Congressional failure to pass legislation before the end of 1948 would have had the effect of returning agricultural policy to the Agricultural Adjustment Act of 1938. That possibility gave a certain urgency to the process but did not lead to a workable compromise. Instead, Congress passed legislation that forced no one to immediately yield their position. Under the leadership of Congressman Clifford Hope of Kansas, representing the high support advocates, and Senator George Aiken of Vermont, representing advocates of a flexible price support system, Congress simply extended high fixed supports at 90 percent of parity for the 1949 crop year and mandated a flexible scale of 75 percent of parity or lower, depending on supplies, for subsequent years. Both Hope and Aiken agreed to a new definition of parity based on the previous ten-year period rather than the traditional base period calculated from pre–World War I ratios.[15]

Agricultural policy debates have seldom taken place as simply a discussion of economic alternatives. Since the earliest debates on land policy at the beginning of the nation's history through the passage of the Homestead Act of 1862 and Farm Bloc activities of the 1920s, to the massive intervention of the New Deal years, farm policy debates have taken place in the larger context of social policy. One of the most remarkable and persistent notions in United States social history has been the strong bias toward agrarian values. While the country remained predominantly rural, such values were not surprising. Yet the presumption that the "family farm" provided a moral and ethical base for American society persisted into the twentieth century, even as industrial labor and urban life increasingly dominated most people's experience. The postwar debates over farm policy were no exception. In 1949, Secretary of Agriculture Charles F. Brannan initiated debate over a comprehensive agricultural program that reflected the persistence of agrarian values.[16]

Brannan began his professional career as a lawyer in Denver. In 1941, he became the Western Regional counsel for the Farm Security Administration (FSA), the successor agency to the Resettlement Administration, designed to help small and marginal farmers and to provide relief for farm laborers. In 1944, Brannan came to Washington, D.C., as the assistant administrator of the FSA, and later he chaired a number of USDA policy studies committees. When Secretary of Agriculture Clinton B. Anderson resigned to run for the Senate from New Mexico, President Truman appointed Brannan his successor. While it is difficult to pinpoint precisely the sources of Brannan's philosophy, he clearly understood that a move to flexible and lower price supports could only make life more difficult for his former clientele. He was also aware of commercial producers' hostility toward programs designed to maintain small farms. He had witnessed the emasculation of the FSA in 1944. Whatever his motivation, Brannan presented Congress with a proposal designed to address three basic propositions. The Brannan Plan envisioned government policies that stabilized rural populations and maintained relatively high farm income, while providing adequate supplies at relatively low market prices.[17]

The essence of the Brannan Plan was to move government support from commodity prices to income maintenance. Brannan proposed abandoning the idea of parity and substituting an income standard based on a ten-year rolling average beginning with the period 1938–47. Market demand and supply would determine commodity prices. The government would directly pay farmers for the difference between market prices and the income standard. The plan contained a limit on the volume of commodities the government would use to calculate any payment, initially set at 1,800 units. Varying amounts of commodity constituted a unit valued at a uniform price. Brannan anticipated that small farmers would produce below the maximum unit limit and receive payment for their entire production, thereby producing sufficient income for most to remain in the industry. Presumably, larger, efficient producers would receive payment to the maximum limit and could further profit from the market price for production over the limit. The plan obligated all participating producers to employ certain conservation practices.[18]

The Brannan Plan received a cold reception in Congress and, except for the Farmers Union, from spokesmen of organized agriculture. Western cattlemen opposed any kind of direct government payment, and most large commodity producers objected to both the support limits the plan contained and the overt exposure of the level of income support they would receive. They preferred a price support system within which personal income was less visible. Large producers, who were rapidly investing in new or larger technologies such as self-propelled combines and cotton pickers, were probably equally uninterested in seeing smaller farmers remain in agriculture, consequently making less land available for their own expansion. The potential cost of the plan unnerved many of Brannan's allies in Congress.[19]

By midsummer 1949, opposition to the Brannan Plan had solidified sufficiently to ensure its failure. Congress was unwilling to consider even a modest test, involving a limited number of crops, of the ideas contained in the plan.

Instead, in October 1949, with farm prices falling rapidly, Congress extended 90 percent of parity support through 1950 and mandated price supports of 80 to 90 percent for 1951. The beginning of the Korean War in June 1950 and renewed demand for agricultural products postponed any further debate between high fixed support advocates and those seeking lower, flexible supports or the Brannan Plan. In 1950, 1951, and 1952, Congress, through the "Defense Production Acts," simply extended 90 percent of parity supports each year.[20]

The election of a Republican president and Congress in 1952 gave proponents of flexible price supports renewed life. It also encouraged western cattle and farming interests to renew their efforts to gain control over grazing lands and more water at public expense. President Dwight D. Eisenhower's appointment of Ezra Taft Benson of Utah as the new secretary of agriculture and Douglas McKay of Oregon as secretary of the interior gave western ranchers and farmers a sympathetic ear in Washington, D.C.

Soon after the new Republican Congress assembled in 1953, Congressman Leslie D'Ewart of Montana introduced legislation increasing the authority of Stockmen Advisory Boards to supervise Forest Service grazing policy similar to Taylor Grazing Act boards. Basically, along with expanding advisory board authority, D'Ewart's bill vested rights to any improvements on grazing ranges with the stockmen who held permits. It also effectively froze permits in the hands of current holders, making it difficult for the Forest Service to lower the number of cattle or sheep permitted on the range.[21]

Western cattlemen lined up in favor of D'Ewart's bill in a series of hearings held by Senator George Aiken of Vermont, chairman of the Senate Agricultural Committee, throughout the summer of 1953. The D'Ewart bill failed to pass in 1953 but was reintroduced in milder form in 1954. When it appeared that Congressman Clifford Hope, chairman of the House Agricultural Committee, would not act on the bill in the House, Senator Clinton Anderson of New Mexico, the former secretary of agriculture, attached the bill as a rider to the farm bill then under consideration. The D'Ewart rider failed to survive a Conference Committee on the farm bill but was effectively put into place administratively by Secretary Benson.[22]

Western irrigation farmers continued to pursue water development projects and elimination of acreage restrictions. California agribusiness interests were particularly active. They attacked the limitation on several fronts. Four California irrigation districts filed suit in California courts, seeking to invalidate the limitation. Although the California Supreme Court held the limitation invalid, in 1958 the United States Supreme Court sustained the limit's constitutionality. In the meantime, Senator Clair Engle of California successfully added a provision to the 1956 Small Reclamation Projects Act that effectively allowed irrigators to receive subsidized water in excess of the limit. California growers also joined with environmentalists in stopping a Bureau of Reclamation project that would have flooded Dinosaur National Park. California growers were afraid

Although government agricultural policy has enabled western sheep raisers to graze their flocks cheaply on federal lands, wool and lamb production has never been an important aspect of agriculture in the West. Few Americans eat lamb, and foreign competition has kept wool prices low. In June 1945, this flock grazed near Bridgeport, California, on the eastern slope of the Sierra Nevada. *Courtesy, United States Department of Agriculture.*

that a dam on the upper Colorado drainage would decrease available water for themselves downstream.[23]

Finally, California agribusiness interests began to actively support state water projects. Although state water appeared more expensive than federal water, most state proposals carried no acreage limit and, in actuality, were designed to furnish water for irrigation at rates comparable to federal rates. Through the 1950s, however, before state projects were in place, California growers simply evaded the federal law.[24]

The Agricultural Act of 1954, to which Senator Anderson tried to attach a grazing lands rider, was the first agricultural legislation to contain a flexible price support mechanism. Secretary of Agriculture Benson's proposals attacked agricultural surpluses in two ways. The Agricultural Act of 1954 pegged price supports at 82.5 to 90 percent for 1955 and at 75 to 90 percent of parity, depending on levels of production, after 1955. A peculiar section of the act provided a Brannan Plan approach to wool. Sheep raisers received direct income payments based on the difference between market prices and government-determined fixed support price. The wool provision of the 1954 act, funded by tariffs on imported wool, remained basically unchanged through 1995.[25]

Earlier in the session, Congress passed the Agricultural Trade Development and Assistance Act (PL-480) to stimulate the movement of stored commodities into international channels through sales and relief. Although PL-480 contained no fundamental new ideas, it nevertheless signaled a more aggressive effort to move domestic surplus production into international markets. It also initiated a process that tied agricultural policy more firmly to U.S. foreign policy. Officials among the president's foreign policy advisers would not necessarily hold the same goals as the secretary of agriculture.[26]

The relative prosperity that farmers enjoyed in the decade after World War II allowed many to invest heavily in new technologies and apply the fruits of scientific discoveries in the form of improved seed varieties, fertilizers, pesticides, and herbicides to their farm operations. Agricultural production per acre increased dramatically in the postwar years. By the mid-1950s, production had reached levels that flooded the Commodity Credit Corporation's storage facilities with nonrecourse loan crops. As prices fell through 1955, it was evident that flexible price supports alone would not significantly contain production. Consequently, Congress, with the Eisenhower administration's blessing, reintroduced government acreage retirement programs, in contrast to Benson's stated policy of moving agriculture toward a market-oriented structure. Congress passed the Agricultural Act of 1956, commonly referred to as the Soil Bank. The combination of flexible price supports coupled with acreage retirement was a variation on the provisions of the Agricultural Adjustment Act of 1938.[27]

The Agricultural Adjustment Act of 1938 continued to provide the legislative basis for acreage allotment for certain crops. Congress amended the act on several occasions to adjust the allotments but left imposition of allotments to the discretion of the secretary of agriculture. This proved particularly advantageous for large-scale producers in Arizona and California. When acreage allotments had not been applied between 1950 and 1954, California and Arizona cotton planters and California rice producers had rapidly expanded acres devoted to these two crops. Consequently, when allotments returned, the USDA calculated their share of the national allotment from a larger base.[28]

The Soil Bank program consisted of two parts: one to retire land planted to crops then in surplus (the so-called basic crops of corn, wheat, cotton, rice, tobacco, and peanuts), and a longer-term effort to permanently retire marginal land into a "conservation reserve" to protect "soil, water, and forest and wildlife resources."[29]

The reimposition of allotments, Soil Bank reserves, and flexible price supports did not produce any of the results anticipated by Benson and the Eisenhower administration. Agricultural production continued to rise, suppressing price supports to the minimum allowed, while creating huge stockpiles of excess commodities. In effect, the price support mechanism was not high enough to allow smaller farmers to stay in the industry and not low enough to induce large producers to voluntarily decrease the acreage they planted. The result was lower farm income and the acceleration of small-scale farmers' departure from agriculture.

The Soil Bank and flexible price supports instituted after 1956 proved extremely unpopular with farmers and some town merchants who wanted high fixed price supports. Many farmers placed their entire farms in the conservation reserve and thus ceased to be customers for machinery, seed, and fertilizers. As a result of numerous complaints from town and country voters, Congress passed legislation in 1958 that essentially abandoned the Soil Bank and the lower range of flexible price supports. The Agricultural Act of 1958 again proved particularly beneficial to large-scale cotton and rice planters in Arizona and California. The act provided for 2 million acres in cotton allotments above what previous legislation would have allowed. Similarly, the act maintained rice at a level more than 650,000 acres above what previous legislation mandated. The act also established fixed parity payments for cotton at 80 percent for 1959 and 75 percent for 1960. Cotton planters were allowed to plant up to 40 percent above their allotment in return for parity support at 65 percent for 1959 and 60 percent in 1960. The secretary of agriculture had discretion to set parity rates for rice between 75 and 90 percent of parity. Western agribusiness again proved a major beneficiary of southern-dominated committees in Congress.[30]

By 1960, the federal government had essentially abandoned serious efforts to lower production through acreage control and nearly abandoned flexible price supports. Farm productivity during the 1950s consistently overwhelmed Congress's political will to reduce acreage sufficiently to induce downward production. Flexible price supports, because of high production levels, generally meant lower price supports. When a new Democratic administration entered office in 1961, government-stored crops were at an all-time high, while farm income had steadily declined.

President John F. Kennedy and his secretary of agriculture, Orville Freeman of Minnesota, concluded early in 1961 that acreage reduction was not an effective mechanism to control production. The administration pushed Congress to enact legislation designed to control the volume of crops marketed regardless of planted acres. The Kennedy-Freeman plan had the residual effect of shifting control of farm policy from Congress to the White House and commodity producers. Local farmer committees and referendum votes among commodity producers would be the vehicle for setting specific policies. Neither Congress, the organized commodity groups, nor the general farm organizations supported reordering the political apparatus of farm policy in such a manner.[31]

The Kennedy-Freeman approach to production control failed to gain congressional approval in 1961 and did so only for wheat in 1962. In May 1963,

The wheat lands of the Pacific Northwest, particularly in Washington and Oregon, exceed those of any other region in scale. In 1968, this wheat farmer in Wasco County, Oregon, used a combine capable of cutting on a hillside to bring in the harvest. *Courtesy, United States Department of Agriculture.*

wheat producers voted against imposing mandatory controls. A provision of the act initiating the referendum was designed to reduce parity support to 50 percent if mandatory controls were not approved. Early in 1964, however, Congress passed legislation providing for voluntary acreage diversions and a complicated wheat certificate program designed to support commodities, particularly wheat and cotton at different rates depending on whether the product was sold on the domestic or foreign market. The effect was to set price supports between 65 and 90 percent of parity. Actual support in 1964 and 1965 was just under 80 percent of parity. Farmers, gambling that neither Congress nor the administration would allow farm income to decline further, had won.[32]

In 1964, Congress, as part of Lyndon Johnson's War on Poverty, passed legislation that indirectly affected agricultural policy and helped cement an alliance of urban and rural congressmen in support of agricultural legislation. That year, Congress established a food stamp program that began as a modest subsidy to encourage consumption and improve nutrition among the poor; the program eventually grew into the largest single program administered through the USDA. For the next two decades, the incorporation of Food Stamp and related programs in general agricultural legislation sustained an uneasy coalition between farm, state, and city politicians.[33]

The 1964 legislation also contained a structure reminiscent of the Brannan Plan. Price supports through loans and government purchase of wheat and cotton were designed to bring domestic agricultural prices generally in line with prices on the world market. Farmers who participated in voluntary land retirement programs received a direct payment from the government that reflected the difference between previous high price supports and lower supports. The idea did not abandon price supports but did legislate the Brannan idea of income maintenance.[34]

The Food and Agricultural Act of 1965 incorporated lower price supports designed to level domestic prices with world prices and direct payments to maintain farm income. The 1965 legislation also attempted to bring some stability to the policy-making process. It provided for a comprehensive four-year program covering most commodities rather than the multitude of single-crop acts that had characterized agricultural legislation since 1958.

By 1965, the debate over flexible price supports or fixed rates had basically come to an end. Most legislation after 1965 contained provisions for lower fixed rates with minimal elements of flexibility. Attempts to control the quantity of production eligible for price supports had failed, but the Brannan concept of income maintenance became permanently affixed to agricultural legislation.

In part, the Food and Agricultural Act of 1965 was the compromise that Congress and postwar administrations had failed to achieve between the flexible and fixed price support advocates. It also recognized that the structure of American agriculture had changed dramatically in the previous twenty years. The most significant change had occurred in the number of people engaged in agricultural production. By the 1960s, less than 5 percent of the population earned the majority of their income from agriculture. Farms were visibly larger, represented substantial capital investment, and engaged in the kind of specialization usually associated with industry. The manner in which the government worked out agricultural legislation also changed. The voices that engaged in agricultural debate reflected the increased specialization. A growing number of commodity organizations spoke for their constituents rather than a few general farm organizations. More congressional committees, with more urban representatives, insisted on playing a larger role in constructing agricultural programs. The USDA evolved into a source of expert information and the administrator of programs devised largely by others. Constructing agricultural policy and achieving legislative majorities became more complex, more participatory, and less certain.[35]

With more interest-group participation in agricultural policy determination, it became difficult to institute fundamental change in the structure. The various commodity interests, urban welfare advocates, and environmentalists established an equilibrium in agricultural policy that militated against more than minimally altering the specifics.

Clifford Hardin, President Richard Nixon's first secretary of agriculture, initially proved reluctant to suggest fundamental change or offer an administration blueprint for agricultural policy. As the 1965 act neared its terminal date in 1970, however, the Nixon administration proposed legislation that reflected conservative commitments to lower price supports, less restriction on production, and renewed emphasis on moving agricultural surpluses into the world market.

The debate over the Agricultural Act of 1970 proved long and contentious. Secretary Hardin emphasized the administration's goal of less government regulation of the agricultural market, while many congressmen from farm states insisted on relatively high price supports and strict control over production. At the same time, urban congressmen voiced severe criticism of the large payments some farmers received, in many highly publicized cases amounting to more than $1 million. The farm bill that emerged from Congress reflected all three views. The Agricultural Act of 1970 ended acreage allotments but instituted a set-aside of acres as a condition to qualify for price supports. Farmers were free to plant whatever they wished on their remaining acres. For many that meant bringing into production acres that had never been part of an allotment program. Urban legislators demanded and gained a limit of $55,000 in total payments an individual could receive under the act.[36]

Agricultural policy had reflected the closer integration of the United States economy to world economic events at least since 1965. In the years immediately following passage of the Agricultural Act of 1970, farmers and other Americans discovered just what such integration could mean. The dollar's declining value, coupled with a world agricultural shortfall, rapidly drove much of the U.S. stored production into the world market. After two decades of dealing with surplus production, world events in 1972–73 seemed to introduce an era of agricultural shortages and reinvigorated those who desired a market-driven agricultural economy.

In 1973, Secretary of Agriculture Earl Butz, a protégé, of former Secretary Ezra Taft Benson, urged Congress to adopt policies designed to move agricultural policy toward a more market-oriented structure. This entailed removing acreage restrictions, encouraging increased production, and in general limiting government participation in the agricultural economy. With domestic food prices increasing rapidly, in part driven by extraordinary foreign demand, Butz argued effectively that it was appropriate to change the direction of agricultural policy.

The Agricultural and Consumer Protection Act of 1973 incorporated most of Butz's ideas while retaining a minimum program of income support and standby authority to reintroduce allotments and price supports. Urban congressmen were able to further reduce the limit on government payments to individuals from $55,000 to $20,000. The act continued the nonrecourse loan provision, a device farmers had come to rely on for necessary capital to invest in their operations, established a new system of "target prices" for basic commodities, continued the set-aside program, and retained the "deficiency payment" scheme of direct payments to farmers when prices fell below the stated target price. Basically, however, the act was designed to encourage production in the belief that market mechanisms alone would encourage adequate supplies at an acceptable price.[37]

So long as foreign demand, such as the massive sales to the Soviet Union in 1972, characterized the world market, Butz could savor his partial victory for free-market agriculture. Instead of stability in the agricultural market, however, volatile demand produced chaos and invited speculative grain futures trading and less than virtuous activity in foreign grain trading. Nevertheless, while prices remained relatively high, the government did indeed play a minor role in the agricultural economy. That condition, however, lasted barely two years. By 1975, when foreign agriculture recovered from the shortfalls of the early 1970s, coupled with substantially increased domestic production, domestic prices tumbled once again.[38]

Many farmers, including western wheat growers, urged President Gerald Ford to invoke the standby authority available under the 1973 legislation and reinstitute acreage restrictions and higher price supports, but Ford refused to do so. In addition, he vetoed legislation that would have raised the "target price" of commodities, creating a greater differential between the market price and target prices, thereby increasing the level of government deficiency payments. Ford's refusal to intervene in a declining farm economy probably helped explain his defeat in 1976. Farm interests may have expected more sympathy from his successor, a Georgia peanut farmer, but they were soon disappointed.

President Jimmy Carter and Secretary of Agriculture Robert Bergland of Minnesota proposed legislation that only moderately altered the program inherited from Nixon and Ford. Carter agreed to modest increases in target prices, established a "farmer-owned" reserve to keep surplus production off the market, and proposed a major expansion of federally subsidized crop insurance to replace direct government disaster payments. It was nowhere near what many farmers and farm state congressmen demanded. In 1977, Congress passed the Food and Agricultural Act of 1977, which contained a compromise between administration-recommended target prices and what farm state congressmen sought. Otherwise, along with expanded disaster insurance that included farmer-paid premiums, the 1977 act essentially was a continuation of the 1973 Agriculture and Consumer Protection Act.[39]

Both the entanglements of foreign policy and the growing influence of consumer and environmental groups became evident in the Carter administration. Consumer advocate Carol Tucker Foreman became an assistant secretary of agriculture in charge of a new consumer affairs department. Foreman used her position to develop nutrition programs that infuriated western beef producers and others. Carter challenged western water users when he created a "hit list" of water projects that he recommended be either terminated or not started.

Nine of the twelve projects on the final list (there had been thirty-nine originally) were in the Mountain States. Carter and Interior Secretary Cecil Andrus, former governor of Idaho, also endorsed the Ford administration–sponsored Federal Land Policy and Management Act of 1976, which western grazing interests had bitterly opposed. Although the act had no direct effect on western grazing, it did have the potential to substantially increase wilderness areas from which cattle and sheep raisers were barred. The Department of the Interior soon began a series of administrative changes designed to improve the western range based on the study that had led to the Federal Land Policy and Management Act. By 1979, western public land and water users were in open rebellion. After January 1980, when Carter embargoed grain shipments to the Soviet Union in protest of the invasion of Afghanistan, western agricultural interests were united in opposition. Western grazers reopened their demands for transfer of public lands to the states and possible further transfer to private interests. Western farmers participated actively in the formation of the American Agriculture Movement and drove their huge tractors in protest to Washington, D.C.[40]

The so-called Sagebrush Rebellion also received a good deal of public press exposure and rekindled the debates of 1946 and 1953. Western grazers, however, cooled their ardor for private ownership of western lands when they realized that in a bidding war for private ownership there was no guarantee that they would be the successful bidders. The Carter administration's "war on the west," however, provided much political fodder for Ronald Reagan and the Republican quest to regain the White House and control Congress. In 1980, western farmers and ranchmen moved to support Reagan as rapidly as they had moved to support Carter in 1976.

Ronald Reagan rode into office on a wave of discontent. Republicans captured control of the Senate for the first time since 1953 and decreased the Democratic majority in the House. Reagan's appointment of John Block, a midwestern hog farmer, as secretary of agriculture and James Watt, an outspoken opponent of government land and water policy, as secretary of the interior pleased most western farmers and ranchers. Reagan and Watt had declared themselves part of the Sagebrush Rebellion, and western farmers and ranchers waited in anticipation for Sagebrush-inspired programs to emerge from the Interior Department. Watt's programs fell well short of transferring public land to states or private hands, but his virtual suspension of restrictive regulations governing grazing and water use quieted most Sagebrush rebels.[41]

At the same time, the Agricultural Act of 1977 was nearing its terminal date. Construction of an agricultural act in 1981 took place within a different atmosphere than had occurred in the past. The Reagan administration was committed to cutting federal spending generally. Reagan's pledge to end the Carter embargo on grain shipments to the Soviet Union dramatized the influence of foreign policy in domestic agricultural matters. In the 1970s, United States agricultural production increasingly went into foreign markets and became a major positive item in the country's trade balance. The importance of agriculture in United States foreign policy was already evident early in the decade. In 1974, when a meeting in Rome addressed the problems of world markets, the American position was presented not by the secretary of agriculture but by Henry Kissinger, the secretary of state.[42]

A vigorous Office of Budget and Management directly intervened at the expense of the Department of Agriculture in setting spending limits on agricultural programs. The president's Council of Economic Advisors also became more active in determining agricultural budgets. The agricultural subcommittees of the House and Senate Appropriations Committees had always participated in agricultural policy, but the adoption of a budgetary process that established fixed overall levels of funding dramatically increased their influence in determining agricultural policy.[43]

In the past, commodity groups had generally cooperated in supporting each other's program requests. The final agricultural budget reflected the combined costs of whatever the commodity groups could negotiate with the House and Senate Agricultural Committees. In devising the 1981 farm bill, however, the agricultural committees were obligated to fit each commodity request within a fixed budget. The result was a near-complete breakdown of cooperation, replaced by a system of intemperate attack and counterattack that nearly ended with no agricultural bill reported out of the House Agricultural Committee. With Jesse Helms, Republican of North Carolina, and Kika de la Garzia, Democrat of Texas, leading the Conference Committee, it took sixteen days of near-continuous meeting to produce a bill. A Republican-dominated Senate acted quickly to pass the bill, but in the House prolonged debate preceded a two-vote margin of approval.[44]

The Food and Agricultural Act of 1981 proved to be the most contentiously constructed and short-lived agricultural act since 1949. The hearings on the bill illustrated how complex agricultural policy had become. Over 230 separate organizations and 240 individuals representing farm and urban constituencies testified on the bill. Urban and rural interests faced off bitterly over the food stamp program. Republicans insisted on separating food stamps from agricultural legislation and reducing the program's cost. Democrats, particularly in the House, insisted on maintaining the coupling at a higher level of funding. Faced with serious declines in farm income and growing numbers of farm failures, Congress and the administration began to fashion a new agricultural bill within months of the passage of the 1981 legislation.[45]

John Block and other administration officials had come into office expressing a policy intended to move agriculture toward a more market-oriented structure, including fewer restrictions on acreage limits and abolishing target prices and farmer-owned grain reserves. Target prices, however, remained in the 1981 bill, although at a lower level than commodity groups wanted. The administration achieved its goal of removing restrictions on acreage devoted to production. Then, in 1982, foreign demand for U.S. production dropped dramatically, while farmers were producing at a record level. Rather than decreasing the costs of farm programs, deficiency and land-diversion payments increased the cost of agricultural programs to record levels even while farm income spiraled downward. Government-held commodities reached levels that had not occurred since 1960. This combination of events, along with continuing high interest rates, forced the administration to abruptly return to price supports and acreage limitations.

In January 1982, Secretary Block announced new acreage-reduction programs. In the Mountain and Pacific States, acreage reduction affected wheat, cotton, and rice farmers. These producers had to reduce their acreage by 10 percent to gain eligibility for price supports. Even with reduced acres, farmers produced at record rates. Farm income continued to decline, while the cost of the government's farm program increased. Operating on the assumption that high production levels would continue, the administration moved to further reduce crop acreages.

The following January, Secretary Block announced the payment-in-kind (PIK) program, designed by the USDA to encourage farmers to dramatically reduce their cultivated acres in return for payments derived from the massive stores of commodities in the government's possession. The program was similar to the certificate program of the 1960s, although under PIK farmers actually received commodities without the option of a cash alternative. Government officials had estimated the impact of the PIK program based on normal production expectations. A severe drought throughout the country, however, encouraged many more farmers, who found themselves without a crop to sell, to sign up for PIK payments than the administration expected. In the end, PIK obligation forced the government to purchase supplies from the farmer-owned reserves to cover PIK transfers. Although PIK was a major program nationally, its effect on the Mountain and Pacific States, with the exception of the drought-stricken Southwest, was minimal. Winter wheat, which dominated the wheat-growing areas of the Far West, largely escaped the drought. Farmers preferred to produce rather than trade acres for PIK.[46]

Westerners, however, gained a major victory in their long-term effort to improve their access to federally subsidized water. In 1982, Congress passed legislation that changed the maximum acreage allowed water from 160 to 950 acres and eliminated the residency requirement for eligibility. In effect, the legislation legalized the common practice of western water users to evade the limits contained in the 1902 Reclamation Act.[47]

While the USDA hustled to purchase sufficient commodities to fulfill PIK obligations, Congress geared up to address farm legislation once again. The 1981 farm act expired in 1985. The same political division in Congress, a Republican Senate and Democratic House, prevailed as in 1981. However, neither Republicans nor Democrats were anxious to return to the chaotic process that characterized the 1981 debate.

Senator Jesse Helms, chairman of the Senate Committee on Agriculture, Nutrition, and Forestry, characterized the 1985 Food Security Act as a "slow but decisive transition to market-oriented farm policy." The act, however, as it applied to commodity support closely resembled earlier farm legislation. The government relied on deficiency payments to maintain farm income, retained a lower-rate but still effective nonrecourse loan program, and vigorously pursued foreign markets to relieve surplus production. The act also returned to large-scale land retirement in the image of the soil bank and conservation diversion programs of the past. The act allowed the secretary of agriculture to enter into long-term contracts to place cropland in a Conservation Reserve Program (CRP), removing the land from production. The government also paid half the cost of seeding the reserved land in grass or trees.[48]

The Mountain States that contained High Plains grazing and wheat lands quickly responded to the CRP. By 1992, the far western states had placed more than 6 million acres, representing over 15 percent of the national total, in the CRP. Montana, Colorado, and Idaho alone placed over 3 million acres in the CRP.[49]

By 1990, the terminal date of the Food and Security Act of 1985, Congress seemed in no mood to make substantial changes in agricultural programs. Congress had designed the 1985 act in part to ease farmers away from deficiency payments by a scheduled drop in target prices. In the intervening years, however, Congress passed legislation maintaining target prices at the 1985 level. The Food, Agriculture, Conservation, and Trade Act of 1990 fixed target prices at the 1990 level. The 1985 act and some previous agricultural legislation provided for cross-compliance—that is, farmers had to participate in all or most programs authorized within the legislation to be eligible for others. The 1990 act ended this requirement. The 1985 act had limited nonrecourse loan rates to between 75 and 85 percent of world prices for a given commodity. The 1990 act set the loan rate at 85 percent of a five-year moving average of market prices. The 1990 act also continued the CRP.[50]

As Congress, controlled for the first time since 1946 by Republican majorities in both the House and the Senate, neared consideration of the extension of the 1990 farm act, Americans heard a familiar tune. Senator Richard Lueger of Indiana, the chairman of the Senate Committee on Agriculture and Forestry, sounded the first dominant note, insisting that agriculture be weaned from government programs and prepared to compete in a system dominated by market forces. Western livestock raisers had already successfully beaten back one attempt by Secretary of the Interior Bruce Babbitt to raise grazing fees. Western congressmen raced to pass legislation fixing grazing lands more firmly in control of permit holders before Babbitt could administratively impose limits and conditions on users. Western water users held little fear that their victory in 1982 was in jeopardy. The state of Nevada once again passed legislation demanding that the federal government transfer public land to the states, and the secretary of agriculture remained silent.[51]

Republican leaders since the 1950s had little success in fashioning agricultural policy that relied on a market-oriented agricultural economy. In 1996, however, Republicans seemed more determined than in past years. The result was the first comprehensive change in agricultural policy since 1949. Congress sent President Bill Clinton a measure, known as the Agriculture Improvement and Reform Act of 1996, that provided a descending federal payment to farmers over seven years regardless of commodity supplies or market prices. At the end of the seven years, presumably, the government payments to farmers would come to an end. In the meantime, farmers were free to produce whatever they wished, on as many acres as they desired, although CRP contracts remained in force. In a year of relatively high commodity prices, farm organizations voiced little opposition to the scheme. President Clinton reluctantly signed the act, while announcing that he would propose legislation in 1997 to restore a "safety net" for farmers.[52]

In the past, farmers had gambled successfully on Congress's willingness to provide government assistance when prices fell, regardless of the agricultural program then in force. In 1996, farmers reasoned that they could take advantage of government payments during a period of relatively high commodity prices and still find relief in the future if low commodity prices reappeared. President Clinton's lack of enthusiasm for the new farm act, and his proposal for a safety net in the future, offered a good bet.

NOTES

1. U.S. Department of Commerce, *Statistical Abstract of the United States: 1949* (Washington, D.C.: Government Printing Office, 1949); 614; U.S. Department of Commerce, *Census of Agriculture, 1992*, vol. 1, part 5.

2. Compiled from U.S. Congress, *Congressional Directory*, for the years 1965–95.

3. U.S. Congress, *Congressional Directory*, 1965–92; U.S. Department of Commerce, *Census of Agriculture, 1992*.

4. William Voigt, Jr., *Public Grazing Lands: Use and Misuse by Industry and Government* (New Brunswick, N.J.: Rutgers University Press, 1976), 3–7.

5. Ibid., 76–79, 196,

6. Ibid., 140–41.

7. U.S. Department of Commerce, *Census of Agriculture, 1992*.

8. Donald Worster, *Rivers of Empire: Water, Aridity, and the Growth of the American West* (New York: Pantheon, 1985), 266.

9. Ibid., 294; Gary D. Weatherford et al., *Water and Agriculture in the Western U.S.: Conservation, Reallocation and Markets*, Studies on Water Policy and Management No. 2 (Boulder, Colo.: Westview Press, 1982), 25–27.

10. Worster, *Rivers of Empire,* 287–89; Michael C. Robinson, *Water for the West: The Bureau of Reclamation, 1902–1977* (Chicago: Public Works Historical Society, 1979), 102.

11. 52 Stat. 31 (16 February 1938); Douglas Bowers, Wayne Rasmussen, and Gladys Baker, "History of Agricultural Price-Support and Adjustment Programs, 1933–84," U.S. Department of Agriculture, *Agricultural Information Bulletin 485,* December 1985, 16.

12. Congressional Quarterly, *Farm Policy: The Politics of Soil, Surpluses, and Subsidies* (Washington, D.C.: Congressional Quarterly, 1984), 119.

13. Willard W. Cochrane and Mary E. Ryan, *American Farm Policy, 1948–1973* (Minneapolis: University of Minnesota Press, 1976), 73–74.

14. Ibid., 27, 74–75; Congressional Quarterly, *Farm Policy,* 109–10.

15. Bowers, Rasmussen, and Baker, "History of Agricultural Price-Support and Adjustment Programs," 17–18.

16. Karen J. Bradley, "Agrarian Ideology and Agricultural Policy: California Grangers and the Post–World War II Farm Debate," *Agricultural History* 69 (Spring 1995): 240–56.

17. For a full discussion of the Brannan Plan and the political fallout it engendered, see Reo M. Christensen, *The Brannan Plan: Farm Politics and Policy* (Ann Arbor: University of Michigan Press, 1959); Allen J. Matusow, *Farm Policies and Politics in the Truman Years* (Cambridge, Mass.: Harvard University Press, 1967).

18. Brannan outlined his plan in a presentation to a joint session of the House and Senate Agricultural Committees on 7 April 1949.

19. Cochrane and Ryan, *American Farm Policy,* 87–98.

20. Bowers, Rasmussen, and Baker, "History of Price-Support and Adjustment Programs," 19–21; Cochrane and Ryan, *American Farm Policy,* 74–76.

21. Advisory Boards had been part of the administration of the Taylor Grazing Act from the beginning. The Granger-Thye Act of 1951 gave legal status to such boards regarding grazing lands administered through the Forest Service. See Voigt, *Public Grazing Lands,* 204–5.

22. Ibid., 215–29.

23. Robinson, *Water for the West,* 93, 102–3.

24. Ellen Liebman, *California Farmland: A History of Large Agricultural Landholdings* (Totowa, N.J.: Rowman and Allanheld, 1983), 147–48, 159–60.

25. 68 Stat. 897 (28 August 1954).

26. 68 Stat. 454 (10 July 1954); Edward L. Schapsmeier and Frederick H. Schapsmeier, *Ezra Taft Benson and the Politics of Agriculture: The Eisenhower Years, 1953–1961* (Danville, Ill.: Interstate Printers and Publishers, Inc., 1975), 99–109.

27. 70 Stat. 34 (2 March 1956).

28. Liebman, *California Farmland,* 136–37, 139; Cochrane and Ryan, *American Farm Policy,* 143–44. Allotment legislation in 1953 had a similar effect for wheat, an important crop in Montana, Oregon, Idaho, Washington, and Colorado. The legislation raised the minimum national allotment from 55 million acres to 65 million acres. See 67 Stat. 151 (14 July 1953).

29. 70 Stat. 188 (28 May 1956).

30. Cochrane and Ryan, *American Farm Policy,* 78; 72 Stat. 81 (7 April 1958).

31. Bowers, Rasmussen, and Baker, "History of Agricultural Price-Support and Adjustment Programs," 23–24; Cochrane and Ryan, *American Farm Policy,* 80–81.

32. Cochrane and Ryan, *American Farm Policy,* 80–81.

33. Ibid., 159–60; Congressional Quarterly, *Farm Policy,* 76–79.

34. 78 Stat. 173 (11 April 1964).

35. James T. Bonnen, "Observations on the Changing Nature of National Agricultural Policy Decision Process, 1946–1976," in *Farmers, Bureaucrats, and Middlemen: Historical Perspectives on American Agriculture,* ed. Trudy H. Peterson (Washington, D.C.: Howard University Press, 1980), 309–29. Bonnen sees the fragmentation of agricultural interests and the influence of nonagricultural interests (environmental and urban welfare) in the policy-making process as a detriment to sound policy. He generally would leave the process primarily in the hands of experts (agricultural economists) and the congressional chairs of the principal agricultural committees. A reader need not agree with Bonnen's conclusions to appreciate the insight of his analysis.

36. 84 Stat. 1358 (30 November 1970); Cochrane and Ryan, *American Farm Policy,* 83; Liebman, *California Farmland,* 137–40.

37. 87 Stat. 221 (10 August 1973); Congressional Quarterly, *Farm Policy,* 135; Bowers, Rasmussen, and Baker, "History of Agricultural Price-Support and Adjustment Programs," 29–31. In early 1976, Congress passed legislation establishing a set-aside and price support system for rice that also contained a $55,000 limit.

38. Congressional Quarterly, *Farm Policy,* 136–38.

39. Bowers, Rasmussen, and Baker, "History of Agricultural Price-Support and Adjustment Programs," 31–34; Congressional Quarterly, *Farm Policy,* 139–40.

40. C. Brant Short, *Ronald Reagan and the Public Lands: America's Conservation Debate, 1979–1984* (College Station: Texas A&M University Press, 1989), 47–48; Worster, *Rivers of Empire,* 326; Marc Reisner, *Cadillac Desert: The American West and Its Disappearing Water* (New York: Viking, 1986), 325–42; Congressional Quarterly, *Farm Policy,* 142–43; U.S. Department of the Interior, *Range Condition Report Prepared for the Senate Committee on Appropriations* (Washington, D.C.: Government Printing Office, 1975).

41. Congressional Quarterly, *Farm Policy,* 147; Short, *Ronald Reagan and the Public Lands,* 36–37. See also R. McGregor Cawley, *Federal Land, Western Anger: The Sagebrush and Environmental Politics* (Lawrence: University Press of Kansas, 1993).

42. Congressional Quarterly, *Farm Policy,* 137, 141.

43. Dale E. Hathaway, "Government and Agriculture Revisited: A Review of Two Decades of Change," *American Journal of Agricultural Economics* 63 (December 1981): 782–85; Congressional Quarterly, *Farm Policy,* 80. See also William P. Browne, *Cultivating Congress: Constituents, Issues, and Agricultural Policy Making* (Lawrence: University Press of Kansas, 1995).

44. R. G. F. Spitz, "Agriculture and Food Act of 1981: Continued Policy Evolution," *North Central Journal of Agricultural Economics* 5 (July 1983): 67–69; John G. Peters, "The 1981 Farm Bill," in "Food Policy and Farm Programs," ed. Don F. Hadwiger and Ross B. Talbot, *Proceedings of the Academy of Political Science* 34 (Fall 1982): 157–73.

45. Spitz, "Agriculture and Food Act of 1981," 68; Congressional Quarterly, *Farm Policy,* 152–53.

46. Bowers, Rasmussen, and Baker, "History of Agricultural Price Support and Adjustment Programs," 40–41; Congressional Quarterly, *Farm Policy,* 159–60.

47. Christopher E. Leman and Robert L. Paarlberg, "The Continued Political Power of Agricultural Interests," in *Agriculture and Rural Areas Approaching the Twenty-First Century,* ed. R. J. Hildreth et al. (Ames: Iowa State University Press, 1988), 50–53.

48. Jesse Helms, "The 1985 Farm Bill," in *Is There a Moral Obligation to Save the Family Farm?* ed. Gary Comstock (Ames: Iowa State University Press, 1987), 381; John A. Schnittker, "The Long-Run Political, Economic and Technological Environment for U.S. Agriculture," in *Impacts of Farm Policy and Technological Change on U.S. and California Agriculture,* ed. Harold O. Carter (Berkeley: University of California Press, 1987), 13–20; Rodney B. W. Smith, "The Conservation Reserve Program as a Least-Cost Land Retirement Mechanism," *American Journal of Agricultural Economics* 77 (February 1995): 93, 102, 104.

49. U.S. Department of Commerce, *Census of Agriculture, 1992.*

50. M. C. Hallberg, *Policy for American Agriculture: Choices and Consequences* (Ames: Iowa State University Press, 1992). Hallberg provides a crop-by-crop summary and comparison of the 1985 and 1990 agricultural acts.

51. U.S. Department of the Interior, *Rangeland Reform '94: A Proposal to Improve Management of the Rangeland Ecosystems and the Administration of Livestock Grazing on Public Lands* (Washington, D.C.: Bureau of Land Management and the Forest Service, 1993). See, for example, a wire service story in the *Great Falls (Montana) Tribune,* 12 July 1995. Interested parties may also use the Internet to review the fears, speculations, and prognostications of those interested in and involved with formulating farm policies for 1995 and after.

52. *Billings (Montana) Gazette,* 5 April 1996, 3A.

5

Ranch and Farm Women in the Contemporary American West

Sandra Schackel

In 1981, historian Joan Jensen made the point that women have been "active participants in every stage of agricultural production and in every period of agricultural history." In a society that views farming as a male occupation, however, farm women's lives often have been ignored or misunderstood. As the agrarian economy of the seventeenth century has evolved into the present urban industrial economy, major changes have occurred in the agricultural production system. Over time, women's productive roles have changed, causing a shift in the sexual division of labor. As a result, the workday roles of women and men have altered life on the family farm.[1]

Historians have been slow to acknowledge the significance of farm women's lives. Since the 1920s, rural sociologists have looked at the part of culture that agricultural historians have not—the families and communities within which rural people lived out their lives. In the 1980s, when a few historians began to study rural women, they drew on the work of sociologists, anthropologists, folklorists, and others. As the field has grown, historians have begun to uncover a rich and varied tapestry that demonstrates the significance of women's work on farms and ranches. To date, much of this work has focused on America in the eighteenth and nineteenth centuries.

The past fifty years represent a period of rapid agricultural change in the United States characterized by, among other factors, a steady decline in farm population, the disappearance of small-scale family farms, and the identification of large-scale operations with agribusiness. How have farm women fared in this new agricultural age? How have the structural changes in agriculture altered their lives, most particularly the patriarchal nature of farming? How have women adapted to the new technology that has shaped agriculture in the twentieth century? Historian Katherine Jellison, in her recent study of midwestern farm women, pointed out: "Farm women as well as men have played a role in modernizing farm life and changing forever the face of rural society and the character of its relationship to urban America." Jellison's work can be extended to the American West, using the voices of farm women in Idaho and New Mexico as a model for further study. Oral history interviews can help show the effect of technology on women's role as consumers and the link between such consumerism and the pattern of their off-farm work.[2]

At the close of World War II, farmwives throughout the nation were poised to become consumers in a new era of prosperity. In 1946, for example, a Nebraska farm mother and her daughter wrote to the editors of *Wallaces' Farmer* regarding postwar home improvements that were beginning to alter lifestyles for some farm families. "When Dad got the new manure scoop, the elevator and other modern farm tools, daughter and I approved, feeling that one of these days it would be our turn to enjoy electricity and a few modern conveniences. Just when we thought we had him convinced, what does he do? Orders another new tractor for the boys!" This farm wife obviously had looked forward to sharing in the postwar technological bounty awaiting war-weary consumers after four years of sacrifice and rationing. When the war ended, women began to discuss what they wanted to purchase "now that the war [was] over . . . and there [would] be all kinds of new equipment on the market." Such expectations were typical of farmwives in a period of rising prosperity and technological change that would alter life on the farm in postwar America.[3]

Much is known about the consumer habits of postwar urban families. Nationwide, American families were growing and spending; that is, family size increased dramatically as the soldiers returned home, and consumer spending rose to accommodate both the larger families and the bigger appetites that postwar affluence encouraged. Significant increases in discretionary spending power marked the postwar years. Between 1947 and 1961, the number of families rose 28 percent, national income increased over 60 percent, and the group with discretionary income (those with money for nonnecessities) doubled. Rather than spending for personal luxury items, Americans bought for the home. In the five years after World War II, consumer spending increased 60 percent, but the amount spent on household furnishings and appliances rose 240 percent. Between 1946 and 1950, consumers purchased 21.4 million automobiles, more than 20 million refrigerators, 5.5 million electric stoves, and 11.6 million television sets, a trend that continued into the 1950s.[4]

Many of these new items could be found in fast-growing suburban cities. Here, in a crabgrass-free, three-bedroom, two-bathroom ranch home, young families could raise children in a nice neighborhood complete with cars, washing machines, refrigerators, television sets, and other appliances associated with the good life. Yet farm families also desired to, and in fact did, purchase many of these same commodities, assuming, of course, they had electricity. By 1954, 91.4 percent of rural families in the Mountain West (Montana, Idaho, Wyoming, Colorado, New Mexico, Arizona, Utah, and Nevada) and 96.7 percent in the Pacific West (Washington, Oregon, and California) had electric power. Farm families were not without many of the new consumer items their city counterparts were enjoying.[5]

Still, U.S. Department of Agriculture (USDA) officials estimated in 1946 that only middle- to high-income farm families would benefit from increased farm incomes. In the corn and wheat belts, which led all other areas of the country in increased farm incomes and wartime savings, only "farm families with the largest savings look[ed] forward to having the conveniences that [were] generally available in cities—central heat, automatic hot water, telephone, electricity, and an all-weather road to the door." One study listed the appliances now expected by middle-class rural families in this order: refrigerators, washing machines, irons, radios, deep-freeze units, brooders, and churns. As it did for their urban counterparts, increased income gave farm women "the opportunity," as one woman put it, "to get some of the things we've always wanted."[6]

How widespread was this pattern of consumerism in the West? Limited sources suggest at least some farms and ranches shared in the bounty. Martha Ascuena, who in the 1950s lived on a sixty-acre ranch south of Mountain Home, Idaho, felt very content with her refrigerator and conventional washing machine. However, she lacked a dining room set, so her husband determined that they should have one, went to town, and purchased a set that Martha has loved ever since. When asked if she ever thought women in town had more or better things than she, Martha replied: "I never in my life wanted things anybody else had; that never bothered me one bit. They definitely lived better, there's no doubt about that. They dressed better, they went more, they did things that way but that didn't bother me because I didn't miss it. And I think farm women of my time didn't miss it."[7]

Perhaps farm women did not miss those things because many of them already had at least the basic comforts prior to World War II. In her article "How're You Gonna Keep 'Em Down on the Farm?" historian Cynthia Sturgis notes that by 1931 in Utah, 96 percent of homes had electricity, more than three-fourths of the families had electrical equipment, and more than two-thirds of the homes had running water. In addition, 94 percent of the homes had sewing machines, 80.4 percent had electric washing machines, and 43 percent had vacuum cleaners. This is not to suggest that rural living was easy, compared with urban standards, but that life on Utah farms and ranches had greatly improved by World War II.[8]

Yet this standard was not met in all western states. On the Great Plains, for instance, as late as 1940, only 15.7 percent of Kansas farm homes had running water and 27.3 percent had electricity. The situation was even more dismal in the Dakotas, where just 6 percent of homes in North Dakota had running water and 27.3 percent had electricity; the corresponding numbers for South Dakota were 11.8 percent and 17.9 percent. In the 1930s, however, the creation of the New Deal's Rural Electrification Administration (REA) provided a major breakthrough for rural people. Speaking directly to farm women in 1936, Secretary of Agriculture Henry A. Wallace promised that "rural electrification [would ease] the burden of the farm wife more and more." According to one North Dakota woman, the coming of the REA "really changed [housekeeping], because then we got electric stove, electric refrigerator, electric iron and electric lights. It was just wonderful. [Especially the] electric stove. Push that button and there you had heat. Didn't have to chop wood or carry coal to get some heat to cook on."[9]

For an Arizona widow, the REA provided a lifeline for her general store. Violet Irving led an extensive campaign in the 1940s to bring electricity to her remote rural area in Skull Valley. When the local power company declined to extend power lines to the area, Irving and others solicited subscribers at five dollars apiece and built a powerful coalition. "[I was the leader in the electrification movement from] let's call it necessity. I had the one business there that really [needed it]. By that time there were frozen foods and that meant a lot to my business. It was a necessity as far as I was concerned. . . . I was the one who was going to benefit the most." For Irving, determination and effort toward a public cause brought not only personal power but economic power as well.[10]

Government efforts to make life easier on America's farms began early in the twentieth century when Progressive Era reformers initiated the Country Life Movement, an attempt to stem the flow of population from farms to cities. Overall, the Country Life Movement failed to keep people "down on the farm," not because farm life could not be made more appealing through modernization but because the movement's supporters failed to recognize the strong pull of economic opportunity in the city. Embedded in this early reform movement were two goals that ultimately proved contradictory—"to preserve traditional agrarian ideals in the face of industrialism and to adapt agriculture to the modern age." Another less overt force was at work, however, in the form of reformers' attempts to prop up the patriarchal farm family by encouraging women to become modern homemakers. Over the next several decades, the message to farm women was intended to reinforce their traditional role as homemakers, one they persistently resisted. In time, many women would in fact leave the farm to take jobs in town in order to allow the family to stay on the farm.[11]

As life was made easier for the farmwife with the introduction of laborsaving devices, improved technology also altered the way farmers farmed. Two studies conducted in the 1970s in the Palouse, a rich dryland wheat-farming region in western Idaho and eastern Washington, note that accepted roles for men and women have not changed, but the content of their roles has. As Corlann Bush found in " 'The Barn Is His, the House Is Mine': Agricultural Technology and Sex Roles," the value or importance of men's work was enhanced as they moved from animal-powered farming to using mechanized equipment, while new household technology eliminated much of women's traditional work that was formerly crucial to the economic functioning of the family.

Women have always played an active role in eastern agriculture, but new forms of technology, such as tractors and combines, often relegated them to the home or to seeking jobs off the farm. Many western farm women, however, still consider themselves partners in the farm operation. In July 1996, Ramona Martinez, with sons Arthur and Roy, repairs a hay baler near Mora, New Mexico. *Courtesy, Sandra Schackel.*

Hence, as the husband/farmer moved from using horsepower and hired men to purchasing expensive combines, threshers, tractors, and other specialized equipment, the farm operation became far more complex. At the same time, the demands on the farmwife's role as one who "helped out" by working in the fields and cooking for large harvest crews declined.[12]

Sue Armitage, in "Farmwomen and Technological Change in the Palouse, 1880–1980," demonstrates the connection between increased technology on the land and technology that transformed the home. She found that technological change in the form of tractors and then combines occurred in the farmer's sphere first, resulting in more productivity and income. The most significant technological change to the domestic sphere came in the form of electricity, and in the Palouse region this came later than the technology that transformed farming. Farm men and women both welcomed changes that made their work-day lives easier—he on the tractor and she in a kitchen surrounded by laborsaving devices. The irony lay in the fact that her increased productivity was not in demand, since his technological improvements had eliminated the basis for her efforts. She no longer was required to feed farmworkers, since machinery had taken the place of manpower. Hence, as Bush noted, the value or importance of her role had been eroded.[13]

Yet, according to prevailing cultural values, women's primary postwar role remained that of homemaker. An editorial in *Wallaces' Farmer* in March 1953 described the farmwife's situation in this way:

> What does the "little woman" do with her time now that she has a cleanfuel stove and cake mixes have come on the market? With clothes dryers to save trips to the clothes lines, freezers to bring forth frozen pies and casseroles for hurry-up meals, a great many women hours are spent each year on tractors. Perhaps more important are the hours spent on trips to town for repairs for all the new machinery. . . . And then somebody—guess who—has to take time to make the good rolls, and the angel food cakes and the casserole dishes that come out of the freezer on busy days.[14]

Still, many farm women resisted the full-time homemaker status. They saw themselves in partnership with their husbands and believed that outside farm work, self-described as "helping out," brought more status and personal satisfaction, and demonstrated their importance to the family economy. They continued to run errands, pick up machinery parts, shut off the tank, or chase the hogs when they got out. By "helping out" in these ways, women were able to deny that they actually performed farm work and could then claim that they were living up to the postwar domestic ideal. Perhaps that is why they supported decisions to spend family income on new agricultural equipment before making repairs on the farm home, although new or improved equipment would lead to greater income.[15]

The patriarchal nature of agriculture assumes the male farmer's control of the labor of women and children. To many farm women, the phrase "He's the boss" is of secondary importance to the recognition that farm women play an important role in farming and in passing that knowledge on to their children. Farmwife Helen Tiegs of Nampa, Idaho, would agree, and describes her marriage as a partnership shaped by distinct gender roles. Her husband works in the field, and she runs the household, which at one time included six children. Although she prefers not to get on a tractor—"I have but it's been a disaster!"—and has never driven the beet truck during harvest, she considers herself "the hub of the wheel. I kinda keep things going because I'm the one that chases to town for parts; I really am the 'gofer'. . . . Instead of them having to leave their jobs, they send me. So I've been the one who has to run for parts and it gets pretty hot and heavy—they're always breaking chains, they're always breaking something." Tiegs is there to provide the needed labor at a crucial time.[16]

Martha Ascuena of Mountain Home, Idaho, would concur with Tiegs and, in fact, also referred to herself as a "gofer" as well as a farmer. Although she did not operate the farm by herself during the years when her husband also

Since the frontier period of the nineteenth century, rural women have fought isolation caused by distance and low population densities by joining service organizations, churches, and literary societies in the small towns across the West. In 1994, these women in Monte Vista, Colorado, spent time together while making a comforter. *Courtesy, Sandra Schackel.*

taught school, she helped him irrigate, cut corn, drive the truck, and work their hundred head of cattle. She views their relationship as balanced, noting that she has supported his decisions regarding farm purchases because "he knows more about those things and would not buy what we could not afford." Overall, Ascuena praises farm life and cannot imagine another way of making a living. "I always thought I would be a farmer's wife. . . . It was all that I knew and I loved it from the very start."[17]

Few farmwives today are disadvantaged by a lack of utilities (as their mothers and grandmothers were) or by an absence of laborsaving devices such as refrigerators, washing machines and dryers, home freezers, radios, or television sets. They have, like their urban counterparts, become "good consumers." Clearly, consumerism appears to be part of a larger, more complex issue—one that is related to issues of power, to gender roles, and, at a deeper level, to a strongly held belief in agriculture as a way of life. Whether the farmer orders another tractor at the expense of remodeling the farm kitchen is perhaps less important than how both farm people view their roles on the land and their ability to stay on the farm in the face of continuing change.

Lila Hill and her husband, Earl, know firsthand how change can alter gender roles. Hill and her husband live on a 147–acre farm in Meridian, Idaho, west of Boise. Together they operate a dairy farm caring for about 100 head of cattle. When they married in 1968, they were clear on the division of labor on the farm. Earl was the farmer and worked outside, Lila the farmwife who worked inside with the exception of the garden and yard. For more than fifteen years, Lila gave music lessons to augment the family income, carrying as many as fifty students a week at one time. By the early 1980s, Lila and Earl agreed that Lila would take a job off-farm, one that would produce greater income in a time of rising farm costs and falling dairy prices. To prepare herself for the job market, Lila took a computer course under the Job Training Partnership Act (JTPA), then took a series of jobs serving as secretary for several area churches, a position she continues to hold today.[18]

Now, in the 1990s, their roles have altered as Earl is "easing into" retirement while Lila continues to work off the farm. She still teaches music to a few students after school, both because music defines part of who she is and for the income the lessons produce. She no longer has time to do yard work, so Earl has taken over that responsibility. The farm, originally homesteaded in 1891 by Angus Hill, will pass to the oldest son, Martin, who currently lives in a home on the property. Lila and Earl have already sold several parcels of land and foresee the distinct possibility that the farm will be sold to developers as urban growth creeps up to their property line, a common situation in metropolitan areas in the West today.[19]

Lila Hill is typical of many farmwives who recognize that their most important contribution to farming may be taking a job in town. Working off the farm to augment the farm income is not a new development but one that has been taking place for several decades as American agriculture has undergone dramatic changes. At the turn of the century, almost half the population lived on farms. This figure dropped to 30 percent in 1920 and has declined to less than 2 percent in the 1990s. At the same time, small family farms have given way to very large farms now recognized as part of the sector known as agribusiness. In 1935, there were 6.8 million farms averaging 155 acres. In 1960, there were just under 4 million, and, by 1982 the figure had dropped to 2.4 million farms averaging 433 acres. According to government definitions, however, there is great variation in the type of farms. The current definition, first used for the 1974 census, is any place from which $1,000 or more of agricultural products were produced and sold or normally would have been sold during the census year. On these terms, farms range from the very large ($500,000 or more annual gross farm income) to large, medium, and small family farms (annual gross farm sales ranging from $499,000 to $10,000), to what the USDA classifies as a rural residence with less than $10,000 gross income. The trend in the last half century has been an increase in the very large and large family farms, while medium and small family farms and rural residences have declined. The result is that farming has become more productive, concentrated, centralized, and dependent on hired rather than family labor, with corporate farms accounting for increased farm production.[20]

Still there is a great deal of sentiment among Americans for farming as a "way of life." The notion that small to medium-sized farms are indispensable to

American democracy is part of the heritage of the Jeffersonian agrarian ideal. Although the number of small, part-time farms has increased, the total number of farms in the United States has been dropping since the 1930s. Since 1950, it has declined by half, from more than 5 million to fewer than 3 million farms. Still, it is not likely that the family farm will disappear from view despite the "farm crisis" that has persisted for much of the twentieth century, accelerating since World War II. Indeed, one farmwife responded to my query about the farm crisis by commenting that being raised on a farm meant "it was always a crisis, all my life."[21]

One important factor that has allowed family farms to stay in business is working off-farm for wages. Men as well as women have taken jobs off-farm in order to be able to stay on the farm. Martha Ascuena's husband, for example, taught school in Mountain Home for many years while continuing to farm. From the beginning of their marriage, Elizabeth Lloyd's husband did part-time and later full-time work while continuing to raise dairy cattle on their farms in both eastern Idaho and eastern Oregon. When a back injury in 1956 prevented him from returning to farm work, Elizabeth went to work full-time for Ore-Ida Foods in 1957 and continued at the potato processing plant until her retirement in 1986. Still, they continued to farm and to care for a family of seven children. Earl worked the evening shift, while Elizabeth worked nights, which allowed her to see the children off to school in the mornings and be there when they returned later in the day. Equally important, Elizabeth was able to maintain the role of mother and wife that was expected of farm women while contributing to the farm income.[22]

Lloyd is one of many women who fit Katherine Jellison's study of mid-western farmwives between 1913 and 1963. Jellison found that women taking jobs off-farm was a new phenomenon in the 1950s that drew mixed responses. Editors at *Wallaces' Farmer* took the position that wage work was acceptable but only as a temporary measure until the young couple could "establish themselves." By the mid-1950s, however, farm women of all ages were increasingly becoming permanent members of the small-town labor force in midwestern communities. In Illinois, 10 percent of that state's farm women were wage earners, most of them working as retail clerks, teachers, or factory workers. Although wages were low, women could still make more money at town jobs than they could by selling dressed chickens, cottage cheese, or eggs—the traditional types of economic activities for farm women. Nor did they expect to quit their town jobs soon, even when a forty-mile round-trip commute was part of the job. According to the *Wallaces' Farmer* editor, "It isn't for a TV set or a home freezer that Harriet Sellers, R.N. and homemaker, is spending her salary. It's for school clothing, groceries, tractor fuel and farm payments. . . . Practically speaking, it seems that mom has come to town so dad and the kids can stay on the farm." Many Idaho farm families fit this midwestern pattern as well.[23]

More recent studies show that a substantial number of farm women continue to hold full- or part-time jobs off the farm, jobs that benefit both farm families and local businesses. A 1976 survey of rural women in the small communities of Wendell and Jerome in south central Idaho showed that 45 percent from small farms—those with an annual production below $25,000—were employed away from the farm. Women on larger farms were less likely to have outside employment. The survey showed that income from the farmwife's off-the-farm job may be necessary for a small farm to remain in operation. At the same time, such employment strengthens the bonds between farm and non-farm sectors of the economy.[24]

Not only is off-farm work important to keep a small farm going; it can be crucial to establishing a family farm given the high costs of getting into business as a farmer. Linda and Gary Murgoitio of Meridian, Idaho, struggled and scrimped for nearly fifteen years to build a financial base that would enable them to invest in land and farm equipment. During this period, when they worked on Gary's parents' farm, Linda worked off-farm first at a bank, then at a trucking company, and later at an insurance company, usually for low wages. They delayed starting a family, again because all their energy and assets were directed toward building up capital to purchase their own farm. Once their two children were born, Linda quit work in town to care for them, as well as to help Gary with farm work, a working relationship she values highly. When asked if she would work off-farm again, perhaps when the children were grown, she was hesitant to commit to the possibility, preferring to maintain the warm partnership they have created. She went on to say, "When I was working outside the home I think my relationship with Gary suffered. Gary and I are terribly close now and I don't want to jeopardize [that by] going back [to work]. . . . I really like hanging out with him and doing whatever he's doing. . . . We seem to be pretty close."[25]

Like many others, Linda questions how small farmers today can amass the capital needed to enter agriculture under present conditions. Several of the older farm women interviewed for this study spoke of younger women who work off-farm as a matter of fact rather than necessity. Helen Tiegs described her daughter-in-law, who works for an insurance company, as "a good farm wife. She knows how to irrigate, how to do siphon tubes and everything" and is a "very good business gal" in addition to keeping the books for a local farm organization. In Martha Ascuena's view, "three-quarters of the girls are [working off-farm] because the farm just isn't enough to pay expenses. . . . I'm sure that income is taking care of the house expenses or even the groceries. It's certainly a different way of life." Elizabeth Lloyd was even more direct, saying, "The farm was just a place to live really because even people today that have small farms—a lot of their living they get from outside work."[26]

Rosalie Romero of Chacon, New Mexico, was eighteen when she first went to work off-farm at the local hospital in nearby Las Vegas in the early

1950s. There she worked for fifty cents an hour but remembered that "we did a lot with it." Her mother-in-law kept her children while her husband worked his father's land. Gradually Rosalie and Alfonso took over the 800-acre farm, mostly sheep, and both continued to seek out wage labor to meet their modest expenses. When Alfonso went to work for the Forest Service, the extra income helped buy "coffee, sugar, the basics." Rosalie held a variety of jobs over her lifetime as a maid, a waitress, a nutrition aid to the agricultural extension agent, in the Senior Citizen Center in Mora, and until her retirement in May 1995, as a school bus driver.[27]

The Romeros did not, and still do not, have mechanical equipment, just horses and wagons. When their children were small, Rosalie would take them with her on horseback to deliver lunches to the sheepherders in the mountains. Like most farmwives, she tended a large garden and canned, although she no longer cans as much as she used to. The family did not install running water in their home until 1982 but carried water from a nearby river and used outdoor plumbing. She recalled washing diapers outside in tubs and cooking over a wood-burning stove. The stove is still present in her kitchen, right next to a modern electric stove. Rosalie is cheerfully optimistic when asked about the character of their lives. She has had a hard life, but it has brought satisfaction as well. The presence of a large extended family nearby has been important to her as a source of support. As her husband did, their children—four sons and one daughter—will take over the farm at their parents' deaths, perpetuating this family farm for yet another generation.[28]

Taking over the family farm is not as clear for many families, given the increasing costs associated with farming. Irene Getz of Elgin, Illinois, married a sheep and cattle rancher in 1930 and came west, to Monte Vista, Colorado, to begin a new life. Initially, her husband, Floyd, worked for his father for cash wages, fifty dollars a month, until they were able to acquire land of their own. At one time, the family farm consisted of two operations of 5,000 acres where they raised approximately 500 head of cattle and 1,200 sheep. After Floyd's death in 1975, their four sons continued to run the two operations. Later they sold one ranch. In the 1980s, one son left ranching and moved into town, where he became a businessman and local politician. Although her husband arranged for all five children to inherit the land, Irene is not sure how long the Getz ranch will remain in the family. Her daughter, Marilyn, has two sons, one of whom may go into the family agricultural enterprise; he is currently finishing a college degree. At present, the grandsons represent the only hope that this family farm will continue in its present form.[29]

In cash-poor Mora County in northeastern New Mexico, small family farms dot the high-mountain countryside. Mora, thirty miles north of Las Vegas, is the largest town in the valley at 800 people. In 1970, nearly 60 percent of the residents lived in what the federal government officially defined as poverty; nationally less than 11 percent of the population fit that category. Over home-made tortillas, red chile, and *posole,* Alice and Frank Trambley relate some of their forty-two years together. Alice grew up on her family's farm eight miles south of Mora. She met Frank while baling hay (with horses), married him at age twenty-two, and settled into farm life. After three of their six children were born, the family moved into "town," where they have resided since, although they continue to make daily trips to the farm. They raise cattle and hay on about 600 acres. Half the land is under irrigation; cattle graze the other half.[30]

Like many of the other families in heavily Hispanic Mora Valley, this family has always had income from off-farm work. In the 1960s, they opened a slaughterhouse in Mora, drawing on family labor. All the children went to work when they were small; the sons learned to cut meat at age fourteen. Alice divided her time between raising the children and working at the business. There were long days, especially in the fall, when eighty head of cattle a week were slaughtered. For twenty-five years, she helped with the slaughter on Mondays and wrapped meat on Thursdays. Today she is free of this task, since one of the sons took over full management of the business in 1992. Her "free" labor, unaccounted for in census terms, helped this farm family to survive. The work of family members reduced labor costs, and thus "The slaughterhouse gave them a cushion."[31]

Twenty years ago, the family invested in another income-generating business, a small mobile home park adjacent to their home in Mora. Today they have space for thirty-three units; they own fifteen units and rent out the remaining spaces. Alice and Frank agreed early on in their marriage that she would do the "inside" work; it is Alice's task to clean the rental units when tenants move out. Despite the discomfort of sometimes noisy, rowdy renters, the extra income has been important. Along with the slaughterhouse business, off-farm work has allowed this family to maintain their agricultural roots through difficult periods and in a challenging environment. Alice made it clear that "we can't make it without these sources of income." As a result, their children will inherit a working family farm, one that has been maintained by outside income. Two of the sons live nearby and are actively involved in the daily management of the cattle and hay operation. Yet they, too, live and work off-farm.

Of the Trambleys' eight grandchildren, will any of them be willing to return to the Mora Valley and commit to the demanding tasks of maintaining the family farm? Frank and Alice are unsure. Reflecting on the reality of farming in the late twentieth century, they suggest that "maybe the grandchildren will be smarter and will sell out." They note the large number of young people who leave the valley because of a lack of jobs: "Even the ones that finish high school and college have to go out and look for jobs." Farm expenses are simply too great. In this valley, as in other agricultural areas, local families sell out to newcomers, people who have retired from jobs elsewhere, saved their money, and can afford to buy up large parcels.[32]

Alice Trambley's willingness to serve as a cheap source of labor is key to the survival of small farm families. Cornelia Butler Flora and Jan L. Flora, in their 1988 study of agriculture and women's culture in the Great Plains, suggest three factors that allow the family farm to survive in a society dominated by capitalist relations of production: provision of a flexible labor force; absorption of risk; and heavy capital investment relative to the profit generated. Women play key roles in each situation. Since agricultural production differs from industrial production as regards a flexible labor force, the family is the ideal basic production unit. As part of a flexible labor force, shaped by the cyclic nature of farming and dictates of weather, women and often children are "available" to "help out" at harvest or calving time, or to serve as the ones to go for parts or supplies. Once the peak season has ebbed, women can then assume the role of "dependent" during the rest of the agricultural cycle, as Alice and her children did after the fall slaughter.[33]

Farm women take pride in "helping out" in this manner and have created a variety of cultural structures around the role of farmwife. Basic to agrarian ideology is the notion that "the family working in harmony as a production unit is the best possible way of life even though that unit may be defined by the male in the household." Unlike in industry, management, labor, and capital are bound up in the agricultural enterprise—the family—so all in the family are expected to contribute to the whole to make it work. Alice Trambley, as well as her children, have been integral to this system, helping to mobilize needed labor at peak periods in the production cycle. At the same time, the demand for labor in "her sphere" continued—cooking, cleaning, child care, laundry, and numerous other tasks associated with being a farmwife. While cultural norms allow women to do men's work, men perform women's tasks less often.[34]

Along with their role as part of a flexible labor force, women play a key role in the absorption of risk through diversification in production. Examples of this diversification include the production and sale of butter, cream, eggs, poultry, and vegetables. Historically, women have been actively involved in some aspect of agricultural production. Dairying, poultry raising, and truck farming were often an integral part of all farm families' work up through the 1950s and 1960s. Women participated in the marketplace and received monetary compensation. Irene Getz was typical: she raised turkeys and sold cream and butter in town to cover household expenses. When insects attacked the crops or drought occurred, profits from selling chickens, eggs, or butter contributed to the family economic base. These diversified enterprises also allowed women to control one portion of family income while reducing risk for the farm operation as a whole.[35]

Another form of diversification is in the off-farm jobs women take to supplement agricultural income. Wage labor has often meant the difference between staying in agriculture and losing the family farm. Lila Hill went to work in town when her family's dairy operation was threatened in the 1980s. She also contributed to diversification by giving piano lessons for many years.

Rosalie Chacon's wage labor has been key to her family's stability throughout their lifetime.

Finally, according to the Floras, women's patterns of consumption affect the welfare of the agricultural enterprise. Because the nature of farming is land-extensive, it requires a relatively large investment to reach the volume of production necessary to support a family. Women's willingness to support investment in land and machinery before household improvement is an integral part of their commitment to agriculture. Sometimes that acceptance comes at the expense of their own sacrifice. The house will have to wait, as the Nebraska farm mother and daughter quoted earlier experienced. For Sylvia Ortega of Guadalupita, New Mexico, supporting her husband's decision to buy land rather than install running water in their farm home paid off in time. As she describes it now, "We were buying land and I still didn't have running water. He'd buy more land and I'd complain and get mad, then I'd give in. Which I'm glad I did because otherwise we wouldn't have the land we have. . . . We did get the water eventually." Clearly, her husband prevailed in the larger decision of land purchase. Ultimately, they installed indoor plumbing. Although Sylvia was initially resistant, she eventually acquiesced to the larger use of land as capital for investment.[36]

The lives of the women in this study mirror some of the findings of Rachel Ann Rosenfeld's 1980 national study of farm women, published in 1985 in *Farm Women: Work, Farm, and Family in the United States*. This study, carried out through telephone interviews with 2,509 women and 569 men, has provided researchers with material that the federal census did not cover. In general, census data have centered on farms rather than farm families. The Bureau of Census did not ask the sex of the farm operator until 1978. In that year, 128,170 women listed themselves as farmers and farm managers, or 5.2 percent of all American farmers. In the West, 17,037, or 5.9 percent, of the area's farm operators were female. As part of the nationwide trend toward smaller farms, women tend to run even smaller farms than their male counterparts. They also earn less, are older, and are more likely to be full owners of the land they farm. While the majority of women farmers are in the South, western farm women have the largest average-size farm, perhaps due to the large number of commercial farms in the West.[37]

Rosenfeld's work also draws on statistics compiled by Judith Z. Kalbacher. Both studies show the number of women farmers and ranchers increasing between 1950 and 1980, from 3 percent of total operators to almost 10 percent. The largest increase occurred between 1970 and 1980 when the numbers nearly doubled, from 71,000 to over 137,000 female farmers and farm managers. Although not yet completely documented, it is possible that this period of high land prices, easier access to credit, and greater availability of federal programs encouraged women as well as men to expand their agricultural holdings.[38]

Gretchen Sammis exemplifies the modern woman farmer/rancher in the West. She is sole heir to the historic Chase Ranch near Cimarron in northeastern New Mexico. Her great-grandfather, Manley M. Chase, came to New Mexico in 1866. He built a notable reputation as a rancher, businessman, and local politician, while the Chase family women created orchards and poultry flocks. Manley's wife, Theresa, planted fruit trees that developed into one of the finest orchards in the Southwest. Daughter-in-law Nettie Chase built up a prosperous poultry business, while the cattle and sheep enterprise continued to thrive. In the next generation, Zeta Chase, Gretchen's grandmother, ran a dairy. Gretchen, born in 1925, was active in ranching activities at an early age and developed a close working relationship with her grandfather, Stanley Chase. When he died in 1964, she took over management of the family Hereford cattle ranch.[39]

At that time, Gretchen was teaching high school in nearby Cimarron, working on the ranch before and after school. Although her grandfather had relied on animal power, she quickly turned to mechanized equipment as a more efficient and timely way to carry out ranch work. In 1965, she took on a partner, Ruby Gobble, who shares the work and satisfaction of running the Chase Ranch. According to Gretchen, "We do it all. Right now, the ranch is a little over 11,000 acres and we still run straight Hereford cattle. We also farm a little bit, irrigate a little bit, raise alfalfa, oats for the cattle and raise oats for the turkeys—we have lots of wild turkeys. . . . I used to do all of the irrigating and most of the farming and Ruby is really good with heavy equipment . . . we still do all our own cattle work." Gretchen continued to teach and ranch until 1972, when she gave up teaching to give full attention to the ranch, but she "still misses the kids."[40]

Gretchen Sammis fits Kalbacher's profile, which shows that women who farm or ranch are older than their male counterparts. They also inherit a significantly greater proportion of their land than do men. Sammis's situation is unique in that she was much younger than the average heir at time of inheritance. Many women inherit their farm operations after a husband's death, and they usually are older than fifty-five; Gretchen was just thirty-nine when her grandfather died. In 1978, only 5.2 percent of farm operators nationally were female, with a median age of fifty-nine; the median age for men in this category was almost fifty. (Gretchen was then fifty-three.) In 1992, the average age of female operators dropped to 57.6. So, unlike most (older) women farmers or ranchers, Gretchen has been the operator, with Ruby's help, for more than thirty years.[41]

The Chase Ranch, like many other western outfits, has become more than a working ranch. Gretchen has allowed hunting on the ranch since the early 1970s. Deer and elk hunting "pays a lot of the bills. The way cattle prices are right now, we'd be in bad shape if it wasn't for hunting." For the Sammis operation, "It's a secondary income as far as this ranch is concerned, not primary yet but it's pretty close to being as good." Talli Manning of Big Piney, Wyoming, is equally supportive of this form of diversification because "with ranching, there's not a guaranteed income. You have to keep a good nest egg or you could end up out of business."[42]

Few western women have been ranchers on their own. Gretchen Sammis is an exception. In 1986, she operated the Chase Ranch near Cimmaron, New Mexico, with a combination of frontier independence and twentieth-century business skill. *Courtesy, Barbara Van Cleve, photographer.*

Obtaining an outfitter's license gives the landowner the right to charge money to take people fishing, on pack trips, or hunting. Gretchen is enthusiastic about combining hunting and cattle ranching, finding them compatible activities. "We lease it to an outfitter and he worries about everything. If we wanted to worry about everything ourselves, we'd make more money but it wouldn't be worth the hassle." In Sammis's view, hunting benefits both humans and animals because "anything that grows has to be harvested. I don't care if it's animals or grass or people or anything. If it grows, it has to be harvested or it falls apart."[43]

Seventy miles south of Cimarron, in the small Mora County village of

Rociada, lies the 4,000-acre Gascon Ranch now owned and managed by Editha Bartley and her son John and his wife, Tamara. The Gascon Ranch is also a diversified operation that includes a sawmill; from the early 1940s until 1989, it also included a guest ranch. Editha's husband, Jim, built the sawmill in 1984; since his father's death in 1993, John has managed the sawmill and the cattle ranch. Adjacent to the Santa Fe National Forest, the ranch has served as a gateway into the wilderness for visitors for five decades. Originally owned by the Gascon family, it has served as a summer respite for midwestern and eastern doctors who came to New Mexico to visit patients they had referred to nearby Valmora Sanitarium early in the twentieth century. Dr. William T. Brown, Editha's grandfather, himself a tuberculosis patient, founded the sanitarium, twenty-five miles from Las Vegas, in 1904; it stayed in family hands until the Bartleys sold it in 1991. The Gascon Ranch, just over the ridge from Valmora, continues to be a working cattle ranch.[44]

Editha Bartley dreamed of becoming a veterinarian; her father, Carl H. Gallenthien, wanted her to become a physician like himself. Instead, Editha met and married Jim Bartley, an electrician, and moved to Las Vegas, New Mexico, although they spent the summer months at Gascon Ranch. After the birth of their three children in the 1950s, they bought the Gascon property and continued to run it as a guest ranch. New to this type of ranch management, they drew on the experiences of other westerners in the same business and quickly developed a loyal clientele, including groups of children who "needed to be in the wilderness for a while." All the Bartley children helped with the enterprise, and Editha "practiced a lot of medicine without a license, especially on animals." Inexperienced in the kitchen when first married, she soon learned to cook for large groups of twenty or more guests and developed into a gourmet cook.

For over twenty-five years, the guest ranch provided the family with extra income and at the same time allowed them to remain on the ranch. In Editha's words, "We make it with moonlighting, with the guest ranch and the sawmill." Although she had to close the facility in 1989 because of her father's illness, she hopes to reopen it as a bed-and-breakfast inn in the near future, continuing the pattern of diversification that has marked many western operations in the twentieth century.[45]

Clearly, life on a family farm in the 1990s is a challenge. It is apparent from the foregoing accounts that farm women do not make the choice to work off-farm in order to provide the family with luxury items. Instead, farmwives, and some husbands, work at wage labor to increase farm income because the costs associated with farming are so high. Post–World War II accounts demonstrate that farmwives in the 1950s were working to pay bills, clothe their children, buy farm supplies, and generally support their families in ways similar to farmwives four decades later. These farmwives take pride in and find satisfaction with wage work, which in turn brings them a measure of power within the patriarchal structure of agriculture. Similarly, those women who describe their farm work as "helping out" in times of need have made a commitment to agriculture as a way of life. They place great value on this lifestyle despite the hardships. Seventy-four-year-old Elizabeth Lloyd, now living with a daughter, made it clear: "Right now I'd rather be on the farm; that's all I knew." When asked if she had missed anything by living in a rural area, Martha Ascuena responded, "I don't think a thing, no, I think that my life has been just about as complete as anyone's could be." Editha Bartley put it this way: "Those of us that have that feel[ing], I don't think it will ever change. . . . I love being in the country. I love people and working with people, but I love the quiet and isolation. I love this kind of country." Although it may appear that the demise of family farms is at hand, farm and ranch women in New Mexico and Idaho reaffirm a commitment to a way of life that has long shaped our perception of the United States as an agrarian nation.[46]

NOTES

1. Joan Jensen, *With These Hands: Women Working on the Land* (Old Westbury, N.Y.: Feminist Press, 1981), xxiii.

2. Katherine Jellison, *Entitled to Power: Farm Women and Technology, 1913–1963* (Chapel Hill: University of North Carolina Press, 1993), xx.

3. Ibid., 151–52.

4. Elaine Tyler May, *Homeward Bound: American Families in the Cold War Era* (New York: Basic Books 1988), 165; Susan M. Hartmann, *The Home Front and Beyond: American Women in the 1940s* (Boston: Twayne, 1982), 8.

5. U.S. Bureau of the Census, *Statistical Abstract of the United States: 1957* (Washington, D.C.: Government Printing Office, 1957), 641.

6. Jellison, *Entitled to Power,* 150.

7. Interview with Martha Ascuena, Mountain Home, Idaho, 26 June 1995.

8. Cynthia Sturgis, " 'How're You Gonna Keep 'Em Down on the Farm?': Rural Women and the Urban Model in Utah," *Agricultural History* 60 (Spring 1986): 182–99.

9. Katherine Jellison, "Women and Technology on the Great Plains, 1910–1940," *Great Plains Quarterly* 8 (Summer 1988): 145–57.

10. Mary Logan Rothschild and Pamela Claire Hronek, *Doing What the Day Brought: An Oral History of Arizona Women* (Tucson: University of Arizona Press, 1992), 85–86.

11. Sandra Schackel, *Social Housekeepers: Women Shaping Public Policy in New Mexico, 1920–1940* (Albuquerque: University of New Mexico Press, 1992), 115; Jellison, *Entitled to Power,* 184.

12. Corlann G. Bush, " 'The Barn Is His, the House Is Mine': Agricultural Technology and Sex Roles," in *Energy and Transport: Historical Perspectives on Policy Issues,* ed. George H. Daniels and Mark H. Rose (Beverly Hills, Calif.: Sage, 1982), 235–59.

13. Sue Armitage, "Farm Women and Technological Change in the Palouse,

1880–1980" (paper presented at the Fifth Berkshire Conference on the History of Women, Vassar College, Poughkeepsie, New York, 16–17 June 1981); Bush, " 'The Barn Is His, the House Is Mine'," 235–59.

14. Quoted in Jellison, *Entitled to Power,* 164.

15. Ibid.

16. Sarah Elbert, "Women and Farming: Changing Structures, Changing Roles," in *Women and Farming: Changing Roles, Changing Structures,* ed. Wava G. Haney and Jane B. Knowles (Boulder, Colo.: Westview Press, 1988), 245–64; interview with Helen Tiegs, Nampa, Idaho, 29 June 1995.

17. Ascuena interview.

18. Interview with Lila Hill, Meridian, Idaho, 13 September 1995.

19. Ibid.

20. Rachel Ann Rosenfeld, *Farm Women: Work, Farm, and Family in the United States* (Chapel Hill: University of North Carolina Press, 1985), 12; U.S. Department of Commerce, *Census of Agriculture, 1987,* vol. 1, Geographic Area Series, part 51, United States Summary and State Data (Washington, D.C.: U.S. Department of Commerce, Bureau of the Census, 1989); Harold D. Guither and Harold G. Halcrow, eds., *The American Farm Crisis: An Annotated Bibliography with Analytical Introductions* (Ann Arbor, Mich.: Pierian Press, 1988), 2; Rosenfeld, *Farm Women,* 12–13.

21. *Lewiston Tribune,* 7 September 1981, 2B; interview with Elizabeth Lloyd, Ontario, Oregon, at the home of her daughter, Jeanette Moore, in Boise, Idaho, 18 September 1995.

22. Ascuena interview; Lloyd interview.

23. Jellison, *Entitled to Power,* 165–67.

24. *Idahonian,* 21 October 1976.

25. Interview with Linda Murgoitio, Meridian, Idaho, 20 September 1995.

26. Tiegs interview; Ascuena interview; Lloyd interview.

27. Interview with Rosalie Romero, Chacon, New Mexico, 3 October 1995.

28. Ibid.

29. Interview with Irene Getz, Monte Vista, Colorado, 28 September 1995.

30. William Eno DeBuys, *Enchantment and Exploitation: The Life and Hard Times of a New Mexico Mountain Range* (Albuquerque: University of New Mexico Press, 1985), 211; interview with Alice and Frank Trambley, Mora, New Mexico, 3 October 1995.

31. Trambley interview.

32. Trambley interview; DeBuys, *Enchantment and Exploitation,* 210–11.

33. Cornelia Butler Flora and Jan L. Flora, "Structure of Agriculture and Women's Culture in the Great Plains," *Great Plains Quarterly* 8 (Fall 1988): 195–205.

34. Ibid., 197.

35. Madeline Buckendorf, "The Poultry Frontier: Family Farm Roles and Turkey Raising in Southwest Idaho, 1910–1940," *Idaho Yesterdays* 37 (Summer 1993): 2–8; Jensen, *With These Hands;* Getz interview.

36. Flora and Flora, "Structure of Agriculture and Women's Culture in the Great Plains," 197–98; interview with Sylvia Ortega, Guadalupita, New Mexico, 4 October 1995.

37. Rosenfeld, *Farm Women,* 36; Judith Z. Kalbacher, "A Profile of Female

Farmers in America," Development Division, Economic Research Service, *USDA Rural Development Research Report No. 45* (Washington, D.C.: Government Printing Office, 1985); the average size of a female-operated farm in the West is 701 acres; in the South, 226 acres. The national average for women is 285 acres; for men, 423 acres.

38. Kalbacher, "A Profile of Female Farmers," 2; Rosenfeld, *Farm Women,* 3.

39. Interview with Gretchen Sammis, Cimarron, New Mexico, 5 October 1995.

40. Interview with Gretchen Sammis, Cimarron, New Mexico, 25 October 1995.

41. Kalbacher, "Female Farmers," 7–9.

42. Ronnie Farley, ed., *Cowgirls: Contemporary Portraits of the American West* (New York: Crown, 1995), 26.

43. Sammis interview.

44. Interview with Editha Bartley, Rociada, New Mexico, 5 October 1995. For a fuller discussion of dude ranching in the West, see Robert G. Athearn, *The Mythic West in Twentieth-Century America* (Lawrence: University Press of Kansas, 1986).

45. Bartley interview.

46. Lloyd interview; Ascuena interview; Bartley interview.

6

Federal Water Policy and the Rural West

Donald J. Pisani

World War II had a profound effect on American agriculture. The increased demand for food and fiber wiped out the agricultural surpluses of the 1930s. Moreover, the armed forces and defense industries drained off many tenant farmers and owners of marginal lands, and the war contributed to the long-term agricultural trend of replacing men with machines. Farmers produced at maximum capacity and still received high prices. Their income more than doubled from 1939 to 1945, and the value of their farms more than tripled. This period of agricultural prosperity—one of the longest in the nation's history—lasted into the early 1950s. Europe's postwar demand for food helped sustain the boom and avert a sharp agricultural depression like the one that had followed World War I.[1]

The region between the Rocky Mountains and the Pacific Ocean came of age, agriculturally, in the decades after World War II. Irrigation already dominated western agriculture in 1940. Virtually all crops raised in Arizona and Nevada were irrigated, along with most of the crops cultivated in California, Utah, Idaho, Wyoming, and Colorado. In Montana, New Mexico, Washington, and Oregon, "artificial rain" nourished from 35 to 50 percent of agricultural land. From 1940 to 1980, however, irrigated acreage in the western half of the nation more than tripled to 45 million acres, and irrigated crops returned more than half the total value of the region's agricultural production. Because the easily accessible alluvial land adjoining major streams had been taken up in the late nineteenth and early twentieth centuries, and because the water in those streams had long since been claimed, land opened to cultivation during or after World War II was more expensive to water. Much of it required pump systems to tap underground water or move water up hundreds of feet from streams to bench or plateau land. Few farmers could afford to pay the soaring costs, and California was the only western state wealthy enough to build its own dams and canals. Therefore, the federal government assumed new responsibilities for the growth of western agriculture. The Reclamation Bureau's original mission was to turn the West into a region dominated by family farms. Ironically, in the decades after World War II it did far more to promote agribusiness, urbanization, and industrial growth.[2]

In 1933, Congress created the Tennessee Valley Authority (TVA) to combat poverty in one of the poorest parts of rural America. The Tennessee Valley's average farm was worth only 25 percent of the national average, and more than half the valley's farm families were on relief. The enabling legislation authorized the new agency to produce *and market* power and fertilizer in the Tennessee River basin, which included parts of Tennessee, Alabama, Mississippi, Kentucky, Virginia, North Carolina, and Georgia. The TVA was also expected to improve transportation on the region's major rivers, fight soil erosion, restore cutover forests, and build flood control works. Between 1933 and 1944, nine

Water is the life-giving blood of agriculture in the West. Since the 1940s, however, urbanites have increasingly demanded affordable water that agriculturists claim as their own. This irrigation ditch in Maricopa County, Arizona, has been lined with concrete to prevent the loss of water from seepage, much in the tradition of the prehistoric Indians who packed their irrigation ditches with clay. *Courtesy, U.S. Department of Agriculture.*

major dams and many smaller ones were constructed on the main river and its tributaries.

Although the TVA enjoyed widespread popularity during the 1930s, by the end of the decade many of its friends were disappointed. Congress refused to appropriate money to lay out model communities, valley residents often opposed the suggestions of TVA officials regarding how they should run their farms and their lives, and the proponents of river basin development could not agree on what they wanted to accomplish. Should TVA be a relief agency, an object lesson in the benefits of public power, a model for regional economic development, an experiment in scientific agriculture, a new kind of government, or an exercise in social planning? For example, if one cause of the Great Depression had been the concentration of factories and financial institutions in a handful of eastern cities, why not use river basin authorities to decentralize industry? The national economy could be stabilized, this theory ran, by moving industry into the countryside, where it would benefit from cheap land, power, and labor. Or should the paramount goal of river basin authorities be to restore the small, family farm as rural America's dominant economic institution—even in an age of crop surpluses?

There were also problems of governance. The TVA was sold to valley residents as a way to stimulate "grassroots democracy" by encouraging farmers to take responsibility for their own lives. Yet how could "home rule"—building up such state and local agencies as land-grant colleges, agricultural and engineering experiment stations, state extension services, school boards, library boards, departments of health, park and conservation commissions, and municipal power boards—be accomplished without fragmenting authority and forfeiting national leadership? Equally important, how could an autonomous TVA be reconciled with the increasing power of federal agencies with a strong interest in rural development, such as the Soil Conservation Service, the Resettlement Administration, and the Agricultural Extension Service? The TVA depended on a very fragile institutional partnership.[3]

In April 1933, when he proposed the TVA to Congress, President Franklin D. Roosevelt emphasized that the legislation was experimental. "If we are successful here," Roosevelt predicted, "we can march on, step by step, in a like development of other great natural territory units within our border." In 1937, following a year of heavy flooding in 1936 and an overwhelming victory in the presidential election, Roosevelt announced a plan for seven regional authorities covering the Atlantic seaboard; the Great Lakes and Ohio Valley; the TVA; the Tennessee and Cumberland Rivers; the Missouri Basin (including the Red River of the North); the Arkansas Basin (including the Red River and the Rio Grande); the Colorado; and the Columbia. Only the Mississippi River was excluded; it was left under the authority of the Mississippi River Commission. Roosevelt justified the proposal on the grounds of institutional efficiency rather than regional planning. "This proposal is in the interest of economy and the prevention of overlapping or one-sided developments," he announced. "My rec-ommendations in this message fall into the same category as my former recom-mendations relating to the reorganization of the Executive Branch of the Government." Two regional authority plans appeared in Congress, one spon-sored by Senator George Norris and the other by Congressman Mike Mans-field. Each provided for the creation of regional authorities at the behest of the president, and each permitted him to define and amend the territorial boundaries.[4]

Given the nation's crop surpluses, the increasing antagonism of business and power companies toward the TVA, and a general lack of sympathy for planning in Congress, the 1937 "trial balloon" never got off the ground. Roosevelt nominally remained a supporter of regional authorities, and in the fall of 1940 he asked David Lilienthal to draft legislation to create an Arkansas Valley Authority modeled after the TVA. Regional authorities seemed particularly well suited to the West and South, whose economies were primarily extractive. In 1941, a congressman from Arkansas observed: "After the war I think we shall see a rebirth of democracy, a democracy in which the people shall see to it that there is more universality of opportunity, more universality in the use and enjoyment of our rich stores of God-given resources. . . . We are historically poor because of our development along the lines of an agricultural and raw-materials economy. We have been the area to be exploited. We have been the colonial empire of these United States."[5]

The end of the war posed both problems and opportunities. From 1945 to 1950, the supporters of river basin authorities portrayed them as a necessary part of demobilization and a response to the new military threat posed by the Soviet Union. The fear of massive postwar unemployment and a return of the depression of the 1930s contributed greatly to support for public works projects. Water projects would provide millions of jobs, particularly after the pent-up demand for consumer goods and for exports had abated. Supporters thought that valley authorities would create vast new supplies of power and thus would produce jobs in manufacturing as well as construction.[6]

Residents of the Pacific Northwest and the Missouri River valley antici-pated particularly severe postwar problems. No part of the country gained faster in population during the war than the Pacific Northwest, whose labor force increased by 50 percent. The value of water projects to the war effort had been enormous. The region's prewar economy had been heavily dependent on lumbering and wood products. However, during fiscal year 1944, the Grand Coulee and Bonneville Dams had provided power to five aluminum-reduction plants that produced about one-third of the nation's output of that metal. Nearly all the aluminum had been used to build ships and airplanes. In effect, the region's interior had been drained of rural residents to supply the war industries of Seattle, Portland, and other communities along the coast. Therefore, boosters argued that the postwar regional economy depended on simultaneously expand-ing farming and industry to compensate for the defense jobs lost during demobilization. The lesson was obvious. One writer warned: "Some sort of effective action in the political as well as the economic field must be taken—and soon—if there is not to be that mass exodus from the Northwest which forward-looking citizens fear when the curtain finally drops on the war." It was not hard to predict what would happen when the war was over and the defense plants closed their doors.[7]

Nor was it hard to predict what would happen if private power companies gained control of the hydroelectric plants built by the government in the 1930s and during World War II. In the minds of many advocates of public power, river basin authorities represented a struggle for the very future of the West. Control over power might enslave a region if it fell into the wrong hands. "If private companies control it," Max Lerner warned, "it can mean staggering wealth and domination. It belongs in public hands. It belongs to the people." The Columbia River had the potential to produce fifteen times the amount of power it generated at the end of the war and more than three times all the power generated in the entire United States in 1945.[8]

The Missouri River valley was very different from the Columbia. The river originated at the juncture of the Jefferson, Madison, and Gallatin Rivers in Montana, then flowed east and south for nearly 2,500 miles, passing through Montana, Wyoming, Colorado, North and South Dakota, Nebraska, Iowa, Kansas, and Missouri. The drainage basin covered one-sixth of the nation's land mass but only one-twentieth of the nation's population. The value of the region's manufactured goods declined by 30 percent from 1929 to 1939, and the region's population dropped by 10 percent during World War II. To make matters even worse, basin residents suffered massive floods in 1943 and 1944. Upstream there was too little water, downstream too much; therefore, residents of St. Louis had very little in common with Dakota wheat farmers or ranchers in the foothills of the Rocky Mountains. "Incomes, tax receipts and industrial production are dropping," one writer noted, "and since 1940, 1,000,000 people have left the area. There are few Americans, even these days, who do not remember the dust bowls of a decade and more ago in the Upper Valley, while year after year we hear of floods which ruin thousands of acres of rich farmland nearer the river's mouth." Advocates of a Missouri River Authority promised that regional water planning would open up 5 million acres of virgin land to cultivation and simultaneously drive up the value of farmland already cultivated.[9]

That promise was not enough, and river basin authorities never enjoyed broad regional or national popularity. Roosevelt originally proposed river basin governments for all parts of the nation, but they were far better suited to the West, which depended heavily on public power and irrigation. This posed the danger of regional imbalance. Using cheap power generated at federal dams to expand the West's agriculture and industry would encourage people and businesses to leave the East. Presidential adviser Raymond Moley maintained that "both the new river Authorities and the [national] highways are efforts to decentralize the population—to make big cities smaller and to take business away from large cities and 'channel' (a good New Deal word) it into the countryside. They would take tax money from urban centers and spend it elsewhere." Such institutions offered little political payoff to the Democratic Party. The Democratic coalition built up during the 1930s included an alliance between the rural South and big cities of the Northeast. Much of Roosevelt's vacillation on river basin authorities—he provided public support in speeches but little direction in Congress—grew from the fact that there was little irrigable land or undeveloped water power along the eastern seaboard.[10]

The events of the 1930s and World War II made Americans particularly receptive to fears of "collectivization," "sovietization," and what came to be called "creeping socialism" in the 1950s. The 1948 Republican platform promised to eliminate "arbitrary bureaucratic practices" and support "greater local participation in the operation, control, and eventual local ownership of reimbursable, federal-sponsored water projects. We vigorously oppose the efforts by this national Administration . . . to establish all-powerful Federal socialistic valley authorities." Many Republicans regarded such institutions as a legal ruse by federal agencies to win control over the transmission and sale, as well as the generation, of electricity. They feared that centralized control over electricity would result in centralized control over basic industries and, inevitably, the entire national economy.[11]

Private power companies strenuously lobbied against river basin authorities, claiming that such schemes were unconstitutional and a perversion of the American system of government. Authority bills created government corporations beyond the control of Congress and the individual states. They would, in effect, preempt existing institutions of government. Most river basin legislation permitted the president to appoint the administrator and boards of directors of each authority without confirmation by the U.S. Senate; the authorities would also bypass or ignore existing congressional committees on flood control, irrigation, and rivers and harbors. The taxing power of the states, counties, and municipalities would be undermined; state control over water rights would be disrupted; the boards would likely be composed of "carpetbaggers" with little knowledge of, or attachment to, the regions they served; agriculture would be shortchanged in the name of industry; and there would be no assurance that each state would receive a fair share of the benefits doled out by those who administered the river basin governments. The directors could use power revenue as an almost unlimited source of funds that would permit them, according to Raymond Moley, to engage in "almost any activity that might occur to the directors."[12]

The West was not united. Many westerners feared that river basin authorities would delay the construction of water projects pending at the close of the war by several years because a whole new set of surveys and reports would be commissioned by the authority. Others resented comparisons between their region and the Tennessee Valley because such an admission might frighten off private capital. Colorado and Wyoming, located at the headwaters of the West's major streams, worried that regional authorities would transfer water from upper-basin states to states downstream, limiting their agricultural development. In the Columbia Basin, the Oregon Grange and Oregon Federation of Labor supported an authority, while most of Portland's commercial interests opposed it. Farm groups hoped that a Columbia Valley Authority (CVA) would integrate power from Grand Coulee and Bonneville, standardizing rates throughout the valley. Businessmen already enjoyed cheap electricity and feared that a uniform rate would increase their energy costs and reduce their competitive advantage over businesses in Seattle, Tacoma, and Los Angeles. Flat rates benefited rural areas and the agricultural economy, while graduated rates favored urban and industrial areas. Since farmers could not afford to pay the full cost of irrigation works, other rate payers within the basin would be called upon to subsidize agriculture at the possible cost of industrial development.[13]

Strong opposition to regional authorities also came from Washington. River basin authorities threatened to duplicate the work of existing agencies. Officials in the U.S. Department of Agriculture (USDA) worried about their programs to retire submarginal land, combat soil erosion, and administer wildlife refuges. The Bureau of Reclamation dreaded losing control over hydroelectric power revenues—which allowed the bureau to pay for water projects it could not afford in the days before the "high dam era." River basin authorities would also prevent the bureau from assuming control over all federal drainage projects. "Reclamation, for one, shudders at the thought of organizing a game with the cards thus stacked," Commissioner of Reclamation Michael Straus wrote to Assistant Secretary of the Interior William Warne in May 1951, "and then inviting itself to sit in as the principal loser." Plans would be sent from the river basin commissions to a board of review in Washington, D.C., without any consideration by the existing federal agencies interested in water planning. "River Basin Commissions . . . having administrative duties and an appropriation of [their] own, would sooner or later tend to influence, if not usurp, departmental responsibilities with regard to the preparation of budget estimates, financing, and the control of the kind and rate of surveys to be included in the departmental program." Interior Department officials demanded the creation of a Department of Natural Resources before they would consider river authorities. They were reluctant to support any authority that would do more than coordinate investigations and give a voice to state officials.[14]

While President Harry S. Truman (1945–53) nominally supported the creation of river basin authorities—at least in the Missouri and Columbia Basins— in 1950 the Korean War intervened to demonstrate that communism was, indeed, on the march. In 1952, the Republican Party's presidential candidate, Dwight D. Eisenhower, insisted that federal tax dollars raised from all over the country

Farmers and urbanites have argued considerably over water rights since 1940, and the use and control of water have created complicated legal, political, and economic problems. Although a host of dams provide water for irrigation, only large-scale farmers or growers with considerable capital can afford to use it for their crops. Furrow irrigation, such as this, enables sugar beet production where it would otherwise be impossible, but water rights remained a volatile economic and political issue in California and other western states during the late twentieth century. *Courtesy, U.S. Department of Agriculture.*

should not be used to reward the residents of one section of the nation. The Republican landslide buried the river basin authority, and the cold war ensured that it would not be resurrected.[15]

If the history of the TVA is any guide, western river basin governments could not have rescued the family farm. Romanticism and nostalgia limited the effectiveness of the TVA as much as the American aversion to social planning. Some New Deal thinkers saw the family farm as an antidote to the corrupt values of the Jazz Age—an age that worshiped business, reveled in the excitement of the city, and relentlessly pursued the ethic of "getting ahead." The TVA unquestionably improved the lives of the people it served, but agricultural income increased much faster in other parts of the country; the region's farm income fell from 32 percent of the national average in 1940 to only 29 percent in 1949. Neither the TVA nor any other government program could curb the inexorable migration from the countryside to the city. The basin's farms declined from over 300,000 in the early 1930s to little more than 100,000 in the 1970s. The TVA demonstrated that it was easier to attack rural poverty by allowing people to take factory jobs than by subsidizing the family farm. It took much more to make rural life attractive than giving people a secure home on the land and furnishing them with cheap power and fertilizer.[16]

To be sure, the Tennessee Valley was not a fair test of the federal government's ability. The family farm had much more potential in parts of the arid West than in the Tennessee Valley. In the West, irrigation had long been recognized as a tool to allow farmers to raise more crops, and more valuable crops, on less land. Beginning in the late nineteenth century, social reformers had touted reclamation as a tool to break up large landholdings, restore the family farm, and provide rural families with independence and a subsistence. However, the policy contained two other objectives that often clashed with these goals. Watering desert land usually drove up the value of that land; therefore, it was immensely attractive to land speculators and real estate developers. Simultaneously, it was an instrument of regional economic growth. Since irrigation permitted relatively small farms, it promised to lure new residents into the West and lay a solid foundation for industrialization. In this way, the West could escape subordination to the East. Prior to the 1930s, irrigation was largely a private affair, the work of corporations, mutual water companies, and irrigation districts. In 1930, the federal government watered only a few million acres—no more than 10 percent of the total irrigated in the western half of the nation.[17]

The federal government's presence in the West increased dramatically during the 1930s and World War II. In the 1930s, the Bureau of Reclamation spent three times as much on dams and canals as it had from 1902 to 1932. By the end of the decade, water projects constituted almost 40 percent of the nation's public works budget. The 1930s witnessed two fundamental changes in federal reclamation policy. With the completion of Boulder Dam in 1935, proceeds from the sale of power were used to subsidize the cost of irrigation. This contributed to the dramatic expansion of irrigated acreage in the West after the war. Then, in 1939, Congress decided that the cost of flood control as well as navigation should be nonreimbursable; after the war, it added fish and wildlife conservation to the list of nonreimbursable expenditures, for which farmers and other water users did not have to pay back project costs. Since most large water projects designed and constructed in the 1930s and after provided many benefits, this proved a windfall to farmers by reducing construction costs.[18]

Many water projects had a profound influence on the rural West. In 1935, only 11 percent of the nation's farms enjoyed electric service. Ten years later, with help from the Rural Electrification Administration, nearly half did. The power plants constructed at Hoover, Bonneville, Shasta, and other dams furnished farmers with the energy to heat homes and power radios, electric ranges, refrigerators, washing machines, milking machines, cream separators, and a host of other machines and appliances. Equally important, it provided cheap energy to drive irrigation pumps. The war made electricity even more important. "The War Production Board authorized a crash program to complete Shasta Dam [at the headwaters of the Sacramento River] and to enlarge the generating capacity of a number of other reclamation projects," historian Donald Swain has observed. "During the war the expansion of reclamation power accounted for 84 percent of the total expansion of electrical power in the eleven far-western states." By the end of the war, the Bureau of Reclamation was the single largest producer of power in the world.[19]

By World War II, the small-scale farmer was an anachronism. During the 1930s, critics of reclamation pointed out that the immigrant-fueled population growth at the beginning of the century had abated and that the population had stabilized for the first time in American history. A 1940 survey of government reclamation projects settled between 1931 and 1940 revealed a 30 percent turnover in owners during that decade, and many projects exhibited unmistakable signs of poverty. On one project in eastern Oregon, 75 percent of the houses cost less than $350, nearly half had only one or two rooms, and 40 percent of the farms had no wells. Project residents suffered from many chronic ailments, including typhoid fever, but they were too poor to obtain medical help.[20]

Congress tacitly abandoned the family farm ideal when the Reclamation Bureau took over construction of California's Central Valley Project (CVP) in 1935. Large corporations owned much of the land within the CVP, and the project was designed mainly to benefit agribusiness. Then, in 1938, Congress explicitly exempted land under cultivation within the Colorado–Big Thompson Project from the 160-acre limitation contained in the Reclamation Act of 1902. Even though more than 300,000 farm families had been displaced by drought and dust, Congress refused to use federal reclamation to help what Roosevelt described as "indigent but worthy farm families."[21]

During the war, water projects became symbols of nationalism and patriotism, and, once again, the family farm became a symbol of democracy and social stability. Congressman Clyde T. Ellis of Arkansas suggested that western water projects would provide homes for hundreds of thousands of people and might mean "the difference between saving the democracy and losing it during the inevitable economic chaos that shall accompany peace.... [W]e are going to have to buckle our belts and dig in as we have never dug before to prevent the sight of increasing millions of unemployed, poor, hungry, ill-clothed, and ill-fed men, women, and children."[22]

The memory of the Great Depression was not the only fear. The declining farm population and increasing farm size during the war seemed to pose grave dangers for the future of American agriculture. In 1945, a group of Roman Catholics, Protestants, and Jews led by Edwin V. O'Hara, bishop of Kansas City and founder of the National Catholic Rural Life Conference, proclaimed that "access to land and stewardship of land must be planned with the family unit in view. The special adaptability of the farm home for nurturing strong and wholesome family life is the reason for the universal interest in land use and rural welfare.... The family's welfare must ... have the first consideration in economic and social planning." The group agreed that large landholdings were "undemocratic and unsocial" and should be discouraged.[23]

Many officials in the Reclamation Bureau agreed. "The ultimate objective of the Bureau of Reclamation and its staff," one writer in *Reclamation Era* remarked in 1946, "is to develop the West through creation of permanent family farms on Federal Reclamation projects." At the end of the war, the bureau had immediate plans to reclaim 4 million acres and create 45,000 new farms on government reclamation projects—nearly as many new homes as had been created from 1902 to 1945 under the Reclamation Act of 1902. Veterans received a ninety-day preference to file on all new land opened to settlement on federal reclamation projects, which included the Klamath (California), Yakima (Washington), Minidoka (Idaho), and Shoshone (Wyoming) projects. Veterans with more than nineteen months of active duty were allowed to shorten the period of residence needed to perfect title from three years to one year. Nevertheless, they had to meet the same standards of industry, experience, and capital as other settlers. Between 1945 and 1950, returning veterans filed nearly 23,000 applications for government land, but only one of every twenty-eight was approved. Many veterans lacked the capital required by the Bureau of Reclamation, and there was little public land left to reclaim. Over three times the number of World War I veterans took up government farms after that conflict.[24]

The Columbia Basin was expected to create the most family farms. In 1943, Congress enacted the Columbia Valley Project Act, which authorized the Interior Department to purchase more than 1 million acres of privately owned, dry-farmed land north of Pasco, Washington, and subdivide it into 15,000 to 20,000 small farms. It was hoped that the towns and farms within the project area would provide homes to more than 300,000 people. The enabling legislation recognized two fundamental changes in federal reclamation policy: the public domain contained no more large blocks of land suitable for reclamation, and settlers would be unable to pay more than a fraction of project costs. Power from Grand Coulee Dam, which was completed during the war, would pay most of the cost of pump systems and canals. The legislation did not permit the Bureau of Reclamation to engage in social planning on a large scale, such as building farmhouses or designing model towns, but it did address the chronic problem of land speculation that plagued so many of the reclamation projects undertaken by the federal government before the 1930s. The Bureau of Reclamation was authorized to set the price of farmland within project boundaries for five years after water became available.[25]

The project was filled with disappointments. Construction began in 1946, and the first 6,000 acres were opened in 1948. The project was designed, in part, as a refuge for those who worked marginal lands on the Great Plains, but over half the applicants came from Washington state and, most who came from outside Washington were from Utah. Some were veterans, but the median age was forty, and they were not "poor"—over half claimed family assets of at least $20,000. Nor were they willing to accept a subsistence income; they wanted to live in comfort. The 40-acre plots authorized in the original project legislation were too small, and in 1957 Congress allowed a husband and wife to own as much as 320 acres. By leasing land from those who left the project, it was possible to control far more than that. Over 25 percent of the original settlers left their land within four years, and the average farm increased from 84 acres in the 1950s to more than 240 acres by 1970. About one-third of the farmers lived in cities, and a 1974 study found that 25 percent of the landowners received 75 percent of the benefits.

In 1968, the federal government tacitly conceded that the project would never be completed when it turned the hydraulic works over to the water users, organized into three irrigation districts. Only about half of the more than 1 million acres originally set aside for reclamation had been watered. In 1945, the cost of the project had been estimated at $280 million; by 1967, it was pegged at more than a billion dollars. In 1945, farmers were expected to pay 25 percent of the project's total cost; by 1959, the amount had fallen to only 10 percent. It soon became clear that the cost of watering the entire 1 million acres would far exceed the benefits. Farmers paid a minuscule share of the total cost, and future diversions for irrigation would sharply reduce the amount of power that could be generated at Columbia River dams downstream from the project. While the Grand Coulee Dam had been expected to provide power to central Washington that would permit the marriage between agriculture and industry contemplated in the 1930s, the dam in fact delivered most of its power to cities on the coast, draining off potential settlers and industries.[26]

In his excellent recent history of Grand Coulee Dam, historian Paul Pitzer points out that while the Columbia Basin Project locked out large-scale corporate agriculture, it stood little chance of becoming the "planned promise land" many had anticipated when the project first took shape. True, the Bureau of Reclamation made many mistakes. World War II interrupted geologic and soil studies that might have foreseen costly drainage and alkali problems later encountered on the project, but planners could not anticipate that the collectivist dreams of the 1930s would become the socialist nightmare of the cold war era. Nor could they anticipate that the labor surplus anticipated at the end of the war would never materialize. As always, farmers were quick to accept subsidies but slow to accept direction. They thought that the high cost of reclamation was due to waste and bad planning by federal bureaucrats. Despite half a century of experience, the Columbia Basin Project suffered from many of the same problems encountered on the nation's first reclamation projects. Yet had the project "succeeded," Pitzer notes, "it would be a collection of family farms ranging from forty to eighty acres, none of them capable of supplying their owners with a satisfactory living. The area would be a rural slum. It is for the best that this aspect of the project failed."[27]

The Columbia Basin Project was not alone. The Bureau of Reclamation encountered similar problems on the Riverton Project in Wyoming. "There was a good deal of fanfare connected with this rebirth of the irrigated homestead," one historian has commented. "It turned out to be a rebirth of all the old troubles. Before the year [1950] was out, the veterans were complaining to their senators that the project was waterlogged." A subsequent survey revealed that much of the land was not suitable for irrigation without an expensive drainage system and that the Bureau of Reclamation had known as much when the project was opened. Following protests from veterans who had lost thousands of dollars and several years of their lives trying to reclaim poor land, Congress provided the settlers with homesteads on other federal projects. Nevertheless, most Reclamation Bureau projects launched after World War II did not attempt to create new farms. For example, in the decade after World War II, the bureau completed twenty-three midsize dams in the Missouri Basin, but added only 2,000 acres to the 657,000 acres in federal reclamation projects within Colorado, Wyoming, and Montana. Most of the water stored behind the new dams went to land in private ownership that previously had been dry-farmed or only partially irrigated.[28]

The Columbia Basin Project revealed a deep division between those who wanted to preserve or restore the family farm at virtually any price and those who wanted to encourage industrialization and urban growth. The West became a testing ground because only there did the government produce enough power to have a choice. Many urbanites argued that their cities could not continue to grow if the Bureau of Reclamation followed a policy of building up rural areas. In a paper presented to the American Political Science Association in August 1951, Leland Olds, a member of President Truman's Water Resources Policy Commission, insisted that in the future most water conflicts would focus on this issue. "The problem is already before us in a small way in Southwest Texas, where lands have been withdrawn from irrigated agriculture to assure water for El Paso's expanding needs," he observed. "In a larger way it involves the future of Southern California urbanism against Arizona agriculture. Even in the East, where water seems abundant, whole watersheds are being withdrawn from natural rural and recreational life to provide an untreated water supply for great urban-suburban constellations and lovely streams are being transformed into waste carriers."[29]

Thus, the Bureau of Reclamation's brief flurry of interest in creating new homes on the land after World War II was largely a relic of New Deal idealism, tempered by the pervasive fear that rapid demobilization would lead to massive unemployment and a new depression. The cold war soon killed the planning ideal, just as a robust postwar economy undermined the need to use agriculture as a "safety valve." Changes in government were also important. The future of the family farm in the West hinged on bureaucratic rivalries in Washington. To satisfy its friends in Congress, and to compete with rival agencies in the field, the Bureau of Reclamation appealed to the largest constituency possible. That meant courting established farmers and urbanites.

During the 1930s, as hydroelectric power and flood control became important features of national water policy, the Reclamation Bureau, Army Corps of Engineers, Soil Conservation Service, Federal Power Commission, and other federal agencies came into conflict. In 1910 or 1920, it was easy to separate the responsibilities of the Corps and the Reclamation Bureau: the Corps concentrated on navigation work in the rivers and harbors of the eastern United States, while the Reclamation Bureau built dams and canals for irrigation in the arid and semiarid West. However, the vast water projects of the 1930s emphasized multiple-use reservoirs that could perform many functions and serve many different groups of water users. Inevitably, more and more agencies became involved in the planning, construction, and operation of these projects.[30]

Prior to the 1930s, water projects were evaluated solely in terms of direct benefits, such as the crops raised from irrigation or the value of land saved from floods. The Reclamation Bureau pointed with pride to the ways irrigation increased business in the vicinity of irrigated land—including within the towns adjoining the farms it created—but the relationship of cheap power to industrial production, national defense, and the cost of living was rarely considered. World War II forced planners to think nationally, and cheap hydroelectric power changed the way politicians looked at water projects. Federal water projects had become powerful tools of regional economic development, not just agricultural subsidies.

Multiple-use projects allocated water according to a complicated set of priorities; no reservoir could serve all functions equally well. Reservoirs used predominantly for flood control had to be kept empty most of the time. Those used for power had to be kept as full as possible most of the time. Reservoirs used for irrigation were filled during the winter and early spring and drawn down during the growing season. Conflict arose not just over which agency should build a dam but also over which agency would operate it, which set of water users would receive preference, and, most important, who would pay for it. It was difficult to determine the exact cost of irrigation in relation to flood control, navigation, or wildlife protection, and there were many ways to measure benefits. For example, water users could be charged for a certain amount of storage space in a reservoir, or their assessment could be based on the value of water in use. (Farmers who raised cotton could be charged more than those who grew wheat.) It was equally difficult to measure the indirect benefits of water projects. To compound the problem even further, after the war there was considerable pressure on Congress to increase nonreimbursable benefits from water projects, including recreation, pollution abatement, and national defense, to name just a few.

In 1945, the Bureau of Reclamation had big plans for the western half of the nation. It wanted to dam every major western stream, irrigate 6.7 million acres of new land, and provide a supplemental supply to another 9.3 million. However, many western farmers and landowners, represented by such powerful water-user organizations as the National Reclamation Association, favored the Corps over the bureau. They had many reasons for doing so. In particular, the Corps was not bound by the 160-acre restriction in the 1902 law, and it did not require farmers to repay the full cost of structures that provided some water for irrigation but whose *primary* justification was flood control or navigation. This put the Reclamation Bureau at a disadvantage. As Secretary of the Interior Harold Ickes noted in a memo to the president in 1939: "Irrigationists are being weaned from the Bureau by the promise or the hope that they can get stored water for little or nothing if the Corps of Engineers builds the dams." If the Bureau of Reclamation was to survive and flourish in the postwar world, it would have to abandon the 160-acre limitation and emphasize benefits other than irrigation, such as work relief and low-cost power for industry. The agency was at a crossroads.[31]

During the 1930s, Roosevelt argued that it was wrong to place too many water projects under U.S. Army supervision because, should war come, the civilian responsibility would clash with its military work. The Corps, he insisted, should be limited to water projects involving navigation, though such projects might have flood control and power as secondary benefits. He ordered the two agencies to exchange information about multiple-purpose projects, and he also used interagency committees to promote cooperation. Nothing worked until the end of the war was in sight. Anticipating the end of the war, the 1944 Flood Control Act declared Congress's intention "to facilitate the consideration of projects upon a comprehensive and coordinated development." Plans for water projects had to be circulated among all interested agencies, federal and state. The legislation contained a massive appropriation for flood control—

prompted in part by the 1943 and 1944 floods in the Missouri Basin—but it also placed limits on the Corps. Section 5 gave the secretary of the interior the responsibility for marketing all power generated by dams constructed by the Corps, and Section 8 stipulated that while the Corps could build dams that stored water for irrigation (so long as that was not the primary purpose of the structure), only the Interior Department could construct the canals to carry that water to the land benefited.[32]

Later in 1944, the two agencies forged an alliance and presented to Congress a consolidated or composite scheme for developing the Missouri River—the Pick-Sloan plan (named in honor of the two officials who negotiated the pact). In 1940, the Corps of Engineers had built the first major dam on the stream, a flood control structure, at Fort Peck in the middle of Montana. During the war it became clear that the Bureau of Reclamation wanted to dam the upper tributaries of the Missouri, particularly the Republican River, to generate as much power as possible. Proceeds from power would subsidize the expansion of irrigation in Montana and the Dakotas. The Corps favored downstream communities between Omaha and St. Louis; both flood control and channel improvements would encourage commercial use of the river. The two agencies did not reconcile their plans or work out a coherent, overall plan for developing the basin's water resources. Instead, they reached a $1.26 billion accommodation that included dams, levees, and other hydraulic works—many of questionable value. For example, after long insisting that the Corps of Engineers' proposed Garrison Dam would lose more water to evaporation than the structure could store, the Reclamation Bureau accepted the dam without a murmur.[33]

The *Chicago Sun* described the accommodation as "the most shameless sort of quid pro quo. The two agencies behaved exactly like two big business competitors, dividing up territory to form a cartel. . . . The result is that the joint plan will cost millions more than a unitary plan." A special executive commission charged with suggesting ways to reorganize the structure of the federal government concluded: "Analysis of that [1944] plan reveals the fact that it contains many projects which previously had been subjected to devastating criticism by one or the other. . . . [T]here is serious question in this case whether agreement between the two agencies is not more costly to the public than disagreement."[34]

The 1944 Pick-Sloan plan did not represent a permanent settlement. Conflict continued, especially after Harold Ickes stepped down as secretary of the interior in 1945. For example, despite the fact that the Flood Control Act of 1944 gave the secretary of the interior exclusive authority to sell all power produced by Corps of Engineers dams, in late 1948 or early 1949 the Corps conducted a survey of the power potential and markets of the Missouri Basin, despite strong protests from the Interior Department. In Texas, the Corps and the Department of Agriculture blocked a Bureau of Reclamation drainage project on grounds that drainage within farms was the Agriculture Department's job and outside farms a Corps' responsibility. The Reclamation Bureau insisted that drainage was a necessary part of arid land reclamation, and the Interior Department's desire to extend its control over drainage posed as much of a challenge to the Corps as the Corps' threat to invade the realm of arid land reclamation posed to the Bureau of Reclamation. From 1945 to 1953, the Corps reclaimed about 3 million acres of land from flooding in the Missouri River valley alone— more than the 2.7 million acres of land irrigated by the Reclamation Bureau during the same years.[35]

In the San Luis Valley of Colorado, Congress had authorized the Bureau of Reclamation to construct a dam at Wagon Wheel Gap in 1941. However, local interests, encouraged by statements of army engineers, urged Congress to give the job to the Corps so they could secure free water as a "by-product" of flood control. The Corps was even more welcome in the San Joaquin Valley, where it contended that flood control was the *primary* function of most multiple-purpose reservoirs. All across the West, conflict increased in the late 1940s and 1950s. Like Roosevelt, President Truman nominally favored the Interior Department and Bureau of Reclamation. For example, after the Corps finished building the Pine Flat Dam on the San Joaquin Valley's Kern River, he gave the secretary of the interior the responsibility for negotiating repayment contracts with water users. When he approved the construction of Folsom Dam near Sacramento, another Corps' flood control job, he required that the completed dam be turned over to the Bureau of Reclamation for operation as part of the Central Valley Project. The bureau would then construct the dam's power plant.[36]

In 1949, the continuing conflict between the Corps of Engineers and the Bureau of Reclamation prompted the Hoover Commission—which had been created to draft a plan to reorganize the executive branch of the federal government—to propose that the civilian functions of the Corps be merged with those of the bureau in a Water Utilization and Development Service within the Interior Department. The commission, however, was deeply divided. Three members urged that the Interior Department be abolished and that the new agency be located within a Department of Natural Resources, and two others filed a minority report that strongly opposed stripping the Corps of its civilian functions.[37]

At the beginning of January 1950, President Truman appointed a temporary Water Resources Policy Commission under the leadership of Morris Cooke, a public power advocate and former head of the Rural Electrification Administration. Since the end of the war, the federal government had spent an average of more than $1 billion annually on water projects, which made coordination and planning imperative. Truman charged the commission with determining better standards for evaluating the costs, benefits, and feasibility of water projects, as well as for allocating the construction costs of multiple-purpose projects. He had many other objectives as well. He wanted to create, in his words, a "stable and expanding national economy"; determine the extent to which hydroelectric power was important to national security and the extent to which it should subsidize other water users; promote agricultural production and establish criteria by which federal agencies could evaluate the agricultural benefits of water projects nationwide—not just for irrigation but also for drainage and flood control; establish uniform standards by which federal agencies could decide whether to aid or salvage existing nonfederal irrigation projects; and modify the traditional 160-acre limitation on the amount of water individual farmers could purchase from federal projects, taking into account variations in climate and crop potential in different parts of the West. The president ordered the committee to submit its final report by the beginning of December 1950.[38]

The Cooke Commission consisted of two engineers, three economists, a biochemist, and a geographer. It recommended the creation of up to fifteen river basin commissions, each with nine members. Six would come from federal agencies: the Federal Power Commission and Public Health Service, as well as the departments of War, the Interior, Agriculture, and Commerce. Two would represent the states or local interests involved, but so might the ninth member, who would be appointed by the president with the approval of the Senate. The chair's term would be ten years; other members would serve for six years, though all could be reappointed. Local interests would also be represented by a twenty-five-person advisory committee chosen by the governors of the states within each river basin to represent agriculture, business, labor, recreation, and fish and wildlife, as well as local governments. Each commission would be required to prepare a twenty-year plan for the development of natural resources within its boundaries, and coordinate the work of federal agencies therein. A federal board of review would oversee the work of the individual commissions; nothing could be done without its approval.[39]

Soon before leaving office, President Truman endorsed many of the Cooke Commission's recommendations in his last message to Congress. His speech was a blend of old and new. The new was the menacing cold war world, and Truman reminded Congress that the nation's natural resources constituted "a foundation, on which rest our national security, our ability to maintain a democratic society, and our leadership in the free world." The old was the need for cheap power to promote regional economic development. The TVA, Truman insisted, had proved the value of unified management and demonstrated the correlation between abundant electricity and economic health. Without naming specific rivers, he urged the creation of basin authorities "in those parts of our country which need much improvement." While he proclaimed that "the Government should continue to help make available new family farms at reasonable prices and on reasonable terms," he also urged that "the cost of resource projects should be paid more directly by those who benefit from them." This implied the need for better procedures for project selection and repayment. The economy of 1953 was very different from that of 1933, and the range of options open to Truman was far narrower than that available to Franklin D. Roosevelt. In the

1930s, selection criteria were less important because of the compelling need for jobs; in effect public works were their own justification. Not so in 1953.[40]

The Republican president and Congress elected in 1952 showed little sympathy for comprehensive planning, and existing federal agencies were no more enthusiastic about river basin authorities than they had been in 1944 or 1937. The Reclamation Bureau applauded many of the Cooke Commission's recommendations, especially its insistence that public projects should be treated differently from private ones and that repayment contracts ought to distinguish between private and public purposes. The Corps of Engineers and other federal agencies already resented the bureau's monopoly over the generation and transmission of power in the West and the subordination of power to irrigation. The commission threatened to expand the bureau's power even further. It had concluded that since reclamation projects served the public interest by providing homes and keeping the price of food low, they should not have to meet any financial feasibility test at all. This frightened the Corps of Engineers and other agencies. Removing economic feasibility as a test for irrigation projects, they feared, would permit the Bureau of Reclamation to launch massive new irrigation projects in the West at a time when land in the East and South could be made productive at a far lower cost. The Corps also worried that the bureau would persuade Congress to extend the 160-acre limitation from irrigated lands to lands the Corps reclaimed by flood control.

The Cooke Commission's recommendations were moot. The 1952 campaign had promised to decentralize power and restore faith in private enterprise. When the Republican Party took power at the beginning of 1953, it scrapped Truman's twelfth-hour proposal to expand river basin authorities and, in the words of a leading historian of conservation policies, "immediately laid plans to cut every aspect of the . . . water development program. [The Republicans] appealed to eastern representatives of both parties who resented spending money on western projects."[41]

Nevertheless, the Republican call for economy and localism did not stall the federal water program; the momentum of the postwar boom in public works carried over into the 1950s and 1960s. In absolute terms, the Bureau of Reclamation's budget did decline during the 1950s, but the level of funding was still far above that of the 1930s. In 1940, Congress allocated $79 million to the bureau. That fell to $27 million in 1945 but reached $373 million in 1950. The Korean War and the change in administrations reduced the budget to $166 million in 1955, but by 1960 it was again on the rise, reaching $260 million. Thereafter, appropriations steadily climbed until they peaked at $490 million in 1975. As political scientist Daniel McCool has pointed out, the bureau formed an "iron triangle" with congressional committees and its clientele, an alliance that proved remarkably effective in securing new water projects and remarkably persistent.[42]

Many projects authorized in the 1950s and 1960s were staggering in scope.

For example, in 1968, at the height of the Vietnam War, Congress approved the most expensive water bill ever authorized, the omnibus Colorado River Basin Project Act. The cornerstone was the Central Arizona Project, a 300-mile-long aqueduct linking the Colorado River with Tucson via Phoenix. The water was pumped uphill more than 1,200 feet through some of the driest land in Arizona. The Colorado River Basin Project Act also included a dam in the Gila Wilderness of New Mexico, a canal from Lake Mead (Hoover Dam) to Las Vegas, and two major irrigation projects in Utah. The legislation represented horse-trading on a massive scale. Rural areas upstream attempted to reserve water for future agricultural use, while southwestern states moved to capture water for immediate urban as well as farm use. Although the project contained something for almost everyone, the increasing political clout of the lower basin states soon became evident. The Central Arizona Project was nearly finished when construction began on the first of five major diversions slated for the upper Colorado.[43]

Some of the boldest water projects were never built. The Pacific Southwest Water Plan (1964) included hydroelectric dams at either end of Grand Canyon National Park to take advantage of the 1,000-foot drop between Glen Canyon and Hoover Dam. The scheme also included diverting the wild rivers of far northern California to farmers in the San Joaquin Valley and building an aqueduct from the Columbia River to southern California. New irrigation projects would be strung along the latter canal like beads on a necklace, with Oregon and Nevada receiving most of the benefits. Budgetary constraints imposed by the war in Vietnam, as well as strong opposition from environmental organizations led by the Sierra Club, killed the plan by the end of the 1960s.

The grandest dream of the hydraulic age was the North American Water and Power Alliance, a project conceived by a Los Angeles Department of Water and Power engineer in the early 1950s and nominally supported by both the Bureau of Reclamation and the Corps of Engineers. It promised to reverse the flow of the Susitna, Copper, Tanana, and Yukon Rivers in Canada, turning them south into the United States with a massive reservoir and pump system. Most of the water would travel 2,000 miles through the Rocky Mountain Trench into the American Southwest. The project's cost was estimated at between $100 and $200 billion—more than the entire annual national budget in the 1950s. The cost, environmental risks, and opposition in Canada blocked the project. Luna Leopold, a professor of hydrology at the University of California, Berkeley, observed: "The environmental damage that would be caused by that damned thing can't even be described. It could cause as much harm as all of the dam-building we have done in a hundred years."[44]

As historian Donald Worster has pointed out, the Reclamation Bureau did not simply abandon the family farm ideal; in parts of the West—especially in California and Arizona—it contributed to its destruction by providing massive subsidies to corporate farms. When Congress gave the Reclamation Bureau authority to construct California's Central Valley Project in the mid-1930s—a project originally launched by the state—it did not empower the bureau to purchase and subdivide private land and resell it to small farmers, as did the Columbia Valley Project legislation of 1943. The 160-acre limitation applied, but it was easy to evade. In 1952, the Westlands Water District was formed in the San Joaquin Valley of California. The 600,000-acre district was even larger than the gigantic Imperial Irrigation District north of the California-Mexico border, and it served corporate landowners such as the Southern Pacific Railroad, Standard Oil, the Boston Ranch, and Southlake Farms. It was hoped that the mere act of irrigating the land would lead to the breakup of large holdings. Instead the project enriched the established landowners. Federal reclamation constituted a subsidy of $2,200 an acre, or more than $350,000 for a quarter section.[45]

The boom years of western water development came to an end in the 1970s. By that time, most runoff subject to storage had been claimed and the best dam sites had been taken. The 1976 collapse of Teton Dam on a tributary of the Snake River—a dam built by the Bureau of Reclamation on a porous foundation—suggested that the boom years were over. Most pending irrigation projects threatened to flood as much land as they irrigated; their cost was much higher than potential benefits. Equally important, the nascent environmental movement pointed to the high price westerners had paid for cheap water and power in the destruction of marshes and fisheries, altered wildlife habitats, and rampant urban growth.

Environmentalists saw clear limits to economic growth and worried about such problems as siltation, alkali buildup, and the poisoning of groundwater with herbicides and pesticides. Once water projects had been seen as a panacea that would allow the colonial West to make the giant leap from a pastoral and mining economy to agricultural and industrial independence. Now they were a bulwark of the agricultural status quo. Cheap water did exactly the opposite of what had been intended. By driving up the value of land and increasing its productivity, it reduced the likelihood that those large corporations that owned much of the best land in California and Arizona would sell it. And while these states constituted only a small part of the West, they were the most likely home to the family farm. There a small farm was capable of producing tremendous revenue from fruits and vegetables. There the economies of scale were far less compelling than in parts of the West that raised field crops.

Jimmy Carter has often been portrayed as the president who put an end to the era of giant water projects. But as Donald Worster points out, Congress had not authorized a single major project during the five years prior to Carter's term as president. In an age of inflation, tight budgets, crop surpluses, and rising concern for the environment, massive dams and canals no longer made sense to most Americans. Between 1945 and 1950, an average of 1 million acres a year was added to the West's stock of irrigable land. Surface water withdrawals peaked in 1955, and, thereafter, most new irrigation came on the High Plains of Texas, Oklahoma, New Mexico, Colorado, and Kansas. There about 80 percent of the water came from underground sources. The High Plains accounted for more than 40 percent of the new acres irrigated in the West between 1945 and 1974, and an even higher percentage in the 1960s and 1970s. This growth, too, had its limits. The deeper the well, the higher the cost. Moreover, center-pivot irrigation and "big gun" systems—designed to water lands with rough or irregular surfaces—imposed large additional expenses on would-be irrigators.[46]

By the 1980s, then, the federal government irrigated only 25 percent of the land watered in the West, and most of that land had been cultivated before the Reclamation Bureau provided it with cheap water. The federal role varied enormously from state to state. The bureau served four out of every five acres irrigated in Washington and three out of five in Idaho. On the other hand, it watered almost no land on the Great Plains, where the Department of Agriculture was much more powerful than in the Far West. Statistics can be misleading, however. While the government provided water to only 30 percent of California's irrigated farmland, that land was among the most productive and valuable in the world. Still, the Bureau of Reclamation probably had more impact on the rural West by building up cities that provided farmers with alternative job opportunities than by subsidizing agribusiness.[47]

Much of what happened in the West, of course, was beyond government control. Throughout the nation, the machine triumphed over the countryside as well as the city, the farm as well as the factory. Technology—remorseless, unrelenting, and ever more efficient—transformed American agriculture. It was technology that doubled the nation's production of wheat and tripled the production of potatoes during the three decades between 1940 and 1970, and it was technology that reduced the need for agricultural labor and made farming ever more expensive. The average tractor cost $1,000 or $1,500 in the late 1940s; by the 1970s, the largest models cost as much as $100,000. Such machines made it possible to plant or harvest 150 acres of many field crops in a single day.[48]

As capital costs rose, so did the size of farms. And as the size of farms increased, the rural population dwindled. From 1940 to 1960, the average-size American farm increased from 174 to 302 acres, and the number of farms fell from 6.1 to 3.7 million—with the sharpest decline in those of 100 acres or less. As late as 1945, labor represented 53 percent of the cost of doing business in agriculture; by 1960, that figure fell to 30 percent. Put another way, in 1940 one farm worker could feed eleven people, but in 1960, with the aid of high-powered tractors, hybrid corn, and herbicides, he fed twenty-six. Despite the shrinking farm population, in the mid-1960s the per capita earnings of farm residents—from all sources of income—were only 58 percent of those who lived in towns and cities. Nonfarm families had a median income 86 percent higher than that of farm families, and over 43 percent of farm families lived below the poverty level (compared with 17 percent of nonfarm families). Black families living in central cities larger than 1 million enjoyed higher incomes than the average for both black and white farm families.[49]

The dilemma facing agricultural planners was whether the United States should have more farmers, even though many of them could not earn a decent living by national standards, or fewer farmers who were more prosperous. The historian Vernon Carstensen put it well in 1956 when he observed: "Assuredly the family [farm] unit has been an effective and satisfactory way of operating a farm, but it is hard to see the special advantages enjoyed by the families on the two million farms with incomes of less than $720 a year if the farm is the only source of income. In fact, anyone uninfluenced by the sentimental litera-ture dealing with the virtues of the family farm might be tempted to speak of this group as comprising the rural slums." In the late 1970s, less than 20 percent of the nation's farmers earned more than 75 percent of the total farm income. And a majority of farm families earned more than half their annual income off the farm; they took jobs in town to make ends meet. To many critics of American agricultural policies, the message was obvious. If farmers could not afford to buy enough land or equipment to make a decent living, what could government do to help? The "farm bloc" had all but disappeared by the 1980s, and increasing numbers of urban politicians opposed price support pro-grams. Even some farmers wanted the federal government out of agriculture.[50]

Of course, there were many forces besides technology that undermined the small farm. Farmers, like other Americans, had a hard time countering the argument that bigger was better or, at least, more efficient. Moreover, the inter-state highway system, television, chain stores, branch banking, and countless other innovations obliterated the line between country and city, contributing to the decline of rural America. In the 1980s, many small towns near major pop-ulation centers flourished, while farm towns were dying. Farm work was widely perceived as drudgery, lacking in status as well as in economic, educational, and cultural opportunities.

This is not to suggest that western agriculture simply reflects the same patterns and problems as the rest of the nation. There were and are regional differences. Those differences are as much the legacy of the extractive western economy of the nineteenth and early twentieth centuries, compounded by re-gimes of western landownership and tenure, as the product of post–World War II federal water policies. Years ago, the great agricultural historian Paul Wallace Gates published an exhaustive series of essays demonstrating that rural society never really had a chance in California. For a variety of reasons, Mexican land grants prevented the emergence of the family farm and served as the foundation for agribusiness. Monopoly triumphed even before irrigation became a com-mon feature of California agriculture.[51] From the 1850s, the Golden State was as urbanized as many eastern states. Other western states where mining was the principal economic activity demonstrated similar characteristics. Oregon and

Utah were the only states in the Far West where the family farm became dominant. Western agriculture changed dramatically after World War II, but it had always been different. Irrigation and federal water policies contributed to those differences, but they did not create them.

NOTES

1. Gilbert Fite, *American Farmers: The New Minority* (Bloomington: Indiana University Press, 1981), 80, 88.

2. Alfred R. Golze, *Reclamation in the United States* (New York: McGraw-Hill, 1952) 51; Kenneth D. Frederick, "Irrigation and the Future of American Agriculture," in *The Future of American Agriculture as a Strategic Resource,* ed. Sandra S. Batie and Robert G. Healy (Washington, D.C.: Conservation Foundation, 1980), 157–58, 165; John Opie, *The Law of the Land: Two Hundred Years of American Farmland Policy* (Lincoln: University of Nebraska Press, 1987), 119.

3. Standard works on the Tennessee Valley Authority include Roy Talbert, *FDR's Utopian: Arthur Morgan of the TVA* (Jackson: University Press of Mississippi, 1987); Arthur E. Morgan, *The Making of TVA* (Buffalo, N.Y.: Prometheus Books, 1974); David Lilienthal, *TVA: Democracy on the March* (New York: Harper and Brothers, 1944); and Thomas K. McCraw, *Morgan vs. Lilienthal: The Feud Within the TVA* (Chicago: Loyola University Press, 1970).

4. Franklin D. Roosevelt hoped that the second regional authority would be created in the Columbia River valley. The TVA was just part of his overall effort to make rural life more attractive. Early in 1933, he informed George Norris that he wanted "one more bill which would allow us to spend $25 million this year to put 25,000 families on farms, at an average cost of $1,000 per family. It can be done." See Arthur M. Schlesinger, Jr., *The Coming of the New Deal* (Boston: Houghton Mifflin, 1959), 364. Also see Paul Conkin, *Tomorrow a New World: The New Deal Community Program* (New York: Da Capo Press, 1976); FDR to Congress, 3 June 1937, General Correspondence File, 1930–1945, Box 708, RG 115, National Archives, Washington, D.C. (hereafter NA-WDC); H. R. 7365 (Mansfield); S. 2555 (Norris); H. R. 7392 (Rankin, Miss.). The latter two bills were twins.

5. *Congressional Record,* Appendix, 23 October 1941, A5128.

6. Edward Skillin, Jr., "Missouri Valley Authority," *Commonweal* 42 (24 August 1945): 448; Ernest Kirschten, "From TVA to MVA," *Christian Century* 62 (30 May 1945): 649; *Chicago Sun,* 16 November 1944.

7. Elmo Richardson, *Dams, Parks and Politics: Resource Development and Preservation in the Truman-Eisenhower Era* (Lexington: University Press of Kentucky, 1973) 19–38; McAlister Coleman, "Rank-and-File Kilowatts," *Nation* 158 (29 January 1944): 127–29; Carey McWilliams, "Power Is the Banker," *Nation* 160 (9 June 1945): 645; Carey McWilliams, "The Northwest Needs a CVA," *Nation* 160 (2 June 1945): 622–23; Joe Miller, "The Growing Need for CVA," *New Republic* 120 (11 April 1949): 14–16.

8. Max Lerner, "Reaction Shows Its Hand in the Battle of the Valleys," *PM* (New York), 4 December 1944; Max Lerner, "The Battle of the Valleys, III," *PM,* 6 December 1944; "Bid for Power," *Business Week* (New York), 20 May 1944, 18.

9. Joseph Kinsey Howard, "Golden River: What's to Be Done About the Missouri?" *Harper's Magazine* 190 (May 1945): 513; *Post Dispatch* (St. Louis), 5 May 1944; Edward Skillin, Jr., "Missouri Valley Authority," *Commonweal* 42 (24 August 1945): 446–49; James E. Murray, "The Missouri River Authority," *Congressional Record,* Appendix, 10 April 1945, A1817–20.

10. Raymond Moley, "The Coming New Deal," *Wall Street Journal,* 22 November 1944.

11. Richardson, *Dams, Parks and Politics,* 73, 114.

12. Raymond Moley, "Death Sentence for State Government," *Newsweek* 34 (15 August 1949): 84; "Comments of L. Ward Bannister on S. 2226, Arkansas Valley Authority Act," 5 March 1942, General Correspondence File, 1930–1945, Box 708, RG 115, NA-WDC; "Resolutions Adopted by Conference of Governors of Western States," 7 February 1941, Box 709, NA-WDC.

13. James O'Sullivan (Secretary, Columbia Basin Commission) to John C. Page (Acting Commissioner of Reclamation), 11 March 1936, General Correspondence File, 1930–1945, Box 710, RG 115, NA-WDC; "A TVA for the Columbia Valley," *Business Week,* 23 April 1949, 91–93.

14. Commissioner of Reclamation Michael Straus to Assistant Secretary [William] Warne, 25 May 1951, Office of the Secretary, Central Classified Files, 1937–1953, Box 589, RG 48, NA-WDC; "Report of the Department of the Interior Reviewing the Report of the President's Water Resources Policy Commission," 26 June 1951, Box 585, NA-WDC; Walter Seymour to the secretary of the interior, 24 March 1950, Box 60, NA-WDC; Michael Straus, assistant secretary of the interior, to James E. Murray, 16 February 1945, General Correspondence File, 1930–1945, Box 714, RG 115, NA-WDC.

15. Richardson, *Dams, Parks and Politics,* 119.

16. William Droze, "TVA and the Ordinary Farmer," *Agricultural History* 53 (January 1979): 197, 200.

17. Donald J. Pisani, *From the Family Farm to Agribusiness: The Irrigation Crusade in California and the West, 1850–1931* (Berkeley: University of California Press, 1984); Donald J. Pisani, *To Reclaim a Divided West: Water, Law, and Public Policy, 1848–1902* (Albuquerque: University of New Mexico Press, 1992).

18. See National Resources Committee, Press Release 054, 11 March 1938, General Correspondence File, 1930–1945, Box 672, RG 115, NA-WDC. On the impact of the New Deal on the West, see Richard Lowitt, *The New Deal and the West* (Bloomington: Indiana University Press, 1984); Golze, *Reclamation in the United States,* 106–7, 219–20.

19. Judson King, "The Record of the REA," *Nation* 159 (8 July 1944): 41–43; "Power to Burn," *Fortune* 31 (February 1945): 140–44, 219; Sidney D. Larson, "The Meaning of Power Utilization," *Reclamation Era* 32 (December 1946): 266–67; Donald C. Swain, "The Bureau of Reclamation and the New Deal, 1933–1940," *Pacific Northwest Quarterly* 61 (July 1970): 146.

20. "Planning Considerations, Reclamation Projects, National Planning Board," memorandum dated 7 September 1933, Department of the Interior, Central Classified Files, 1907–1937, Box 517, RG 48, NA-WDC; Golze, *Reclamation in the United States,* 345–46, 381.

21. The 1902 law limited landowners within government irrigation projects to sufficient water to irrigate up to 160 acres, depending on the size of project farms designated by the secretary of the interior. This requirement was impossible to enforce, and many private landowners watered many times this amount; Lowitt, *The New Deal and the West,* 157–71.

22. *Congressional Record,* House, 5 May 1941 Appendix, A2236.

23. "State Principles for Rural Living," *Christian Century* 62 (5 September 1945): 1019–20.

24. Goodrich W. Lineweaver, "The Human Side," *Reclamation Era* 32 (May 1946): 110. On the family farm ideal in the Interior Department after World War II, see Charles Coate, " 'The New School of Thought': Reclamation and the Fair Deal, 1945–1953," *Journal of the West* 22 (April 1983): 58–63. In 1943, the National Resources Planning Board estimated that if the runoff of western streams was properly conserved the federal government could provide water to 12 million acres of land that suffered from chronic water shortages and another 22 million acres of virgin land. It would also increase the amount of power generated at government dams more than fivefold. The board estimated that the cost of fully developing the nation's water resources, for power as well as irrigation, would run at least $25 billion. This was a massive amount of money, but less than had been spent each year on the war. See *National Resources Development Report for 1943* (Washington, D.C.: Government Printing Office, 1943), 45–46; John R. Murdock, "Veterans—Here's Your Farm," *Reclamation Era* 32 (May 1946): 95–96; "Return of the Homesteader," *Reclamation Era* 32 (July 1946): 149–50; Orin Cassmore, "Gold Mine in the Sky," *Reclamation Era* 33 (February 1947): 25–29; Golze, *Reclamation in the United States,* 369–72.

25. "Columbia Basin Reclamation," *New Republic* 113 (13 August 1945): 175; "A Giant Revives," *Business Week,* 25 August 1945, 41–43; Rafe Gibbs, "Million-Acre Boom," *Collier's* 119 (1 March 1947): 14–15, 58; Richard L. Neuberger, "To the West, Water Is Life and Death," *New York Times Magazine,* 24 October 1948, 15, 60.

26. Paul C. Pitzer, *Grand Coulee: Harnessing a Dream* (Pullman: Washington State University Press, 1994), 280, 286–89, 295, 297–99, 308–10, 313, 327–29, 364–67.

27. On the concept of the "planned promise land," see Richard Lowitt, *The New Deal and the West,* 138–52; Pitzer, *Grand Coulee,* 367.

28. Henry Hart, *The Dark Missouri* (Madison: University of Wisconsin Press, 1957), 155–56, 159.

29. Leland Olds, "Recommendations to the President's Water Resources Policy Commission with Emphasis on Planning Conceptions and Procedure," speech to the Annual Meeting of the American Political Science Association, 28 August 1951, Department of the Interior, Office of the Secretary, Central Classified Files, 1937–1953, Box 589, RG 48, NA-WDC.

30. "Time to Modernize," *Reclamation Era* 32 (December 1946): 279–80.

31. "Irrigation Warfare Renewed," *Business Week,* 17 November 1945, 19–20; Stephen Raushenbush, "Memorandum for Assistant Commissioner Warne, Bureau of Reclamation," 7 September 1944, General Correspondence File, 1930–1945, Box 714, RG 115, NA-WDC.

32. "Facts Respecting Attempts at Cooperation Between the Bureau of Reclama-

tion and the Corps of Engineers," 17 October 1944, Records of the Office of the Secretary of the Interior, Program Staff Central Files, 1947–1953, Box 53, RG 48, NA-WDC.

33. For discussions of the infamous Pick-Sloan plan, see Marian E. Ridgeway, *The Missouri Basin's Pick-Sloan Plan* (Urbana: University of Illinois Press, 1955); Hart, *The Dark Missouri*, 120–35; and Marc Reisner, *Cadillac Desert: The American West and Its Disappearing Water* (New York: Viking, 1986), 176–221.

34. "Missouri Deal," *Business Week*, 18 November 1944, 20–21; *Chicago Sun*, 3 December 1944; Commission on the Organization of the Executive Branch of Government (Hoover Commission), *Organization and Policy in the Field of Natural Resources* (Washington, D.C.: Government Printing Office, 1949), Appendix L, 24.

35. Since 1902, the Reclamation Bureau hoped to extend its authority over reclamation to all the states and include drainage as well as irrigation. See Vernon D. Northrup to Secretary of the Interior Oscar L. Chapman, 2 June 1952, Office of the Secretary, Central Classified Files, 1937–1953, Box 590, RG 48, NA-WDC. Also see "Missouri Valley Project Goes On While Politicians Debate," *Business Week*, 20 March 1954, 120–25.

36. "Evaluation of Interagency Cooperation in the Development of Water Resources, with Special Emphasis on the Relations of the Bureau of Reclamation and the Corps of Engineers," 9 January 1950, Program Staff Central Files, 1947–1953, Box 60, RG 48, NA-WDC.

37. Samuel Trask Dana, *Forest and Range Policy: Its Development in the United States* (New York: McGraw-Hill, 1956), 333.

38. Press release, 3 January 1950, announcing the formation of the Water Resources Policy Commission, Office of the Secretary, Central Classified Files, 1937–1953, Box 588, RG 48, NA-WDC; "The President's Water Resources Policy Commission," *Land Economics* 26 (August 1950): 295–99. The preoccupation with comprehensive planning was partly a reflection of the cold war and the Korean War. As Secretary of the Interior Oscar Chapman noted in a 20 February 1950 letter to Director of the Bureau of the Budget Frank Pace, "the government must organize its responsibilities for resource conservation and development work on just as an effective basis as it does its responsibilities for national defense. . . . We are trying to carry out programs required by problems of today and tomorrow with administrative vehicles of yesterday." Program Staff Central Files, 1947–1953, Box 60, RG 48, NA-WDC.

39. "Draft of a Water Resources Act of 1951 Prepared by the President's Water Resources Policy Commission, February, 1951," Office of the Secretary, Central Classified Files, 1937–1953, Box 588, RG 48, NA-WDC; Leland Olds, "Recommendations of the President's Water Resources Policy Commission with Emphasis on Planning Conceptions and Procedure," 28 August 1951, Box 589, NA-WDC; *New York Times*, 18 February 1952.

40. Harry S. Truman, Message to Congress, 19 January 1953, *Congressional Record*, 83 Cong., 1st sess., Part I, 438–41.

41. Richardson, *Dams, Parks and Politics*, 26.

42. Daniel McCool, *Command of the Waters: Iron Triangles, Federal Water Development, and Indian Water* (Berkeley: University of California Press, 1987), 79.

43. Reisner, *Cadillac Desert*, 300–316.

44. Ibid., 13, 283–300, 510 (quote).

45. It should be noted that all the West was not California. Unlike most other western states, whose major streams were interstate, California's largest rivers emptied into the Pacific Ocean. Therefore, the Golden State had a much larger water supply for its own uncontested use. Equally important, California was wealthy enough to build its own hydraulic systems. Los Angeles, San Francisco, and Oakland had expended massive sums to tap the Colorado, the Owens, the Tuolumne, and the Mokelumne Rivers. And the 400-mile-long California aqueduct, approved as part of the State Water Plan in 1960, was funded by the state. This encouraged federal agencies to seek a financial partnership with California. For an excellent survey of water projects in California see Norris Hundley, Jr., *The Great Thirst: Californians and Water, 1970s–1990s* (Berkeley: University of California Press, 1992). Many other fine books on water have appeared in recent years, many of which are cited in the notes. Two of the best are Daniel Tyler, *The Last Water Hole in the West: The Colorado–Big Thompson Project and the Northern Colorado Water Conservancy District* (Niwot: University Press of Colorado, 1992); and James Earl Sherow, *Watering the Valley: Development Along the High Plains Arkansas River, 1870–1950* (Lawrence: University Press of Kansas, 1990); Donald Worster, *Rivers of Empire: Water, Aridity, and the Growth of the American West* (New York: Pantheon, 1985), 294.

46. Worster, *Rivers of Empire,* 308–11; Frederick, "Irrigation and the Future of American Agriculture," 160–63, 170.

47. Paul Wallace Gates, *History of Public Land Law Development* (New York: Arno Press, 1979), 692, 698.

48. Willard W. Cochrane, *The Development of American Agriculture: A Historical Analysis* (Minneapolis: University of Minnesota Press, 1979), 122–69; Gilbert C. Fite, *American Farmers: The New Minority* (Bloomington: Indiana University Press, 1981), 88, 111–12, 181–83. Irrigation farmers faced heavy additional costs. For example, one historian estimates that on a typical dryland farm of 320 acres on the Texas High Plains the average investment in equipment in the 1950s was $6,615. But on a 320-acre irrigated farm, the amount reached $18,000. See Donald E. Green, *Land of the Underground Rain: Irrigation on the Texas High Plains, 1910–1970* (Austin: University of Texas Press, 1973), 158.

49. Earl O. Heady et al., *Roots of the Farm Problem: Changing Technology, Changing Capital Use, Changing Labor Needs* (Ames: Iowa State University Press, 1965), 10, 12, 20–21; Leon H. Keyserling, *Agriculture and the Public Interest: Toward a New Farm Program* (Washington, D.C.: Conference for Economic Progress, 1965), 7, 8, 12; Thomas R. Ford, "Priorities of Rural Welfare," in *The 70's: Challenge and Opportunity* (Ames: Iowa State University Press, 1970).

50. Vernon Carstensen, "The Changing Nature of the American Farm," *Current History* 31 (September 1956): 138; Fite, *American Farmers,* 143, 146, 180.

51. Gates's essays, published from the late 1950s to the 1970s, have been collected in *Land and Law in California: Essays on Land Policies* (Ames: Iowa State University Press, 1991). Also see Donald J. Pisani, "Land Monopoly in Nineteenth-Century California," *Agricultural History* 65 (Fall 1991): 15–37.

7

Migrant and Seasonal Farm Labor in the Far West

Anne B. W. Effland

Most Americans are familiar with the descriptions of Dust Bowl refugees working as migrant farm laborers in California during the 1930s from John Steinbeck's *The Grapes of Wrath.* In some ways the story of migrant and seasonal farmworkers in the West has changed little since Steinbeck's time. Migrant and seasonal farmworkers remain among the poorest workers in the West, with little power to influence their incomes or the conditions under which they work. Yet in other respects, the story has changed substantially during the last half century, reflecting the revolutionary changes in agriculture during this period, as well as political and demographic developments that have altered the world in which migrant and seasonal farm laborers work and live. If anyone is to understand the history of the rural West in the twentieth century, they must know about the regional and ethnic differences of farmworkers, as well as the laws and programs that affect their lives and those of the growers, in addition to the effects of technological change and immigration.

Definitions of migrant and seasonal farmworkers vary widely. Seasonal farmworkers are generally considered to be employed in farm work for only part of the year, ranging from less than six months to as many as 250 days. Casual farm laborers, who do farm work for only a few days or weeks a year, may even be considered seasonal in some cases. Migrant farmworkers range from those who stay away from home for most of the year to do farm work to those who do farm work on a series of farms in different counties or states during a season but are still able to return home each night. Nearly all migrant farmworkers are seasonal farmworkers, but many seasonal farmworkers are not migrants.

Seasonal hired labor has been part of agriculture in the West almost from the earliest Anglo settlement. Particularly in California, farms became large enough by the 1870s to require seasonal crews for planting, cultivating, and harvesting of wheat and such specialty crops as fruits, nuts, and hops. By the early twentieth century, increasing specialty crop production in the Pacific Northwest added to the demand for seasonal labor, as did widespread development of irrigation throughout the West, which opened new land to large-scale agriculture. Continued urbanization and understanding of the nutritional value of fruits and vegetables have also combined to steadily increase demand for specialty crops over the century and, consequently, demand for seasonal farm labor.

Farm labor in the West has been drawn from a succession of ethnic and racial groups. Early efforts to acquire needed seasonal farm labor focused on imported Chinese and, following the Chinese Exclusion Act of 1882, Japanese workers. By the early twentieth century, Mexican and Filipino workers became the preferred source, supplementing local workers and transient single men. In parts of California, Sikh workers from India added to the mix. Government-facilitated importation of Mexicans began during World War I, spurred by fears of wartime farm labor shortages and authorized by an exemption for temporary foreign agricultural workers in the Immigration Act of 1917. Continued informally after the wartime exemption ended in 1921, the process was reversed in the 1930s, when the onset of the Great Depression brought a large pool of domestic workers from among refugees of the Dust Bowl. Mexicans began to be seen as competition for these domestic workers as the economy worsened in the United States, and they were forcibly deported throughout the decade.

By 1942, however, as the United States entered World War II, wartime production jobs and military service became increasingly available to domestic farmworkers. A new farm labor crisis once again altered the makeup of migrant and seasonal agricultural labor in the West. Authorization of renewed large-scale emergency farm labor importation from Mexico set the stage for a long-term transition to the use of Mexican immigrant labor. Special legislation in 1943 provided for an emergency labor supply program through the end of the war, and amendments to that legislation extended the program to 1947 for the purpose of postwar adjustments. Growers in the western states of California, Arizona, Washington, Oregon, Idaho, Nevada, and Utah used the largest share of temporary Mexican farmworkers during the war emergency, accounting for 75 percent of the total contracted from 1943 to 1947 (172,342 out of 228,774). The remaining Mexican farmworkers (56,432) were divided among fifteen Great Plains and midwestern states.[1]

Farm employers, particularly in the Southwest, argued their continuing postwar need for access to imported Mexican labor so effectively that recruitment continued after 1947 through a special international agreement. Under this agreement, individual growers secured workers directly from Mexico, without the involvement of the United States that had been required under the wartime program. Mexican government concerns about conditions for workers under these individual agreements, coupled with a renewed fear of wartime

labor shortages following the outbreak of the Korean War, led to the renegoti-
ation of a formal government-to-government agreement.

Under the new agreement, established under Public Law 78 and more
informally known as the *bracero program*, temporary employment of Mexican
agricultural workers increased dramatically. The greatest single-year use of
temporary Mexican agricultural workers under the World War II emergency
program had been 62,170 in 1944. During the individual recruitment period of
1948–50, the annual number of temporary workers rose as high as 107,000 in
1949. In the first year under Public Law 78, 192,000 temporary Mexican farmworkers entered the United States. That number rose to a peak of 445,197 in
1956 and did not again fall below the 1951 number until 1963, one year before
the program ended.[2]

The larger numbers of the 1951–64 program partly compensated for the
reduced supply of domestic labor created by a postwar economy that offered at
least the expectation of better wages and working conditions for American
workers outside agriculture. The high numbers also reflected federal immigration policy. Many supporters of Public Law 78 recommended it as a method for
stemming the rising tide of illegal immigration from Mexico by creating a legal
means for Mexicans to enter the United States for agricultural employment.
Using the program to reduce illegal immigration required certification of sufficiently large numbers of Mexican nationals to work in the United States to
remove the incentive for illegal entry.

Provision of legal means of temporary entry to the United States, however,
eventually encouraged further immigration of Mexicans, both by providing
direct experience of the opportunities to be found in the American economy
and by establishing personal relationships between Mexican immigrant workers
and particular employers and communities. Many temporary workers simply
did not return to Mexico and remained in the United States as undocumented
workers, serving as a conduit for family and friends to enter the United States
as well. Others returned according to their contracts but continued to migrate
annually to the United States for work or eventually settled in the communities
where they had found seasonal employment.

From its inception, Public Law 78 had been unpopular among western
advocates for domestic migrant and seasonal farmworkers. Mexican American
farmworkers in California and Arizona, in particular, found themselves competing for work with imported Mexican workers. The availability of this govern-
ment-sponsored labor supply eliminated the need to increase wages or improve
working conditions to attract domestic labor. Moreover, imported workers, despite contract guarantees, had little recourse against their employers if wages
and working conditions did not meet their expectations, providing further opportunity for employers to reduce their labor costs. Some domestic farmworkers simply left for the cities; others traveled as migrants to northern states,
where recruitment and transportation expenses made imported Mexican work-

ers less attractive. Still others, however, with the support and assistance of the labor movement, advocates for the poor, and Chicano and other community organizations, agitated for repeal of the bracero program. Following a protracted and bitter political battle between traditional agricultural powers in Congress and the U.S. Department of Agriculture (USDA) on one side and representatives of a rising urban sympathy for the plight of the rural poor in Congress and the Department of Labor on the other, the program ended in 1964.

Large western growers, however, had become accustomed to Mexican labor both through their participation in the labor importation programs and as a result of rapidly increasing numbers of Mexican and Mexican American farmworkers available in the postwar period. Gradually these workers came to dominate seasonal employment in western agriculture. In the Pacific Northwest (Washington, Oregon, Idaho, and northern Utah and Nevada), migrant Mexicans and Mexican Americans traveling from the Southwest made up most of this labor supply. In the Southwest (California, Arizona, and southern Nevada and Utah), Mexican labor might be either local Mexican American farmworkers or immigrant Mexican farmworkers, documented and undocumented.

Analyzing the ethnic makeup of the population of migrant and seasonal farm labor is not an easy task. Researchers who have attempted to collect data on these workers confront the difficulties of surveying a workforce that is transient, moving at least from job to job if not from residence to residence, and employed sporadically during the year. Many employer surveys count workers more than once, since employees are reported by each farmer who hired them. These surveys, however, miss workers if they are taken at slack times of year for seasonal farm work. Workers living in unconventional housing, or living outside the country during the survey period, are less likely to be counted. Moreover, undocumented workers tend to avoid contact with survey enumerators because of their illegal status and many surveys have not been effective at reaching non-English-speaking workers. Finally, many surveys of farmworkers include all hired farm labor, not just migrant and seasonal workers, making it difficult to identify differences in wages and demographic characteristics between year-round hired hands and short-term, transient harvest workers.[3]

Some trends are apparent, however, despite the limitations of the data. The Hired Farm Working Force surveys conducted by the Census Bureau for the USDA from 1945 to 1987, for example, show that the hired farm labor force in the West has increased as a proportion of the national hired farm labor force. Those surveys also indicate that relatively few African Americans have been hired as farmworkers in the West, in contrast to the Southeast, and that the western hired farm labor force has became progressively more Hispanic over time.

While most national surveys have not been able to provide much detail on the migrant and seasonal farm labor force in the West, case studies offer a close

Migrant workers have been important to western agriculture since the nineteenth century. Most migrant or seasonal workers, however, have been Mexicans or Mexican Americans. Few African Americans have followed the western harvests. In 1943, these black women picked peas in a thistle-laden field in Montana. *Courtesy, Montana State University.*

look at these farmworkers in particular times and places. For example, in 1948, the USDA's Bureau of Agricultural Economics joined with the Institute of Industrial Relations of the University of California to survey the agricultural labor force, including both seasonal and year-round hired workers, in the San Joaquin Valley of California. Using direct interviews with a representative sample of farmworkers, they hoped to learn about the characteristics of the workforce, their employment mix of farm and nonfarm work over a season, and how much they moved from place to place to find work. Only 9 percent of the sample held year-round paid farm jobs; the remaining 91 percent worked at seasonal farm work or at a combination of farm and nonfarm work.[4]

Within the group interviewed, 15 percent were Latin American, 5 percent African American, 3 percent Filipino, and the remainder, 77 percent, Anglo-American, primarily from Oklahoma, Texas, Arkansas, and Missouri. Only 4 of the 393 Anglo-Americans in the sample had been born in California, compared with 20 percent of the Latin Americans. An additional 40 percent of the Latin Americans had come from the southwestern states of Texas, New Mexico, and Arizona, while 30 percent had come from Mexico. The African Americans had come from the same states as the Anglo-Americans. The largest percentage of Latin Americans (30 percent) had come to California before 1929, compared with Anglo-Americans, nearly all of whom had arrived between 1935 and 1945. Most of the African Americans had not come to the state until 1944.

Among the workers interviewed for this study, 30 percent lived in single-family dwellings, and most of these either owned or were buying their homes. Of the 70 percent living in grower, government, or labor contractor camps, one-third considered their mobile or temporary dwellings their homes. Most of the remainder identified their homes as the family home place in the southern Plains states which they visited annually, often during the slack season. A few identified home as Mexico or other parts of California and the Pacific Northwest.

The number of days farmworkers were employed per year varied. The small percentage of year-round workers averaged 263 days of farm work per year, but at the other extreme, those workers employed just for the harvest found only an average of 124 days of work per year. Migrancy, race or nationality, age, and size of a worker's household also affected average days of work, but the range of averages for all heads of households fell between 122 and 186 days per year. Since 50 to 60 percent of these farmworkers were in the labor market for 300 days a year or more, these averages of days worked reflect a good deal of involuntary unemployment. Forty percent of surveyed workers, however, did some nonfarm work during the year, generally construction, oil-field labor, and truck driving, and for 18 percent of those workers, nonfarm work had been their primary employment.

San Joaquin Valley farmworkers followed a wide range of crops in search of work. Workers could begin their year in January, harvesting oranges and cotton either in the southern valley counties or in Arizona. The pea harvest stretched from February to May, after which cherries, apricots, and potatoes became available. For those workers willing to travel north, cherries, berries, beans, and pears provided harvest jobs through the summer in Oregon and Washington. Hops, apples, and olives then matured in September, October, and November in Washington, Oregon, and Montana, while grapes, prunes, tomatoes, and apples demanded workers in California. The year ended (or began again) in December with oranges and cotton.

An interview-based survey of seasonal agricultural workers in California, part of the National Agricultural Workers Survey commissioned by the Department of Labor in response to the Immigration Reform and Control Act of 1986, offers a comparative picture of seasonal farm labor in California in 1990. From October 1989 to October 1991, researchers interviewed 1,844 seasonal farmworkers employed as field workers on perishable crop farms in California. Interviewers found that over 80 percent had been born in Mexico, although these Mexican-born workers had been in the United States an average of twelve years. Nearly 90 percent of California seasonal farmworkers spoke Spanish as their native language, and only a little more than 10 percent spoke English fluently. Hispanics, including Mexicans, made up over 90 percent of the seasonal farm workforce; of the remaining 10 percent, 9 percent were Asian and only 1 percent were white. Two-thirds of farmworkers had completed seven or fewer years of formal schooling, but one-third, drawn from all education levels, had participated in adult education. Parents with children made up more than half the workforce.[5]

Five out of six seasonal farmworkers in California were employed on fruit, nut, or vegetable farms, and half worked in harvest jobs. One-third reported some form of health insurance coverage through their farm jobs, but fewer than 20 percent lived in employer-provided housing. The average California seasonal farmworkers spent two-thirds of the year working in seasonal agricultural work and one-third unemployed. Nearly half of these workers spent part of their unemployed time out of the country. Only 15 percent of farmworkers found jobs outside seasonal farm work for part of the year, but those who did averaged between four and five months at those jobs. Although 71 percent of California farmworkers wanted to do more seasonal farm work, 78 percent would not leave home overnight to find that work, a reflection of the largely nonmigratory structure of California's seasonal farm labor market. Almost half of all California seasonal farmworker families had incomes below the poverty level, even with more than one worker in a family, yet only one in eight received public assistance.

Several case studies over time in the Pacific Northwest reveal both similarities and differences with the California story. In 1959, for example, the Oregon Inter-Agency Committee on Agricultural Labor surveyed migrant farmworkers in Oregon to determine the need for legislation regulating working and living conditions. Based on their interviews, the committee estimated Hispanic American workers made up between 25 and 30 percent of Oregon's migrant farm labor force. The committee described Anglo-American single men and families separately from Hispanic American single men and families, comparing their characteristics and experiences.[6]

According to the committee's survey, between 80 and 90 percent of migrant farmworkers, both Anglo and Hispanic, averaged eight to ten months a year working in Oregon. Anglo-American families noted that in addition to work in Oregon beans, berries, and cherries, they had worked in California and Arizona cotton, California peaches, and Washington apples over the migrant season. Hispanic American families had worked in Texas, Arizona, and California cotton and Idaho potatoes and onions, as well as Oregon sugar beets, beans, berries, and potatoes. Interviewers found Anglo-Americans came primarily from California, Oregon, and Oklahoma. They spent winters, however, wherever work was available, most often in Oregon, California, and Arizona. Hispanic Americans usually came from California and Mexico. Unlike the Anglo-Americans, they chose their winter residence more often on the basis of proximity to friends and family rather than the availability of work.

Hispanic American singles and families generally earned more than Anglo-Americans from seasonal farm work, but their advantage disappeared with

Prior to the widespread adoption of the sugar beet harvester during the 1950s, workers cut the tops off the beets after a machine had lifted them from the soil to facilitate loading and transport to the processing plants. In 1945, migrant workers provided this labor in Montana. *Courtesy, Montana State University.*

lower earnings during the winter months. While 87 percent of Anglo-American families provided their own transportation in family cars to Oregon, only 60 percent of Hispanic Americans could do so. About 17 percent of both Anglo and Hispanic families owned or were buying houses in their home communities. Most (41 percent) worked as seasonal farm laborers because they could not find other work. Many (34 percent of Anglo-Americans and 37 percent of Hispanic Americans) took the work because they could make more money at it than at other jobs, particularly when family members' wages were counted. Still others (24 percent) preferred farm work because they could work outdoors and were free to leave and move as they pleased.

One-room cabins typified housing for farm work for 75 percent of all migrants, both families and single groups. A substantial additional number of both Anglo and Hispanic migrants lived in tents, cars, and in the open. Only 17 percent of all migrants had some kind of medical care coverage, and immunization levels were well below the average for nonmigrant residents of Oregon. Although Anglo-American adults had educational levels well above those of Hispanic American adults, neither reached the average education for the general population. Among children attending school, Anglo-American migrant children attended more regularly than Hispanic American migrant children, and more Anglo migrant children were expected to complete at least ten grades. A higher proportion of Anglo-American children, however, had quit school completely.

Details about conditions for a group of migrant farmworkers in the same Pacific Northwest area during the 1970s and 1980s were recorded by Toby Sonneman, a college graduate who turned to fruit picking for work in the early 1970s. The people with whom Sonneman traveled were Anglo, children of the Dust Bowl refugees who migrated to the West Coast in the 1930s. They still called themselves Okies and Arkies (derived from their Dust Bowl origins in Oklahoma and Arkansas) and maintained ties with family in the southern Plains, considering that region their home. Nearly all of them had been raised as migrants on the same "runs," returning with their parents year after year, until they married, usually into other migrant families, and began traveling with their own children. Parents and children worked together in the fruit orchards of the Pacific Northwest from April to November and picked citrus in Florida, Texas, and Arizona through the winter, following migration routes established by an earlier generation.[7]

For the migrants Sonneman met, specialization in fruit picking had been a recent development, occurring since the 1960s. Many of their parents had worked in cotton and other row crops but had seen work become dominated by Mexican workers, initiated by the bracero contracts of the 1950s, they believed. By the 1970s, a third generation had started families on the road, but few expected them to finish their working life picking fruit. These workers traveled because they had been raised to a seasonal life on the road, but they sensed that their migrant way of life was dying out. They explained that Mexican nationals willing to work for lower wages had begun taking even the fruit-picking jobs, changing the character of life in the camps and orchards and making the work too unprofitable to continue. Even within the second generation, many had other trades they sometimes utilized during the winter when they could not find agricultural work. By the end of the 1980s, nearly all of Sonneman's friends had settled in permanent homes, working at full-time, nonagricultural jobs.

In 1991, thirty years after the Oregon committee report, the Walla Walla, Washington, *Union-Bulletin* hired Isabel Valle, a freelance journalist, to live and work with a Mexican American farmworker family on their annual migration from their home in southern Texas to Washington and Oregon. The family traveled not because they were attached to a migrant lifestyle but because family members had no work during the winter months in Texas. They found work in fruit and vegetable crops, including potatoes, tomatoes, onions, asparagus, raspberries, and apples, between March and October along a route they had followed for years. The family traveled with the three youngest of their thirteen children, but only the father and fifteen-year-old son worked regularly in the fields. The younger children, aged ten and seven, attended local schools during the year and special migrant centers during summer months to maintain their educational progress. The older son worked in the fields only when he had to leave his part-time job at a local recreational center, secured through an employment training program, because of the family's movement in search of work for the father. That son later returned to Texas ahead of the rest of the family to attend high school in his home community, a priority for the family. The mother of the family primarily cared for the younger children, kept up the living quarters, bought groceries, and generally tended to the family's household needs.[8]

The family lived in local housing, ranging from grower-provided trailers to state-assisted rental housing, all of relatively good quality. They found regular medical care available while they traveled, deliberately scheduling children's annual physicals for the summer months at health clinics in Washington and Oregon. Although they preferred to find work at home in Texas, they anticipated continuing migrant farm work for the foreseeable future, until employment opportunities expanded in south Texas. Some of their older children, who had all graduated from high school, continued to travel doing farm work, both because there were so few jobs at home and because they enjoyed the life, much like the second-generation Anglo farmworkers.

These case studies reflect the economic insecurity of seasonal farm work but at the same time suggest that a relatively small number of seasonal farmworker families have looked to general assistance programs for aid. Other forms of specialized government social services, however, have helped to improve conditions. Such programs, directed at migrant and seasonal farmworkers, arose during the 1960s in the context of public concern for civil rights and poverty. Although efforts to improve working conditions through agricultural labor laws brought important protections during the same period, for many farmworkers, particularly migrant farmworker families, the programs that offered health care, improved housing and sanitation, educational opportunities, and day care made the most obvious changes in their lives.

The earliest of these assistance programs provided limited health care to migrant farmworkers by funding primary-care clinics established in areas of heavy migrant travel or in places where migrant farmworkers might have settled recently or lived during the off-season. Authorized by the Migrant Health Act in 1962, these health clinics became one of the most stable and accepted programs provided solely to migrant farm labor. Much wider-ranging in the scope of programs authorized, the 1964 Economic Opportunity Act, the cornerstone of the War on Poverty, included a title specifically funding programs to assist migrant and seasonal farmworkers. The only group targeted by the poverty programs based on occupation rather than income, migrant and seasonal farmworker programs served both current farmworkers and those recently settled and trying to enter other occupations.

Projects encouraged by the Office of Economic Opportunity (OEO) migrant program included rest camps on migrant routes, experimental migrant camp designs and field sanitation facilities, self-help housing, and day care and summer schools for children and adults. Educational programs ranged from preschool adjustment to adult basic literacy, job training and job-search methods, and personal and community relations. In communities in California and Texas that served as "permanent" homes for many migrants working seasonally in western agriculture, programs authorized by the Community Action section of the OEO provided leadership opportunities and social and educational services similar to those offered along the migrant work routes. California received the largest single OEO grant in 1965: $3,485,623 to fund the construction of 1,000 mobile housing units on state land.[9]

In some cases, OEO grants funded the actual services offered to farmworkers. In other cases, OEO grant recipients employed their staffs in coordinating access to other funds available to migrants through the Migrant Health Act and through special educational programs authorized in the Elementary and Secondary Education Act of 1965, designed to provide federal support for educating disadvantaged children. Coordination with other federal educational, job-training, employment, health, nutrition, and housing programs for which migrants might be eligible based on their incomes, rather than simply their occupation, allowed migrant programs to offer as comprehensive an array of programs as possible. Despite the perennial inadequacy of funding and the problems of reaching the eligible populations, advocates of federal assistance for migrant and seasonal farmworkers found many reasons to support the OEO migrant programs as a first step in alleviating the worst effects of the migrant lifestyle.

Among the most valuable aspects of the OEO programs were the opportunities they offered to farmworkers for leadership and experience in working with government and private assistance agencies. For many migrants, work with these programs offered a way out of seasonal agricultural jobs, both through formal educational assistance and through direct employment opportunities, as these community-based programs tried to include farmworkers within their own administrative and employment structures. All OEO community action programs were required to adhere to the concept of "maximum feasible participation," in which members of the clientele population—in this case migrants— served on policy-making boards and worked as aides in whatever programs operated in their areas. Beginning in 1966, agencies receiving OEO program funds had to appoint migrant farmworkers, or at least former migrants, to one-third of the seats on their boards of directors to comply with this directive. In addition, migrant aides, often mothers of children enrolled in day care and summer school programs, were to make up as much as possible of the nonprofessional staff of local programs.

Most of these programs remained essentially the same throughout the 1970s and 1980s. Additional funding and expansion of coverage marked the success of migrant assistance programs, however, and new programs also joined the original War on Poverty initiatives over time. In 1977, for example, the rural legal services program of the Legal Services Corporation began to provide free legal aid to farmworkers. Some legal services operations, notably California Rural Legal Services, expanded beyond the originally envisioned family and small-claims cases, however, to initiate class-action lawsuits against employers and government agencies for failure to comply with laws protecting farmworkers from such conditions as poor housing, lack of sanitary facilities, unsafe work environments, unfair withholding of wages, inadequate services, and discrimination. Free legal services became perhaps the most controversial of government migrant and seasonal farmworker assistance programs.

Equally controversial, arising out of the battle to end the bracero program and growing community empowerment movements of the 1960s, came perhaps the most notable event in the story of migrant and seasonal farm labor in the West since 1940: the United Farm Workers (UFW) organizing campaign led by Cesar Chavez. Labor organizers had attempted to unionize farmworkers in the West, particularly in California, periodically throughout the twentieth century, generally without much success. California growers maintained powerful associations dedicated to resisting organizing efforts by farmworkers and almost always found willing support from state authorities to enforce their control over the labor supply. Strikes led by the socialist Industrial Workers of the World in 1913 and the Communist-led United Cannery and Packinghouse Workers of the 1930s ended in the face of such enforcement. Further sporadic strike efforts under the leadership of the National Agricultural Workers Union in the 1940s and 1950s met the same resolute response from growers and government.[10]

Other problems confronted organizers trying to work with seasonal farmworkers during this period. Most of these farmworkers migrated frequently to new locations and depended on employers for housing and sometimes credit in each new community. Labor organizers had difficulty recruiting a stable core of workers who were independent enough of their employers to sustain themselves during lengthy strikes. By the 1960s, however, those conditions had changed, at least in the southern and central California agricultural valleys where Chavez worked. A relatively stable community of seasonal agricultural workers had evolved there, in which farmworkers moved only short distances from home, perhaps not even staying away overnight, to find work. Living in settled communities, workers could establish and build on long-term relationships with each other and with growers.

Cesar Chavez also developed a new organizing strategy for the UFW, one tailored to the political climate of the 1960s that seemed to hold great promise for achieving lasting success. That strategy consisted of allying the community organizations that fostered solidarity and cooperation among the farmworkers with the movements for empowerment of the poor and minorities that were rising out of the civil rights movement and antipoverty initiatives. Chavez built on the publicity surrounding the poverty of American farmworkers that politicians and journalists had been cultivating since the end of the 1950s. Such publicity had evoked compassion and a commitment to ending poverty among farmworkers. At the same time, the civil rights movement in the South had attuned Americans to the need for direct action and mass demonstrations to gain political power for traditionally powerless groups. Thus, when the Farmworkers Association (the predecessor organization to the UFW) began strike activity against grape growers in 1965, the movement could rely both on sympathy for the justice of their cause and acceptance of nonviolent, mass demonstration tactics to mobilize liberal support for farm labor unionization.

Perhaps the most effective use of the external connections cultivated by Chavez came in the mobilization of the public behind the grape boycotts of the late 1960s. Throwing most of the union's resources into the boycott, organizers called on the support of other unionized workers to refuse to handle shipments of California table grapes, appealed to grocery store owners to refuse to stock the grapes, and asked consumers to refuse to either buy California grapes or shop in stores that continued to sell those grapes. The strategy brought success in little more than a year, resulting in contracts for grape workers that recognized the union, established union hiring and grievance procedures, limited pesticide use, forced rehiring of strikers and contributions to a union health fund, and instituted a twenty-five-cent-per-hour raise.

The subsequent passage in 1974 of an Agricultural Labor Relations Act in the California legislature assisted the UFW efforts to secure better wages and working conditions for farmworkers by guaranteeing the UFW's right to organize and represent workers in collective bargaining with growers. The Agricultural Labor Relations Board (ALRB), charged with adjudicating cases based on California's labor relations law, seemed to work to the advantage of the UFW for its first six years, during the tenure of Democratic Governor Edmund (Jerry) Brown, Jr., who supported collective bargaining for farmworkers. After the election of Republican Governor George Deukmejian in 1982, the political climate swung toward support of employers; as he made more conservative appointments to the ALRB, decisions began to hinder UFW efforts rather than support them.

The UFW had reached the high point of its success in organizing and bargaining for California farmworkers by 1973, when it claimed 67,000 members and held 180 contracts covering 40,000 jobs. By 1987, membership hovered somewhere between 6,000 and 10,000, and the union held approximately sixty contracts covering only 5,000 jobs. Competition from other unions, including the Teamsters, with whom the UFW had violent confrontations and jurisdictional battles throughout the early 1970s, reduced the UFW's effectiveness. As Chavez increasingly sought political solutions for farmworker problems, traditional organizing work slowed and the membership ranks of the union suffered. Meanwhile, many farms went out of business, or changed ownership and crop mixes, shedding union contracts in the process. Constant replenishment of the farm labor supply through immigration also undermined the UFW's ability to establish stable labor relations with growers, as more and more growers turned to labor contractors to simplify their labor relations and reduce their record keeping, as well as to avoid legal responsibility for the hiring of undocumented workers.[11]

During the same period that California experimented with agricultural labor relations legislation in response to successful union organizing, the federal government began to consider covering migrant and seasonal farmworkers under labor laws as well. Most industrial workers had been protected by laws prescribing minimum wages and maximum hours, restricting child labor, protecting health and safety, providing unemployment, old-age, and disability insurance, and guaranteeing the right to collective bargaining since the New Deal of the 1930s. Agricultural workers did not begin to receive such protections until the 1960s, and many exemptions for agricultural employers continued into the 1990s. Amendments to the Social Security Act in 1950 extended old-age, survivors, and disability insurance to most farmworkers, but the Fair Labor Standards Act provisions for a minimum wage and restrictions on child labor did not include farmworkers until 1966, and then only on larger farms. The Occupational Safety and Health Act of 1970 did include enforcement provisions for farm labor housing and later added field sanitation and hazard communication standards, and unemployment compensation coverage began for farmworkers on larger operations in 1976. All of these laws have been expanded and modified since their initial passage, but most share one general characteristic: they apply only to larger farms with a threshold level based on number of employees, number of man-days of labor, or expenditures for farm labor.[12]

California and other western states passed their own legislation as well, in some cases to cover farm labor in areas not addressed by federal laws, particularly workers' compensation, and in other cases to create regulations more stringent than federal standards. By 1965, most states covered agricultural workers to some degree under child labor, workers' compensation, minimum wage, wage payment, labor relations, unemployment insurance, and disability insurance laws. Many states also provided special protections for migrant farmworkers, including regulation of labor contractors, transportation, labor camps, and field sanitation. Among western states, California and Oregon provided for regulating contractors, transportation, labor camps, and field sanitation. Nevada regulated labor contractors and labor camps. Arizona, Idaho, and Washington regulated only farm labor camps. Only Utah had no specific laws protecting migrant farm labor. All western states except Washington included agricultural work in their child labor laws. Washington and Oregon covered all agricultural laborers under workers' compensation; Arizona covered farm employees working with machinery. California, Oregon, Utah, and Washington allowed for administrative orders to set minimum wages in agriculture for women and children. Arizona, California, Idaho, Nevada, Oregon, and Washington protected farmworkers under wage payment laws, and California, Nevada, Oregon, and Washington also included farmworkers in wage collection (back wages) laws. In 1965, no western states included farmworkers under labor relations laws or required unemployment insurance for farmworkers (although they did allow for voluntary coverage with approval of the state). Only California covered farmworkers under its temporary disability insurance law.[13]

By 1988, all seven western states provided at least some minimum wage and maximum hour protection for children and required school attendance. Oregon, Nevada, and California also included adult agricultural workers in minimum wage legislation, and both California and Nevada included agricultural workers under maximum hour laws. All seven states provided unemployment insurance coverage, and all but Idaho and Nevada provided workers' compensation for agricultural workers. Moreover, all but Idaho passed farm labor housing standards or included farmworker housing under general employee housing standards. Only Idaho did not include some coverage for agricultural labor under workplace safety laws, and only Nevada did not require minimum sanitation facilities at field work sites. Arizona, California, and Washington also had passed laws prohibiting use of the short-handled hoe, a field tool that required working in a stooped position. Both a health concern and a matter of worker dignity, the short-handled hoe had become a symbol of arbitrary work requirements by farm employers, and its prohibition became a symbol of farmworker empowerment. These same three states also passed labor relations laws protecting and regulating collective bargaining rights for farmworkers. Additional protection for farmworkers came with farm labor contractor regulation, passed by all seven states either as special agricultural labor contractor legislation or as part of general employment agent licensing law.[14]

Due to the transient and intermittent nature of much seasonal farm labor, many farmworkers traditionally worked in crews organized by a crew leader who secured work for the group. Small crews consisted primarily of extended family members; larger crews, particularly in the large-scale agricultural operations of the Southwest, were recruited from among unrelated individuals and families who responded to informal information about available work. Crew leaders provided a structure to the labor market, offering the farm employers a single individual with whom to arrange conditions for work and on whom to rely for supervision of the crew, both in the field and in camps. Workers without their own employer contacts, or without English-language skills or proper documentation, could find work by joining a crew.

The crew leader system, however, offered many opportunities for abuse. Since crew leaders distributed work assignments and wages, provided transportation to jobs, and extended credit until paychecks came in, they held tremendous power over their crew members. Stories of abuse abounded by the mid-1960s, leading to passage of the first federal crew leader registration legislation, the Farm Labor Contractor Registration Act of 1964. The legislation required farm labor crew leaders to register with the United States Department of Labor and to follow regulations that protected workers against arbitrary withholding of wages, misleading recruitment tactics, and unsafe transportation. The Migrant and Seasonal Agricultural Worker Protection Act of 1983 superseded the 1964 legislation and added new rights for farmworkers to pursue legal recourse for injury or illness resulting from employer negligence.

Farm labor contracting increased rapidly in the West during the 1980s. In California, 90 percent of the increase in seasonal agricultural employment since the mid-1980s occurred through farm labor contractors. In 1987, three of the six states with counties in which $10 million or more was spent on contract labor were in the West (California, Arizona, and Washington). In the same year, nine of the twelve counties in which contract labor expenses reached $20 million or more were in California. The county with the largest contract labor expenses in 1987, $87 million, was Fresno County, California. Such widespread use of farm labor contractors arose partly in response to the increasing record-keeping requirements of farm labor laws and partly in anticipation of changes in immigration law that threatened sanctions against employers who knowingly employed undocumented workers. By acquiring labor through an independent contractor, large farm employers could shift the burden of record keeping and withholding for social security, unemployment insurance, income taxes, and some legal liability for employing undocumented farm workers to the contractor.[15]

The large share of the migrant and seasonal labor employed on American farms in western states, through both labor contractors and direct employment by growers, results from the concentration of large-scale farming operations, particularly in crops with heavy seasonal manual labor needs. Apples, peaches, strawberries, grapes, citrus fruits, tree nuts, onions, potatoes, lettuce, tomatoes, asparagus, peas, beans, hay, wheat, hops, sugar beets, and cotton are prominent in a long list of crops produced in the West that have historically required intense hand labor for short peak periods, usually planting, weeding, and harvesting, and longer-term, but still seasonal, labor for maintenance between these periods of peak demand. Livestock operations in the West also have used seasonal hired workers, although in much smaller numbers. Sheep ranchers in the interior western states of Utah and Nevada, for example, hired seasonal sheepherders and shearers as supplemental labor during spring lambing and shearing and for summer herding.

The work that migrant and seasonal farmworkers perform for western growers varies considerably from crop to crop and has changed over time. Although many workers have specialized, particularly in California, others still move among the varieties of crops, following traditional seasonal work patterns— planting, thinning, pruning, cultivating, harvesting, and packing from early spring asparagus through late fall apples. For these workers, the tasks may vary from year to year, depending on the size and quality of a crop and the availability of workers. For example, the Martinez family profiled by Isabel Valle arrived in Pasco, Washington, in late March of 1990 to prepare for the asparagus harvest, a difficult type of skilled work involving choosing the salable plants, cutting them the proper length, and packing them carefully in the fields. The family secured the asparagus harvesting job by returning to a satisfied previous employer. Following asparagus, the family moved to find work harvesting onions and raspberries. They had heard of jobs in these crops around Walla Walla from other migrants they worked with harvesting asparagus. They found work by asking around at local operations on arrival in Walla Walla. When they could find no more work, the family moved to Boardman, Oregon, where they had located work the previous year and where their eldest son had a steady seasonal job on a large farm. They hoped their family relationship would bring them work on that farm, which it did, in the form of hoeing and harvesting potatoes, tomatoes, and onions. Their landlord in Boardman then recommended the family to a grower for the apple harvest; they had never picked apples before but planned to do it again, since it paid well, despite their difficulty adjusting to working from a ladder. By October, harvesting season had ended and the family returned to Texas, where they lived on their earnings and odd jobs.[16]

The Anglo fruit pickers described by Toby Sonneman often spent their winters on the road, perhaps in southern California, Arizona, or Florida picking citrus fruit, or in the Northwest following pruning jobs in the orchards where they would later pick. Some occasionally returned to homes in Missouri, Texas, Oklahoma, or Arkansas and found relatively steady, but itinerant, nonagricultural work as varied as carpentry and preaching. These families began their farm work season harvesting cherries in late April in Stockton and Lodi, California, then followed the ripening fruit north through Oregon, Washington, and Montana. After cherries came plums, pears, and finally apples, tracing a route back from Montana south through Washington and Oregon until late October. Second-generation pickers remembered harvest seasons as children that could be filled simply by traveling up and down the state of California, starting with peas in March in the southern valleys, followed by fruit all summer in the central and northern valleys, and ending with cotton in southern California again in the late fall. By the 1970s, cotton was no longer harvested by hand, and these Anglo migrants had abandoned the physically taxing "stoop" work of harvesting vegetables to Mexican migrants, concentrating instead on more lucrative jobs in the fruit orchards of the Pacific Northwest.[17]

As Sonneman's Anglo migrants had seen with cotton, technological developments have altered the ways in which crops are farmed, increasing seasonal labor demand in some cases and significantly reducing it in others. Mechanization, adoption of hybrid or bioengineered seed, increased use of chemical fertilizers and pesticides, and changes in farm management practices have led overall to less labor use. Cotton and tomato production offer particularly good illustrations of the dramatic effects of technological developments on seasonal farm labor in the West. Mechanization of the cotton harvest began in the 1950s and became widespread by the early 1960s; between 1949 and 1966, the average peak labor demand for cotton harvesting in California fell by 86,510 workers, a change of 89.1 percent. Machinery to harvest tomatoes for processing became common in the late 1960s; between 1964 and 1969, the average peak labor demand for tomato harvesting in California fell by 24,130, a loss of 49.7 percent.[18]

In other crops, however, the effect of technological change was seen primarily in the reduction of family labor; consolidation to take advantage of new technologies led to fewer farms and smaller families providing fewer unpaid family workers. Yet the increased yields made possible by such consolidation and technological change required increased use of hired seasonal labor to make up for lost family labor. In California, for example, between 1950 and 1977, the number of family workers in agriculture fell from 132,100 to 69,700, while the number of seasonal hired workers was slightly higher in 1977 at 118,300 than the 116,600 it had been in 1950. Such increases in the total number of hired seasonal farmworkers, however, masked changes in the seasonal demand for farm labor that affected individual workers. Although total numbers of farmworkers employed in a year might increase, that demand was concentrated during a shorter period, reducing the length of time any one worker might be employed over a year.[19]

In any case, by the late 1970s many more crops were on their way to being mechanized from planting through harvest, and even the annual total number of hired seasonal farmworkers began to decline. Yet it was a different technological development that began to emerge as the primary issue for migrant and seasonal farm labor in the West in the 1980s. UFW representatives had included pesticide exposure and illnesses among farmworkers in their list of grievances against growers throughout their organizing campaign of the 1960s and early 1970s. Although farmworker pesticide poisonings had been documented in western agriculture by the late 1960s, protection through federal environmental safety laws suffered from a jurisdictional dispute between the Occupational Safety and Health Administration (OSHA) and the Environmental Protection Agency (EPA) over which agency bore responsibility for enforcing regulations against farmworker exposure. OSHA traditionally protected workers from hazardous chemicals in the workplace, but the EPA acquired responsibility for farmworkers' pesticide exposure in 1972, when jurisdiction over pesticide use was transferred from the USDA. The EPA won the dispute with OSHA in a 1974 court decision and began regulating pesticide exposure, prohibiting spraying of workers in fields, establishing reentry intervals, requiring personal protective equipment, and requiring notification of pesticide exposures. By 1980, the EPA had established labeling requirements to protect workers; in 1983, it began a process to rewrite worker protection standards based on studies showing earlier standards were not adequate. By 1990, however, new regulations establishing rules for pesticide safety training, decontamination sites, emergency assistance, notification, restricted entry intervals, and the use of personal protective equipment were the subject of intense debate between growers and farmworker advocates, delaying implementation of the new, stricter standards.

Along with the pesticide exposure issue, immigration control developed as one of the leading issues for both growers and workers in the West and other border states in the 1980s. In the early 1950s, fear of uncontrolled immigration from Mexico had helped support farm employer arguments in favor of the bracero program. In opposition, domestic farmworkers and their advocates, both Anglo-American and Mexican American, had argued that any form of increased immigration of workers into United States agriculture, even sanctioned nonimmigrant worker programs like the bracero program, adversely affected their livelihoods by increasing the supply of seasonal farm labor. Rather than reduce immigration, they charged, the nonimmigrant programs facilitated it. Many nonimmigrant workers would become undocumented immigrant workers when they failed to return to Mexico, and the work and community contacts made even by those workers who did return would become a conduit for further immigration.

Public discussion of the problems of undocumented immigration from Mexico resurfaced soon after the termination of the bracero program in 1964. By 1971, calls for action led to congressional efforts at immigration reform. Although legislation failed to pass during the 1970s, Congress did appoint a commission to investigate appropriate immigration reforms. That commission (the Select Commission on Immigration and Refugee Policy) recommended employer sanctions and legalization of unauthorized immigrants residing in the United States. When immigration reform legislation finally succeeded, in the form of the 1986 Immigration Reform and Control Act (IRCA), both recommendations had been incorporated into the law.

Western growers showed particular concern about access to agricultural workers during deliberations over the 1986 legislation, since they considered Mexican workers necessary to fill what they viewed as gaps in the domestic labor force. Provisions in the 1986 immigration act allowed for a special legalization program for undocumented farmworkers who could show they had done at least ninety days of seasonal farm work in the year preceding the passage of the IRCA. As a further protection against farm labor shortages, undocumented immigrants who did not qualify as special agricultural workers (SAWs) could become replenishment agricultural workers (RAWs) if too many SAWs left farm work for other jobs after becoming legal immigrants. Such a shortage never materialized, however, and the RAW provisions of the IRCA were never invoked.

Program administrators expected over 1 million SAWs to be legalized, with over half of those in California alone. Since SAWs were required to have worked illegally in the United States before being legalized, the program provided an additional incentive for undocumented workers to immigrate into the American farm labor market, hoping that they, too, might eventually acquire legal status. As a result, the IRCA apparently spurred unauthorized immigration, rather than controlled it, particularly among seasonal agricultural workers. Domestic farmworkers and their advocates had hoped that legalization of undocumented farmworkers would improve conditions for all by removing the fear of deportation among illegal farmworkers that made them vulnerable to employer exploitation. They found, instead, that legalization led to an even greater supply of undocumented farmworkers and no change in earnings and working conditions for domestic farmworkers.

The issue of immigration reform and agricultural labor supply brings us essentially full circle, reaching back to the controversy surrounding the establishment and eventual termination of the bracero program. Such a return to the past might seem to reflect a lack of progress in migrant and seasonal farm labor issues in the West from 1940 to the present. The case studies described here suggest slow change at best, with many seasonal farmworkers in the 1990s still living in poverty and without stable sources of income from year to year. Seasonal migration patterns, the tradition of labor crews, word-of-mouth recruitment, and alternating shortages and oversupply of labor at particular times and places have changed little since World War II, and although technological changes have altered the use of seasonal labor in some crops, other crops continued to be harvested in much the same way in the 1990s as they were in 1940.

Yet, despite the persistence of many of the problems related to agricultural labor in the West, the story recounted here illustrates change more than permanence. Perhaps the most dynamic transformation has been the increasing proportion of Hispanics in the migrant and seasonal farm workforce. Although Mexican labor has historically played an important role in the supply of seasonal farmworkers to western agriculture, by 1990 Hispanics, mostly Mexican, had virtually replaced Anglo workers in California. During the same period, primarily Mexican American farmworkers successfully organized the UFW and achieved negotiated improvements in labor conditions in some parts of California, as well as winning state recognition of their right to bargain collectively. Although collective bargaining efforts witnessed serious setbacks during the 1980s, the union and the California Labor Relations Act remained in place in 1990. Moreover, federal and many other state laws enacted since the 1960s supported additional labor protections and provided a range of social services that generally improved the living and working conditions for migrant and seasonal farmworkers. Families who tried to make a living from farm work still faced severe difficulties in the 1990s, but without a doubt, conditions of life and work for migrant and seasonal farm labor in the West had changed since 1940.

NOTES

1. Wayne D. Rasmussen, "A History of the Emergency Farm Labor Supply Program, 1943–1947," USDA, Bureau of Agricultural Economics, *Agriculture Monograph 13,* September 1951, 226.

2. Vernon M. Briggs, Jr., "Non-Immigrant Labor Policy in the United States," *Journal of Economic Issues* 62 (September 1983): 612.

3. For a thorough review of data sources on agricultural labor, see Victor J. Oliveira and Leslie A. Whitener, "Appendix B: Agricultural Labor: A Review of the Data," in "Immigration Reform and U.S. Agriculture," ed. Philip L. Martin et al., University of California, Division of Agriculture and Natural Resources, *Publication* 3358, 1995, 487–525.

4. William H. Metzler and Afife F. Sayin, *The Agricultural Labor Force in the San Joaquin Valley, California: Characteristics, Employment, Mobility, 1948,* U.S. Department of Agriculture, Bureau of Agricultural Economics and University of California, Institute of Industrial Relations, February 1950.

5. "California Findings from the National Agricultural Workers Survey: A Demographic and Employment Profile of Perishable Crop Farm Workers," U.S. Department of Labor, Office of Program Economics, Office of the Assistant Secretary for Policy, *Research Report 3,* 1993.

6. Tom Current and Mark Martinez Infante, . . . *and Migrant Problems DEMAND ATTENTION,* Oregon Bureau of Labor, September 1959.

7. Toby F. Sonneman, *Fruit Fields in My Blood: Okie Migrants in the West* (Moscow: University of Idaho Press, 1992).

8. Isabel Valle, *Fields of Toil: A Migrant Family's Journey* (Pullman: Washington State University Press, 1994).

9. Anne B. W. Effland, "The Emergence of Federal Assistance Programs for Migrant and Seasonal Farmworkers in Post–World War II America" (Ph.D. diss., Iowa State University, 1991), 164.

10. The literature on Cesar Chavez and the United Farm Workers union is abundant, much of it for popular audiences and published during and immediately after the successful grape boycotts of 1965–66 and 1967–70. Among the more scholarly studies, Linda C. Majka and Theo J. Majka, *Farm Workers, Agribusiness, and the State* (Philadelphia: Temple University Press, 1982), and J. Craig Jenkins, *The Politics of Insurgency: The Farm Worker Movement in the 1960s* (New York: Columbia University Press, 1985), are particularly good.

11. Philip L. Martin, Suzanne Vaupel, and Daniel L. Egan, *Unfulfilled Promise: Collective Bargaining in California Agriculture* (Boulder, Colo.: Westview Press, 1988), 35, 40.

12. For a readable review of the provisions of farm labor laws, see Jack L. Runyan, "A Summary of Federal Laws and Regulations Affecting Agricultural Employers, 1992," U.S. Department of Agriculture, Economic Research Service, *Agriculture Information Bulletin 652,* August 1992.

13. "Status of Agricultural Workers Under State and Federal Labor Laws," U.S. Department of Labor, Bureau of Labor Standards, *Fact Sheet 2,* December 1965.

14. William John Craddock, ed., *Federal and State Employment Standards and U.S. Farm Labor* (Austin, Tex.: Motivation Education and Training, April 1988).

15. P. L. Martin, "Farm Labor Contractors Play New Roles in Agriculture," *California Agriculture* 49 (September/October 1995): 37; Victor J. Oliveira, "Hired and Contract Labor in U.S. Agriculture, 1987: A Regional Assessment of Structure," U.S. Department of Agriculture, Economic Research Service, *Agricultural Economic Report 648,* May 1991, 15–16.

16. Valle, *Fields of Toil,* 2–9, 13–19, 171.

17. Sonneman, *Fruit Fields in My Blood,* 39–51.

18. Paul Barnett et al., *Labor's Dwindling Harvest: The Impact of Mechanization on California Fruit and Vegetable Workers* (Davis, Calif.: California Institute for Rural Studies, 1978), 67.

19. John W. Mamer and Varden Fuller, "Employment on California Farms," in *Technological Change, Farm Mechanization and Agricultural Employment,* University of California, Division of Agricultural Sciences, July 1978, 14. The number of family workers declined steadily over the entire period, while the number of seasonal hired workers increased steadily to a peak of 152,200 in 1956, then declined, with only occasional minor annual fluctuations for the rest of the period.

8

Agricultural Science and Technology in the West

Judith Fabry

Before undertaking an examination of the ways in which science and technology affected rural westerners after World War II, a brief consideration of terms may be helpful. In the common parlance of the 1990s, science and technology are often uttered in the same breath and are perceived to be a monolithic force that drives our society, whether we like it or not. More accurately, though, science and technology are not external forces, acting on society for good or ill. Rather, they are embedded in our culture and are products of it. The desires of the majority have determined the direction of our society's science and inspired its technology.

The chief purpose of American technology has been to increase production of a particular commodity while maintaining or decreasing inputs. Technology need not be something tangible, such as a manufactured good. It also may be a new way of doing something, or simply newly acquired knowledge that aids decision making. For most rural westerners, technological change primarily influences the production of crops and livestock.[1]

Regardless of their intentions, the adoption of new technologies by western farmers and ranchers had more far-reaching effects than simply expanding production and cutting expenses. Their decisions increasingly systematized, specialized, and enlarged operations. During the nineteenth century, farmers adopted new technology in a piecemeal fashion, adding a desirable piece of equipment or implement when their income allowed. Beginning in the early decades of the twentieth century, and more predominantly after 1945, agricultural producers adopted *systems* of technology, not pieces of equipment. These systems generally involved machines to reduce labor, specially bred plants or animals, and chemicals to protect and increase the production of the commodity. The inputs of production were so interrelated that one input could not function effectively in the absence of some or all of the other inputs.[2]

Adoption of new technologies also increased specialization and spurred enlargement of operations. Farmers focused on a certain crop or advantageous rotation of crops, or a certain breed of livestock. The purchase of expensive equipment associated with these specialties demanded that it be used as much as possible, which most often meant acquiring or leasing more land or livestock. During the latter half of the twentieth century, producers purchased most of the new inputs of production, and their use frequently required better education or management skills than had former modes of production. Expansion of successful operations and increased financial and managerial demands on those who remained forced many producers out of business. From 1940 to 1987, the number of farms in the twelve western states decreased from 511,000 to 273,000. The total farm acreage, however, increased from approximately 258 million acres to 310 million acres.[3]

No technologies, however, have touched as many rural lives as three that were already well on the way to becoming ubiquitous in 1940: electricity, motorized transportation, and tractors. Although their significance has been well documented in other places, brief mention is made of them here because the adoption of other technologies often hinged upon their presence. In 1940, due to the widespread availability of hydroelectricity, a number of western states had unusually high percentages of electrified farms: 75 percent of the farms in California, 57 percent of the farms in Washington, 54 percent of the farms in Idaho and Utah, 50 percent of the farms in Oregon, and 46 percent of those in Arizona. Nearer the national average was Nevada, with 35 percent. The Rocky Mountain states lagged behind, however, with fewer than 20 percent of the farms in those states having electricity. During the next twenty years, the gaps in rural electrification narrowed, and by 1976 all states of the West approached 100 percent, except Arizona, where 85 percent of farms were electrified. The availability of electricity as a dependable source of power simplified many tasks, changed methods of production, made possible new ways of processing and storing food, enhanced communication, and gave the rural population new ways in which to use leisure time.[4]

Similarly, the automobile, the truck, and the road system that was built to accommodate them permeated the rural West after 1950. Like electricity, these technologies changed modes of production, simplified tasks, increased communication, and changed the ways people used leisure time. After World War II, trucks replaced the railroad as the most common means of moving agricultural products to market. Rail technology did not offer the flexibility or time savings that truck and air transport provided.[5]

The tractor was another technology that became omnipresent in the rural West and had far-reaching effects. By the late 1940s, rubber tires, power take-offs, power-lift mechanisms, and three-point hitches were standard equipment on most models. During the next forty years, no fundamental changes in tractor technology occurred. Tractors increased in size as available horsepower increased, manufacturers offered alternative wheel arrangements to facilitate different tillage practices, and concern for the operator's comfort brought about closed, air-conditioned cabs and stereo sound systems.[6]

Acquisition of a tractor, as with other new technologies, led to changes in farm management. As farmers eliminated draft animals from their farms, the need for forage crops declined. In the West, this change in cropping became particularly significant in California and in the wheat-growing region of the Columbia Plateau, the primary wheat-producing region in the Pacific Northwest, which stretches from northeastern Oregon through southeastern Washington and into northern Idaho. Producers could devote greater portions of their land to high-value crops. Other effects of the adoption of tractor technology included increased agricultural unemployment and a decrease in the size of farm families as labor needs declined.

The acquisition of a tractor often marked the beginning of a farmer's move toward more systematized production. The systematization, specialization, and enlargement of crop and livestock operations that occurred after 1945 can be illustrated by four commodities: dairy products, beef, wheat, and processing tomatoes. The first three have been mainstays of the agricultural economy of the West. The fourth, processing tomatoes, serves as an example of the myriad specialty crops California produces for the nation.

In 1990, dairy products were the highest-value agricultural commodity in both California and Washington. At that time California was the leading dairy producer in the nation, and since 1973 it had maintained the lowest costs of

After World War II, rapid technological change began to solve labor problems for some growers in California, but at the end of the twentieth century many crops still required hand labor. Here migrant workers follow a tractor-powered conveyor that takes the harvested vegetables to wagons pulled alongside. *Courtesy, U.S. Department of Agriculture.*

production of any state. Also, by the end of the 1980s, the output of milk per cow was greater in the Pacific and Mountain States than anywhere else in the country. These achievements were due primarily to adoption of an evolving series of technological innovations that led to larger-scale operations than existed in other dairy regions of the nation.[7]

A technology that dairy farmers began to adopt in the 1950s was artificial insemination (AI). Refinement of techniques for semen collection, storage, and freezing enhanced widespread acceptance of this method of herd improvement. At the same time, dairy producers in the West were testing their herds and submitting production data to the Dairy Herd Improvement Association (DHIA), a national organization formed to maintain breeding and production records of the nation's dairy cows. The use of DHIA records and AI narrowed the number of breeds favored by American dairy producers so that by the late 1980s, Holsteins constituted 90 percent of the herds. Artificial insemination maintained genetic diversity within the breed, however, by reducing inbreeding and making individual herds less susceptible to disease. Embryo transfer, a method of impregnating unproven or inferior cows with embryos from a genetically superior female, also obtained common usage during the 1980s, but its economic advantage was primarily to breeders of dairy cattle and not milk producers. Artificial insemination remained the most economical method of herd improvement for milk producers.[8]

Innovations in methods of feeding dairy herds brought about changes in the scale of dairy operations in the West. By 1990, herds in the Pacific States averaged 500 to 1,000 cows and were among the largest in the nation. Soon after World War II, southern California dairy producers abandoned the practice of allowing dairy cows to graze in a pasture and began what became known as *drylot feeding.* They confined their herds to lots where food and water could be delivered. The feed consisted of large amounts of concentrates, rations designed to provide balanced nutrition at the least cost, which became widely available after World War II. Adoption of forage choppers and field wagons made bringing forage to the cows feasible. Gradually, alfalfa replaced pasture grass as the primary forage for western dairy cattle, a shift that led to the entrenchment of alfalfa as one of the staple cash crops of irrigated agriculture in the western states.[9]

By the 1970s, drylot feeding was common practice for large dairy producers in the West. In these operations, nearly all feed components were purchased. Mechanized systems moved various forage components and concentrates from silos to a mixing station, then on to the feeding areas. These systems controlled the proportions and quality of feed components, as well as the frequency and location of delivery to the cows. Later, more sophisticated systems could identify animals that had already received their ration for the day and deny them any additional feed.[10]

New technologies also changed milking practices. By the 1980s, milking parlors operated sixteen to twenty hours per day, milking cows three times daily. Milking parlors involved channeling cows into stations where dairymen milked them using machines, and the fluid traveled through stainless steel cooling tubes to holding tanks. Tanker trucks transported the milk from the holding tanks to processing facilities.

Establishment of drylot feeding facilities and milking parlors entailed large capital outlays and encouraged enlargement of dairy producers' scales of operation. After 1950, many small dairy producers who could not afford to adopt these new technologies left the business. In California, the number of dairy farms dropped from 20,000 in 1950 to fewer than 3,000 in 1980.[11]

In 1990, another technology with the potential to further reduce the numbers of dairy farmers awaited governmental approval: recombinant DNA bovine somatotropin, or bST. This synthetically produced version of the major hormone responsible for milk production boosted production of a cow in a well-managed herd by as much as 25 percent. Its introduction by the scientific community in the early 1980s created a controversy of unprecedented proportions within the dairy industry. Concerns for food safety, animal safety, the safety of the hormone manufacturing process, and the effect of bST on the dairy industry prompted a decade of investigation and analysis.

Although bST was not available to dairy producers in 1990, in February 1994 the federal government completed its review of bST and determined to allow its use. Concerning bST's projected effects on the dairy industry, analysts found that its use required a higher level of management from the producer and that the technology would benefit large producers disproportionately because they would have better access to information and finance. Forecasters predicted rapid acceptance (five years) of the technology among dairy producers and as much as a 30 percent decline in the number of dairy farms nationwide during that period.[12]

Analysis of this type resulted from growing concern among Americans during the 1970s about the environmental pollution and economic dislocation created by previous technologies. It came from the Office of Technology Assessment (OTA), a federal agency created in 1972 to examine the potential economic, social, and environmental consequences of new technologies. To facilitate such assessments, social scientists and economists worked to develop analytic models that could be used for predicting the effects of these technologies.[13]

Dairy production in the West became more systematized as producers adopted mechanized methods of milking and feeding their herds. The only significant division of labor that took place was in the production of feedstuffs and forage, which became the province of manufacturers and farmers who specialized in alfalfa production. Breeders provided some top-quality breeding stock to the milk producer, but calf production, that is, herd enlargement, remained in the hands of the dairy manager. Purchased inputs in the form of machinery and buildings, feed, and veterinary chemicals increased in importance.

While dairy products were the largest source of agricultural income in California and Washington in 1990, the production of beef held first position in every other western state but Alaska. Although large portions of land in the West are suitable only for grazing, between 1940 and 1990 cattle production took place in many varied situations, from irrigated pastureland to arid desert, from the rolling foothills of the Rockies and Sierra Nevadas to their high-altitude valleys.[14]

Some of the technology adopted by dairy producers also affected the production of beef. Ranchers soon accepted artificial insemination after the pioneering work of dairy scientists and farmers. However, whereas in the dairy industry AI produced a homogenization of breeds, in the beef industry it prompted a proliferation of foreign breeds and crossbreeds, particularly from Europe. Into the 1990s, Black Angus, a traditional mainstay of the American beef industry, still held first position in breed registrations, but Limousin and Simmental, two breeds introduced after the 1950s, held second and third place, respectively. Beef producers also began using prostaglandins to improve their herds. Injections of this hormonelike substance controlled the time of calving and increased calf production.[15]

In 1940, much western rangeland was in poor condition, the result of drought and overgrazing. Efforts to improve the forage on the open range brought about an evolution in management techniques during the decades after World War II. In some places, controlled burning of brush became an accepted method of restoring grass production and water sources. Also, ranchers planted their range with new varieties of grasses imported from Australia and South Africa. For most of the post–World War II period, ranchers used chemical herbicides to control range weeds, but by the 1980s integrated pest management (IPM) gained increasing importance. Integrated pest management involved the use of both biological and chemical controls, in combinations that depended on the severity of the infestation and the effectiveness of each method. Use of IPM demanded high levels of management to monitor pest damage, observe activity of biological controls, and decide when chemical intervention was necessary. Biological controls were more appropriate for weeds in rangeland than in field crops. They did not provide quick pest eradication, but once established they provided long-term protection. Introduction of the *Chrysolina* beetle brought about permanent control of the toxic weed *Hypericum perforatum L.* (Saint-John's-wort or Klamath weed), which infested much western rangeland. Throughout the West in 1990, insects or microbial agents controlled at least eleven other common range weeds.[16]

In addition to improving the quality of their range forage, ranchers also raised grasses, peas, and alfalfa for winter feeding and adopted new ways of harvesting and storing them. Portable electric fences powered by solar batteries became a way to protect stacks of hay in the field until needed for winter feeding. Integrated pest management also became important in the production of alfalfa. During the 1950s the spotted alfalfa aphid threatened virtually all of the alfalfa in the West. It proved resistant to insecticides, but scientists identified parasitic insects and fungi pathogens that brought the infestation under control. Biological controls remained important even after scientists developed aphid-resistant plant varieties.[17]

During the 1980s some ranchers adopted systems of grazing that required dividing their land or pastures into small segments and limiting the amount of time that livestock grazed each segment. Portable electric fences created the pasture segmentation. Rate of plant growth, acreage, and number of animals determined the period of grazing, with the ideal being to graze no grass plant more than once. As with IPM, this system was management-intensive and required the rancher to have a high level of botanical knowledge.[18]

Perhaps the most significant technological change to affect beef production after 1945 was the rise of the feedlot, a place for intensive feeding of cattle to bring them to slaughter weight in a short time. Cattle raisers in southern California adopted feedlot technology from the Midwest soon after World War II. The region's warm, dry climate and the availability of cheap roughage and agricultural by-products for feed enhanced adoption of the system; the booming population with a high per capita income provided a ready market for top-grade beef. By 1965, California had 563 feedlots and marketed nearly 2.3 million head of cattle per year. However, as the technology spread to other parts of the nation, the number of feedlots in California declined, as did the number of cattle marketed. By 1980, 101 feedlots in California marketed 1.25 million head of cattle. At that time, feeders received the largest number of cattle from Texas, followed by Arizona, Oregon, and Nevada.[19]

Feedlot finishing of beef was similar to drylot dairy feeding, where mechanized systems delivered least-cost feed concentrates to the livestock. During the early 1950s, a significant technological change in beef feeding took place when feeders adopted antibiotics and growth stimulants. Also in 1954, the federal government approved the use of the growth hormone diethylstilbestrol (DES) in cattle feed. Within a decade, the Food and Drug Administration (FDA) estimated cattle producers treated 80 to 85 percent of their stock with DES; at that time, 85 percent of commercial feed also contained antibiotic or hormone additives. The low cost of feed additives made them attractive. For a small investment, producers enjoyed increased growth rate, more meat product per pound of food fed, and a reduction in disease. These factors greatly enhanced feedlot operations, where large numbers of animals were kept in confined spaces and disease could spread rapidly. The DES culture collapsed in 1973, however, when the FDA determined the hormone was carcinogenic and banned its use in feed.[20]

During the decades after World War II, technology brought about a division of labor and vertical integration of beef production. Individual ranchers handled cattle for shorter periods but utilized more systematic breeding, veterinary, and range management technologies to bring cattle to feedlot specifications. Trucks moved the cattle long distances from grazing land to feedlots. There, veterinary and nutritional experts took care of finishing the beef with a system of purchased inputs, including computer-operated mechanisms and specially formulated mixes of feedstuffs.

After the early 1940s, technological innovations also significantly altered wheat growing and harvesting on the Columbia Plateau. This region was one of the major wheat-producing areas in the country, with yields of about one-and-one-half times the national average. Rainfall on the plateau varies from ten to thirty inches per year. The soils are fine loam and the terrain is hilly, often with steep slopes.[21]

Soil conservation measures were among the first technological changes adopted by wheat growers during the 1940s. The light, dry soils and hilly terrain of the plateau made them especially susceptible to erosion. At first farmers used green manure crops to increase the organic content of the soil and to reduce erosion, but during the 1950s the widespread use of nitrogen fertilizer eliminated this practice. Wheat varieties in use during the 1940s left tall stubble after harvest, which was difficult to plow with conventional moldboards. Until the 1960s, many farmers burned their stubble, but as new implements became available and short-strawed wheat varieties were developed, farmers increasingly left the harvest "trash" on their fields. High-clearance cultivators and tine-tooth harrows made working a trashy surface possible.[22]

Conservation tillage was another soil technology that some western farmers began to adopt during the 1970s and 1980s. In 1985, in Washington, Oregon, and Idaho, from 24 to 30 percent of the total land in cultivation was under some type of conservation tillage. Although many of the techniques involved were not innovative, systematization of certain planting and tilling practices took place when tillage equipment became available that could handle trashy surfaces. Conservation tillage incorporated a range of practices, each designed for specific soils, climates, and crops. Fundamentally, they were systems of tillage and planting that maintained 30 percent plant residue on the soil surface during periods when erosion might occur. Besides preventing erosion and enhancing the organic content of soils, the systems reduced the amount of labor and fuel required to produce a crop. Growers who practiced conservation tillage, however, used herbicides to control weeds, with the highest level of use in no-till field preparation. Determining the minimum amounts of herbicide needed for weed control required high levels of management. The chief disadvantages of no-till agriculture were the costs of inputs: specialized equipment for planting and fertilizing in an undisturbed trashy surface, and chemical herbicides. Also, fungi destructive to wheat persisted in the undisturbed soil. Reduced tillage, the system most commonly adopted by western farmers, lessened the risk of fungal diseases and was cheaper than no-till methods because conventional implements could be used for tillage and planting.[23]

The plants used by wheat producers also changed from the 1950s into the 1970s. A series of high-yielding varieties rose in popularity, then fell from favor when they became susceptible to disease as well as failed to produce a consistent high-quality grain. Clogging of the straw in the combine also became a problem when heavy fertilization encouraged the growth of long-stemmed varieties. The 1960s brought the semidwarf varieties that solved the problems of lodging and shattering, but these, too, eventually became subject to diseases. Fungicides controlled pythium, which caused the most common soilborne disease, and during the 1980s, biological controls also were being studied.[24]

Anhydrous ammonia, a synthetic source of nitrogen, became the fertilizer of choice during the 1950s. By the mid-1960s, fertilizer use on the Columbia Plateau had increased sixfold. The combination of the semidwarf varieties and fertilizer stepped up yields from less than thirty bushels per acre in the 1940s to fifty-three bushels per acre during the years 1965–75. By 1990, yields in Washington and Idaho were between sixty and seventy bushels per acre.[25]

After 1980, the use of irrigation also enhanced wheat production, particularly in Idaho. By 1990, producers there irrigated nearly one-half of the state's 1.37 million acres of wheat with wheel-line or center-pivot systems.[26]

Wheat harvesting technology also changed after World War II. Although grain combines were available before 1940, after 1950 they become more powerful, self-propelled, and specialized for use on different terrains. In 1970, wheat harvest on a ranch on the Columbia Plateau was accomplished by seven men, three self-propelled air-conditioned combines, and a diesel-powered machine similar to an earth mover that moved the grain from the combines to three trucks waiting at the edge of the field. Fifty years earlier, a similar harvest required more than 100 men and 300 draft animals.[27]

The technological changes that occurred in wheat production after 1940 were primarily evolutionary, building on technologies that existed previously. Techniques of soil conservation became more systematized and required better knowledge of soil characteristics and plant biology for implementation. Producers used higher-yielding and disease-resistant wheat varieties and adopted more specialized and powerful implements. Ultimately, all of these systems worked most efficiently in concert with the new chemical technologies: fertilizers to enhance growth of high-yielding varieties, fungicides to control the diseases that attacked the new varieties, and herbicides to control the weeds.

Unlike the evolutionary process of technological change in wheat production, mechanization and systematization of the production of processing tomatoes took place in a relatively short time due to the coordinated efforts of growers, engineers, horticulturalists, agronomists, and processors. After the 1960s, the processing tomato industry became both a model of technological development and a focus of debate about who should pay for such development and who should profit from it.

Tomatoes were one of the early staples of California's commercial agriculture. During the 1940s, growers realized that it might be possible to handle

Vegetable production in the West has reached a factory or industrialized scale since World War II. During the 1960s, growers in California began using mechanical tomato pickers to reduce labor costs and eliminate the need to hire temporary workers. Tomatoes picked by these machines, however, were suitable only for processing into ketchup, sauce, and paste. *Courtesy, U.S. Department of Agriculture.*

tomatoes intended for processing differently from those that would be used fresh, since blemishes and bruises were not significant in fruit that went directly to processing vats. Therefore, at the request of growers, several groups at the University of California began to work on mechanizing the harvest of processing tomatoes. Horticulturists bred a tough-skinned, pear-shaped tomato. Its vine was determinate, which meant all of the fruit ripened at the same time. Engineers developed a once-over picking machine. Experimentation with cultural practices brought about systematization of planting, fertilizing, irrigating, and controlling weeds to facilitate machine picking.

Producers began to adopt the new plants, cultural systems, and harvesting machinery during the late 1950s. Processors accepted the lower-quality, machine-harvested tomatoes to encourage growers to adopt the technology. Widespread acceptance of the new technology came after 1964, when the federal government terminated the bracero program of imported Mexican labor. Faced with the alternative of using higher-priced domestic laborers who were beginning to unionize, growers rapidly adopted the mechanical picking technology. By 1973, machines harvested 100 percent of California's processing tomato crop. Introduction of an electronic sorter in 1975 further mechanized the harvest. Besides displacing labor, mechanization brought about a decrease in the number of growers and, in combination with expanded irrigation, increased the amount of land planted in tomatoes.[28]

During the 1970s and 1980s, the model of technological development represented by mechanization of the processing tomato industry became the focus of debate and litigation. Pointing out that between 1964 and 1972 the number of tomato workers declined from approximately 50,000 to 18,000, critics condemned the spending of public funds to develop a technology that displaced workers. Agricultural economists defended mechanization, arguing that it had not displaced domestic laborers and that the expansion of labor-intensive agriculture in California during the 1960s had more than compensated for any domestic jobs lost. Economists also cited the benefits to consumers of lower prices for tomato products. In 1979, a group of fifteen farm laborers, represented by attorneys of California Rural Legal Assistance, sued the University of California to prevent tax dollars from being used for research that benefited private rather than public interests. The suit was not resolved until 1987, when a California superior court judge ruled in favor of the farmworkers, saying that in the future the university must give "primary consideration . . . to the interests of the small family farm." Another economic analysis of the results of mechanization, released earlier in 1987, showed that the growers had benefited more than previously calculated.[29]

The debate swirling around mechanization of the tomato processing industry had implications for producers of iceberg lettuce, another labor-intensive specialty commodity. In 1978, no doubt due to the controversy surrounding the tomato harvester, agricultural experiment station researchers at the University of California–Davis abandoned more than fifteen years of work and a prototype lettuce harvester that had been in the field for three years. At nearly the same time, the California Department of Food and Agriculture denied the request of the Iceberg Lettuce Research Advisory Board for a self-imposed tax on lettuce producers to fund manufacture of a prototype harvester. The state agency's estimated retail cost of a harvester—$40,000—probably would have been beyond the means of small-scale producers who would have been subject to the tax. Decisions such as these, the establishment of the Office of Technology Assessment, and the close scrutiny given bST reflect the increasing concern of the American public with the effects of technological change. By the 1980s, introduction of new technologies was considerably more complicated than before, but market forces continued to determine the direction of technological development.[30]

Two themes recur in the descriptions of the technological changes that took place in the production of dairy products, beef, wheat, and processing tomatoes: the increased reliance of producers on machines to reduce labor and their use of chemicals to promote growth and reduce losses due to pests and disease. These practices affected not just the producers of major commodities but all agricultural producers in the West. The following summarizes the changes in output and use of labor, machines, and chemicals for the Pacific States (California, Oregon, and Washington) and the United States as a whole from 1945 to 1975.[31]

	Pacific States	United States
Output	+109%	+63%
Labor	−47%	−70%
Machines/power	+66%	+93%
Chemicals	+860%	+535%

While the figures for the Pacific region may not apply to all western states during this period, they are useful indicators of some of the changes that took place in the West. Mechanization and the use of power, while showing a significant increase, did not change as much in the Pacific States as in other parts of the United States. Early electrification and early adoption of grain harvesting machinery undoubtedly affected this statistic.

Mechanization had a significance beyond simple adoption of laborsaving devices. In the West after World War II, mechanization of the harvest of a crop signaled that its production had been well systematized. For machine harvesting to be cost-effective, it was necessary for plants or fruits to have matured evenly. Growers accomplished this by first preparing fields or orchards for the type of irrigation system that would be used. Then they planted special high-yielding seed precisely, often with a machine, to ensure the desired amount of space between plants, timed and placed fertilizer to optimize plant growth, used herbicides to eliminate weeds that might interfere with operation of harvesting machinery, and applied insecticides and fungicides to protect the health of the plants. In some cases they applied herbicide again to defoliate plants before harvest.

Mechanization of the harvests of cotton and sugar beets, which took place during the 1950s and 1960s, have been well documented elsewhere. In both cases, modifications of the plant materials and cultural practices accompanied mechanization. Harvesting of many of California's fruit and vegetable crops became mechanized during the period following World War II. "Once-over" machines, similar to those used in the tomato industry, were most commonly used for annual row crops. The cultural technology necessary for this type of harvesting (uniform plant maturity) also transferred to hand-harvested crops, where once-over picking also was desirable.[32]

Mechanical harvesting technologies affected the scale and location of production. The size of operations usually increased to optimize use of equipment. However, some small-scale operators mechanized without increasing the size of their operation by leasing, custom harvest work, or cooperative purchase of expensive machinery. Areas of production also shifted. Shake-catch harvesting of prunes, for example, was not feasible in the coastal areas of California because the fruits did not ripen uniformly there. As a consequence, prune production moved from the coast to the Sacramento Valley, where conditions encourage uniform maturity. The Pacific Northwest replaced the Northeast as a center for green pea production because the larger and more level fields there were better adapted to machine technologies. Similarly, potato production increased in Idaho because soil conditions there were favorable to mechanical harvesting equipment.[33]

Irrigation was another area in which mechanization brought increased systematization. Irrigation was well established in all of the western states by 1940 and had been responsible for bringing into production land that otherwise could have been used only for grazing. With the exception of four states, irrigated acreage remained relatively stable from the 1950s through the 1980s. Increases occurred in Washington (32 percent), Idaho (38 percent), and Nevada (37 percent), while in Arizona, irrigated acreage decreased by 22 percent. The availability of inexpensive hydroelectricity for pumping contributed to much of the expansion of irrigated land. In the years after 1954, urbanization brought about the loss of more than 5 million acres of irrigated land in Arizona.[34]

The desire to reduce the cost of irrigation drove changes in irrigation technology. At the simplest level, concrete linings improved or pipelines replaced earthen ditches, which were prone to seepage and evaporation. More powerful pumps replaced or supplemented gravity-flow systems, making water delivery more reliable. By the 1960s, electrically timed and controlled water delivery became possible. Besides cutting labor costs, changes such as these also conserved dwindling water resources and lessened soil erosion. In other cases, however, the same innovations made increased irrigation possible. In Idaho during the 1960s, the Ore-Ida Foods corporation began using large-capacity pumps and pipelines to lift water 500 feet from the Snake River to new fields established on formerly arid benchlands.[35]

The use of sprinklers—spraying water through perforated pipe or a nozzle—instead of furrow or flood irrigation began during the 1930s in the Pacific Northwest and in southern California. During the 1950s, orchard growers in Washington and Oregon quickly adopted sprinkler systems because they could be used on steep or rough land or where the topsoil was too thin to level. Also, delivery of water through sprinklers was especially useful in the loose, sandy soils of the West, where porosity kept water from being held on the surface and large volumes of water caused erosion. The advent of center-pivot irrigation (CPI) in the early 1950s further systematized sprinkler technology by rotating the wheel line—several hundred feet of pipe rolling on five-foot wheels that alternated every eighty feet with sprinkler heads—around a central pump. Later innovations permitted application of fertilizer during irrigation.[36] The following shows the percentages of irrigated acreage on which sprinkler systems were being used in 1990.[37]

Many western farmers use sprinklers to irrigate their crops and improve production. Pumps draw water from wells or streams in the absence of reservoirs that permit ditch irrigation. In June 1949, an Idaho farmer pumped water from the Weiser River to irrigate his fields. *Courtesy, U.S. Department of Agriculture.*

	Irrigation by Sprinklers
Washington	76%
Oregon	55%
Idaho	50%
Utah	21%
Arizona	12%
Nevada	10%

Although comparable figures for 1990 are not available for California, in 1993 producers there depended about equally on sprinklers and low-flow systems (microspray or drip), which constituted 34 percent of their irrigation. Montana, Wyoming, Colorado, and New Mexico are not included in these statistics because most sprinkler irrigation in those states took place east of the Rockies.

Although the growers and farmers in California were the nation's largest groundwater users by the mid-1980s, with those in Idaho and Arizona not far behind, the social costs of CPI in the Far West have been high. The irrigation technology that dominated the first half of the twentieth century encouraged smaller, closely spaced, owner-operated farms. Center-pivot irrigation and wheel-line technologies encouraged investor-owners and management from a distance, with a single set of farm buildings to serve many thousands of acres of land. Center-pivot irrigation technology was expensive ($61,000 to acquire a single unit plus high annual operating costs in 1976) but required little labor for operation. Thus, a 10,000–acre development such as the one Ore-Ida established on the Snake River Plain was owned by a corporation, managed by persons who commuted to the site from distant business centers, and operated by itinerant workers who lived in dormitories at a central location on the project.[38]

Sociologists have found that CPI in the Pacific Northwest had two effects on the cost of electricity to nonagricultural users. The increased demand for water from the region's rivers decreased the water available for hydroelectric generation; therefore, the cost of electricity went up. Also, power companies actively encouraged irrigation development by lowering rates to large users of power, then passed their losses along in higher rates to other customers.[39]

As extensive as were the mechanical innovations adopted by western producers during the decades after 1940, chemical innovations had the greatest impact. As shown earlier, chemical use in the Pacific States increased by 860 percent from 1945 to 1975. The use of chemicals to increase crop production took two forms: fertilizer and pesticides. During the early twentieth century, most western farmers depended on manure and nitrogen-fixing crops to fertilize their fields. However, during the 1930s a new form of nitrogen—anhydrous ammonia—became commercially available in California. Among the first to use anhydrous ammonia were citrus growers in the southern part of the state, who injected it into their irrigation water. The use quickly spread to other crops and other places. For crops grown on dry land, machines were devised to inject the liquid directly into the soil, where it dissipated as a gas. As a result of the effectiveness and low cost of this form of fertilizer, its use in California increased nearly twentyfold from 1940 to 1980. Producers in all of the western states spent increasing amounts of money on fertilizer into the early 1980s. However, between 1982 and 1987 the amount spent on fertilizer declined by 35 percent. Changing cultural practices, such as conservation tillage in grain production and the substitution of less expensive urea for anhydrous ammonia, may account for this decrease. Urea, usually used in granular form, was easier to transport than ammonia. It also contained twice as much nitrogen as ammonia, so it could be applied in lesser quantities.[40]

Although the importance of fertilizers should not be minimized, pesticides were the driving force behind the chemical revolution of American agriculture that took place after World War II. By 1987, producers in the twelve western states spent only one-tenth as much for fertilizers as for pesticides. In that year their fertilizer bill was $90 million dollars while their pesticide bill was $1.03 billion.[41]

Chemicals had not been an important cost of production before World War II. Farmers relied on planting whichever variety of their crop was most insect- and disease-resistant. To control weeds, they cultivated. The few pesticides that were available were difficult to use and toxic, and their effectiveness was unreliable.

Two chemical products that came on the market in 1945 bear the responsibility for beginning farmers' heavy dependence on chemical inputs: the insecticide DDT and the herbicide 2,4-D. DDT, the effectiveness of which became apparent during World War II, killed a wide range of insect pests, whether on plants, animals, or humans. It seemingly had no deleterious effects; could be dusted, sprayed, or atomized; and within a few years became very inexpensive. The herbicide 2,4-D (also a product of wartime research) killed a broad spectrum of plant pests without apparent damage to humans, animals, or desirable plants. Unlike earlier contact herbicides that burned or poisoned plant tissues, 2,4-D caused abnormally rapid growth that exhausted a plant's food reserves and brought about death.

Rapid adoption of these two products gave rise to an industry that created an endless stream of chemical solutions to the problems of agriculture. However, during the 1960s the long-term negative effects of pesticide use began to be apparent: pollution of water and soil resources, destruction of beneficial insects and animals, and the emergence of chemical-resistant pests. In the early 1970s, after a decade of studies and deepening public concern for protecting the environment, the federal government banned DDT and a list of related products from public use.

In one generation's time, pesticides had changed the practice of agriculture immeasurably. The systems associated with their use were so entrenched that neither the manufacturers nor the consumers of agricultural chemicals considered abandoning them and giving up the profits they brought. Instead, scientists and technologists sought to revise the systems. Plant scientists shifted the focus of their research from developing higher-yielding varieties of plants to breeding for pest resistance. Agricultural chemical manufacturers began to develop less toxic pesticides that could be used in lower concentrations. Instead of using only one herbicide, farmers rotated products on a regular basis to prevent development of herbicide-resistant weed varieties. By 1980, manufacturers offered 30,000 products representing 1,200 active pesticide ingredients. New products also led to new systems of production. By the 1980s, many western producers were using systems that incorporated pest-resistant plants bred for specific soil and climatic conditions, precision fertilizing, integrated pest management that combined biological and chemical controls, and specialized crop rotations and soil management techniques that minimized chemical use.[42]

In 1990, two other technologies, computers and biotechnology, stood poised at the threshold of acceptance and had the potential to revolutionize American agriculture in the same way that chemicals did earlier. Computers were not new. Forecasters for the USDA predicted in 1970 that by 1990 every agricultural producer in the United States would have a computer, but their forecast proved incorrect. In fact, only a small number of farmers owned computers in 1990, and most used them for bookkeeping and calculating ration balances. More often farmers benefited from computers through the better service they received from vendors who used them, such as farm management accounting services. However, the advent of expert systems, programs that simulated the problem-solving ability of a human expert, promised to put the findings of agricultural science at the fingertips of individual producers. Also, adoption of full-text retrieval systems on CD-ROM could make the latest agricultural research publications readily available to farmers and extension agents.[43]

Agricultural producers began to be aware of biotechnology's possibilities in the early 1980s. "Biotechnology" is a broad term applied to the products of genetic engineering and tissue culture. Agricultural biotechnology includes plants and animals that have been genetically altered by recombinant DNA techniques to create varieties and breeds that are resistant to diseases, insect pests, or chemicals. Tissue culture is a technique by which specific cells are grown in the laboratory to produce substances that previously were available only from plants and animals. In 1990, veterinary vaccines made from monoclonal antibodies (products of tissue culture) were the chief products of biotechnology available to agriculturists.

By 1995, the federal government had approved several more bioengineered products: bST, and genetically engineered corn, tomatoes, cotton, squash, and canola. In spite of long periods of review by the USDA, the FDA, and the EPA, the products remained subjects of controversy. Opponents of bST feared that residues of antibiotics used to treat the udder infections that are common in bST-treated cows would contaminate milk supplies. The chief objection to genetically engineered plants was their unknown effect on the environment. Some scientists believed the approved varieties of plants, all of which but tomatoes were engineered for insect or herbicide resistance, would not harm humans or the environment and would, in fact, benefit them by reducing the need for chemical pesticides. Environmentalists worried that cross-pollination could create pest-resistant weeds and genetic selection would create insects resistant to control measures.[44]

Computers and biotechnology lie at opposite ends of the technological spectrum that confronted agricultural producers from 1945 through 1990. At the computer end were systems of management that required farmers to have intimate knowledge of the natural processes underlying production—such things as grazing systems, conservation tillage, and IPM. At the biotechnology end of the spectrum were manufactured solutions to specific problems: machines, chemicals, new plants and animals. From 1945 until the 1970s, farmers tended to support the development of technologies of the latter type. By 1990, however, the commonly used systems of production fell closer to the middle of the spectrum; they required more intensive management of natural resources but utilized mechanical and chemical technologies when they were cost-effective. The systematization—industrialization, if you will—of agriculture that took place between 1945 and 1990 was the result of farmers' management decisions. The systems in use in 1990 represented the best bets of the producers who had survived the economic culling process of the previous three decades. Making a profit, which was the only way producers could persist, required minimizing all inputs but knowledge. Today, computers and biotechnology represent the most sophisticated responses of science and technology to the apparent desires of agricultural producers. They offer new ways of acquiring knowledge and decreasing inputs. It remains for the producers and consumers of agricultural commodities to determine, just as they had during the previous fifty years, whether and how these technologies might be used.

NOTES

1. Deborah Fitzgerald provides a useful definition of agricultural technology in her essay "Beyond Tractors: The History of Technology in American Agriculture," *Technology and Culture* 32 (January 1991): 115.

2. For a general discussion of the significance of technological systems during the latter half of the twentieth century, see Alan I Marcus and Howard P. Segal, *Technology in America: A Brief History* (San Diego: Harcourt Brace Jovanovich, 1989), 260–61.

3. U.S. Bureau of the Census, *Statistical Abstract of the United States: 1992* (Washington, D.C.: Government Printing Office, 1992), 646; U.S. Bureau of the Census, *Statistical Abstract of the United States: 1963* (Washington D.C.: Government Printing Office, 1963), 614. The tally of Western states includes Alaska.

4. U.S. Department of Agriculture, *Farmers in a Changing World: The Yearbook of Agriculture 1940* (Washington, D.C.: Government Printing Office, 1940), 802; U.S. Department of Agriculture, *Agricultural Statistics 1959* (Washington, D.C.: Government Printing Office, 1960), 588; U.S. Department of Agriculture, *Agricultural Statistics 1976* (Washington, D.C.: Government Printing Office, 1976), 500. For more information about electrification of rural areas of the United States, see David E. Nye, *Electrifying America: Social Meanings of a New Technology, 1880–1940* (Cambridge, Mass.: MIT Press, 1990), 287–335.

5. Marcus and Segal, *Technology in America*, 291–95.

6. R. Douglas Hurt, *Agricultural Technology in the Twentieth Century* (Manhattan, Kans.: Sunflower University Press, 1991) 20–21, 25–28. For a discussion of the slower adoption of tractors in California, see Robert E. Ankli and Alan L. Olmstead, "The Adoption of the Gasoline Tractor in California," *Agricultural History* 55 (July 1981): 215.

7. U.S. Bureau of the Census, *Statistical Abstract of the United States: 1992*,

653; Ronald Knutson, Robert D. Yonkers, and James W. Richardson, "The Impact of the Biotechnology and Information Revolutions on the Dairy Industry," in *Biotechnology and the New Agricultural Revolution,* ed. Joseph J. Molnar and Henry W. Kinnucan, American Association for the Advancement of Science (AAAS) Selected Symposium 108 (Boulder, Colo.: Westview Press, 1989), 121; U.S. Congress, Office of Technology Assessment, *U.S. Dairy Industry at a Crossroad: Biotechnology and Policy Choices,* OTA-F-470 (Washington, D.C.: Government Printing Office, May 1991) (hereafter OTA-F-470), 19.

8. George E. Seidel, Jr., "Biotech on the Farm: Geneticists in the Pasture," *Current* 316 (October 1989): 24; Knutson, Yonkers, and Richardson, "The Impact of the Biotechnology and Information Revolutions on the Dairy Industry," 125–26.

9. Ann Foley Scheuring, ed., *A Guidebook to California Agriculture* (Berkeley: University of California Press, 1983), 196–97.

10. H. B. Puckett, K. E. Harshbarger, and E. F. Olver, "Automatic Livestock Feeding," in *Science for Better Living: The Yearbook of Agriculture, 1968,* 90th Cong., 2d sess., 1968, House Document No. 239, 126–28.

11. Scheuring, *A Guidebook to California Agriculture,* 197.

12. Knutson, Yonkers, and Richardson, "The Impact of the Biotechnology and Information Revolutions on the Dairy Industry," 125–26; Frederick H. Buttel and Charles C. Geisler, "The Social Impacts of Bovine Somatotropin: Emerging Issues," in *Biotechnology and the New Agricultural Revolution,* ed. Joseph J. Molnar and Henry W. Kinnucan, AAAS Selected Symposium 108 (Boulder, Colo.: Westview Press, 1989), 138–39.

13. For a more detailed description of the establishment of the Office of Technology Assessment and its role, see Marcus and Segal, *Technology in America,* 352–53; two studies that examine and utilize forecasting models are William H. Friedland, Amy E. Barton, and Robert J. Thomas, *Manufacturing Green Gold: Capital, Labor, and Technology in the Lettuce Industry,* (Cambridge: Cambridge University Press, 1981); and Gigi M. Berardi and Charles C. Geisler, eds., *The Social Consequences and Challenges of New Agricultural Technologies* (Boulder, Colo.: Westview Press, 1984).

14. U.S. Bureau of the Census, *Statistical Abstract of the United States: 1992,* 653.

15. Sherm Ewing, *The Ranch: A Modern History of the North American Cattle Industry* (Missoula, Mont.: Mountain Press Publishing, 1995), 150–61, 254.

16. George S. Wells, *Garden in the West: A Dramatic Account of Science in Agriculture* (New York: Dodd, Mead, 1969), 27–39; Suzanne W. T. Batra, "Biological Control in Agroecosystems," *Science* 215 (January 1982): 136; U.S. Congress, Office of Technology Assessment, *A New Technological Era for American Agriculture,* OTA-F-474 (Washington, D.C.: Government Printing Office, August 1992) (hereafter OTA-F-474), 54–58.

17. Wells, *Garden in the West,* 11–18; Scott Evans and John Workman, "Helping Ranchers Make the Right Choices," *Utah Science* 52 (Fall 1991): 113; U.S. Congress, Office of Technology Assessment, *A New Technological Era for American Agriculture,* 54–55.

18. Gretel Ehrlich, "Growing Lean, Clean Beef," in *Our Sustainable Table,* ed. Robert Clark (San Francisco: North Point Press, 1990), 110.

19. Scheuring, *A Guidebook to California Agriculture,* 191.

20. Terry G. Summons, "Animal Feed Additives," *Agricultural History* 42 (October 1968): 307–10; for a study of the DES controversy, see Alan I Marcus, *Cancer from Beef: DES, Federal Food Regulation, and Consumer Confidence* (Baltimore: Johns Hopkins University Press, 1994).

21. James F. Shepherd, "Soil Conservation in the Pacific Northwest Wheat-Producing Areas: Conservation in a Hilly Terrain," *Agricultural History* 59 (April 1985): 230–31.

22. Ibid., 235–37, 241.

23. Charles Little, *Green Fields Forever: The Conservation Tillage Revolution in America* (Covelo, Calif.: Island Press, 1987), 58, 161–62, 166.

24. James F. Shepherd, "The Development of New Wheat Varieties in the Pacific Northwest," *Agricultural History* 54 (January 1980): 59–61; Little, *Green Fields Forever,* 58.

25. Alex C. McGregor, "From Sheep Range to Agribusiness: A Case History of Agricultural Transformation on the Columbia Plateau," *Agricultural History* 54 (January 1980): 25–26; U.S. Bureau of the Census, *Statistical Abstract of the United States: 1992,* 662.

26. "1994 Irrigation Survey: Overall Growth a Continuing Trend," *Irrigation Journal* 45 (January/February 1995): 31.

27. McGregor, "From Sheep Range to Agribusiness," 26.

28. Hurt, *Agricultural Technology in the Twentieth Century,* 88–97; Wayne D. Rasmussen, "Advances in American Agriculture: The Mechanical Tomato Harvester as a Case Study," *Technology and Culture* 9 (October 1968): 531–43; Andrew Schmitz and David Seckler, "Mechanized Agriculture and Social Welfare: The Case of the Tomato Harvester," *American Journal of Agricultural Economics* 52 (November 1970): 569–77; Jon A. Brandt and Ben C. French, "Mechanical Harvesting and the California Tomato Industry: A Simulation Analysis," *American Journal of Agricultural Economics* 65 (May 1983): 265–72.

29. Eliot Marshall, "Berglund Opposed on Farm Machine Policy," *Science* 208 (May 1980): 580; Philip L. Martin and Alan L. Olmstead, "The Agricultural Mechanization Controversy," *Science* 227 (February 1985): 601–6; "Out of Order," *The Economist* 305 (November 1987): 38; C. S. Kim et al., "Economic Impacts on Consumers, Growers, and Processors Resulting from Mechanical Tomato Harvesting in California—Revisited," *Journal of Agricultural Economics Research* 39 (Spring 1987): 39–44.

30. Anne Fredricks, "Technological Change and the Growth of Agribusiness: A Case Study of California Lettuce Production," in *The Social Consequences and Challenges of New Agricultural Technologies,* ed. Gigi M. Berardi and Charles C. Geisler (Boulder, Colo.: Westview Press, 1984), 259–60.

31. Harold O. Carter and Warren E. Johnston, "Agricultural Productivity and Technological Change: Some Concepts, Measures and Implications," in *Technological Change, Farm Mechanization and Agricultural Employment* (Berkeley: University of California, Division of Agricultural Sciences, July 1978), 97–99.

32. For descriptions of the mechanization of the sugar beet industry, see Hurt, *Agricultural Technology in the Twentieth Century,* 78–85; Roy Bainer, "Science and Technology in Western Agriculture," *Agricultural History* 49 (January 1975): 61–63; Wayne D. Rasmussen, "Technological Change in Western Sugar Beet Production," *Agricultural History* 41 (January 1967): 31–35; and Scheuring, *A Guidebook to California Agriculture,* 123–24. For

mechanization of cotton production in the West, see Hurt, *Agricultural Technology in the Twentieth Century,* 38–40; Willis Peterson and Yoav Kislev, "The Cotton Harvester in Retrospect: Labor Displacement or Replacement?" *Journal of Economic History* 46 (March 1986): 205; Charles R. Sayre, "Cotton Mechanization Since World War II," *Agricultural History* 53 (January 1979): 110–18; Bainer, "Science and Technology in Western Agriculture," 64–65.

33. Paul Barnett et al., *Labor's Dwindling Harvest: The Impact of Mechanization on California Fruit and Vegetable Workers* (Davis, Calif.: California Institute for Rural Studies, 1978), 41–42, 44; Scheuring, *A Guidebook to California Agriculture,* 266–67.

34. U.S. Department of Commerce, Bureau of the Census, *1987 Census of Agriculture,* vol. 1, Parts 2, 3, 5, 6, 12, 28, 31 (Washington, D.C.: Government Printing Office, 1989), 7.

35. David Lawrence Smith, "Superfarms vs. Sagebrush: New Irrigation Developments on the Snake River Plain," *Proceedings of the Association of American Geographers* 2 (1970): 129.

36. Hurt, *Agricultural Technology in the Twentieth Century,* 65–66.

37. "1994 Irrigation Survey," 28, 29, 31, 35, 37, 39, 40.

38. U.S. Department of Agriculture, *Using Our Natural Resources: 1983 Yearbook of Agriculture* (Washington, D.C.: Office of Information, 1983), 21; Charles C. Geisler et al., "Sustained Land Productivity: Equity Consequences of Alternative Agricultural Technologies," in *The Social Consequences of New Agricultural Technologies,* ed. Gigi M. Berardi and Charles C. Geisler (Boulder, Colo.: Westview Press, 1984), 220–21; Smith, "Superfarms vs. Sagebrush," 129.

39. Geisler, "Sustained Land Productivity," 220.

40. Scheuring, *A Guidebook to California Agriculture,* 269–71.

41. U.S. Department of Commerce, Bureau of the Census, *1987 Census of Agriculture,* 7; Bureau of the Census, *Census of Agriculture, 1987, on CD-ROM* (Washington, D.C.: Bureau of the Census, 1990), County Data, State, State Total, County Summary Highlights, Farm Production Expenses, for Montana, Oregon, Utah, Washington, Wyoming.

42. Scheuring, *A Guidebook to California Agriculture,* 273.

43. For a brief discussion of the computer technologies that appeared to hold promise for agricultural producers, see U.S. Congress, Office of Technology Assessment, *A New Technological Era for American Agriculture,* 6–8. For a description of an expert system already in use, see Peter B. Goodell et al., "CALEX/Cotton: An Integrated Expert System for Cotton Production and Management," *California Agriculture* 44 (September/October 1990): 18–21.

44. For overviews of the agricultural biotechnologies of the 1990s and the issues surrounding them, see U.S. Conress, Office of Technology Assessment, *A New Technological Era for American Agriculture;* and Bette Hileman, "Views Differ Sharply over Benefits, Risks of Agricultural Biotechnology," *Chemical and Engineering News* 73 (August 1995): 8–17. For an in-depth critique, see Jack Kloppenburg, Jr., "The Social Impacts of Biogenetic Technology in Agriculture: Past and Future," in *The Social Consequences and Challenges of New Agricultural Technologies,* ed. Gigi M. Berardi and Charles C. Geisler (Boulder, Colo.: Westview Press, 1984), 291–321; and Jack Doyle, *Altered Harvest: Agriculture, Genetics, and the Fate of the World's Food Supply* (New York: Viking, 1985).

9

Cattle Raising and Dairying in the Western States

Mark Friedberger

In the early twentieth century, a continuous wave of technical innovations shaped the development of large-scale, systematic, that is, industrial agriculture. The pace of technological innovation and adoption slackened in the difficult decades of the twenties and thirties but quickened after 1945. Farmers found themselves on a treadmill that forced them to either adopt the latest techniques to survive economically or surrender and leave agriculture for some other occupation. Indeed, farming became intensely competitive, and that competition caused agricultural industry manufacturers to produce innovations to capture the market and improve efficiency.[1]

Some farmers were drawn onto the treadmill of technological adoption sooner than others. Since World War II, the major changes in livestock raising and dairying in the western states have involved innovation and competition. The process of rapid modernization in some forms of agriculture and slower development in others can be seen in relation to cattle feedlots and dairying in California, as well as cattle raising on ranches in Utah, Nevada, Colorado, Wyoming, Montana, New Mexico, and Arizona. Cattle feeding and drylot dairies came closest to the ideal of industrialized agriculture, where the production process in corrals was divorced from the land. Animals became machinelike in their role of producing beef and milk for the consumer-driven market. In contrast, ranching for the purpose of raising calves and stocker cattle on large tracts of land remained divorced from the fast-paced, technological changes that took place in other agricultural areas.[2]

It is important to emphasize why livestock production changed after 1940, when consumer demand largely determined the nature of the food and fiber chain in American farming. Agriculture, like other facets of the economy, was influenced by a high wage-scale economy, which enabled consumers to buy durable goods and food items that reflected a high standard of living. The population boom in California and the Pacific Northwest began even before the declaration of war in December 1941 and continued until the economy crashed in the early 1990s. The growing western population required basic foodstuffs— including beef and dairy products. As a result of the economics of feeding and transportation, pork products could be shipped cheaply to the western states from the corn belt. On the other hand, the economics of beef feeding and dairy production made California a prime location for these activities.[3]

California has always been in the vanguard of innovations in agriculture. Agribusiness, that is, large-scale agriculture-related businesses, in the state had pioneered the use of cooperative marketing, the Bank of America had actively encouraged business-oriented agriculture, bonanza wheat farms had used industrialized production methods, and, at the end of the Great Depression, elaborate irrigation projects were being planned to turn the Central Valley into a region of year-round agricultural production. At the same time, in 1940, California's livestock producers remained fairly traditional in their operations. Thousands of small dairy farmers, many of them Dutch and Portuguese immigrants, eked out a living supplying fluid milk to the growing Los Angeles and San Francisco milksheds and cream for butter and cheese.[4]

In 1940, western cattle raisers and dairymen had not climbed on the agricultural treadmill as had the fruit growers or cotton producers in the San Joaquin Valley. Dairy operations remained small and catered to local markets. Cattle raising depended on methods of production that had not changed much since the turn of the century. However, marketing remained both regional and national in scope. For instance, Mountain State cattlemen located east of the Continental Divide shipped their livestock to the corn belt or Great Plains states for fattening and to Midwest packing plants for slaughter. Cattlemen west of the Continental Divide transported their livestock to California for fattening on grass and then to packing plants catering to coastal urban markets.[5]

World War II began the process of modernization and differentiation in each of these areas of cattle raising. At the same time, the treadmill's impact remained less intrusive in cattle ranching than in cattle feeding and dairying. Competition had a greater effect on western ranching than industrialization, although many ranchers remained handicapped by their dependence on federal rangeland for their livelihood. For years ranchers managed to control federal land policy. After 1960, with the rise of the environmental movement, livestock producers were put on the defensive. Ranchers found themselves caught between Bureau of Land Management (BLM) and Forest Service personnel and environmental advocates. Cattle ranching, even in the West, also succumbed from the mid-1960s onward to a trend that had an influence wherever cattle were reared: it became a consumptive rather than a productive activity. Many producers did not need to depend on livestock income for their livelihood. Especially in the years 1954–86, income tax regulations encouraged investment by nonagriculturists in cattle operations. Some became ranchers because they enjoyed the lifestyle and prestige, worrying less about the monetary rewards it brought. To be sure, the "old-fashioned" ranch that depended on marketing calves and young cattle remained a force in the West, but it was often at some disadvantage when competing with well-financed outsiders who did not need to make a profit.[6]

The population explosion on the West Coast encouraged entrepreneurial activity for both cattle raising and dairying. Ever since the settlement of the Midwest and the emergence of the corn belt as a prime grain-producing area, farmer feeders had fattened cattle. For them cattle feeding was a convenient method of marketing their grain and utilizing excess corn. Farmer feeders brought their animals from the West, fed them in small numbers, and then dispatched them to terminal markets such as Chicago and Kansas City. Before 1950, the corn belt, with its small operations and ready supply of corn and roughage (hay and silage), dominated cattle feeding. However, this advantage would not last. Scientific and technological breakthroughs would soon permit other areas to intrude.[7]

The large-scale features of western feeding became a staple in cattle magazines. The Tovrea feed yard, for example, caught the notice of the *American Cattle Producer* in May 1950 and received glowing treatment. The Tovrea family opened a large feedlot in the Salt River valley near Phoenix. Pioneers to the state in the nineteenth century, they had been involved in ranching and meatpacking for many decades, but the Tovreas had turned to cattle feeding when the market became depressed. Their first yard was designed to "hold" cattle until prices improved. By 1950, the yard, with a 25,000-head capacity, probably had become the largest in the country. As custom feeders the Tovreas serviced other ranchers' cattle. Ranchers paid them for the grain and care that the livestock received.[8]

Unlike the Midwest, where farmer feeders possessed primitive equipment, and where unprocessed corn still made up the bulk of the ration, the Tovrea's feed yard used a mix of locally grown products supplemented by molasses. The mill, where the feed ingredients were mixed to uniform specifications, lay at the center of the operation, and it produced a nutritious and digestible ration for maximum gains in the shortest time. The Tovreas tailored the ingredients to the owner's requirements with the flick of a switch. Shaped like a grain elevator, the mill utilized chutes from the mixer to bring the rations to trucks that transported the feed to the corrals.[9]

Soon after the war, agribusiness men perfected this technique for cattle feeders, not only in the West but also across the country. These "tailored beef factories," or feedlots, brought a revolution to the cattle business. Feedlot operators introduced several new features to cattle feeding. First, they provided more services for their rancher customers. Second, they could hold animals if owners needed to wait out a poor market. In addition, the large number of cattle fed meant that costs could be minimized because unit costs decreased as the volume of business increased.[10]

Innovative management provided the key to bringing these new industrial feedlots to the West. The dry, hot climate provided a healthier environment than the mud and cold of the Midwest. An ever-increasing urban population along the West Coast encouraged the establishment of technologically modern feedlots. For example, the capacities of Arizona yards increased from 59,000 in 1950 to 220,000 in 1957; California's grew from 196,000 to 496,000 during the same years. Not only had western feedlots solved the problem of feed requirements by the innovative use of local products such as citrus pulp and cotton hulls, but operators had also eliminated the problem of climatic stress in the hot summer months. New feeding regimens, the increased use of shade, the introduction of crossbred cattle, and the widespread use of implants and antibiotics improved the productivity of the yards.[11]

In the 1950s, feedlot operators made efforts to alleviate heat stress by using shades of various types. They also introduced water sprays for cooling purposes. Temperatures in the Imperial Valley averaged 90 degrees in July and August, with minimums never below 71 degrees. Sometimes in the early afternoon the thermometer reached 126 degrees, and mean summer temperatures often exceeded the body temperature of cattle. In feedlots, livestock not only must survive in such heat but also must gain weight in order to be slaughtered on schedule. In hot temperatures ruminal animals like cattle cannot absorb roughage. Hay and alfalfa makes them hotter at a time when they have difficulty striking a balance between the rate of heat produced and the rate of heat lost. Thus feedlot operators in the Imperial Valley had to carefully balance summer diets by supplementing grain only with the highest-quality roughage.[12]

By 1964, California had 603 feedlots—mostly small-scale—but the larger 10,000-plus lots had become common in the hotter and drier areas of the state. These lots increased from 20 in 1958 to 54 in 1963—all the larger lots custom-fed cattle. In California, cattle usually arrived at the feedlots weighing 600 to 700 pounds. They then received an average of 24 pounds of feed per day during a stay that averaged 152 days. Typical rations consisted of barley, milo, beet pulp, cottonseed meal, and alfalfa, all of which could be grown under irrigated conditions in the San Joaquin and Imperial Valleys.[13]

During the early 1960s, the logistics and expense of moving cattle and grain great distances caused producers and processors to make some important strategic decisions that would have great implications for the feeding and slaughtering business in California and Arizona. The sleeping giant of the industry was the High Plains, which rapidly became the center of the feedlot industry in the United States. In 1962, Texans and Oklahomans traveled to Arizona and California to study feedlot management. They realized that rather than sending their cattle to those states for feeding and slaughter, they could adapt western methods to the Great Plains and compete with advantage. As a result, by the late 1960s the Arizona and California cattle-feeding complex began to contract as the pioneers in industrialized feeding succumbed to competition from the

The rangeland cattle industry remains an important part of livestock production in the West. Although feedlots often are used to fatten cattle with grain after they come off the range, by the late twentieth century some consumers hailed the beef from grass-fed cattle as healthier because it had less marbling, that is, fat. *Courtesy, U.S. Department of Agriculture.*

Plains. In the 1970s and 1980s, innovations in packing plants—especially the introduction of boxed beef, where packers instead of butchers fashioned cuts of meat—streamlined the marketing process. This allowed packers to supply the West Coast from plants on the Great Plains cheaper than shipping live cattle to western slaughterhouses.[14]

In 1980, only 101 feedlots remained in California—47 in the southern San Joaquin Valley and 34 in the Imperial Valley, for 80 percent of the total. Moreover, change in the economics of feeding cattle in the late 1980s caused further restructuring of the industry in the West. In Washington, Idaho, and New Mexico, as well as California and Arizona, cattle feedlots supplied a regional packing industry with products for an increasingly specialized market in which "chemical-free beef" had found a niche.[15]

The entrepreneurial spirit also found a home in the California dairy industry. As historian Anne Scheuring has suggested, Californians were the "renegades" of the dairy business. Farmers have often said that cows needed individual attention to produce milk. Certainly, small-scale farmers in the Midwest believed this dictum. There the farmer, his wife, and children labored with their cows seven days a week; dairying under these conditions lived up to its reputation as slave labor. In the 1940s, many dairies in California worked on this model. On the Kings River in the Central Valley, however, small dairy farms used ditch irrigation from the river to grow alfalfa. Small herds and the rigid routine and trying work regimen provided an ideal vehicle for large Portuguese families to make their way out of poverty.[16]

In the 1950s, dairying in the San Joaquin Valley began to approximate the custom feedlot industry in southern California. As land in the Los Angeles basin became too expensive for paddocks, drylot dairies took their place. Several innovations made this possible. Californians proved they could feed concentrates to dairy cows and increase production. While the drylot still needed hay and alfalfa, both could be produced elsewhere, and new machines helped improve production. Field choppers shortened harvesting time and enabled irrigation alfalfa growers to improve quality.[17]

The warm, dry climate ensured that the cows could remain outside year-round, which permitted a revolution in milking. Rather than utilizing a large barn where the cows remained for long periods, as in the cold winters of the Midwest, the California milking shed remained small. Dairymen now drove their cows into stanchions for milking, then ushered them back to the corral. California dairymen took advantage of the new technology in refrigeration and the methods of moving milk both on the farm and from the farm gate to the processing plant. Pipelines brought the milk from the cows to stainless steel tanks; then refrigerated trucks collected milk daily from the farm for processing.[18]

Dairying lent itself to other efficiencies. An individual cow's production could be monitored, and feed could be tailored to an animal's needs. Dairymen analyzed herd records to make necessary adjustments. Thus milk production soared in California, herd size grew, and the number of dairies decreased. In 1945, 25,000 dairies averaged 32 head. In 1979, only 2,864 dairies existed, and herd sizes had increased to an average of 304. The importance of innovative management became evident when California cows produced 37 percent more milk than Midwest cows in 1978—25 percent more than the national average. By then the state had become second only to Wisconsin in milk production and receipts.[19]

This movement for efficiency can be best studied in the Los Angeles milkshed after World War II. All the characteristics described earlier—market demand, rising land values, and increasing hay costs spurred the introduction of factory-type operations. Dairymen used large amounts of capital, modern equipment, high labor efficiency, and sophisticated feed to attain the greatest possible production with the highest-quality milk per cow.[20]

The typical dairy near Los Angeles consisted of a milking barn, a milk house for storing and cooling, corrals and lanes for feeding, holding, and moving the cows, and other structures such as hay barns, calf sheds, and feed storage buildings. Dairy animals were fed a concentrated diet of grains, meal, and molasses, with alfalfa and hay as roughage. With continuous urban sprawl engulfing the dairies, operators not only lost the ability to produce feed for themselves but also faced environmental problems that began to cause great concern among their neighbors. Odors, flies, and animal noises drove the nearby residential population to complain, which caused local authorities to curb

As the population rapidly increased after World War II, dairying became a major agricultural endeavor in the West. In California, as land values and property taxes increased, dairymen moved away from the cities, often to areas zoned for agriculture. Drylot dairies, that is, operations that confined cows to corrals and fed them grain and hay, replaced dairy farms, such as this one in Montana, where the farmer grazed his cows on lush pastures. *Courtesy, United States Department of Agriculture.*

these nuisances. As a result, county governments devised a new system of zoning for dairies, designating sections of counties some distance from residential populations as dairying areas. Los Angeles County opened Dairy Valley, an 8.75-square-mile area for 241 operations. Dairyland in Orange County permitted twenty cows per acre in an area 2 miles square, and Cypress, also in Orange County, measured 7 square miles, allowed ten cows per acre, and contained 50 dairies. Later, another dairy area in the Chino Valley in San Bernardino County contained 70 square miles of desert.[21]

The advantages of the new zoning regulations were obvious. They solved the problem of harassment and complaints from a public impatient with environmental problems, and they placed a break on the steep rise in land values that had forced dairymen to relocate because of increased tax assessments. Even in the 1950s, producers realized that the termination of dairying outside these designated areas would eventually occur and all operators outside the zoned land would be forced to relocate.

The Los Angeles milkshed stretched farther than the immediate area surrounding the city and included several areas that specialized in different production functions. During the late 1930s, the San Joaquin Valley had shipped cream south to Los Angeles. In World War II, military needs made dairymen in the San Joaquin hard-pressed to supply fluid milk to Los Angeles and the Bay Area. By the end of the 1950s, the San Joaquin Valley had become the most productive milk-producing area in the state. Dairies were found in the Tulare-Hanford region and near Los Banos, Newman, and Modesto. In the 1960s, these dairies converted from pasture-type operations to drylot. Many dairymen found it more profitable to grow irrigated cotton, buying alfalfa from specialists elsewhere in the West. By the 1970s, a discernible migration of dairies from Los Angeles to the San Joaquin could be seen. Dairymen took advantage of the intrusion of urban sprawl to accept high land prices and finance their move.[22]

The outstanding success of the California dairy industry brought with it a certain amount of controversy. California's distance from other population centers permitted the state to run its own system of milk marketing orders. (Marketing orders are part of the federal government's dairy program designed to regulate marketing practices, including the conditions of sale and the setting of minimum prices for grade A milk). Until 1960, California remained primarily a fluid milk state, with most of its milk drunk rather than processed into other products.[23]

After 1960, the federal and state governments became even more involved in regulatory activity in milk production. In addition, the federal government provided a full array of price supports. Within this highly regulated market, California's milk production continued to soar from 8 million pounds in 1960 to 17.2 million pounds in 1986. Virtually all California milk was designated as grade A for use in the fluid market. However, with milk consumption declining, producers channeled a growing percentage of this milk into the industrial pool for the manufacture of butter, cheese, condensed milk, and ice cream. Thus, while the state remained removed from the Midwest-based structure of the federal marketing program, its production overload channeled into the national surplus of milk and affected the whole country. By the 1980s, California supplied the Commodity Credit Corporation (the government surplus program) with 16 percent of its stocks, such as butter and cheese, while the state produced only 12 percent of the nation's milk. California dairying also took advantage of the dairy buyout program. Introduced in the mid-1980s to cut milk production by culling herds in the upper Midwest, the program spent considerable funds in the San Joaquin.[24]

The overproduction problem would continue to plague dairymen after the mid-1980s. The prospects for any solution looked bleak. Dairy cows became even more productive when the U.S. Department of Agriculture (USDA) approved biotechnological innovations. California dairymen made artificial insemination with prize bull semen for cows a routine procedure. Given the continued drop-off in fluid milk consumption by the public, the only bright spot in the industry seemed the continued expansion of pizza consumption and the increased need for Italian-type cheese. In California, cheese production climbed from 17.3 million pounds in 1970 to 137 million pounds only eight years later.[25]

If innovation and competition played key roles in the transformation of dairying in the West, both played different roles in cattle ranching. The lengthy time required to move an animal from birth on the range to the slaughterhouse remained the same wherever cattle raisers operated. Therefore, innovation, except in the introduction of more vigorous breeding stock, had less importance than competition from other regions in the country. Westerners had a competitive disadvantage in ranching compared with other livestock producers because cattle raising in the region took place on public land. Some argued that the Jeffersonian land distribution system proved inappropriate for the West. Compared with the Spanish colonial commons, whose operations permitted extensive operations and flexibility in their administration, Congress's continued insistence that small-scale land distribution remain the standard in the arid West resulted in endless conflict that brought disadvantages to western ranchers.[26]

Passage of the Taylor Grazing Act of 1934 opened a new chapter in western ranching. The act attempted to bring order to the western federal lands. Because western ranchers usually depended on federal land for grazing, they often thought of themselves as dependent on the bureaucratic agencies that oversaw the public grazing lands. Ranchers did not own permits, and this made their operations risky, as well as causing them some humiliation in view of their symbolic role as rugged individualists. In addition, their record for the use of public land had become controversial. For years they were able to control the boards that administered public land. Only with the emergence of the environmental movement in the 1960s did some redistribution of power occur. The environmental movement attacked ranchers for their casual regard for the land ethic. In attacking ranchers, urban environmentalists often failed to fully understand the viewpoint of cattle raisers, who thought of themselves as environmentalists in matters of conservation.[27]

Cattlemen, however, were hardly an undifferentiated mass. They included the affluent and the hard up, commercial operators and registered breeders, those who depended on cattle production as their sole means of support and those who looked for a tax write-off, as well as hobbyists with fewer than twenty cows. Cattlemen traditionally espoused a conservative management style. The nature of the operation made them fatalistic. The long-drawn-out process of raising calves, together with risks from weather, predators, economic downturns, and the effects of government policy, forced ranchers to be frugal.[28]

Frugality and lack of innovation from the 1940s to the early 1960s could partly be blamed on the shadow of the Great Depression, whose psychological legacy made a deep impression on livestock raisers. Many cattlemen lost ranches or, if they were lucky enough to survive, had to scale down operations. Although from 1943 to 1951 the cattle market boomed, many ranchers were in no mood to take risks. The boom after World War II made western ranches attractive places for investment by a moneyed elite. For many, the recreational features of ranching became more important than the monetary rewards, especially for investors who desired that their ranches retain traditional modes of operation. Consequently, they discouraged the use of new techniques such as electric branding and the use of motor vehicles so that their operations would retain the ambience of the old-fashioned ranch.[29]

Since the 1940s, however, fundamental differences have remained between northern and southern areas of the West where cattle-raising operations have been conducted. Northern ranchers in Wyoming, for example, need winter feed. Operations there are more labor-intensive than in southwestern New Mexico, where in years of normal precipitation cattle require little attention and supplemental feed. In addition, the movement of nonranch interests—corporations, affluent outsiders, and small recreational hobby ranchers—into a branch of agriculture where previously full-time ranchers predominated has altered perspectives. Also, the volatility of the economy and the cattle market affected all those engaged in cattle raising. Often ranchers with substantial financial resources suffered as much from economic downturns as did those with less capital. A fourth important characteristic of western ranching remained the presence of federal and state land for supplemental grazing. In most western states the federal government owned millions of acres on which ranchers grazed their cattle in the summer and fall. The administration of these lands and the tug-of-war between bureaucrats, ranchers, and the general public grew over the years as environmental concerns found a place in conventional thought.

Methods that worked in the southwestern desert had little applicability to more northern areas. In the north, good feed was available all year. Cows weighed more because hay produced in irrigated fields made winter feed abundant. Hay production, however, also meant increased labor requirements at certain times of year. In the deserts of New Mexico and Arizona, drought became the enemy, which could cripple an operation after a year. During the 1950s, below-normal precipitation proved especially hard on cattle raisers. The drought caused a scramble for land because a successful operator often acquired more land during years of low moisture. In northern states such as Colorado and Wyoming, harsh winter weather conditions forced continuous feeding and monitoring of cattle. Winter weather could drag on into April and May, making calving difficult. Calves born in snowy and wet pastures often suffered from white scours (an infection in the lower alimentary canal) while late snow cover promoted sunburn on the teats of cows.[30]

Although generalizations about ranching operations in such a huge region as the West can be problematic, most studies have indicated that large- and medium-scale cow-calf ranches are more profitable than small ones. The latter, with around 300 cows, are handicapped because they have fewer resources to fall back on when the market fluctuates downward. Large-scale ranches, with around 1,600 cows, give their owners or managers greater flexibility for securing loans, breeding, marketing, and making decisions to improve efficiency.[31]

Following World War II, typical northern ranch conditions could be found

Cattle raising remains an important part of western agriculture. Often, however, ranchers do not own their own land. Rather, they purchase permits that allow them to graze their cattle on the public lands administered by the Bureau of Land Management or the Forest Service. Corrals near highways permit easy loading of the cattle onto trucks for marketing. *Courtesy, Montana State University.*

in the mountain valleys of Wyoming. All ranches depended on Forest Service grazing in the summer, while irrigated alfalfa meadows provided most of the necessary hay for winter feeding. These meadows also enabled cows to graze in the fall and spring before they moved off to feed at higher elevations on government land. As a rule, the breeding herd calved on hay meadows or creek bottoms or in manmade shelters in April and May. Most dehorning, vaccinating, and castrating occurred before the cattle were moved to summer ranges. The cows and their calves then went to the foothills, and finally in June to national forests for three or four months. Here, cattle made their largest and most economical gains on the public range, which reinforced the importance of cheap grazing on federal land for the profitability of cattlemen. In Wyoming fall was a busy time. Cattle came down from the mountains, the yearlings marked for sale were shipped to feedlots, and the breeding herd was then wintered on hay meadows.[32]

Herds were composed of cows, replacement heifers, bulls, the current calf crop, and yearling steers that were late-born holdovers. In Utah the tough climate and its seasonal nature reinforced traditional cattle management practices. Cattle raisers used one bull to service twenty to twenty-five cows. Some ranchers used the high mountain pastures belonging to the Forest Service from June to October. When the weather grew cold, they brought the cattle down to BLM land for grazing from November to May. Usually they located the home ranch near these ranges. In the event of harsh weather, cattle could be fed hay and other supplements to tide them over. The winter months gave ranchers a chance to take stock of their herd's performance. Such chores included the culling of nonperformers, sales of calves in November, and especially solving administrative problems caused by ranching on government property. Because Utah ranchers usually lived in town, their home ranches had a minimum of facilities: stock sheds, corrals, and feeding and watering troughs. They only needed farm equipment for haying and in some instances custom operators provided this service.[33]

Family ranches in New Mexico and Arizona operated by a considerably different system. Although more than 50 percent of the ranchers had grazing permits to use government land, migration and transhumance were not part of the yearly routine. The configuration of state, federal, and Indian land supplemented requirements of the ranchers. In theory, ranges supported grazing year-round. As a result, the costs of winter feeding remained lower than elsewhere. On the other hand, by the 1950s most ranchers fed cattle in the winter. The range would gradually green up after rains, but frequent droughts forced ranchers to utilize browsing plants and shrubs to bolster scanty range feed. Drought caused ranchers to alter their strategies, to remain flexible, and to use land more conservatively. Over the years, the number of cows that each section supported decreased from roughly ten to seven. Even so, about a third of the operators in one study grazed their land continuously throughout the year; the other two-thirds claimed they rotated their herds.[34]

Adverse weather in western New Mexico during the 1950s forced some advances in range management. Most ranches were fenced and cross-fenced; because of the lack of water, wells, pumps, tanks, and windmills were installed where previously minimal improvements had sufficed. At the same time, these ranches remained unsophisticated in their use of machinery. Few owned tractors, and a single pickup or automobile usually proved adequate. The choice of cattle remained conservative as well, with Herefords composing approximately 90 percent of herds. Breeding remained simple. Half the ranchers kept their bulls with the cows all year and many made no special provisions for pregnant cows except when they needed doctoring. In short, capital outlays were minor on southwestern ranches, which averaged 230 cows on 10,000 acres. The high prices for cattle from the war years until the early 1950s sustained these smaller operations. However, the drought of the 1950s cut into profitability.[35]

In the 1960s, a perceptive study of small and midsized ranches in New Mexico showed ranchers to be deeply pessimistic about operations. Their rugged individualism showed itself in their reluctance to work with others. When drought conditions gripped the land, they responded by placing more cattle on the range to maintain income. Any sense that innovations would assist in saving their range habitat never surfaced. To these ranchers, education had little importance. Ranching knowledge came through doing, not through studying.[36]

Whatever their background, cattlemen retained a conservative management style. Many were set in their ways and did not like to alter management methods except as a last resort. Most cultural studies emphasized that ranchers remained rugged individualists whose word was their bond. One mountain Colorado rancher, for example, sold his cattle to the same Iowa feeder thirteen years in succession sight unseen. The quality of the animals and the rancher's reputation remained so high that his integrity was unquestioned.[37]

Another study of eastern Nevada ranchers in the late 1970s and early 1980s showed that even when modern techniques such as electric branding were available, old-fashioned methods were favored. Frugality epitomized the rancher's operating style. One of the largest ranches in the state, if not the nation, the enormous Broken T, used minimalist management procedures. This ranch had 2,300 sections, or 1.4 million acres, that could support only 600 cows. Its cattle often died and decayed on the range. The rancher's philosophy left as much to nature as possible, avoiding vaccinations and dehorning, and relying on horses rather than pickups. Such frugality meant that "the cows had to make a living for themselves." The rancher believed that the best way to survive the ups and downs of the cattle cycle was to manage his herd the "old-fashioned way."[38]

In the West the older and better established the ranch family, the more status they held. Newcomers had to earn their spurs. Eventually, if they stuck with the cattle business through its bad and good years, they were accepted. Ranching remained a masculine pursuit. Most women acted as "gofers" and communications facilitators. The larger the ranch, the less the influence of the women. Once a woman married, she de-emphasized her own kin ties and stressed those of her husband. The male side of the family dominated the ranch inheritance process. Often the isolated position of a ranch in the West tended to cut a family off from the local trading center. Many lived too far from town to join a church, and their children had to board away from home to go to school. Some felt happy with this situation, for they preferred the isolation of the ranch to the gossip in town.[39]

Although western ranching always had corporate and affluent urban investors in its ranks, the years after World War II saw an influx of outside money into ranching. Land began to rise in price—in some areas this inflationary spiral was fueled by oil and gas speculation and exploration. Indeed, the connection between oil and cattle became cemented in this period. As one observer of the scene described it: "Many wealthy easterners acquired ranches. Most had 'little knowledge of the cow.' " They built luxurious homes and drove expensive cars but seldom rode a horse over the range. When old-timers observed the affluent lifestyles of the newcomers, it caused resentment. They usually depended entirely on cattle to make a living. Newcomers joined an industry that from 1946 to 1948 experienced one of the most profitable periods in its history. The fortunate ones hired managers who could take advantage of good times and bad. The Green Cattle Company, a family corporate ranch in north central Arizona, utilized its resources to good effect in these years. Its largest ranch, the 230,000-acre Baca Float, provided the safety net for the company. As a cow-calf operation, all its cows were raised on the ranch. Smaller ranches that belonged to the family were stocked with feeders for short-term gains. Despite the potential that outside money provided for operational modernization, the Baca Float remained a "horseback outfit" whose owners preferred a traditional approach to their cattle ranching.[40]

The same sort of situation prevailed at another family corporate ranch until circumstances forced modernization after 1960. The N Bar in central Montana struggled in the 1930s as the owners attempted to keep the 29,000-acre spread from foreclosure. In the 1940s and 1950s, traditionalism and frugality prevailed. No one could tell whether the cows had calved because the manager kept no records. The philosophy of the ranch minimized working cattle because, the operators thought, cows knew more about their way of life than did ranch managers. As late as the 1960s, only one pickup and two jeeps plied the ranch. Instead, Belgian horses did the heavy hauling, while ranch horses supplied the motive power for the cowboys. Increasingly, labor became one of the most troubling aspects of ranching in Montana. In the early 1960s, the manager of the N Bar processed 120 W-2 forms. The ranch seemed to attract the wildest people in the West. The $123-a-month wage meant only drifters with character flaws signed on. By 1963, a family dispute among the stockholders forced a sale, and this watershed in ownership began the modernization of the ranch.[41]

The N Bar Ranch hired reliable Hispanics to do cowboy work. Financially nonproductive show cattle were eliminated, and, because the frame of Angus cows had grown too large for the equipment in packinghouses, the owners began a new breeding program to produce smaller animals. The ranch inventoried all its livestock and ear-tagged the cows and calves. Even so, modernization had its costs. In the 1970s and early 1980s the owners adopted the latest methods of range and land management. According to the new owner, "A war on weeds was waged with life-threatening herbicides. The cattle were forced to ovulate. Embryos were flushed from superovulating donor cows and transplanted into synchronized recipients." New attitudes about the effect of industrialized methods on cattle raising also made headway. The wholesale application of technology proved expensive and caused stress for animals and humans. According to one observer of N Bar, the adoption of strategies geared to efficiency had "demeaned the cattle and insulated the ranch from its surroundings." Therefore, the ranch reorganized its priorities and introduced alternative methods. The new strategy called for a balance between high-cost inputs and sustainable techniques on pastures and rangeland. The ranch owners, for example, searched for local suppliers and introduced a neighbor's sheep to crop the weeds.[42]

The agricultural recession of the 1980s forced many cattlemen to reevaluate their position. Drought and poor financial prospects forced the restructuring of ranches in the West, as they did on farms in the Midwest. Large operations were particularly vulnerable. In 1981, the Sierra Power Company took control of the Winecap-Gamble ranch in northern Nevada after a severe drought had eliminated the ranch's water supply. The company then placed the 1.2-million-acre ranch and its normal inventory of 10,000 cows on the market; by the end of the decade, however, it still remained in corporate hands. A similar situation occurred at the huge ZX at Paisley, Oregon. Originally part of the Kern County Land Company, this ranch of 100,000 acres of private land and 1.3 million acres of BLM and Forest Service range was taken over by Metropolitan Life in 1986.[43]

The continued intrusion into western ranching by outsiders caused concern among old established operators. The Lane Ranch in the Big Sky Country of Montana had remained in the same family since the nineteenth century. This ranch was organized as a family partnership managed by a father and his sons. It ran 4,500 cattle on 75,000 deeded acres, with 29,000 additional acres leased from the government. The cattle operation, though wiped out in the Great Depression, lived to see another day. In the 1980s, however, competition from nonfamily operators and difficult financial times made ranchers like the Lanes, who were dependent entirely on cattle for a living, economically vulnerable.[44]

This is not to suggest that oil barons and shopping center magnates have dominated the migration into cattle ranching in the past thirty years. Some ranching families were successful despite handicaps of background and showed much ability and good judgment in their climb up the ranching ladder. The Bident family from Wannamucca, Nevada, not only possessed an unlikely background for a cattle baron family but also ran a cattle operation that illustrated the diversity of the modern western cattle operation. The Bidents, who were Basques, originally grazed sheep in the West. In 1946, they ran 12,000 sheep on government land. By the 1970s, however, cattle had become their chief means of livelihood. They worked 1,400 Herefords on 7,000 owned acres, with another 300,000 leased. Their spring, summer, and fall permits allowed them to run a successful cow-calf operation in Nevada. Moreover, their ownership of land in Idaho, where yearlings gained weight for the market, enabled them to retain the cattle until they reached the feedlot. From Idaho wheat pasture, the cattle were sent to finish in Washington feedlots.[45]

The economic problems of the 1970s and 1980s and the gradual reversal of government priorities, such as the BLM's shift from emphasizing cattle raising to multiple use of its lands, provided an excuse for some owners to cut up their ranches for recreational and hobby operations. As the BLM and Forest Service reduced allotments, some operations could no longer compete. In southwestern Montana, the spectacular scenery and the strong desire of out-of-staters to own hobby ranches lured affluent individuals into ranching. Typically they raised a few cows on a 200-acre spread.[46]

The influence of the federal government on ranching in the eleven western states cannot be exaggerated. The government controlled millions of acres, ranging from 60 million in Nevada to 12 million in Washington. In Nevada, federal land in the 1960s provided 49 percent of all forage requirements, and in New Mexico, Nevada, and Wyoming—which all had more than 25 million acres of federal land—the livestock industry served as the chief employer in each state. Before 1960, western ranchers had the political clout to retain tight control of rangeland policy. The Forest Service and the BLM were small bureaucracies run at the local level by friendly administrators who sympathized with and understood ranch culture. The rise of the multiple-use philosophy and the growing power of the environmental movement caused a reshuffling of priorities in the agencies. Ranchers no longer had an inside track. Controversies over fees, allotments of land, overgrazing, wildlife habitat, and increased recreational use tended to crowd out cattle business, which had to compete for the time of agency personnel. The change in the climate of operations and the increased power wielded by the two government agencies often embittered relations between ranchers and bureaucrats. For instance, one Nevadan became so angry with his landlord, the BLM, that he assigned his wife the task of serving as family spokesperson with the agency. The rancher invariably lost his temper, and conversations ended in shouting matches.[47]

Given the competitive nature of cattle business, the volatility of markets, and the importance of the federal permits for the viability of many ranches, increases in fees and the cancellation of allotments could have a debilitating effect on any operation. Grazing fees had a history of being kept low. On BLM land, fees were not introduced until 1935. Until 1947, they remained at five cents per animal unit per season—only then did charges increase to eight cents. Forest Service fees were higher (around fourteen cents per animal just before World War II and thirty cents after 1947); eventually both agencies charged a common fee. After 1960, fees were based on an elaborate formula that was adjusted annually. Forest Service and BLM officials attempted to gauge forage value as well as the difference in range costs between private and federal lands. In the 1970s, several moratoriums on fees prevented the implementation of new rates. The federal government also introduced the concept of "ability to pay," which further delayed fee increases. As a result, despite continual complaints by ranchers, program costs always exceeded fees by a considerable margin ($47 million in 1991 when fees were $1.97 per animal unit, i.e., a cow and her calf). In addition, many ranchers received cheap irrigation water from federal projects, which subsidized the production of hay.[48]

A recent study placed the fee burden for ranchers in clearer perspective. It calculated that those with permits enjoyed higher net earnings than those without them. Permittee costs were lower, a fact directly attributable to cheaper forage bills when animals were fed on the government range. Even though economies of scale made large ranches more efficient, and most permittees operated those ranches, when size was considered, permittees still had lower costs and higher returns. Clearly the lower the range fee, the more advantage the rancher had both with his neighbors and with ranchers in other areas of the country.[49]

However, to give ranchers their due, whether they used federal land or not, healthy ranches meant healthy communities. A common defense against fee and allotment changes in the West clung to the notion that fee increases would hurt local communities. Increased economic pressure on ranches would cause them to falter, leading to fewer ranches. As a result, local service towns would suffer, the tax base would fall, and the economy would dry up. In the West, where larger ranches usually had a better chance of financial success than smaller ones, such an argument was fairly weak. Ranches were often so few and far between that a loss would make only a marginal amount of difference.[50]

Perhaps the real threat to ranchers was not the alteration of fee structures but the risks and uncertainty of ranching on government land. Allotments and permits were not owned, but rather acted as licenses to graze land. In addition, the BLM and Forest Service could adjust the number of cattle grazed each year to meet environmental conditions. Over the years, permittees had often spent considerable sums on range facilities on public land. Before 1960, risk and uncertainty were minimized by the powerful political grip the ranchers had on the agencies. Later uncertainties over the future of grazing multiplied and added to the anxieties of doing business.[51]

Ranchers were natural recruits for a protest movement that developed into the Sagebrush Rebellion of the late 1970s and early 1980s. Many ranchers believed that an alliance with other users of federal lands in the West, particularly mineral interests, would facilitate a loosening of government controls and provide chances for entrepreneurship to blossom. The Sagebrush Rebellion fizzled out in the early 1980s, but a volatile atmosphere that pitted ranchers, bureaucrats, and the environmental movement against each other remained. The privatization of federal lands, a goal of many Sagebrush rebels, remained an attractive proposition for many who chafed under the restrictive conditions of agency controls. Confrontation and controversy about grazing rights continued into the 1990s.[52]

The arrival of environmental consciousness in the 1960s made the public aware of the importance of stewardship for public lands. The historical record of ranching in regard to the degeneration of land remained questionable. As late as the 1970s, the federal government charged ranchers by their head of stocker cattle fattened on government land. As a result overgrazing remained common.

Publicity about ranchers' lack of attention to range management tended to create resentment among the informed general public, which was angry that ranchers abused public land set aside for their commercial gain. But as ranchers became more attuned to public relations, they too adapted and attempted to display themselves as good conservators who, unlike urban-based environmentalists, had the interests of their communities at heart. Ranch fundamentalism increasingly came into vogue. Here a more traditionalist and sustainable approach to ranching gained ground. A respect for nature went hand in hand with a drive for an efficient and profitable operation.[53]

Given the gradual transformation of ranching, what overall trends could be seen in the West? Statistics showed that there remained roughly 30,000 ranches in the region by the early 1990s. These ranches averaged around 15,000 acres for their operations. From 1964 to 1987, little change occurred in the regional distribution of American beef cow herds. It is worth comparing the western region with the South, an area that raised few high-quality cattle before 1940. Since the 1960s, the South and the West both produced a little over 20 percent of the national calf crop. However, herds in the West remained larger. By 1987, 31 percent of all cattle in the West grazed in herds of 500 or more, compared with only 9 percent in the South. Although the South had more livestock than the West, 50 percent of its cattle grazed in herds of fewer than 50 cows, whereas the West's total in this category was only 13 percent. Since the 1960s, a certain proportion of cattle for the national market often came from small, inefficient herds operated by part-timers who raised cattle for a hobby. Although the numbers of these hobbyists increased in the West as well, the region still retained an advantage from a viewpoint of scale because most of its calves were raised on large ranches. Western states could provide a higher standard of animal than the South—the old British breeds continued their yeomanly service—but high-grade beef did not have any particular advantage when fast food established itself as a large player in beef sales. Southerners were also nearer markets; in addition, because they ranched on private land, they were spared the problems of government intrusion in their operations. Cattle raisers in the West, therefore, competed at a disadvantage with a region that before 1940 could not compare with western states in the quality or quantity of its calf crop.[54]

On the other hand, because cattle raisers held a special place in the beef chain, they avoided the buffeting that other agricultural sectors experienced from innovations after World War II. Feeders and dairymen had to adapt to the treadmill of change or go under. Western livestock production had to respond to the dictates of a high-wage economy in which mass production and mass consumption raised American living standards to new heights for most citizens. American consumers shopped at department stores and supermarkets to buy consumer durables, clothing, and large amounts of prepared and unprepared food. The invention of feedlots and the drylot dairy perfectly represented the best efforts of agriculture and food production to cater to consumer needs in an affluent society. At the same time, the postwar economy, with its high wage structure and relatively high levels of employment, began to dissolve after 1965. Financial pressures on the cattle business brought new cut-rate packers into operation, which drove the old firms like Armor and Swift out of business. The movement of feedlots and slaughtering to the High Plains affected the California feeding industry. On the other hand, California dairying held its own, and only distance prevented the state from becoming the milkshed of the entire nation.

The vagaries of economic change have affected cattle raising in the West. Cattlemen in the region had a built-in disadvantage, because they often depended on federal land for their livelihood. Although the costs of doing business on federal land did not prove especially burdensome, uncertainties about land tenure troubled those with permits. Moreover, the environmental issue gained visibility because after 1960 advocates made cattlemen defensive about issues that affected range management on federal land. Like all beef raisers, westerners suffered from competition with other meats because of the long time frame required for the birth and nurturing of calves. Poultry and hogs could be produced more rapidly. In addition, the ever-watchful media portrayed chicken as healthier than beef for the average consumer.

After World War II, full-time ranchers had increasing difficulty surviving without other sources of income. Ironically, although many western cattle raisers fought a defensive battle to preserve their way of life, others met the competition by looking elsewhere for monetary rewards. Tourism provided an option for those with some initiative and innovative spirit. Many utilized the always popular rancher-cowboy image to make money. Some dabbled in real estate to sell ranchettes, others sold western clothing, and still others promoted tourist attractions such as rodeos or spent part of the year running a dude ranch.

NOTES

1. The treadmill analogy comes from Willard W. Cochrane, *The Development of American Agriculture: A Historical Analysis* (Minneapolis: University of Minnesota Press, 1979), 387–95; for the transformation of agriculture in the twentieth century, see David B. Danbom, *The Resisted Revolution: America and the Industrialization of Agriculture* (Ames: Iowa State University Press, 1979); and Robert C. Williams, *Fordson, Farmall, and Poppin' Johnny* (Urbana: University of Illinois Press, 1987). For farm women see Katherine Jellison, *Entitled to Power: Farm Women and Technology, 1913–1963* (Chapel Hill: University of North Carolina Press, 1993).

2. Only limitations of space prevented analysis of cattle raising in California, Oregon, Idaho, and Washington. Historically California rivaled Texas in its influence on range livestock production. The Hispanic presence in both cattle and sheep spread all over the western states from its California base in the nineteenth century. By 1940,

cattle ranching still retained great importance in the state. There were 2.1 million cattle on the California range—no western or mountain state had as many cattle. For the importance of California ranching, see Terry G. Jordan, *North American Cattle-Ranching Frontiers: Organization, Diffusion, Differentiation* (Albuquerque: University of New Mexico Press, 1993), 241–66; for livestock statistics in 1940, see U.S. Department of Agriculture, *Agricultural Statistics, 1941* (Washington, D.C.: Government Printing Office, 1941), 340, 384; Howard F. Gregor, *The Industrialization of U.S. Agriculture: An Interpretive Atlas* (Boulder, Colo.: Westview Press, 1982), 72.

3. M. L. Kenney et al., "Midwestern Agriculture in U.S. Fordism," *Sociologia Ruralis* 29 (Spring 1989): 131–48.

4. Howard F. Gregor, "The Industrial Farm as a Western Institution," *Journal of the West* IX (January 1970): 70–92; Mark Friedberger, *Farm Families and Change in Twentieth-Century America* (Lexington: University Press of Kentucky, 1988), 29–46.

5. Marion Clawson, *The Western Range Livestock Industry* (New York: McGraw-Hill, 1948), 173.

6. R. McGreggor Cawley, *Federal Land, Western Anger: The Sagebrush Rebellion and Environmental Politics* (Lawrence: University Press of Kansas, 1993), 15–33; Karl Hess, *Visions upon the Land: Man and Nature on the Western Range* (Washington, D.C.: Island Press, 1992), 95–120; Philip O. Foss, *Politics and Grass: The Administration of Grazing on the Public Domain* (Seattle: University of Washington Press, 1960), 117–39; Arthur H. Smith and William E. Martin, "Socioeconomic Behavior of Cattle Ranchers With Implications for Rural Community Development in the West," *Journal of American Agricultural Economics* 54 (May 1972): 219.

7. The invention of growth hormones for cattle in 1953 took place in the Midwest at Iowa State University. Ironically, although small midwestern feed yards utilized this new invention, it was western feedlots, with their innovations in other methods of feeding as well as their use of growth hormones, that provided leadership in the industry in the 1950s and early 1960s. For the invention of DES and its importance to the industry, see Alan I Marcus, *Cancer from Beef: DES, Federal Food Regulation, and Consumer Confidence* (Baltimore: Johns Hopkins University Press, 1994), 11–44.

8. See advertisement for Kaufman Feedlots, San Jose, California, in *American Cattle Producer* 31 (December 1949): 29; Richard Schaus, "Tailored Beef Factories," *American Cattle Producer* 31 (May 1950): 9–10, 18.

9. For trends in cattle feeding in other western states in the 1950s, see Frank S. Scott, Jr., "Marketing Aspects of Western Cattle Feeding Operations," Nevada Agricultural Experiment Station, *Bulletin 190,* December 1955; Schaus, "Tailored Beef Factories," 17.

10. Schaus, "Tailored Beef Factories," 10.

11. R. E. Selzer and M. D. Johnson, "Possibilities for Expanding Arizona's Meat Packing Industry," Arizona Agricultural Experiment Station, *Bulletin 291,* November 1957, 7–9; see also Seymour Freedgood, "The New Cattle Business," *Fortune* 61 (April 1960): 222, 228, which predicted the fall of traditional areas of dominance in the cattle business.

12. N. R. Ittner et al., "Methods of Increasing Beef Production in Hot Climates," California Agricultural Experiment Station, *Bulletin 761,* February 1958, 75–77.

13. S. H. Logan, "A Study of Structural Aspects: Beef Cattle Feeding and Slaugh-

tering in California," California Agricultural Experiment Station, *Bulletin 826,* August 1966, 5–23; James A. Petit, Jr., and Gerald W. Dean, "Economics of Farm Feedlots in the Rice Area of the Sacramento Valley," California Agricultural Experiment Station, *Bulletin 800,* May 1964, 11.

14. W. L. Stangel with David Murrah, interview, Oral History Collection, Southwest Collection, Texas Tech University, 19 January, 1973; John P. Walsh, *Supermarkets Transformed: Understanding Organization and Technological Innovation* (New Brunswick, N.J.: Rutgers University Press, 1993), 77–83.

15. Anne Foley Scheuring, ed., *A Guidebook to California Agriculture* (Berkeley: University of California Press, 1983), 189.

16. Ibid., 196; Friedberger, *Farm Families and Change,* 143–47.

17. Howard F. Gregor, "Industrial Dry-lot Dairying," *Economic Geography* 39 (October 1963): 315–16.

18. Scheuring, *A Guidebook to California Agriculture,* 197.

19. Ibid., 197–98.

20. L. B. Fletcher and C. O. McCorkle, Jr., "Growth and Adoption of the Los Angeles Milk-shed," California Agricultural Experiment Station, *Bulletin 787,* June 1962, 34–41.

21. Ibid., 26–33.

22. Ibid., 30–31.

23. James W. Gruebell, "Regionalism in the U.S. Dairy Industry," U.S. House of Representatives Committee on Agriculture, Sub-Committee on Livestock, Dairy, and Poultry, *Review of Regionalism as an Issue in the U.S. Dairy Industry,* vol. 11 (Washington, D.C.: Government Printing Office, 1988), 21–44.

24. Ibid., 25; Scheuring, *A Guidebook to California Farming,* 194; Friedberger, *Farm Families and Change,* 121.

25. Scheuring, *A Guidebook to California Agriculture,* 195; U.S. Office of Technological Assessment, "U.S. Dairy Industry at a Crossroad: Biotechnology and Policy Choices," *Special Report 470* (Washington, D.C.: Government Printing Office, 1991).

26. Paul Francis Starrs, "Home Ranch: Ranchers, the Federal Government, and the Partitioning of Western North American Ranchland" (Ph.D. diss., University of California–Berkeley, 1989), 16–123.

27. Most important, the Taylor Grazing Act terminated the utilization of federal lands by "tramp sheep" outfits, although the transhumance of sheep continued in the West. The classic study of sheep trailing is H. R. Hochmuth, Eric R. Franklin, and Marion Clawson, "Sheep Migration in the Inter-mountain Region," U.S. Department of Agriculture, *Circular 624,* January 1942; Smith and Martin, "Socioeconomic Behavior of Cattle Ranchers," 219; Jill Derby, "Cattle, Kin, and the Patrimonial Imperative: Social Organization on Nevada Family Ranches" (Ph.D. diss., University of California–Davis, 1988), 294–97; for hobby ranches in California, see Robert C. Ellickson, *Order Without Law: How Neighbors Settle Disputes* (Cambridge, Mass.: Harvard University Press, 1991).

28. Derby, "Cattle, Kin, and the Patrimonial Imperative," 268–71.

29. C. L. Sonnichsen, *Cowboys and Cattlemen* (Norman: University of Oklahoma Press, 1950), 13, 18; James R. Gray, "Cattle Ranches—Organization Costs and

Returns: Southwestern Semi-arid Non-migratory Grazing Areas, 1940–1954," New Mexico Agricultural Experiment Station, *Bulletin 403,* February 1956, 21–22.

30. G. Marshall Hartman, *The Making of a Cowman* (Prescott, Ariz.: Ralph Tanner, 1992), 91, 95–96.

31. Detailed information on breeding herds in the West is scarce. According to data from the National Cattlemen's Association from the Pacific Northwest states, 68 percent of herds in 1953 were commercial, 9 percent were registered breeders, and 23 percent were a combination of both. See M. W. Galgin et al., "Patterns and Practices of Washington Cattlemen," Washington Agricultural Experiment Station, *Report 567,* May 1956, 32; Kenneth H. Wendland and James R. Gray, "Economic Aspects of Registered Cattle Enterprises in New Mexico," New Mexico Agricultural Experiment Station, *Bulletin 538,* October 1968; N. K. Roberts and C. Kerry Gee, "Cattle Ranching Using Public Ranges Year-Long," Utah Agricultural Experiment Station, *Bulletin 440,* February 1963, 4–10.

32. Delwin M. Stevens et al., "Mountain Valley Cattle Ranching in Wyoming: Investments, Costs, Earnings, and Management Practices," Wyoming Agricultural Experiment Station, *Bulletin 386,* June 1962, 5.

33. Roberts and Gee, "Cattle Ranching Using Public Ranges Year-Long," 10.

34. Gray, "Cattle Ranches—Organization, Costs and Returns," 19.

35. Ibid., 20–21.

36. Thomas J. Maloney, "Cattle Ranching as a Cultural Ecology Problem in San Miguel County, New Mexico" (Ph.D. diss., Washington University—St. Louis, 1966), 30, 283, 297.

37. John Max Crowley, "Ranches in the Sky: A Study of Livestock Ranching in the Mountain Parks of Colorado" (Ph.D. diss., University of Minnesota, 1964), 57.

38. Carolyn Ann Sprague, "Nevada Ranch Women: A Study of Management Isolation" (Ph.D. diss., University of Illinois–Urbana-Champaign, 1984), 56–58.

39. Ibid., 48, 76. According to Derby, women were kept "inside not outside"; see "Cattle, Kin, and the Patrimonial Imperative," 242.

40. Robert L. Sharp, *Big Outfit: Ranching on the Baca Float* (Tucson: University of Arizona Press, 1974), 134–35.

41. Linda Grosskopf, *On Flatwell Creek: The Story of Montana's N Bar Ranch* (Los Alamos, N.Mex.: Exceptional Books, 1991), 347.

42. Ibid., 347–48, 358–59, 361.

43. Delbert R. Ward, *Great Ranches of the United States* (San Antonio, Tex.: Ganado Press, 1993), 196, 217–18.

44. Ibid., 113–16.

45. Kipp Parker, "Pine Forest," *American Hereford Journal* 62 (July 1971): 146–47.

46. William Wyckoff and Kathleen Hansen, "Settlement, Livestock Grazing, and Environmental Change in Southwest Montana, 1860–1990," *Environmental History Review* 15 (Winter 1991): 65.

47. Darwin B. Nielsen and John P. Workman, "The Importance of Renewable Grazing Resources on Federal Lands in 11 Western States," Utah Agricultural Experiment Station, *Circular 155,* November 1971; Sprague, "Nevada Ranch Women," 79.

48. Foss, *Politics and Grass,* 174–77; Kenneth H. Mathew, Jr., et al., "Cow/Calf

Ranches in 10 Western States," U.S. Department of Agriculture, *Agricultural Economic Report 682*, May 1994, 2.

49. Mathew, "Cow/Calf Ranches in 10 Western States," 2.

50. B. W. Bromley et al., "Effect of Selective Changes in Federal Land Use on a Rural Economy," Oregon Agricultural Experiment Station, *Bulletin 604*, March 1964.

51. Mathew, "Cow/Calf Ranches in 10 Western States," 9.

52. Cawley, *Federal Land, Western Anger*, 92–133.

53. Hartman, *The Making of a Cowman*, 133–34.

54. Kenneth R. Krause, "The Beef-Cow-Calf Industry, 1964–87, Location and Size," U.S. Department of Agriculture, *Economic Research Service Report 659*, June 1992, 12–15.

10

Agribusiness in the American West

Harry C. McDean

Beginning with World War II, western agribusiness, that is, those businesses that financed, marketed, transported, distributed, processed, manufactured, and sold agricultural products and equipment, gradually integrated into the national and international economies. Small owner-operated agribusinesses routinely extended their markets beyond the West, often into international markets that were either small or nonexistent in the prewar period. They grew in scale while cutting overhead costs by diversifying their products. Sometimes western agribusinesses developed new products or bought companies that produced the goods they wished to sell. As these agribusinesses expanded the geographic range of their markets and diversified their products, the corporate leaders often moved their headquarters out of the West to wherever in the nation (or in the world) business strategy dictated.[1]

As western agribusinesses expanded, they often became targets for companies seeking to accomplish similar goals. Hoping to cut overhead costs by extending the range of their product offerings and market areas, both American- and foreign-based companies routinely bought out western agribusiness firms. By the 1970s, business analysts described the frenzy of corporate buyouts as a national mania: common sense seemed to have given way to an emotionally driven passion for control of corporate America. Business analysts could find no strategic or economic explanation for the rage of corporate takeovers sweeping across America.[2]

Regardless of why the takeovers occurred, by the mid-1980s western agribusiness could hardly be distinguished from any other national or even international business. The same company that sold perfume in France also marketed cereal in America. Another that sold snow skis and travel trailers worldwide also offered several hundred internationally recognized, brand-name food products. National and international corporations became so diversified that public opinion pollsters found the average American did not know who owned the businesses that produced historic western products like Carnation, Del Monte, and Sun Maid. Agribusiness no longer could be defined simply as any business that engaged in "financing agriculture, or in the manufacturing, transporting, distributing, and wholesaling or packaging of farm machinery, fertilizers, pesticides, seed, feed" (called "inputs" by economists), and the processing, manufacturing, or marketing of food (called "outputs"). These businesses now were contained within very complicated business structures, ones defined as "large multinational, capital intensive corporations," that continuously sought to diversify and "expand their holdings while concentrating their economic power in the agribusiness market place."[3]

These changes did not go unnoticed by students of western agribusiness. By the 1980s, professors of agricultural economics met routinely not only to discuss the changes but also to ask of themselves the hardest question of all: Had this new world of agribusiness made them obsolete? Were the new trends clearly in the field of business and not agriculture? With the growing force of fundamental business strategies and tactics, did it make sense for university students to study agriculture at all? Perhaps it was best, some pondered, for the schools of agricultural economics to drop agribusiness courses altogether and direct agribusiness students into schools of business, where they could study the subjects that are decisive in today's world of business.[4]

While the debate continues over where in the academic world agribusiness subjects belong, clearly it is difficult to find single-product agribusiness companies located in the West. If anything, it can be argued that in the postwar period western agribusinesses led America into restructuring its businesses into multiproduct, international market operations. Likewise, western agribusinesses in the postwar period showcase the ways in which successful agribusinesses routinely were absorbed by huge business concerns (conglomerates) and thereafter played only a contributing part in large and often unwieldy business operations. They also offer a number of sideshows that typify life in the West: agribusinesses that hid their real operations beneath some kind of facade. Often these were highly capitalized, sometimes publicly held, companies that appeared to operate large-scale farms for "profit," when in reality they held the land for other uses. Such companies generally wanted the gas and petroleum reserves that lay beneath the farms, or they wanted to develop them for sale as residential neighborhoods, shopping centers, and commercial real estate.

Reflecting these historic developments are the basic industries that sell goods and services used by western farmers in everyday operations. They include banks that make loans to western farmers on their land, buildings, and operating equipment; producers of seeds, fertilizers, and chemicals; and manufacturers of farm tools, tractors, planters, tillers, and harvesters.

Toward the end of the Great Depression, the first of these industries, western banks, were erroneously depicted by John Steinbeck as blind, heartless, nefarious institutions that played with farmers like defenseless pawns and bull-dozed them off their land. Nevertheless, federal and western state banking laws after World War II either prohibited banks from engaging in farm operations or made it impractical to do so. Moreover, western banks became so reluctant to take over unprofitable farms that they received criticism from both private and public bank analysts for not foreclosing quickly on failing farm operations.[5]

In the postwar period, Bank of America served as the largest agricultural lender in the West and in the world. Along with other western banks, Bank of America never showed an interest in owning and operating western farmlands. Founded in San Francisco in 1904, it grew rapidly to surpass Crocker National as the largest bank in western America. Maneuvering through gray areas in both federal and state banking laws, Bank of America expanded by reaching into California towns through a system it called "branch banking." Aided by the support of California's superintendent of banks, William Williams, Bank of America branches gradually opened in strategically located, small rural towns, where they offered an uncommon convenience to the Golden State's farmers. So successful was the strategy that, by the late 1920s, the bank operated branches in rural Washington, Oregon, Nevada, and Arizona.[6]

Born at a time when the accepted banking practice permitted loans only to businesses, corporations, and wealthy individuals, Bank of America's branches launched a new era in loan making. Aimed at servicing the average person, the branches provided the growing capital requirements of western farmers. By World War II, the bank had become the largest agricultural lender in the West; in accumulated loans and deposits it also surpassed Chase Manhattan in 1945 to become the world's largest bank.

In its drive to the top, the bank had created a holding company (literally to hold all the stock in any and all Bank of America–related operations) called TransAmerica. This company allowed Bank of America to utilize its presence in western rural towns to sell insurance to farmers through a company it founded, Occidental Life. By offering an additional financial package, the bank offset the heavy overhead expenses it added by operating its many small rural town branches. The Federal Reserve System, however, had voiced concern about the legality of this dual service. Faced in the 1950s with growing legal arguments of the Federal Reserve against the marriage of banking and insurance busi-nesses, Bank of America developed a different financial strategy that enabled it to successfully overcome a federal order to divest itself of Occidental Life in 1957.

Announcing it would become the nation's first "department store of finan-cial services," Bank of America set a course that gradually diminished its branch banking costs. While Bank of America remained the major agricultural lender in the West, gradually its portfolio of farm loans fell in relation to the value of other operations provided in its financial department store. By the 1990s, less than 8 percent of Bank of America's loan portfolio was farm-based; when the value of other operations is added, western farmers contributed less than 2 percent to the value of its business. Even so, western farmers, like so many other Americans, enjoyed the added value of the many new services the bank provided. It created the nation's first bank credit card (BankAmericard—now VISA); the first automatic loan payment system (through which loan payments were deducted automatically from deposit accounts); the first automatic deposit system (through which payments—including paychecks—were automatically deposited in checking or savings accounts); the first fully computerized (1961) branch banking system (so that a client could enter a branch in Longview, Washington, and immediately access information and money in his account in Modesto, California); and the nation's first student loan program. It also bought one of the nation's major discount brokerage firms, Charles Schwab.

While Bank of America calculated that over time the new financial services would drive down the cost of operating its branches, it also utilized the local expertise in its branches to assess the long-term potential for growth in rural western areas. In the 1960s, realizing that its rural branches were dependent on continued growth and sensing that the values of its agricultural portfolio might not increase, Bank of America became an aggressive investor in rural growth and development. It bought huge issues of risky long-term, low-interest-bearing rural development bonds. These investments included bonds not only in water and irrigation districts but also in rural municipal development projects. Moreover, the bank made high-risk, low-interest loans in poverty-stricken western rural areas.

Although this long-term strategy seemed sound, over the short term it proved disastrous. In the late 1970s, start-up costs for these many enterprises combined with the collapsing value of its rural development bond and loan portfolio to nearly bust the nation's largest bank. With interest rates rising fast in the early 1980s, Bank of America was stuck holding risky low-interest, rural bonds and loans. With the value of its assets in rapid decline, it could not make or obtain new loans. As a result, the operating costs of its branch banks rose sharply on a per-client basis. Once the nation's greatest bank, Bank of America was fast going broke. Its stock plunged on the New York Stock Exchange, and the financial world swirled with rumors of its demise. Talk centered on how a mini-mite in the banking world, western-based First Interstate, planned to buy its Goliath brethren.[7]

Bank of America abruptly trimmed its financial sails to raise capital and diminish its appeal to potential buyers. It sold much of its "department store" of financial services, including its most successful operation, Charles Schwab. Over the outraged voices of the bank's founding family, the bank sold its vastly appreciated real estate that headquartered its operations in San Francisco. It wrote down its bad loans and shed its costly corporate clients. Most important for rural westerners and farmers, it closed a quarter of its high-cost rural branch banks. It sold nonperforming rural and farm loans at a discount to other banks, mortgage companies, and savings and loans. And, while it retained most of its risky, low-interest irrigation district and rural development bonds, it stopped buying new issues.

Unfortunately for western farmers, this banking crisis hit at the worst possible time. By the mid-1980s, farm prices had collapsed from the expansion programs urged by schools of agriculture that taught young western farmers about the benefits of leveraging assets for the purpose of expansion. Moreover, the worst drought occurred since the days of the Dust Bowl. When the Bank of America's woes caused rural and farm credit to tighten, it seemed to some farmers and many urban Americans that it was déjà vu—another story like Steinbeck's of the late 1930s.[8]

Once the bank had sold its highly valued "department store" financial assets and written down or sold off its worst bonds and loans, however, it successfully fought off its suitors and became the suitor. Helped by declining interest rates, the value of its remaining assets rose sharply, thereby adding value to its cash-rich reserves generated during its selling spree. Having closed its high-cost branch banks, it now possessed one of the most efficient branch banking systems in the nation. Other western banks and savings and loans that survived most of the 1980s abruptly faced their own difficulties by the early 1990s. As their positions weakened, the new, stronger Bank of America stood ready to purchase their assets at discounts or take over entire operations. In one of the nation's greatest bank mergers, in 1992, a much weakened First Security joined with Bank of America, allowing the parent to close inefficient operations while instantly putting Bank of America into businesses in western states where it had not operated before: Texas, New Mexico, and Hawaii.[9]

Restructured and operating in this new low-interest-rate environment, the bank rapidly restored its historic mission of providing financial services to the ordinary western citizen. Buttressed by the rapid expansion of its low-cost western branch banks acquired in the 1990s, Bank of America became the nation's first bank to create new features that made banking vastly more convenient for western farmers. It extended banking hours into early evenings and Saturdays; it introduced an automatic teller card and machine; and it ranked among the first to link with the ATM system so that farmers could bank at any branch in the West at any hour of the day or night.[10]

While Bank of America provides a revealing case history of trends in the agribusiness of banking, its onetime parent company, TransAmerica, offers a study of the major insurance company that served western farmers in the postwar period. By the 1950s, through its Occidental Life Company, TransAmerica served as the largest insurer of western farmers, but its president, John R. Beckett, soon became devoted to the broader goal of restructuring the company to make it a "department store of finances services." He maintained that strategy even after the company split off from Bank of America in 1957. But Beckett's conception of a "department store of financial services" was different from that held by anyone else. It made sense only if one dropped the term "financial services" and focused on the "department store."

By the 1970s, a western farmer who boarded an airplane operated by Trans International Airlines in fact flew with TransAmerica. When he got off the plane and rented a car from Budget Rental Cars, he rented from TransAmerica. When he went to town to see a motion picture produced by United Artists, he watched a TransAmerica production. Beckett bought these companies and dozens of others in the 1960s and 1970s.[11]

TransAmerica reported stunning losses, and the price of its stock on the New York Stock Exchange (NYSE) went into a nosedive by the late 1970s. In 1981, TransAmerica appointed a new president, James Harvey, who abruptly sold all the aforementioned businesses and pushed a new business strategy. Harvey searched for businesses directly involved in high finance. He especially wanted to acquire high-profile brokerage, mutual fund, and investment banking businesses.

The fundamental simplicity of the strategy worked wonders for TransAmerica, although its day-to-day application proved so tricky that at times it appeared impossible to accomplish. The 1980s and 1990s were a time of immense upheaval in the world of banking and investment institutions. As a prominent player in this tumultuous economy, TransAmerica itself was constantly restructured. As a result, western farmers might not have known just who they were dealing with when they sought loans, obtained a mortgage, bought insurance, or adopted new strategies of buying commodities futures as a hedge against current farm prices (a strategy widely recommended by agricultural economists and farm management specialists in the 1980s and 1990s). At some point in these decades, TransAmerica owned Fairmont Financial (workers' compensation insurance), Criterion (investment management), the Sedwick Group (insurance), the Money Store (loans), and a host of other financial services besides its Occidental Life.[12]

Adding further confusion in this new world of finance was the tendency of some large western farm operations to employ major financial service companies to sell stock in their farms to the public. Farms such as the Tejon Ranch in California raised capital by turning to huge investment banking and brokerage firms that took them public. These companies used traditional means of underwriting the sales (guaranteeing the price for an entire issue) of stock. On occasion, brokerage firms ended up holding the stock in large western farm operations for extended periods—making them for a while the major shareholders in a few of the West's largest farms. Generally, however, they sold this stock in large blocks, often to other financial concerns.[13]

While most buyers of these issues held them in diversified stock portfolios for the sole purpose of appreciation (and therefore had no intention of affecting management practices on the western farms), others not only acquired stock in publicly held western farm operations but also often bought farms outright for the purpose of managing them. Some, like Travelers Insurance, used insurance premiums as funds for investment in southwestern farmlands that its management believed could be converted into housing developments and shopping centers. Others, like Newhall Land and Farming, raised capital on Wall Street for the express purpose of investing in western ranch and farm properties that it planned to operate until they could be successfully developed into residential, commercial, and industrial real estate. Perhaps most important were heavily capitalized business firms that bought western farms to tap into the mineral, oil, and gas reserves that lay beneath them.[14]

Where possible, companies like Chevron Oil preferred to buy only the mineral, oil, and gas rights, leaving the property itself in the hands of western farmers. This policy created a new relationship between western farmers and businesses that once provided them only with petroleum and chemical products. These companies could set up drilling operations miles away from operating farms and tap into the underground reserves. Modern homing devices developed by companies such as Seitel eliminated much of the guesswork in "wildcat" drilling. Armed with accurate detection devices, revenues from oil, gas, and mineral leases proved important sources of income for western farm operations. In some areas, such as the Imperial Valley in California, farmers lucky enough to be located atop a valued reserve sold mineral, oil, and gas rights for three to five times the agricultural value of their property.[15]

Some oil, gas, and mineral firms, such as Tenneco, bought western farm properties outright. Founded in the 1930s by investment bankers in Chicago, Tenneco explored for natural gas in the Southwest. In the postwar period, Tenneco moved its headquarters to Houston and began buying farm and ranch property so it could lay down pipelines and deliver its products to eastern markets. In the 1960s, Tenneco joined the crowd of businesses that sought to diversify operations, and it began to purchase chemical companies. Soon Tenneco bought the Packaging Corporation of America—itself a Fortune 500 corporation—and thereby acquired 400,000 acres of western timberlands. In 1967, Tenneco entered the California natural gas economy by acquiring the farm and ranch corporation with the greatest potential in this area—Kern County Land Company. A firm that also had sought to diversify in the 1960s, Kern County Land Company had recently bought Case Corporation, the venerable midwestern tractor and farm implement manufacturer. In one year, Tenneco became the owner-operator of 2.5 million acres of western farm and ranch property, and it ran one of the nation's major manufacturers of farm machinery.[16]

Even though its San Joaquin property made Tenneco one of America's largest producers of table grapes and almonds, the company had little interest in these operations. Tenneco was more interested in what was beneath the land than what grew or grazed on it, and to get mineral rights, especially for gas, it had to take Case as part of the deal. Running Case seemed less of a challenge a year later when Tenneco acquired Newport News Shipbuilding and Dry Dock

Company, thereby adding management skillful in the field of manufacturing heavy equipment. Even so, this business plan seemed ill conceived during the 1980s, when the agricultural recession joined with flat or falling natural gas prices to drive down the price of Tenneco's stock on the NYSE. With the market price of its stock falling well below the asset value of the company, takeover discussion began on Wall Street. Tenneco management acted swiftly. In 1985, it began by selling a variety of small unrelated businesses that sold insurance, precious metals, and polyvinyl chlorides. In 1987, it sold Kern County Land Company (by now called Tenneco West), and in 1988 it sold its entire oil and gas business. It groomed for sale and then sold Case in 1996 but kept most of its other manufacturing firms. It also kept its original core business—Tenneco Gas Pipeline. Thus in 1996 Tenneco, once one of the dominant players in western agribusiness, left the business altogether.[17]

Other western gas and oil companies tended to be more focused in their operations. They entered diverse operations more tentatively and exited at the first sign of trouble. Atlantic Richfield (ARCO) was typical. Formed in 1966 when Sinclair and Richfield Oil companies merged, ARCO successfully bet its bankroll on a joint venture it formed with Humble Oil (soon to become Exxon) to explore Alaska's North Slope. Making the most of the enormous windfall of cash that it received from this successful venture, ARCO vigorously expanded its western operations to become, by the late 1970s, one of the farmer's primary providers of petroleum products. ARCO also sought to diversify. It bought one of the West's most famous mines, Anaconda, and a major producer of agricultural chemicals, Lyondell Petrochemicals. As ARCO began accumulating these businesses its leadership soon recognized that they could not operate them profitably. In the 1980s, ARCO sold their acquistions and, with the infusion of cash these sales provided, began buying western oil, gas, and mineral properties from distressed conglomerates like Tenneco. ARCO used the cash to build its first major chain of convenience stores, where in a rural western town at any time of day or night residents could buy a tank of gas and, when paying for it, shop for anything from ice cream to razor blades.[18]

Lubrizol, a petroleum company formed in 1942 to provide additives that lengthened the life of engines, was highly respected by western farmers for its useful core products. This company too began to diversify in the 1970s. Lubrizol bought and sold a variety of companies in the 1970s and early 1980s, then astounded the financial world when, in 1985, it bought the even more highly capitalized western-based Agrigenetics Corporation. This agribusiness company had raised a significant capital fund when it made large public stock offerings following its successful effort to splice bean and sunflower genes.[19]

Since its acquisition, Agrigenetics has been more a company of future promise than one providing immediate cash returns. Like other companies in the field of agricultural genetics, the flow of funds into research has exceeded the profits from sales of genetically engineered products to farmers. In fact, some independent western agrigenetics firms, like Calgene and Mycogen, have such heavy cash flows into research and development that product sales to western farmers cannot replenish them. Such companies must regularly make new stock offerings to stay alive. They also must link with public institutions, such as state universities, to help pay the salaries of researchers and provide costly laboratories. While this technique of funding private research raises ethical questions about the rights of public employees, until now the reality of the issue has been that one rarely finds western university research faculty who have become rich from the working relationships they developed with private agrigenetics firms. In any case, the most common outcome for western agrigenetics firms is that they are swallowed up by a larger, more highly capitalized corporation that has the "deep pockets" to fund costly high-risk research and development programs.

Brief case histories of Mycogen and Calgene—two California-based agricultural biotech firms—help explain the transient character of finances in today's world of high-tech agribusiness. Founded in 1991 with a heavy direct investment from Lubrizol (in the form of preferred stock—one that has no voting rights and is not backed by assets but bears a fixed return), Mycogen set up shop near the University of California at San Diego, where it employed a team of scientists to engineer a core technology that could produce insect-resistant crops. Once it became a going concern, Mycogen went public by selling common shares (those that allow holders a voice in management but are neither backed by assets nor provide any form of a guaranteed return) to Wall Street investors. Marketed as a "concept stock"—that is, one in which a company has no meaningful assets or earnings but is pursuing a strategy of great potential value—Mycogen stock appealed to investors, who rushed to buy a company that promised to end the use of dangerous pesticides in American agriculture.[20]

This public offering funded several years of Mycogen's research and development, allowing it to develop *Bacillus thurigiensis* (Bt), a bacteria that, when placed in plant genomes, produces insect-resistant crops. In spite of this breakthrough in plant biotechnology, Mycogen was unable to refine the product for commercial sales and in 1995 reported that its operations would lose $15 million. Realizing that such heavy losses made it all but impossible to make yet another public offering, Mycogen searched for a "deep-pockets" investor–business partner to fund continuing research and help it bring its innovative products to market. The chosen mate was Des Moines–based Pioneer Hi-Bred, the world's largest seed company and the seller of 44 percent of America's seed corn. Hoping to benefit from Mycogen's Bt technology, in 1996 Pioneer Hi-Bred gave its partner $30 million in exchange for 3 million shares of common stock, or 13.5 percent ownership in the company. Mycogen received not only funds for continuing research but the added benefit of a partnership with a company that annually sold seed to farmers valued at $1.5 billion.[21]

These hi-tech agribusinesses not only are designing new ways of financing operations but also, of course, are simultaneously altering the way western farmers plant, maintain, and harvest their crops. Calgene, a company founded in 1986 not far from the University of California's campus at Davis, engineered a number of plants whose fruit is solid enough to be picked by new technologies in harvesting that themselves are being engineered simultaneously by researchers. The company's greatest success to date is an engineered tomato and mechanical harvester whose sales contributed to total revenues of $21 million in 1995. Even so, the company's research and development expenses were so great that it reported a 1995 loss of $30 million—nearly a fifth of its total capitalization. Like Mycogen, Calgene sought out a deep-pockets partner. It found one in Monsanto, a huge, diversified agribusiness whose market capitalization exceeds $17 billion. On 1 April 1996, Monsanto reported it had completed the purchase of 49.9 percent of Calgene's stock and would furnish the funds it needs to realize its research goals.[22]

Some western agribusinesses with high research and development costs were able to meet these expenses by diversifying the range of products they manufactured and sold. Generally, these were western agribusinesses whose roots reached deep into western history. Western farm equipment manufacturers such as Caterpillar found they could meet mounting research and development costs by moving their operations out of the West and restructuring their operations so they could sell products not just to western farmers but also to heavy equipment users throughout the world.

Founded in California in the early twentieth century, Caterpillar was typical of successful American business concerns that were quick to utilize Delaware's laws of incorporation to rapidly expand operations nationwide. Having moved its headquarters to Peoria, Illinois, in the postwar period, Caterpillar continued to diversify its range of equipment offerings until those in agriculture played only a small role in its theater of business. Mining, logging, road building, and construction equipment gradually shoved its agricultural equipment offerings to the bottom of its listings. Taking advantage of the rebuilding that occurred internationally following World War II, Caterpillar hurried to build plants in strategic locations throughout the world. By the 1970s, Caterpillar for the first time faced competitors for its markets, especially Japanese-based, heavy equipment manufacturers that benefited from strong connections with powerful Japanese industries. Meeting this competition caused Caterpillar to turn away from its original mission of serving the western farmer.[23]

While the record shows that by the mid-1990s Caterpillar successfully met the highest level of international competition, it did so by abandoning the farm equipment market in America to the remaining competitors. Case stepped into the void, but did so only in name and not in substance. After reorganizing and restructuring repeatedly in the decades following World War II, the company became the prey of conglomerates. It changed hands several times until (as we saw earlier) it was taken over by Tenneco. Meanwhile, International Harvester, which had always been a midwestern-based firm, failed to do what Caterpillar succeeded in doing; it struggled and reorganized repeatedly, along the way shedding parts of company. Its agricultural division was purchased by Tenneco in 1986. Now having two of the largest farm equipment makers under its corporate wing, and, in the absence of Caterpillar, with only one major competitor remaining, Tenneco merged the two companies and focused operations on meeting the heavy equipment needs of farmers. During the early 1990s, the new Case Company brought fresh, innovative products to the markets and slashed prices to create market share. Having succeeded in this endeavor by the mid-1990s, Tenneco announced it would sell the Case division to Wall Street investors.[24]

Meanwhile, John Deere survived its own problems to become Case's only competitor. While Deere never was a western-based operator, through the toughest times it stuck with its commitment to design and manufacture farm equipment demanded by western farmers. By the 1980s, it operated annually at heavy losses. In spite of its losses, Deere retained its historic mission of researching and developing innovative farm machinery. Even so, the company diversified its product offerings and ventured overseas to market them. By the mid-1990s, nearly a quarter of Deere's revenues came from overseas sales, and more than a third of its domestic sales came from nonfarm equipment.[25]

In spite of the sharp agricultural focus of Case and Deere, two non-western-based, start-up firms helped create one of the most important innovations in western farming. Both companies that raised capital through successful public offerings on Wall Street, Tyler Industries (until 1991 Mertz, Inc.) and Ag-Chem Equipment literally sent their research sights into orbit. Aimed at tapping into America's military satellite system, the companies are developing computerized navigational systems that guide and operate farm machinery. Called "site-specific" farming, the systems enable farmers to employ computer-controlled machines that automatically perform an array of planting, treating, and harvesting according to scientific databases guided by the military's satellite system.

Ag-Chem, having formed a joint venture with computer giant Unisys Corporation, may, with its product "Soilection," have established the early lead. This program allows agronomic data to be fed into a computer aboard a tractor hooked up to specifically designed equipment that chemically treats the soil. This computerized tractor carries another device that feeds information to America's military satellite system. Yet another device taps into the information coming aboard and commands the equipment to deploy location-specific amounts of chemicals as it travels along the computer-generated coordinates that guide the tractor.[26]

Because no firm has earned profits from these inventions, it is likely that profitable products will flow from joint ventures formed by Case, Deere, Ag-Chem, and Tyler, and very probably manufacturers of nonagricultural equipment. The high cost of rapidly changing technology in modern agriculture makes it difficult and often impossible for profits to be earned through single-product innovations. Clearly, through joint ventures and mergers agribusinesses diminish single-product research and development costs by spreading them across national, international, and routinely nonagricultural product lines.

Just as postwar agribusinesses involved with farm production have had to develop an array of innovations to earn profits in an environment of high-cost technical change, so too agribusinesses that provide services to ship, process, distribute, and market agricultural products had their profit-earning capacities severely tested in the postwar markets. Nowhere is this shown more clearly than in the western-favored and time-tested arena of farmer-controlled, agricultural cooperative marketing associations. Cooperatives faced the same economic environment as did other postwar agribusinesses: fast-changing technologies, new competitive products, emerging international markets and competitors, new forms of finance and business organizations, and changing farm and nonfarm populations. For each of these developments, agricultural cooperatives had to either provide a strategic response or face failure. Because western agricultural cooperatives often employed the same responses as privately and publicly held agribusinesses, in the postwar era they became in the minds of many Americans and their legal agencies indistinguishable from private enterprise.

The archetype of a western cooperative—and one might argue the father of all agricultural cooperatives—is Sunkist. This enormously successful organization provides a case study in the effects of postwar economic forces.[27]

Like all western cooperatives, Sunkist saw the changing demography alter its membership. By the early 1970s, the typical member farm was two to three times larger than it had been in the immediate postwar years. Between the latter years of the Great Depression and 1995, the number of citrus growers in the cooperative fell from 14,000 to around 6,500. While during the earlier period nearly all farms were run by families, during the latter period many were operated by general partnerships, syndicates, and corporations. They no longer operated in lush suburbs in southern California but had sold these properties to residential developers. The new generation of citrus growers (in 1980 the average Sunkist grower had been in the business less than fifteen years) was found in the San Joaquin Valley and in southern Arizona. Yet in the 1990s, Sunkist still marketed about two-thirds of the nation's fresh citrus product. In fact, the Sunkist brand was by then the forty-third most recognized in America and the forty-seventh most recognized in the world. The value of its products marketed worldwide surpassed $1 billion. Beneath these simple facts is a complex postwar history of Sunkist.

The rise of the modern chain store supermarket posed the first new business structure Sunkist confronted in postwar America. Prior to the war, Sunkist (until 1952 known as the Southern California Fruit and Citrus Grower's Exchange) employed dealer servicemen who were responsible for helping "mom-

Agribusiness refers to the large-scale and capital-intensive operation of farms, as well as corporate control in terms of processing and marketing of specific agricultural commodities. One of the largest, most successful, and publicly recognized agribusiness firms is Sunkist Growers, Inc. This farmer cooperative provides system and order to the production and marketing of citrus fruits. *Courtesy, Sunkist Growers, Inc.*

and-pop" grocery stores purchase, display, and advertise Sunkist products. Then in the 1960s and 1970s, chain store supermarkets spread across the West, displacing the independent groceries. The supermarkets took complete control over their store shopping environments and ran their own advertising campaigns. By the end of the 1970s, Sunkist's servicemen were misfits in this new environment, so the cooperative phased them out. In their place Sunkist joined with the supermarkets to fund advertising campaigns aimed at attracting customers to particular stores and provided fruit store displays designed in cooperation with the stores' advertising managers.[28]

The chain store supermarkets controlled not only their marketing environment but also the warehousing and distribution of products. As these controls over the market spread from the West to the East Coast, local and regional fresh produce auctions were eliminated. Although Sunkist benefited from cost reductions through the new system of direct purchasing by the supermarkets, the elimination of the auctions on the East Coast forced further changes in Sunkist. In earlier years it had loaded its citrus aboard trucks and headed them east. The drivers sold their produce on the road and marketed the remainder at auction when they arrived on the East Coast. Sunkist used these auctions as its hedge or "safety valve" against surplus product.

With this hedge eliminated, Sunkist had to find new and different ways to handle surplus product. One new tack took Sunkist into the business of researching and developing citrus by-products. Owing to this new emphasis on research and development, Sunkist invented such products as Perma-Stabil citrus flavors, which extended the useful life of peel products, that is, products that have citrus peel. It designed the Sunkist Juicit Extractor, which simply and efficiently extracted juices from fresh citrus. It also developed a range of new citrus-based products, including Sunkist Punches and Sunkist Frozen Fruit Bars. In 1985, it built the world's largest bulk frozen food facility on the docks of southern California's largest harbor, and here it stored not only huge quantities of its own frozen juices but also large quantities of low-cost Brazilian citrus concentrates, which it mixed with its own product and sold in concert with world demand for citrus juices.[29]

The international market for citrus and citrus-based products that emerged in the postwar period was the second major development that encouraged Sunkist to make further changes in its operations. In the years immediately following the war, increasing discretionary income in Europe encouraged Sunkist to construct warehouses and distribution systems in selected countries. By the late 1960s, Sunkist sold 20 percent of its product in Europe. In subsequent years, Brazil invaded the market with heavy supplies and low prices. Sunkist shifted its focus to the Far East, especially Japan. By the 1990s, more than 30 percent of Sunkist's product was consumed in these new international markets.

Despite Sunkist's success in rapidly adjusting to changes in international markets, other corporations that traded in these markets took steps that created yet another problem for the company. These were corporations that decided to meet international competition through a strategy of product diversification. This strategy made Sunkist face huge, highly capitalized conglomerates that attempted to buy up Sunkist affiliates in the West. No sooner had one of these conglomerates, Castle and Cook, bought Sunkist's largest affiliate—Blue Goose Packers—than Sunkist evaluated the problem and took steps to resolve it.[30]

Clearly the conglomerates had the financial resources to provide citrus growers with an array of benefits. Conglomerates could spread operating and capital costs across a field of products, thereby diminishing unit operating costs for each individual product line they sold. Moreover, they could offer to affiliates in their business—in this case new citrus growers lured from Sunkist—low-cost loans and insurance.

To meet the challenge presented by the conglomerates, Sunkist developed new programs and revamped old ones. To help it reduce operating and capital costs on a per-unit product basis, Sunkist diversified its operations. In part this was accomplished by altering the character of old operations so the company no longer performed the role of a vertically integrated business. For example, Sunkist owned nearly 200,000 acres of timber, a resource for the lumber used in making wood crates for citrus products. When Sunkist designed plant technologies that manufactured sturdy cardboard boxes, it sold off its lumber mills and crate-making facilities. Then it negotiated contracts through which it sold "sustained yield permits" that allowed lumber and paper companies to harvest its trees. Earnings from these permits were used to reduce sharply capital charges Sunkist had traditionally made on the citrus products sold for member growers.

Capital and operating charges were further reduced through a trademark licensing program introduced by Sunkist in 1974. Businesses such as the Ben Myerson Candy Company bought Sunkist citrus by-products and used them to manufacture and market candies in wrappers bearing the Sunkist logo. So successful was the original program that agreements were reached with large conglomerates, such as General Cinema, which established new divisions to produce products bearing the Sunkist logo. By the 1980s, these companies manufactured and sold worldwide a range of juices, soft drinks, and confections that bore the Sunkist label.

While payments from Sunkist's licensees helped reduce the capital and operating costs for its members, the cooperative realized that some conglomerates preferred to compete head-on with Sunkist for market share. These companies aimed their sights on the source of Sunkist's revenues—the citrus grower. Due to their size and highly rated bond structure, conglomerates could offer low-cost loans to new entrants or to growers who wished to expand production. The conglomerates also used low-interest loans to entice citrus growers to join them, rather than Sunkist, in marketing their products. In response, Sunkist created the Sunkist Realty Corporation and used its Standard and Poors A+++ bond rating to obtain funds that could be used to make low-interest loans either to current members or to prospective Sunkist growers.

The fourth and final obstacle facing Sunkist in the postwar period was the Federal Trade Commission (FTC). Like most major players in the national economy, Sunkist faced ongoing scrutiny from this watchdog agency. Created in 1914, the FTC investigated businesses to determine if they violated federal laws—especially laws against monopolistic practices. While the Capper-Volstead Cooperative Marketing Act of 1922 excluded agricultural cooperatives from the FTC's legal domain, the agency nevertheless found grounds to prosecute many cooperatives, including Sunkist, beginning in the 1970s. As did other cooperatives, Sunkist fought the FTC throughout the 1970s and 1980s. The results were mixed. On the one hand, Sunkist had to divest itself of one packaging operation and agreed to freeze plans for holding and operating new packaging plants. On the other hand, this agreement freed Sunkist from further investigations and operating constraints.[31]

Although the interests of most agribusinesses range far beyond matters of commodity purchasing, sales, and services, and while many agribusinesses conduct business on an international scale, Sunkist Growers, Inc., remains an important agricultural cooperative that markets most of the citrus fruit produced in California. Note the windmill behind the orange grove, used to generate electricity. *Courtesy, Sunkist Growers, Inc.*

Other western agricultural cooperatives encountered many of the same problems as Sunkist. Each also faced issues particular to the special line of products it marketed. Many confronted an additional problem: they lacked the large capital base of Sunkist and therefore found it either difficult or impossible to compete effectively in national and international markets that demanded a powerful presence in newspapers, magazines, radio, and television (a single advertisement in a major television event might cost as much as the entire cash flow of a small cooperative).[32]

By the end of the 1970s, several of California's venerable specialty crop cooperatives struggled to meet expenses. Some had operated for fifty years or more. A group of them—walnut growers, prune and apricot growers, raisin growers (the reader should recognize the Sun Maid logo), and fig growers—began merging in the 1970s to finally incorporate in 1980 as the Sun-Diamond Growers of California. In 1984, the Hazelnut Growers of Oregon also joined Sun-Diamond.[33]

By the mid-1980s, Sun-Diamond had an annual advertising budget that exceeded $15 million. The cooperative helped spread these and other marketing and distribution costs by emulating Sunkist: it introduced new by-product lines, including processed animal feeds. In addition to such processed raw products, Sun-Diamond developed a host of new manufactured goods, including top-selling bakery products such as Sun Maid raisin bread. In 1985, this consolidated group of cooperatives became a Fortune 500 company.

These achievements failed to build a defense against a broad decline in commodity prices caused, in part, by new high international tariffs erected by the nascent European Economic Community. While Sunkist replaced the loss of European markets in the mid-1980s with ones in Asia, Sun-Diamond had products that were not as easy to market in this area of the world. Worse yet, before the cooperative could build a new market, it announced that in 1985 accounting errors had caused it to pay out to its growers profits they had not earned. This resulted in a mass defection of growers, the termination of key management, and a restructuring of the cooperative that sharply diminished the powers of management over each of the product cooperatives. Once in place, these changes combined with rising commodity prices to generate steady profits for the cooperative's growers in the 1990s.[34]

Ocean Spray Cranberries, Inc., was another cooperative that broke into the Fortune 500 in the 1980s. Like Sunkist, Ocean Spray illustrates how strong demand for a high-quality core product encourages new product ventures that result in a high-profile brand-name presence in national and international markets. It also illustrates how a small group of specialty crop growers (about 1,000) can achieve this lofty status.

While cranberry cultivation originated on the East Coast in the 1850s, it spread west until in the 1880s it became firmly rooted in bogs located in Washington and Oregon. In the early twentieth century, the Ocean Spray Cooperative was founded in Massachusetts; during World War II, growers in Washington and Oregon joined the cooperative, and a few years later the Canadian Cranberry Growers joined Ocean Spray. Demand for both the fresh and the canned product grew steadily until late 1959, when the United States Department of Health, Education, and Welfare released news that cranberries grown in Washington and Oregon contained elements of a cancer-causing weed killer used by the growers.[35]

This news flattened demand for cranberries and nearly destroyed Ocean Spray. In hopes of reviving the co-op through a radical strategy designed to restore the healthy image of Ocean Spray, Edward Gelsthorpe, a former marketing specialist from Colgate Palmolive and Bristol Meyers, was named president. Gelsthorpe launched a campaign some critics thought suicidal: he borrowed heavily against assets to develop, advertise, and market healthful drinks bearing the Ocean Spray logo. By the 1970s, this campaign helped overpower the public's memory of the 1959 debacle, and Ocean Spray was on its way to becoming one of the world's most recognized names by health-conscious and fitness-oriented consumers.[36]

So successful was this new image that Pepsi Co. bought from Ocean Spray a license permitting it to distribute individual bottles of its drink products worldwide. Armed with these funds, Ocean Spray bought Milne Fruit Products of Milne, Washington, one of the nation's major processors of grape and prune juice concentrates. Now a wholly owned subsidiary, Ocean Spray added to this facility concentrate production of cherry, blueberry, plum, raspberry, strawberry, and blackberry juices. Ocean Spray not only blended these juices with cranberry juices to provide a new world of drink variations but also sold the concentrates to other cooperatives (such as Sunkist) and other major food companies (such as Nestle, R. J. Reynolds, and Kraft–General Foods) for development of yet other food product variations.[37]

While Ocean Spray illustrates how western specialty crop growers allied themselves with national cooperatives that tapped into powerful distribution and marketing channels controlled by large corporations, Mid-America Dairymen illustrates why some small, isolated, western cooperatives often made a giant geographic leap to join distant regional ones.

Incorporated in 1968, Mid-America Dairymen typified the regional dairymen's cooperative that resulted from local mergers within a geographic area. Changing health laws, technologies, and supermarkets defined new marketing regions for dairymen's cooperatives, and they found themselves constantly altering their operations to cope with the ever-changing presence of dairy product superpowers such as Beatrice, Borden, and Carnation. As the dairymen's cooperatives changed their configurations to meet these challenges, a few (like the Associated Milk Producers [AMPI] and Mid-American Dairymen) gained superpower status in regional markets. By the late 1980s, Mid-American Dairymen had become the dominant dairy cooperative not only in the Midwest but also in North and South Dakota, Nebraska, Kansas, Oklahoma, and Texas. Recognizing the marketing resources it would gain through a merger with this huge brethren, Glenn Milk Producers Association (located in the tiny Sacramento Valley town of Willows) announced in 1991 that it would merge with Mid-America. In explaining the decision to leap across hundreds of miles of unaffiliated dairymen's associations and join Mid-America, the association's president said it was essential to "increase their scale of operations through consolidations, mergers, joint ventures and marketing agencies."[38]

Many of the same trends framed somewhat different business structures in other western specialty product agricultural cooperatives. American Crystal Sugar Cooperative, which markets more than 15 percent of the nation's sugar, exemplifies the uniqueness of some modern western cooperatives. Founded in the early twentieth century as a private company by the Oxnard family, in southern California, this company expanded throughout the Mountain States as sugar beet growing moved eastward. Eventually, American Crystal Sugar located its headquarters in Denver, Colorado. Following World War II, sugar beet growing moved rapidly northward, and grower cooperatives emerged in competition with American Crystal. These organizations proved more efficient in their operations than American Crystal (the inheritors of the Oxnard wealth did not buy new technologies) and used sinking funds (earnings retained for plant renewal) to begin buying shares of stock in American Crystal. In 1973, the cooperatives bought the remaining shares held by the Oxnard family and began to vigorously merge with other sugar beet growers' cooperatives. Soon American Crystal Cooperative owned major, strategically located processing plants in all the western and midwestern beet-growing regions. Even so, American Crystal sought out alliances with remaining stand-alone sugar beet cooperatives. In one of its most important alliances, it formed a joint venture that built a major beet by-product plant near San Francisco. This plant produced mostly pellets used as cattle feed. By the mid-1990s, nearly two-thirds of its product was sold to Japan, with most of the remainder sold in Europe.[39]

While western specialty crop growers often preferred the business structure provided by cooperatives, other western growers found that the dynamics of the modern, privately held corporation better met their needs. The success story of central California grape growers moves almost in lockstep with the development of Gallo Wineries. Founded during the Great Depression by two brothers, Ernest and Julio Gallo, the company rapidly moved out of the confines of their backyard garage to develop one of the nation's most aggressively expansionist business vehicles. After reaching agreements with local table grape producers to share with them profits made from converting their fresh produce into wine, in 1910 the brothers decided to place their own label (Gallo) on their bottles and build a sales force to make direct sales to liquor stores. Theirs was the first winery to hire salesmen for the express purpose of selling a specific brand-name label at point-of-sale locations, and Gallo wines came to be displayed prominently against the backdrop of a clutter of unknown wine labels.

Meanwhile, Gallo invested profits in research and development. As researchers developed grapes superior to the standard table grape (Thompson seedless), Gallo negotiated new contracts with growers. Beginning in the late 1960s, any growers who agreed to tear out their old vines and plant new varieties were given fifteen-year "fair price" contracts for their product.[40]

Gallo made good on its promises to growers because it vigorously pursued cost-cutting measures while simultaneously developing a range of new products across which it could spread mounting advertising and marketing costs. Gallo bought its own bottle manufacturing plant, its own aluminum foil cap company (to replace the costly standard cork plug), and its own trucking company. It introduced an array of wine-based fruit drinks, thereby helping to drive down the cost of marketing its core wine group. By the early 1970s, Gallo could earn a solid profit selling its Hearty Burgundy for $1.25, which acclaimed critics judged to be the best wine value in America.

Nevertheless, this aggressive and enormously successful enterprise had problems. Beginning in the 1970s, the FTC instigated proceedings against Gallo for alleged monopoly of the low-cost wine retail business. After years of costly litigation, the charges were "set aside." At the same time, the ability of Gallo to develop cheap palatable fruit wines created other problems. Critics singled out its Thunderbird product as an alleged contributor to the rise of alcoholism among low-income urban Americans. Responding to this charge, in the late 1980s Gallo suspended the sale of these wines in low-income areas and intitiated a new business strategy in the 1990s. Playing on the powers of its brand name, Gallo aims to expand the worldwide sale of its premium (high-cost) wines as it diminishes the production of low-cost wines.[41]

Gallo's experience in some ways is paralleled by other privately held specialty crop businesses. Dole Food Company—today located in Westlake Village, California—illustrates a few of the parallels while also showing some of the ways western agribusinesses were restructured in the postwar period. Founded by James Dole just north of Honolulu in the early twentieth century, this pineapple canning firm fell on hard times during the Great Depression and was bought by a local real estate firm (Castle and Cook). The new owners drew on their real estate assets to develop and market a range of new products, including freshly packaged pineapple chunks and fresh juices. When in the mid-1960s it decided to include television spots in its advertising campaign, the company reasoned it would need to cut per-unit advertising costs by adding new specialty crops to its line of Dole products. In the next two decades, it bought company after company, adding a seemingly endless procession of crops to the Dole line—nuts, bananas, vegetables, citrus fruits, sugar, and even beer and canned tuna.[42]

Yet this frenzied effort to spread heavy advertising costs across multiproduct food lines encouraged Dole to borrow heavily to purchase the companies it needed. The debt burden soon grew faster than earnings. Stock in Dole (sold on the NYSE as Castle and Cook) plunged. In 1985, several newly formed investment firms that specialized in buying out troubled companies such as Dole made bids for the company. To fend off the bidders, Dole merged with Flexi-Van. This corporation had a huge fleet of ships, complete with shipping containers, that not only raised sharply the value of the new company's stock on the NYSE but also allowed Dole to reduce international shipping costs.[43]

With this armada Dole now ventured into uncharted international markets. Its field of business operations widened exponentially to include tiny Honduras, the troubled Philippines, and fast-growing markets in South Korea and volatile regions such as the nations in Eastern Europe and the Middle East. Meanwhile, it prepared to sell its real estate holdings. In preparation for the sale of its Castle and Cook operations, in the early 1990s it created construction firms dedicated to the development of specific properties. Beginning in 1994, Dole began to form these real estate ventures into specific corporate entities, which it plans to sell through public stock offerings.[44]

Another western specialty crop business, Del Monte, is one of Dole's toughest competitors, yet it provides a classic example of a company that could not survive the takeover battles fought by corporations during the 1970s and 1980s. Del Monte itself is the product of a merger mania among California fruit and vegetable packers that began in the late nineteenth century. By the early twentieth century, more than seventy-five canneries located in Oregon, Washington, Idaho, Alaska, and Hawaii had merged to produce premium products carrying an identical label—Del Monte.[45]

By World War II, Del Monte had made acquisitions in the Midwest and on the East Coast, and also in countries such as the Philippines, Canada, and Haiti. As companies in the food processing business fought for shelf space in supermarkets during the 1960s and 1970s, Del Monte found itself burdened with growing advertising expenses. To spread these costs across wider offerings, Del Monte bought a range of agribusinesses that allowed it to introduce new products carrying the Del Monte logo. These included canned fruit drinks, frozen french fries, frozen TV dinners, potato chips, and turnovers. To brace itself against fluctuations in commodities prices, Del Monte did what food companies such as Dole already had done—bought agricultural properties with the plan of developing them into commercial property, residential neighborhoods, and shopping centers.

Although Del Monte succeeded better at this effort in diversification than many other food companies, the company learned in 1978 that a sizable block of its stock had been purchased by one of the nation's largest tobacco producers, R. J. Reynolds and Co. (RJR). Seeking to diversify its operations as a hedge against mounting public criticism over the health effects of its core product, RJR determined to buy successful food companies such as Del Monte. Faced with the power of large capital reserves, and fearful of shareholder suits should management fail to recognize how Reynold's pursuit of Del Monte stock drove up its price on the NYSE, Del Monte agreed to the buyout.[46]

During the 1980s, RJR continued to acquire other food companies, until near the end of the decade it held under its corporate umbrella such food giants as Nabisco. Meanwhile, the debt it incurred to purchase these companies at inflated prices mounted faster than its companies' earnings. As the price of RJR-Nabisco's stock sank on the NYSE, several suitors lined up to vanquish the giant. The victor was itself a newly organized, but nonetheless feared, giant: Kohlberg, Kravis, and Roberts (KKR). Consummating the deal in 1988, KKR set about its main business, that of selling RJR-Nabisco parts. Del Monte was partitioned into business segments and sold off to the highest bidders. An inside management group borrowed nearly $1.5 million (called a "bridge loan") against the holdings of one segment—Del Monte's domestic vegetable canning operations—and took the company private. This management group reopened the canning group's historic headquarters in San Francisco in the mid-1990s, but, burdened with huge debts, the company continued to be bantered about as a takeover target.[47]

These abrupt turnabouts in the fortunes of Del Monte illustrate the way in which food companies, expanding operations, and product lines aggressively raised their debt loads in the 1970s and 1980s to diminish mounting advertising and marketing costs, until the debts became unbearable financial burdens. Management repeatedly went forward and then retreated, forever in motion, often seeming to go this way or that, if for no other reason than to keep their jobs, fool investors, and trick those businesses that might seek to buy them out.

Great and powerful names in the food business—Beatrice and Kraft Foods, to name but two—bought up and sold western agribusinesses (and hundreds of other unrelated businesses) with such ferocity that even the most astute business analysts could neither track their operations nor decipher a business strategy that explained them. Put simply, the big agribusinesses in the postwar period have histories that tell little about food production, marketing, or their effects on farmers and much about high finance, management ethics, and business gamesmanship.

Carnation Foods is one of the corporate giants that helps deepen our understanding of American business life. This company originated during the early twentieth century in the state of Washington. By World War II, the company's name had become synonymous with canned condensed milk. Americans identified the product as "milk from contented cows" (in its national ads, Carnation portrayed the cows of its dairymen in romantic, pastoral northwestern settings). In years immediately following the war, Carnation continued its original commitment to researching and developing healthful dairy products and to developing or acquiring dairy product plants. In the mid-1950s, it introduced an "instant dry milk" that dissolved in water, for which it was able to develop a strong international market. Fueled by the financial success of these businesses, Carnation developed an immensely successful powdered "instant breakfast" that could be stirred into a glass of milk, and it came up with a dairy "replacement" product for coffee lovers who feared the cholesterol in cream—Coffee-Mate.

In spite of these successes, during the 1960s and 1970s Carnation joined the phalanx of highly capitalized companies that changed directions. Now headquartered in Los Angeles, it faced a barrage of new problems. First, the FTC ordered it to abort its strategy of further expansion in the dairy products business. Second, chain supermarkets that once happily gave preferred shelf space to Carnation began to insist that the company produce either generic or store-labeled products. Often the supermarkets placed cheaper prices on these products, then placed them next to the Carnation products. On other occasions, the chain supermarkets formed their own dairy products operations and eliminated Carnation products altogether. Third, consumers began to reduce or eliminate dairy products from their diets to reduce cholesterol levels.[48]

To hedge against these threats to its historic operations, Carnation followed the path of every highly capitalized business when threatened: it diversified by acquiring businesses totally unrelated to its core products. When in 1972 a longtime accountant with the firm, H. E. Olson, became the first nonfamily CEO of Carnation, this diversification strategy was pursued vigorously. By 1980, Carnation had produced fourteen varieties of processed frozen potatoes, an array of products marketed as Slender-Diet Foods, Alber's corn meal and grits, Contadina tomato products, and several lines of pet foods, including Friskies. Most of the companies were acquired in takeovers. To make sure it was sufficiently diversified, the company added such businesses as Herf Jones school rings and Dayton Reliable Tool and Manufacturing Company. In 1980, to help finance this expansion, Carnation made its first public stock offering and listed it on the NYSE.[49]

Carnation's management, however, was not keen enough to play successfully in an arena filled with brilliant, professionally trained financiers and lawyers whose domain did not have national or even international boundaries. In fact, Carnation was one of the first food giants to be consumed by these skilled takeover artisans. Nestle Foods in Vevey, Switzerland, bought Carnation in 1985 for $3 billion. Once other acquisitions were completed, Nestle became one of America's largest food companies, doing more than $7 billion in business annually (and about $35 billion worldwide).[50]

This pattern in highly capitalized western agribusinesses repeats itself again and again until it plays much like noontime soap operas on television: the names change, but the plot remains. A few nuances are worthy of note. The McKesson Corporation, a long-standing eastern corporation whose history is filled with such intrigue that a Hollywood screenwriter could not create a better corporate story, was bought in 1967 by Foremost, one of the West's prominent dairy giants. Foremost closed down McKesson's East Coast headquarters and based its new operations in San Francisco. This was not an easy job for a group of dairymen. The range of products it inherited ran from Sparklett's Water to Armor-All products to ORAfix denture adhesives. It even owned a drugstore chain, Valu-Rite, through which it sold this potpourri of products.

Foremost's dairymen managers thought they could run these enterprises without help from McKesson's former managers and so fired them. As the history of American takeovers in the 1970s and 1980s shows, this often proved to be a fatal mistake by the management that staged the coup. McKesson's terminated managers teamed up and went straight to one of the highly capitalized takeover firms staffed with the nation's top financiers, accountants, and lawyers. In this case, the firm was Pennsylvania-based Sharon Steel, which quietly bought 10 percent of Foremost's stock and then announced publicly (to meet Securities and Exchange rules) that it planned to buy the remaining stock in Foremost.[51]

A huge proxy fight (Foremost management and Sharon Steel fought for the vote of shareholders) ensued. Management won a temporary victory when it got stockholders to adopt a charter amendment that prohibited "undesirables" from acquiring more than 10 percent of the company's stock. No matter. This battle was so time-consuming for management and so costly for the company that by 1980 its earnings dove and the price of its stock plummeted as Wall Street analysts derided Foremost as one of the worst-managed companies in America.

Responding to this outcry, Foremost fired the original managers and brought in a new team. They sold its parts hurriedly to pay down debt. Kraft Foods, for example, bought Foremost's entire dairy and food group. Kraft, however, soon mergered with Dart Industries (which sold such products as Duracell batteries), and the newly combined company then bought Kitchen Aid appliances. The stock of this corporate mishmash fell rapidly on the NYSE once analysts dissected its operations. Abruptly, the company sold all its nonfood businesses.

No sooner did Kraft present itself to the public as a pure food company than Philip Morris, like other tobacco companies on the prowl for food product additions to supplant the projected decline in its core business, made an astonishingly high bid for all the stock (called a tender offer) in Kraft. Thus, in the 1990s, Philip Morris became the producer of not only Foremost dairy products but those of Knudsen too, as well as Raisin Bran and Grape-Nuts cereals. Everything from Entemanns and Oroweat, to Cool Whip and Jell-O, to Bird's Eye and Budget Gourmet, to Louis Rich and Oscar Meyer, are food products of Philip Morris.[52]

Clorox Company of Oakland, California, provides a slightly different variation on our recurrent theme in the history of highly capitalized agribusinesses. Clorox has a history of moving in and out of all sorts of businesses—food and nonfood. It is not only a veteran in this high-risk game of musical chairs in business, but it traditionally employs highly talented financiers, accountants, and attorneys. The convergence of these talents gave Clorox an uncanny ability to correctly time the entry into, and the departure from, the many food businesses it has owned. The food companies it retained for long periods were carefully selected niche food product companies such as Cream of Rice cereal and B&B mushrooms. The result has been a strong, western, diversified product company with staying power.[53]

Many of the Goliaths in America's food business in the 1970s and 1980s were shredded in the 1990s until they became mere skeletons. Beatrice Corporation, once the thirty-eighth largest corporation in America and a superpower in food business, is today a figment of its former self; its many parts are owned by other businesses. Some of the acquiring companies succeeded because they focused sharply on the food products business and never ventured out of them. These companies—like Archer-Daniels-Midland—generally were midwestern-based and managed to retain the conservative orientation for which the American heartland is renowned. Other parts were spread about among the conglomerates that survived the heavy tests posed by skilled financiers and their lawyers and accountants. What these businesses will look like in the future defies even the most daring guess by corporate analysts.[54]

Western grocery businesses in the postwar period also faced tough and tumultuous competition, but many avoided the rage for diversification that beset the huge food processing agribusinesses. With a few exceptions, the grocery business has a history of mergers and acquisitions that follow the traditional patterns of horizontal (acquiring a company that operates in the same field of business) and vertical (acquiring a company that provides a cost-cutting product or service) mergers. As western grocery stores entered the postwar period, they were cautiously expanded by managers who had deep personal roots in the grocery business. Indeed, even new businesses in the entire postwar period generally were founded by experienced grocery men.

Vons Stores, established in 1906, operated until 1969 under owner-managers descended from the original founders. Safeway Stores, which the Merrill Lynch investment firm bought in 1926 from the original founder, merged almost immediately with a much larger chain, Skaggs Markets, to utilize the top-flight managerial talent provided by the founder's family. Ralph's Stores, established in 1873, operated as a family enterprise until 1992, when Century City–based Yucaipa Companies bought it.

Along the way, such family-operated groceries either merged with their competitors or were acquired by them. Some of the prewar chains were large even by today's standards. In 1931, MacMan Stores, for example, which merged with Safeway, operated 1,400 grocery stores in the Pacific Northwest. Drawing on generations of experience in operating grocery stores, managers of these chains introduced many modern marketing techniques. They helped design large accessible refrigeration units, and they introduced scales and packaging materials to their stores, each of which allowed customers to serve themselves. They built warehouses and delivery systems that replaced those once provided by independent wholesalers. Despite these cost-cutting measures, the chain store grocery business had one of the lowest profit margins in American industry. The average for the industry was about 1.5 percent, and it was an uncommon chain that could sustain a margin of 3 percent.[55]

Clearly, in the postwar period there was no room for error in the management of America's chain store grocery markets. Even so, competition for the leaders surfaced, usually generated by sharp grocery store managers who had ambitions of their own. One of the first to surface was a single Albertson's store, built freestanding in Boise, Idaho, in 1939. Here a former manager from Safeway joined with another from Skaggs to build a store ten times the size of the average American grocery. In an unusual break with tradition, the store made bread and confections in sight of its shoppers, and it sold various sundry items such as magazines.

While the founders of Albertson's might lay claim to being the creators of the modern supermarket ("super" not only in size but also in providing sizable space for the sale of nonfood items), Smith's Food and Drug Centers challenged it for the title. This business originated as a small "mom-and-pop" grocery in little Brigham City, Utah, early in the twentieth century and continued as such until 1948. In that year, the founder's son, Dee, joined with George Woodward to build a supermarket on the scale of Albertson's. Smith's Food was distinguished by its attempts to provide customers with a wide range of nonfood products. As had other grocery chains, Smith's moved swiftly to establish its own wholesale supply operation. Rather than build its own, Smith's Food simply purchased its chief supplier. In the mid-1950s, Smith's took profits from its single venture in Brigham City and literally "bet the bank" on an unrelated enterprise opening twenty-five miles away—Thiokol Chemical Corporation. The stock it bought in this enterprise soared 1,200 percent in 1960; with these profits, Smith's had the capital it need to fund rapid expansion.[56]

Leveraging heavily against assets, Smith's began buying grocery stores in the intermountain states. Although some of its first ventures failed (it bought a Safeway store located near an Albertson's in Boise, Idaho, but it failed because the store's original manager had used creative accounting methods to make the store appear to be something it was not), over the long haul its basic strategy paid off. Aiming to buy grocery stores that could not hit the aforementioned narrow profit margin of 1.5 percent, Smith's bought groceries that offered pure and simple food products—such as Mayfair Markets—and converted them into supermarkets like the one it founded in Brigham City. Smith's also took advantage of the low job growth rate in the intermountain states during the 1960s. It slashed salaries of workers in the acquired groceries and increased their workloads. Employees who stayed and met targets received incentive pay. Those who did not were replaced with workers willing to aim at the high goals set by Smith's. These and other cost-cutting measures allowed Smith's to offer customers discount pricing, which gave it a competitive edge as the company entered markets where Safeway, Albertson's, and other chains operated. As Smith's moved farther West, however, this edge became blunted as tighter job markets pushed workers' salaries higher and unions resisted the worker speedup programs of the grocery. In an effort to continue offering discount pricing in the face of rising wages, Smith's built huge distribution centers that sold not only to its own stores but also to others. It built or bought food processing and packaging plants that permitted it to produce its own plain-wrapped generic products (more than 200 items were sold as such by 1980). Smith's sharply expanded the size of its supermarkets so it could experiment with "variety products" departments that came and went according to customer demand. It also bought a string of higher-margin Kmart Stores, and Smith's was quick to sell or close down any operation that failed to meet profit expectations.[57]

So intense was the competition among western supermarkets that by the 1990s Smith's announced it planned to phase out its supermarkets altogether. Replacing them would be "combination stores." These were one-stop shopping centers, mammoth enclosures in which any and all nondurable consumer goods might be purchased. This strategy required heavy new investments from a company already burdened with one of the highest debt-to-assets ratios in the industry; therefore, Smith's went public in the early 1990s. To block potential takeover companies from targeting it during this period of great vulnerability, Smith's management issued nonvoting and voting stock, holding nearly 50 percent of the latter. Yet even so financed, in 1996 the company announced it would retreat from its plans to build sixty combination stores in California.

While Smith's combination store strategy gave it a sound footing as it moved into the most competitive western markets, it met failure in California. Already saturated with every imaginable combination of food and nonfood store, the Golden State operated much like a cemetery for failed supermarkets. Of all supermarkets opened during the 1970s, one-third failed within a decade. Making this tight economy even tighter, in 1990 the state entered its biggest recession since the Great Depression, crushing consumer demand as businesses and workers either stopped spending or left the state altogether. Moreover, other conservatively financed supermarkets had a strong grip on the existing market, making penetration by new entrants improbable if not impossible.[58]

Albertson's in California primarily foiled Smith's plans. This conservatively run supermarket had expanded cautiously through the Mountain States in the 1950s, had gone public to raise capital for expansion in 1959, and had arrived in California in 1964. Albertson's aimed its sights on California's two metropolitan centers, Los Angeles and San Jose–Oakland. Here it located supermarkets that were either remodeled or replaced with such regularity that customers began to yawn when temporary store closures were announced. Albertson's dedicated itself to providing customers with freshly designed shopping environments. To keep costs low in pursuit of this policy, Albertson's assembled a team of analysts, engineers, construction firms, planners, architects, and lawyers. This team assessed and reassessed western supermarkets and chose sites where Albertson's would buy, trade, construct, or reconstruct new supermarkets. As for its own stores, the team determined which ones to maintain, redesign, rebuild, lease, sell, or close. Of the stores it kept, only one in ten got through the 1970s without a major facelift. As Albertson's entered the 1990s, it not only had become one of the most successful supermarkets in California's economy but also was firmly entrenched in every major growth area in the West.[59]

Other giants in the western supermarket industry have experienced the turmoil of takeovers and leveraged buyouts. Vons was bought in 1969 by the conglomerate Household Finance, which made the supermarket one of the companies controlled by its merchandising division. There the store remained until 1986, when the supermarket's managers arranged a bridge loan that enabled them to borrow against assets and buy the company from Household. Once freed, the new company vigorously pursued strategies that distinguished its successful competitors. To fund this strategy it went public in 1987. Then it began to expand by purchasing outdated supermarkets (including 172 Safeway Stores) and remodeling them so they provided the fresh, vibrant shopping environments needed to compete with Albertson's. Finally, it began building Pavillion's, or Vons' version of Smith's combination stores.[60]

Partly because of the revitalization of Vons, partly because it failed to respond to the store enhancement policies of Albertson's, and partly because of the new aggressive strategies of upstarts such as Smith's, Safeway steadily lost market share in the West. Through the late 1970s and early 1980s, Safeway was able to avert disaster by expanding abroad (in Australia and England) and by purchasing and operating specialty stores (Liquor Barn and Bon Appetit). But in 1985–86, mounting losses in its supermarkets could not be offset by the earnings of its specialty and foreign stores. As the price for its stock on the NYSE went into a tailspin, it became clear that the company's assets were worth far more than the market value of its stock. Rumors swirled through Wall Street that Safeway stock was being accumulated by takeover firms. First Dart Industries became the alleged suitor, but soon the heaviest hitter in the bunch— Kohlberg, Kravis, Roberts, and Co.—got Dart to step aside in exchange for a 20 percent position in the new Safeway Stores Company it created upon completion of the buyout. In 1987, KKR moved swiftly to sell all of Safeway's overseas operations and more than 1,110 of its supermarkets in California, Oklahoma, Texas, and New Mexico. Then KKR sold a vastly trimmed-down Safeway Stores to the public in an NYSE stock offering.[61]

This intense competition among western supermarkets provides a snapshot of the characteristics found in the history of all western agribusinesses in the postwar period. To meet the competition, heavy capital funds were required. Commonly these were used to expand product lines through either acquisitions or the construction of new facilities. As if trapped in a vicious circle, agribusiness firms found they had to produce and market growing numbers and varieties of products, cut advertising costs, or meet an endless procession of changes in their competitive environments. In many agribusinesses the profit margins became so thin that the slightest errors resulted in losses and, as one became thereby weakened, another stood ready to take advantage. Mergers, friendly takeovers, leveraged buyouts, and hostile takeovers by powerful financial firms created a tumultuous business environment that made anew the western stereotype of a shootout.

NOTES

1. In the postwar period historians expressed a growing interest in the changing structure of American business. They have written a large body of literature that examines the broad historical forces that forged basic structural changes in business. A topical and bibliographic assessment of these histories cannot be covered in the text, but the notes will provide a guide for further research on American business history.

2. See Harry C. McDean, "Beatrice Corporation: Historical Profile of an American-Style Conglomerate," in *Case Studies in American Business History,* ed. Joseph Pusateri and Henry Dethloff (Arlington Heights, Ill.: Harlan Davidson, 1986); and Harry C. McDean, "The History of National Dairy Products Businesses," in *The Handbook of American Business History,* vol. 2, ed. David O. Whitten (Westport, Conn.: Greenwood Press, 1996).

3. Ellen Paris, "Swimming Through Syrup," *Forbes* 132 (21 November 1983):

63–64; McDean, "Beatrice Corporation"; McDean, "The History of National Dairy Products Businesses."

4. While virtually all professional meetings of agricultural economists dealt with these questions in the 1980s and 1990s, the clearest report on the status of education is "Agribusiness Education in Transition: Strategies for Change," *Report of the National Agribusiness Education Commission, June 1989* (Cambridge, Mass.: Lincoln Institute of Land Policy, 1989).

5. Clifford Carlson, "Wells Fargo Hitches Wagon to Commerce on the Net," *San Francisco Business Times,* 16 December 1994; "Waving Goodbye to Wells Fargo," *Business Week* (New York), 1 August 1994, 33–34.

6. The best coverage of this phase in Bank of America's history is provided in Marquis James and Bessie James, *Biography of a Bank: The Story of Bank of America, N.T. & S.A.* (New York: Harper, 1954).

7. The near disaster for Bank of America is examined by Gary Hector, *Breaking the Bank: The Decline of BankAmerica* (Boston: Little, Brown, 1988).

8. *BankAmerica Corporation Annual Reports 1990–1993* (San Francisco: BankAmerica Corporation).

9. *Wall Street Journal,* 4 February 1993; Sam Zuckerman, "Bank of America Adopting Security Pacifics Orphan NonBank Units," *American Banker* 158 (6 April 1993): 1.

10. "New BankAmerica Debuts," *BankAmerican* 29 (22 April 1992): 1.

11. *TransAmerica Corporation Annual Reports, 1974–1979* (San Francisco: TransAmerica Corporation); George H. Koster, *The TransAmerica Story: 50 Years of Service and Looking Forward* (San Francisco: TransAmerica Corporation, 1978), 1–96.

12. *Wall Street Journal,* 20 April 1993; Clifford Carlson, "TransAmerica Set to Shed Unprofitable Unit," *Insurance* 84 (22 January 1993): 4.

13. *Tejon Ranch Company Annual Reports, 1989–94* (Tejon, Calif.: Tejon Company).

14. Frederick Simpich, *Dynasty in the Pacific* (New York: McGraw-Hill, 1974), 38–142; *The Travelers Insurance Company Annual Reports, 1986–1988* (Hartford, Conn.: The Travelers Company); *Newhall Land and Farming Company Annual Reports, 1991–1994* (Newhall, Calif.: The Newhall Company).

15. *Seitel Corporation Annual Reports, 1992–1995* (Houston: Seitel Corporation); *Chevron Oil Corporation Annual Reports, 1979–1990* (San Francisco: Chevron Oil Corporation); W. K. Summers and Sylvia H. Ross, "Getting Up Steam," *Barron's* 49 (17 November 1969): 48–49; *Wall Street Journal,* 10 June 1968; "Magma Generates Powerful Margins," *California Business* 28 (June–July 1993): 33.

16. *Tenneco's First 35 Years* (Houston: Tenneco Co., 1978); Michael Holmes, *J. I. Case: The First 150 Years* (Racine, Wisc.: Case Co., 1992).

17. *New York Times,* 23 January, 16 March, 23 July, and 7 December 1991; *Wall Street Journal,* 18 and 23 March 1993, 15 June 1993, and 7 March 1996; Mike Osenga, "Case Sells Vibromax," *Diesel Progress Engines and Drives* 58 (June 1992): 102–3; Brian Bremner, "Tough Times, Tough Bosses," *Business Week,* 25 November 1991, 174–79.

18. *Atlantic Richfield Corporation Annual Reports, 1988–1994* (Los Angeles: Atlantic Richfield Cos.).

19. *Lubrizol Corporation Annual Report, 1994* (Wickliffe, Ohio: Lubrizol Cos.).

20. *San Diego Union-Tribune,* 19 September 1995.

21. Ibid., 22 March 1996.

22. *Monsanto Corporation Annual Report, 1995* (St. Louis: Monsanto Cos.); *Dow Jones Newswires,* 1 April 1996.

23. "Construction Equipment" and "Agricultural Equipment," *Standard and Poors Industry Surveys* (October 1993): S34–S37.

24. Therese Eiben, "How the Industries Stack Up," *Fortune* 128 (12 July 1993): 102–3; *New York Times,* 23 January, 16 March, 23 July, and 7 December 1991; *Wall Street Journal,* 18 and 23 March 1993, 15 June 1993, 7 March 1996; Osenga, "Case Sells Vibromax"; Bremner, "Tough Times, Tough Bosses."

25. *John Deere and Company Annual Reports, 1989–1995* (Moline, Ill.: John Deere Corp.); "Construction Equipment" and "Agricultural Equipment."

26. *Investor's Business Daily* (Los Angeles), 27 November 1995.

27. Except where noted, the information in this review of Sunkist was extracted from "100 Sunkist Years: 1893–1993," *Sunkist Growers Inc. 1993 Annual Report* (Van Nuys, Calif.: Sunkist Growers); Catherine Merlo, *Heritage of Gold: The First 100 Years of Sunkist Growers, Inc., 1893–1993* (Van Nuys, Calif.: Sunkist Growers, 1994).

28. Interview with Russell Hanlin, CEO and president of Sunkist Growers, "Sunkist's Back in the Supermarket, Driving Sales with Ads," *Supermarket Business* 47 (February 1992): 14–15.

29. "The Sunkist Research Foundation," Dow Jones News Reference #A13933556 (Van Nuys, Calif.: Capital Cities Media Inc., 1993).

30. *Castle and Cook Annual Report, 1980* (Honolulu: Castle and Cook Cos.).

31. Joanna Ramey, "Sunkist Growers Inc. Market Share," Dow Jones News Reference #A11781935 (Washington, D.C.: Fairchild Publications, 1992).

32. *Los Angeles Business Journal,* 2 October 1995.

33. "What Makes Sun-Diamond Grow?" *Business Week,* 9 August 1982, 28–29.

34. *Los Angeles Times,* 11 May 1986.

35. *The History of Ocean Spray Cranberries* (Lakevile-Middleboro, Mass.: Ocean Spray Cranberries, Inc., 1981); "Cranberry Growers Reel under Pre-Holiday Blow," *Business Week,* 15 November 1959, 41–42.

36. Rayna Skolnik, "Ocean Spray's Canny Marketing," *Sales and Marketing Management* 125 (18 August 1980): 31–35.

37. *Washington Post,* 21 November 1990; Jon Berry, "Ocean Spray Joins the Pepsi Generation," *Adweek's Marketing Week* 33 (9 March 1992): 18–21; Peter Hanson, "How Ocean Spray Trims the Risk of Seasonal Borrowing," *Corporate Cashflow* 31 (May 1990): 16–18.

38. Russell Johnston, "Beyond Vertical Integration: The Rise of the Value-Adding Partnership," *Harvard Business Review* 66 (July/August 1988): 94–101; Julie Schlax, "Strategies: A Good Reason to Mess with Success," *Forbes* 142 (19 September 1988): 66–67; James L. Reeves, *The First 20 Years: The Story of Mid-America Dairymen* (Republic, Mo.: Mid-America Dairymen, Inc., 1989); *Annual Report of Mid-America Dairymen, 1991* (Kansas City, Mo.: Mid-America Dairymen, Inc.).

39. *50 Years in the Valley* (Moorehead, Minn.: American Crystal Sugar Company, 1976); Steve Brandt, "Sweet Deal," *Corporate Report Minnesota* 14 (January 1986):

91–96; *Star Tribune* (Minneapolis, Minn.), 19 March 1987, 11 July 1988, 9 July 1989; Norm Alster, "Getting the Middleman's Share," *Forbes* 154 (4 July 1994): 108–9.

40. *New York Times,* 15 and 22 November 1992; "American Wine Comes of Age," *Time* 100 (27 November 1972): 76–85.

41. Jaclyn Fierman, "How Gallo Crushes the Competition," *Fortune* 114 (1 September 1986): 48–49; Marvin K. Shanken, "Gallo's Dramatic Shift to Fine Varietals," *Wine Spectator* 22 (15 September 1991): 22–23; James Laube, "Gallo Brothers Growing Stake in Sonoma," *Wine Spectator* 22 (31 May 1991): 11–13.

42. *The History of Dole* (Westlake Village, Calif.: Dole Food Company, 1992); David Powers Cleary, *Great American Brands* (New York: Fairchild, 1991).

43. Jason Zwein, "Pineapples, Anyone?" *Forbes* 144 (27 November 1989): 286; *Dole Food Company Annual Report, 1985* (Westlake Village, Calif.: Dole Food Company).

44. *Los Angeles Times,* 9 March and 11 October 1991; Dan Koeppel, "Dole Wants the Whole Produce Aisle: Branded Fruits and Vegetables Are Turning the Nation's Supermarkets into Dole Country," *Adweek's Marketing Week* 31 (22 October 1990): 20; *New York Times,* 23 November and 26 December 1991; Lisa Ishikawa, "Pining Away," *Hawaii Business* 19 (August 1992): 35.

45. William Braznell, *California's Finest: The History of the Del Monte Corporation* (San Francisco: Del Monte Corp., 1982).

46. *A Century of Growing* (San Francisco: Del Monte Corp., 1991); *Business Week,* 18 November 1985, 18 September 1989.

47. *Wall Street Journal,* 11 January 1990, 13 September 1991, 28 May 1992; Fara Warner, "What's Happening at Del Monte Foods," *Adweek's Marketing Week* 31 (28 November 1991): 4–8; Fara Warner, "Del Monte Has a Rendezvous with an Italian Suitor," *Adweek's Marketing Week* 32 (1 June 1992): 4; Hope Lampert, *True Greed: What Really Happened in the Battle for RJR Nabisco* (New York: New American Library, 1990).

48. Michael McMenamin and Walter McNamara, *Milking the Public* (Chicago: Nelson Hall, 1980); Alison Otto and Jerry Dryers, "Movers and Shakers," *Dairy Foods* 88 (April 1987): 41–42.

49. *Carnation Corporation Annual Report for 1980* (Los Angeles: Carnation Inc.).

50. *Nestle S.A. Annual Report for 1994* (Vevey, Switzerland: Nestle S.A.).

51. Robert Hof, "McKesson Dumps Another Asset: The Boss," *Business Week,* 25 September 1989, 30–31; Harlan S. Byrne, "McKesson Corp.: Big Drug Distributor Bounces Back from a Bummer Year," *Barron's* 70 (25 June 1990): 51–52.

52. *Kraft, Inc.—Through the Years* (Glenview, Ill.: Kraft, 1988); Julie Liesse and Judann Dagnoli, "Goliath KGF Loses Steam After Merger," *Advertising Age* 63 (27 January 1992): 16–17; Fara Warner, "Kraft General Foods Move to Mend Its Floundering Marriage," *Adweek's Marketing Week* 33 (24 February 1992): 4–5; *Philip Morris Annual Report for 1994* (Lexington, Ky.: Philip Morris).

53. *About the Company on Its Diamond Anniversary* (Oakland, Calif.: Clorox Co., 1988).

54. Laura Sachar, "Top Seed," *Financial World* 157 (3 May 1988): 2–28.

55. *History of Vons Companies, Inc.* (Arcadia, Calif.: Vons Cos., 1992); Elliot Zwiebach, "Vons: Diversifying Formats for Diversified Needs," *Supermarket News* 36

(7 April 1986): 18–21; Elliot Zwiebach, "Vons New Accent," *Supermarket News* 37 (9 February 1987): 9–11; Alan Deutschman, "America's Fastest Risers," *Fortune* 124 (7 October 1991): 71–72; *Los Angeles Business Journal,* 21 August 1995.

56. Harlan S. Byrne, "Albertson's Food and Drug Retailer Boasts Top Earnings Growth, High Rate of Return," *Barron's* 72 (13 April 1992): 55–56; *Albertson's Today* (Boise, Idaho: Albertson's Cos., 1989); Howard M. Carlisle, *The Dee Smith Story: Fulfilling a Dream* (Brigham City, Utah: Ida Smith, 1992).

57. *Wall Street Journal,* 28 September 1989; *Los Angeles Times,* 8 September 1991.

58. "Smith's Scores with One-Hour Photo," *Progressive Grocer* 12 (1 December 1995): 14–16; John H. Taylor, "Mr. Smith Goes to Riverside," *Forbes* 149 (17 February 1992): 61–62.

59. *Los Angeles Business Journal,* 21 August 1995; Melanie Johnston, "Supermarkets Feed Phoenix Glut," *Advertising Age* 60 (13 November 1989): 66; "Albertson's Massive Deployment," *Discount Merchandiser* 31 (March 1991): 26–27.

60. *History of Vons Companies;* Zwiebach, "Vons: Diversifying Formats for Diversified Needs," 18–21; Zwiebach, "Vons New Accent," 9–11; Alan Deutschman, "America's Fastest Risers," *Los Angeles Business Journal,* 21 August 1995; *Seattle Times,* 23 February 1993; Mike Duff, "Superstores," *Supermarket Business* 46 (January 1991): 18–19.

61. Marc Beauchamp, "Food for Thought," *Forbes* 143 (17 April 1989): 73; *Safeway Stores Annual Report for 1994* (Oakland, Calif.: Safeway Stores Cos.).

Selected Bibliography

"Agribusiness Education in Transition: Strategies for Change." *Report of the National Agribusiness Education Commission, June 1989.* Cambridge, Mass.: Lincoln Institute of Land Policy, 1989.

Bernstein, Alison R. *American Indians and World War II: Toward a New Era in Indian Affairs.* Norman: University of Oklahoma Press, 1991.

Braznell, William. *California's Finest: The History of the Del Monte Corporation.* San Francisco: Del Monte Corp., 1982.

Broehl, Wayne G., Jr. *John Deere's Company: A History of Deere and Company and Its Times.* New York: Doubleday, 1984.

Brown, F. Lee, and Helen Ingram. *Water and Poverty in the Southwest.* Tucson: University of Arizona Press, 1987.

Browne, William P. *Cultivating Congress: Constituents, Issues, and Agricultural Policy Making.* Lawrence: University Press of Kansas, 1995.

Cawley, R. McGreggor. *Federal Land, Western Anger: The Sagebrush Rebellion and Environmental Politics.* Lawrence: University Press of Kansas, 1993.

Clark, Ira G. *Water in New Mexico: A History of Its Management and Use.* Albuquerque: University of New Mexico Press, 1987.

Cochrane Willard W., and Mary E. Ryan. *American Farm, Policy, 1948–1973.* Minneapolis: University of Minnesota Press, 1976.

Danbom, David B. *Born in the Country: A History of Rural America.* Baltimore: Johns Hopkins University Press, 1995.

Dunbar, Robert G. *Forging New Rights in Western Waters.* Lincoln: University of Nebraska Press, 1983.

Fite, Gilbert C. *American Farmers: The New Minority.* Bloomington: Indiana University Press, 1981.

Fixico, Donald L. *Termination and Relocation: Federal Indian Policy, 1945–1960.* Albuquerque: University of New Mexico Press, 1986.

Foss, Philip. *Politics and Grass: The Administration of Grazing on the Public Domain.* Seattle: University of Washington Press, 1960.

Friedberger, Mark. *Farm Families and Change in Twentieth-Century America.* Lexington: University Press of Kentucky, 1988.

Gulliford, Andrew. *America's Country Schools.* Washington, D.C.: Preservation Press, 1991.

Hartmann, Susan M. *The Home Front and Beyond: American Women in the 1940s.* Boston: Twayne, 1982.

Harvey, Mark. *A Symbol of Wilderness: Echo Park and the American Conservation Movement.* Albuquerque: University of New Mexico Press, 1994.

Helvarg, David. *The War Against the Greens: The "Wise-Use" Movement, the New Right, and Anti-Environmental Violence.* San Francisco: Sierra Club Books, 1994.

The History of Dole. Westlake Village, Calif.: Dole Food Company, 1992.

Hundley, Norris, Jr. *The Great Thirst: Californians and Water, 1970s–1990s.* Berkeley: University of California Press, 1992.

Hurt, R. Douglas. *American Agriculture: A Brief History.* Ames: Iowa State University Press, 1994.

———. *Indian Agriculture in America: Prehistory to the Present.* Lawrence: University Press of Kansas, 1987.

Iverson, Peter. *When Indians Became Cowboys: Native Peoples and Cattle Ranching in the American West.* Norman: University of Oklahoma Press, 1994.

Jellison, Katherine. *Entitled to Power: Farm Women and Technology, 1913–1963.* Chapel Hill: University of North Carolina Press, 1993.

Jenkins, J. Craig. *The Politics of Insurgency: The Farm Worker Movement in the 1960s.* New York: Columbia University Press, 1985.

Jordan, Terry G. *North American Cattle-Ranching Frontiers: Organization, Diffusion, Differentiation.* Albuquerque: University of New Mexico Press, 1993.

Krimsky, Sheldon, and Robert Wrubel. *Agricultural Biotechnology and the Environment: Science, Policy, and Social Issues.* Urbana: University of Illinois Press, 1996.

Lewis, David Rich. *Neither Wolf Nor Dog: American Indians, Environment, and Agrarian Change.* New York: Oxford University Press, 1994.

Liebman, Ellen. *California Farmland: A History of Large Agricultural Landholdings.* Totowa, N.J.: Rowman and Allanheld, 1983.

Lowitt, Richard. *The New Deal and the West.* Bloomington: Indiana University Press, 1984.

McCool, Daniel. *Command of the Waters: Iron Triangles, Federal Water Development, and Indian Water.* Berkeley: University of California Press, 1987.

McGuire, Thomas R., William B. Lord, and Mary G. Wallace, eds. *Indian Water in the New West.* Tucson: University of Arizona Press, 1993.

McWilliam, Carey. *North from Mexico: The Spanish-Speaking People of the United States.* Philadelphia: Lippincott, 1949.

Majka, Linda C., and Theo J. Majka. *Farm Workers, Agribusiness, and the State.* Philadelphia: Temple University Press, 1982.

Marcus, Alan I. *Cancer from Beef: DES, Federal Food Regulation, and Consumer Confidence.* Baltimore: Johns Hopkins University Press, 1994.

Martin, Philip L., Suzanne Vaupel, and Daniel L. Egan. *Unfulfilled Promise: Collective Bargaining in California Agriculture.* Boulder, Colo.: Westview Press, 1988.

Martin, Russell. *A Story That Stands Like a Dam: Glen Canyon and the Struggle for the Soul of the West.* New York: Henry Holt, 1987.

May, Elaine Tyler. *Homeward Bound: American Families in the Cold War Era.* New York: Basic Books, 1988.

Merlow, Catherine. *Heritage of Gold: The First Hundred Years of Sunkist Growers, Inc., 1893–1993.* Van Nuys, Calif.: Sunkist Growers, 1994.

Nash, Gerald D. *The American West Transformed: The Impact of the Second World War.* Bloomington: Indiana University Press, 1985.

Parman, Donald L. *Indians and the American West in the Twentieth Century.* Bloomington: Indiana University Press, 1994.

Pisani, Donald H. *From the Family Farm to Agribusiness: The Irrigation Crusade in California and the West, 1850–1931.* Berkeley: University of California Press, 1984.

———. *To Reclaim a Divided West: Water, Law, and Public Policy, 1848–1902.* Albuquerque: University of New Mexico Press, 1992.

———. *Water, Land, and Law in the West: The Limits of Public Policy, 1850–1920.* Lawrence: University Press of Kansas, 1996.

Pitzer, Paul C. *Grand Coulee: Harnessing a Dream.* Pullman: Washington State University Press, 1994.

Prucha, Francis Paul. *The Great Father: The United States Government and the American Indians.* 2 vols. Lincoln: University of Nebraska Press, 1984.

Rasmussen, Wayne D. "A History of the Emergency Farm Labor Supply Program, 1943–1947." U.S. Department of Agriculture, Bureau of Agricultural Economics, *Agriculture Monograph 13,* September 1951.

Reisner, Marc. *Cadillac Desert: The American West and Its Disappearing Water.* New York: Viking, 1986.

Richardson, Elmo. *Dams, Parks and Politics: Resource Development and Preservation in the Truman-Eisenhower Era.* Lexington: University Press of Kentucky, 1973.

Robinson, Michael C. *Water for the West: The Bureau of Reclamation, 1902–1977.* Chicago: Public Works Historical Society, 1979.

Rosenfeld, Rachel Ann. *Farm Women: Work, Farm, and Family in the United States.* Chapel Hill: University of North Carolina Press, 1985.

Rowley, William D. *U.S. Forest Service Grazing and Rangelands: A History.* College Station: Texas A&M University Press, 1985.

Schackel, Sandra. *Social Housekeepers: Women Shaping Public Policy in New Mexico, 1920–1940.* Albuquerque: University of New Mexico Press, 1992.

Short, C. Brant. *Ronald Reagan and the Public Lands: America's Conservation Debate, 1979–1984.* College Station: Texas A&M University Press, 1989.

Soule, Judith D., and Jon K. Piper. *Farming in Nature's Image: An Ecological Approach to Agriculture.* Washington, D.C.: Island Press, 1992.

Thomas, Robert J. *Manufacturing Green Gold: Capital, Labor, and Technology in the Lettuce Industry.* Cambridge: Cambridge University Press, 1981.

Voigt, William, Jr. *Public Grazing Lands: Use and Misuse by Industry and Government.* New Brunswick, N.J.: Rutgers University Press, 1976.

Wells, George S. *Garden in the West: A Dramatic Account of Science in Agriculture.* New York: Dodd, Mead, 1969.

White, Richard. *The Organic Machine: The Changing World of Indians and Whites, Salmon, and Energy, on the Columbia River.* New York: Hill and Wang, 1995.

Williams, Robert C. *Fordson, Farmall, and Poppin' Johnny.* Urbana: University of Illinois Press, 1987.

Worster, Donald. *Rivers of Empire: Water, Aridity, and the Growth of the American West.* New York: Pantheon, 1985.

Contributors

Anne B. W. Effland received her Ph.D. in the Graduate Program in Agricultural History and Rural Studies at Iowa State University. She is a social science analyst in the Markets and Trade Economics Division of the Economic Research Service of the U.S. Department of Agriculture and associate editor of *Agricultural Outlook*. She specializes in the history of farm labor, rural women, and agricultural policy.

Judith Fabry earned a Ph.D. in the Graduate Program in Agricultural History and Rural Studies at Iowa State University. She has published, with Richard Lowitt, *Henry A. Wallace's Irrigation Frontier*. Dr. Fabry is an independent scholar, living in Georgetown, Texas.

Mark Friedberger is a research scientist in the Center for Economic Development and Research at the University of North Texas. He is the author of *Farm Families and Change in Twentieth-Century America* and *Shake-out: Iowa Farm Families in the 1980s*. Dr. Friedberger has published widely on the western livestock industry.

David Rich Lewis is an associate professor of history at Utah State University, where he also serves as associate editor of the *Western Historical Quarterly*. Professor Lewis is the author of *Neither Wolf Nor Dog: American Indians, Environment, and Agrarian Change*.

Harry C. McDean is Meritorious Professor of Economic and Business History at San Diego State University. He has published on a range of topics in both agricultural and business history. He specializes in the history of agribusiness.

Paula M. Nelson is an associate professor of history at the University of Wisconsin–Platteville. She is the author of *After the West Was Won: Homesteaders and Townbuilders in Western South Dakota* and *The Prairie Winnows Out Its Own: The West River Country of South Dakota in the Years of Depression and Dust.*

Donald J. Pisani is Merrick Professor of Western American History at the University of Oklahoma. He has published *From Family Farm to Agribusiness: The Irrigation Crusade in California and the West, 1850–1931; To Reclaim a Divided West: Water, Law, and Public Policy, 1848–1902;* and *Water, Land, and Law in the West: The Limits of Public Policy, 1850–1920.*

Sandra Schackel is an associate professor of history at Boise State University, where she specializes in the history of women and the American West. She is the author of *Social Housekeepers: Women Shaping Public Policy in New Mexico, 1920–1940.*

James E. Sherow is an associate professor of history at Kansas State University, where he specializes in environmental history. Professor Sherow is the author of *Watering the Valley: Development Along the High Plains Arkansas River, 1870–1950.*

Thomas R. Wessel is professor of history and head of the Department of History at Montana State University. He is a past president of the Agricultural History Society and the author of numerous works on the history of American agriculture.

INDEX